The Measurement of Equity in School Finance

THE MEASUREMENT OF EQUITY IN SCHOOL FINANCE

CONCEPTUAL, METHODOLOGICAL, AND EMPIRICAL DIMENSIONS

Robert Berne
and Leanna Stiefel

THE JOHNS HOPKINS UNIVERSITY PRESS
Baltimore and London

© 1984 by The Johns Hopkins University Press
All rights reserved
Printed in the United States of America

The Johns Hopkins University Press, Baltimore, Maryland 21218
The Johns Hopkins Press Ltd., London

Library of Congress Cataloging in Publication Data

Berne, Robert.
The measurement of equity in school finance.

Includes index.
1. Education—Michigan—Finance—Evaluation.
2. Education—New York (State)—Finance—Evaluation.
3. Educational equilization—Michigan—Evaluation.
4. Educational equilization—New York (State)—Evaluation.
I. Stiefel, Leanna. II. Title.
LB2826.M5B47 1984   379.1′54   83-24394
ISBN 0-8018-3148-2

For Shelley and My Parents,
Ruth and Buddy Berne

For My Husband, Mel Schoenfeld, and My Parents,
Jane and Donald Stiefel

CONTENTS

List of Figures   *viii*
List of Tables   *xiii*
Preface   *xvi*
1 Equity Analysis in an Era of Fiscal Restraint   *1*
2 A Framework for Organizing Alternative School-Finance-Equity Concepts   *7*
3 Hypothetical Illustrations of the Equity-Measurement Methodology: Alternative Units of Analysis and Objects   *44*
4 Hypothetical Illustrations of the Equity-Measurement Methodology: Alternative Measures of the Equity Principles   *63*
5 Review of Methodologies of Recent School-Finance-Equity Literature   *97*
6 Children's Objects in Michigan and New York   *117*
7 Horizontal Equity in Michigan and New York   *129*
8 Equal Opportunity in Michigan and New York   *169*
9 Vertical Equity in Michigan and New York   *221*
10 Summary and Conclusions   *270*
Index   *291*

LIST OF FIGURES

2.1 Alternative Concepts of School-Finance-Equity for Children   *9*
2.2 Hypothetical Data Illustrating Two Different Combinations of Correlation and Bivariate Elasticity and Slope Measures   *30*
2.3 Hypothetical Relationship between Per-Pupil Objects and Property Values in Two States   *32*
4.1 Relationship between Per-Pupil Dollar Inputs and Per-Pupil Property Values, State E1   *78*
4.2 Relationship between Per-Pupil Dollar Inputs and Per-Pupil Property Values, State E2   *79*
4.3 Relationship between Per-Pupil Dollar Inputs and Per-Pupil Property Values, State E3   *80*
4.4 Relationship between Per-Pupil Dollar Inputs and Per-Pupil Property Values, State E4   *81*
7.1 Table and Graph of the Coefficient of Variation of Current Operating Expenditures in Michigan, 1969–70 to 1977–78   *131*
7.2 Michigan: Range, Restricted Range, Variance, Federal Range Ratio, and McLoone Index for Instructional Expenditures per Pupil   *135*
7.3 Michigan: Coefficient of Variation, Gini Coefficient, Theil's Measure, Standard Deviation of Logarithms, and Relative Mean Deviation for Instructional Expenditures per Pupil   *136*
7.4 Michigan: Atkinson's Index for Instructional Expenditures per Pupil ($E = 0.2, 8, 16, 150$)   *141*
7.5 Michigan: Comparisons among Six Input-Based Dollar Objects Using the Federal Range Ratio as the Horizontal-Equity Measure   *144*
7.6 Michigan: Comparisons among Six Input-Based Dollar Objects Using the McLoone Index as the Horizontal-Equity Measure   *145*
7.7 Michigan: Comparisons among Six Input-Based Dollar Objects Using the Coefficient of Variation as the Horizontal-Equity Measure   *146*

LIST OF FIGURES ix

7.8   Michigan: Comparisons among Input-Based Dollar and Price-Adjusted Dollar Objects Using the Federal Range Ratio as the Horizontal-Equity Measure   *150*

7.9   Michigan: Comparisons among Input-Based Dollar and Price-Adjusted Dollar Objects Using the McLoone Index as the Horizontal-Equity Measure   *151*

7.10   Michigan: Comparisons among Input-Based Dollar and Price-Adjusted Dollar Objects Using the Coefficient of Variation as the Horizontal-Equity Measure   *153*

7.11   Michigan: Comparisons among Input-Based Dollar, Price-Adjusted Dollar, and Resource Objects Using the McLoone Index as the Horizontal-Equity Measure   *155*

7.12   Michigan: Comparisons among Input-Based Dollar, Price-Adjusted Dollar, and Resource Objects Using the Coefficient of Variation as the Horizontal-Equity Measure   *156*

7.13   New York: Coefficient of Variation, Gini Coefficient, McLoone Index, Standard Deviation of Logarithms, Federal Range Ratio, and Relative Mean Deviation for Current Operating Expenditures per Pupil   *161*

7.14   New York: Atkinson's Index with $E = .2, 50, 100,$ and 200 for Current Operating Expenditures per Pupil   *162*

7.15   New York: Coefficient of Variation, Gini Coefficient, McLoone Index, Standard Deviation of Logarithms, Federal Range Ratio, and Relative Mean Deviation for Price-Adjusted Current Operating Expenditures per Pupil   *164*

8.1   Michigan: Equal-Opportunity Measures for Instructional Expenditures with Respect to Wealth—Correlation and Elasticities   *172*

8.2   Michigan: Equal-Opportunity Measures for Instructional Expenditures with Respect to Wealth—Slopes and Adjusted Relationship Measures   *173*

8.3   Michigan: Comparisons among Six Input-Based Dollar Objects Using the Correlation as the Equal-Opportunity Measure with Respect to Wealth   *175*

8.4   Michigan: Comparisons among Six Input-Based Dollar Objects Using the Simple Elasticity as the Equal-Opportunity Measure with Respect to Wealth   *176*

8.5   Michigan: Comparisons among Input-Based Dollar and Price-Adjusted Dollar Objects Using the Correlation as the Equal-Opportunity Measure with Respect to Wealth   *178*

8.6   Michigan: Comparisons among Input-Based Dollar and Price-Adjusted Dollar Objects Using the Simple Elasticity as the Equal-Opportunity Measure with Respect to Wealth   *179*

8.7   **Michigan: Equal Opportunity with Respect to Wealth Using All Teachers per 1,000 Pupils as the Object and Four Equal-Opportunity Measures**   *181*

8.8   Michigan: Equal-Opportunity Measures for Instructional Expenditures with Respect to Income—Correlations and Elasticities   *184*

LIST OF FIGURES

8.9 Michigan: Equal-Opportunity Measures for Instructional Expenditures with Respect to Income—Slopes and Adjusted Relationship Measures *185*

8.10 Michigan: Comparisons among Four Input-Based Dollar Objects Using the Correlation as the Equal-Opportunity Measure with Respect to Income *187*

8.11 Michigan: Comparisons among Four Input-Based Dollar Objects Using the Simple Elasticity as the Equal-Opportunity Measure with Respect to Income *188*

8.12 Michigan: Comparisons among Input-Based Dollar and Price-Adjusted Dollar Objects Using the Correlation as the Equal-Opportunity Measure with Respect to Income *190*

8.13 Michigan: Comparisons among Input-Based Dollar and Price-Adjusted Dollar Objects Using the Simple Elasticity as the Equal-Opportunity Measure with Respect to Income *191*

8.14 Michigan: Equal Opportunity with Respect to Income Using All Teachers per 1,000 Pupils as the Object and Four Equal-Opportunity Measures *192*

8.15 Michigan: Ratios of Average Instructional Expenditures per Pupil and Average Local Plus Total State Revenues per Pupil, by Region *195*

8.16 Michigan: Ratios of Average Price-Adjusted Instructional Expenditures per Pupil and Average Price-Adjusted Local Plus Total State Revenues per Pupil, by Region *196*

8.17 Michigan: Ratios of Average All Classroom Teachers per 1,000 Pupils, by Region *197*

8.18 Michigan: Equal-Opportunity Measures for Instructional Expenditures with Respect to Race *201*

8.19 Michigan: Comparisons among Four Input-Based Dollar Objects Using the Correlation as the Equal-Opportunity Measure with Respect to Race *203*

8.20 Michigan: Comparisons among Input-Based Dollar and Price-Adjusted Dollar Objects Using the Correlation as the Equal-Opportunity Measure with Respect to Race *206*

8.21 Michigan: Equal Opportunity with Respect to Race Using All Teachers per 1,000 Pupils as the Object and Six Equal-Opportunity Measures *207*

8.22 New York: Correlation and Constant, Simple, Quadratic, and Cubic Elasticity for Current Operating Expenditures per Pupil with Property Wealth per Pupil *209*

8.23 New York: Simple, Quadratic, and Cubic Slope and Simple, Quadratic, and Cubic Adjusted Relationship Measure for Current Operating Expenditures with Property Wealth per Pupil *210*

8.24 New York: Correlation, Simple Slope, Simple Elasticity, and Simple Adjusted Relationship Measure for Price-Adjusted Current Operating Expenditures with Property Wealth per Pupil *212*

8.25 New York: Correlation, Simple Slope, Simple Elasticity, and Simple Adjusted Relationship Measure for Current Operating Expenditures per Pupil with Income per Return *214*

LIST OF FIGURES

8.26 New York: Correlation, Simple Slope, Simple Elasticity, and Simple Adjusted Relationship Measure for Price-Adjusted Current Operating Expenditures per Pupil with Income per Return   *215*

8.27 New York: Current Operating Expenditures per Pupil and Price-Adjusted Current Operating Expenditures per Pupil, by Region (with Upstate Nonurban Region as Denominator)   *216*

9.1 Michigan: Restricted Range, McLoone Index, Coefficient of Variation, Standard Deviation of Logarithms, Relative Mean Deviation, and Federal Range Ratio for Instructional Expenditures per Weighted Pupil Using Scheme 1   *235*

9.2 Michigan: Correlation, Simple Slope, Simple Elasticity, Simple Adjusted Relationship Measure, Implicit Weight, and Averaged Implicit Weight for Instructional Expenditures per Pupil Using Scheme 1   *236*

9.3 Michigan: Vertical-Equity Measures for Local Plus Total State Revenues Using Scheme 1—Restricted Range, McLoone Index, Federal Range Ratio, Coefficient of Variation, Correlation, and Averaged Implicit Weight   *240*

9.4 Michigan: Vertical-Equity Measures for Total Revenues Using Scheme 1—Restricted Range, McLoone Index, Federal Range Ratio, Coefficient of Variation, Correlation, and Averaged Implicit Weight   *241*

9.5 Michigan: Vertical-Equity Measures for Price-Adjusted Instructional Expenditures Using Scheme 1—Restricted Range, McLoone Index, Federal Range Ratio, Coefficient of Variation, Correlation, and Averaged Implicit Weight   *245*

9.6 Michigan: Vertical-Equity Measures for All Classroom Teachers per 1,000 Pupils Using Scheme 1—Restricted Range, McLoone Index, Federal Range Ratio, Coefficient of Variation, Correlation, and Averaged Implicit Weight   *248*

9.7 New York: Restricted Range, McLoone Index, Coefficient of Variation, Standard Deviation of Logarithms, Relative Mean Deviation, and Federal Range Ratio for Current Operating Expenditures per Weighted Pupil Using Scheme 1   *257*

9.8 New York: Correlation, Simple Slope, Simple Elasticity, Simple Adjusted Relationship Measure, Implicit Weight, and Averaged Implicit Weight for Current Operating Expenditures per Pupil Using Scheme 1   *259*

9.9 New York: Vertical-Equity Measures for Current Operating Expenditures per Pupil Using Scheme 2—Restricted Range, McLoone Index, Federal Range Ratio, Coefficient of Variation, Correlation, and Averaged Implicit Weight   *261*

9.10 New York: Restricted Range, McLoone Index, Coefficient of Variation, Standard Deviation of Logarithms, Relative Mean Deviation, and Federal Range Ratio for Price-Adjusted Current Operating Expenditures per Weighted Pupil Using Scheme 1   *264*

9.11 New York: Correlation, Simple Slope, Simple Elasticity, Simple Adjusted Relationship Measure, Implicit Weight, and Averaged Implicit Weight for

Price-Adjusted Current Operating Expenditures per Pupil Using Scheme 1   *266*

9.12 New York: Vertical-Equity Measures for Price-Adjusted Current Operating Expenditures per Pupil Using Scheme 2—Coefficient of Variation, Federal Range Ratio, McLoone Index, and Correlation.   *267*

LIST OF TABLES

2.1	Differences among Children by Characteristics and Their "Legitimacy"	*14*
2.2	Formulas for Revenue-Disparity Measures (Pupil Unit of Analysis)	*20*
2.3	Value Judgments Inherent in Eleven Horizontal-Equity Measures	*23*
2.4	Descriptions of Eleven Regression-Based Relationship Measures (Pupil Unit of Analysis)	*28*
2.5	Value Judgments Inherent in Eleven Relationship Measures	*34*
3.1	Basic Data for States A1 and A2	*48*
3.2	Per-Pupil Dollar Inputs by Quintiles for States A1 and A2	*50*
3.3	Basic Data for States B1 and B2	*52*
3.4	Per-Pupil Dollar Inputs by Quintiles for State B2 (District and Pupil Units of Analysis)	*55*
3.5	Calculation of Coefficient of Variation for State B2 (Pupil Unit of Analysis)	*57*
3.6	Calculation of Coefficient of Variation for State B2 (District Unit of Analysis)	*58*
3.7	Basic Data for States C1 and C2	*61*
3.8	Mean, Median, and Coefficient of Variation in States C1 and C2 Using Alternative Input-Based Objects	*62*
4.1	Basic Data for States D1, D2, D3, and D4	*64*
4.2	Horizontal-Equity Measures for States D1, D2, D3, and D4 (Pupil Unit of Analysis)	*65*
4.3	Quintiles of Per-Pupil Dollar Inputs for States D1, D2, D3, and D4	*65*
4.4	Graph of Lorenz Curve for State D1	*67*
4.5	Calculation of Gini Coefficient for State D1	*68*
4.6	Ranking of States D1, D2, D3, and D4 by the Six Horizontal-Equity Measures	*71*
4.7	Basic Data for States E1, E2, E3, E4, and E5	*72*

xiv LIST OF TABLES

4.8 Equal-Opportunity Measures with Per-Pupil Dollar Inputs as Dependent Variable and Per-Pupil Property Value as Independent Variable for States E1, E2, E3, E4, and E5   *73*
4.9 Calculation of Simple Correlation between Per-Pupil Dollar Inputs and Per-Pupil Property Value for State E1   *75*
4.10 Per-Pupil Dollar Inputs by Quintiles Ordered by Per-Pupil Property Values for States E1, E2, E3, E4, and E5   *77*
4.11 Ranking of States E1, E2, E3, E4, and E5 by the Four Equal-Opportunity Measures   *82*
4.12 Calculation of Coefficient of Variation Using Unweighted and Weighted Pupils in State F1   *84*
4.13 Basic Data for States F1 and F2   *86*
4.14 Unweighted and Weighted Dispersion Measures for States F1 and F2   *87*
4.15 Basic Data for States F3 and F4   *88*
4.16 Relationship Measures of Vertical Equity for States F3 and F4   *88*
4.17 Weighted Dispersion Measures of Vertical Equity for States F3 and F4   *90*
4.18 Relationship Measures of Vertical Equity for States F1 and F2   *91*
4.19 Calculation of Averaged Implicit Weight for State F1 and Values of Averaged Implicit Weight for States F2, F3, and F4   *93*
4.20 Ranking of States F1, F2, F3, and F4 by Four Vertical-Equity Measures   *93*
5.1 Frequency of Children's Equity Objects in School-Finance Studies   *99*
5.2 Frequency of Taxpayer Objects in School-Finance Studies   *102*
5.3 Frequency of Various Children's Equity Principles in Studies   *103*
5.4 Frequency of Various Taxpayer Equity Principles in Studies   *104*
5.5 Frequency of Various Equity Measures in Children's Studies, Cross-Tabulated by Principle   *106*
5.6 Frequency of Various Equity Measures in Taxpayer Studies, Cross-Tabulated by Principle   *107*
5.7 Frequency of Alternative Fiscal-Capacity Measures in Studies   *108*
5.8 Summary of Methodological Findings for Single-State, Multistate, and Fifty-State Studies   *110*
6.1 Michigan Teachers per 1,000 Pupils in K–12 Districts (Pupil-Weighted Statewide Analyses)   *120*
6.2 Michigan Per-Pupil Expenditure and Revenue Variables in K–12 Districts (Pupil-Weighted Statewide Averages)   *121*
6.3 Michigan Price Indexes for Selected Districts   *126*
6.4 Michigan Price-Adjusted Per-Pupil Expenditures and Revenue Variables in K–12 Districts   *127*
6.5 New York Current Operating Expenditures per Pupil in K–12 Districts   *128*

LIST OF TABLES

7.1 Michigan: Horizontal-Equity Measures for Instructional Expenditures per Pupil   *134*

7.2 Michigan: Atkinson's Indexes for Instructional Expenditures per Pupil   *140*

7.3 New York: Basic Statistics and Horizontal-Equity Measures for Current Operating Expenditures per Pupil   *159*

8.1 Michigan: Equal Opportunity with Respect to Race for Alternative Input-Based Dollar Objects   *202*

8.2 Michigan: Equal Opportunity with Respect to Race for Alternative Price-Adjusted Input-Based Dollar Objects   *204*

9.1 Definitions of Categories of Handicapping Conditions in Michigan   *224*

9.2 Pupil Weights for Vertical-Equity Assessment in Michigan   *228*

9.3 Michigan: Vertical-Equity Measures for Instructional Expenditures Using Group and Weighting in Scheme 1   *231*

9.4 Michigan: Vertical-Equity Measures for Instructional Expenditures Using Group and Weighting in Scheme 2   *232*

9.5 New York: Vertical-Equity Measures for Current Operating Expenditures Using Group and Weighting in Scheme 1   *254*

10.1 Theoretical and Empirical Groupings of Alternative Dispersion Measures   *276*

10.2 Theoretical and Empirical Groupings of Alternative Relationship Measures   *277*

PREFACE

The seeds of this book germinated in the late 1970s, when we became involved with a community of scholars interested in developing alternative ways to quantify the equity of state school-finance systems. Much of the motivation for our work was provided by the need for states to assess the equity of their school finance systems. Some states wanted to know whether they needed to reform their school finance system; others wanted to learn if the results of their reform were as expected. While troubling to those in search of one answer to the question, Is our school finance system equitable? we stressed from the beginning that the subjective values inherent in any assessment, even a statistical one, logically lead to a multidimensional equity concept.

This book develops the dual themes of the alternative ways of quantitatively measuring equity and the need to understand the value judgments inherent in all measures. It is timely into the 1980s, when many states have switched their emphasis from reform to retrenchment, because it provides a methodology for measuring the equity effects of changes, whether they involve increases or cutbacks in funds. It is also appropriate now that primary and secondary education is under intense scrutiny because the trade-offs among equity and other goals need to be measured and understood.

The book is written for a variety of audiences, including analysts, state and federal legislative and executive staffs, students, and scholars. It contains a conceptual framework applicable to school-finance equity as well as other public policy issues, chapters containing hypothetical examples that allow novices in the field of quantitative measurement to perform calculations with hand calculators, and empirical applications of the framework to the states of Michigan and New York over nine- and fourteen-year time periods respectively. While we hope the parts are well integrated, it is also intended that some can be skipped if readers are not in need of the information.

Partial funding for the actual writing of the book was provided by the National Institute of Education. Much of the preliminary thinking was stimulated by earlier grants from the Ford Foundation. A grant from the Spencer Foundation enabled us to collect the data for New York.

We want to especially thank two individuals without whom our work in this area would not have occurred. James Kelly, now President of Spring Hill Center, in his former position as Program Officer at the Ford Foundation, supported our earlier work emotionally as well as financially and provided numerous forums for lively, sometimes critical, interactions with scholars, analysts, and activists interested in fair schooling. James Phelps, Associate Superintendent of Education for the State of Michigan, not only allowed us access to Michigan's well-developed school-finance data, but to a large extent is the reason for the existence of the data. His curious and energetic mind has stimulated one of the best developed information systems on state school finance. In addition, numerous colleagues read and critiqued part of the book, including Elizabeth Durbin, Anne-Marie Foltz, and Mitchell Moss at the Graduate School of Public Administration, New York University, Dick Netzer at the Urban Research Center, New York University, and Dick Schramm at Tufts University. Allen Odden of the Education Commission of the States helped in early efforts to develop a conceptual framework and to empirically implement it. James Fox and David Mandell of NIE and Thomas Nicol, then of the Michigan Department of Education, also assisted us during our work. Anders Richter, Editorial Director at Johns Hopkins University Press, provided us with timely advice and encouragement. A referee, who remains anonymous, suggested many useful changes. Cynthia H. Foote contributed helpful editorial guidance. Chris Hakusa provided intelligent and reliable computer assistance, and Karen Gruhn helped in both data collection and typing. Suzanne Haray, Noreen O'Keefe, Ruth Sheridan, Theresa Steinbacher, Susan Stock, and Delores Varley also assisted in typing drafts of the manuscript.

Last, but with the most gratitude, we thank our families for the times they spent without us while we thought, wrote, revised, and finally completed this book.

The Measurement of Equity in School Finance

1

EQUITY ANALYSIS IN AN ERA OF FISCAL RESTRAINT

Observers of American social trends in the 1980s might conclude that equity has become a dirty word. Nevertheless, the 1980s ushered in many changes that affect the importance of equity analysis in public education. In the 1970s such analysis was a dominant theme in school finance, as state courts ruled that state systems of funding were unconstitutional and state governments used their often growing revenues to fund larger shares of elementary-secondary (K-12) education and to influence the ways in which the funds were distributed.[1] In the 1980s, many states find themselves in tight fiscal situations, local governments are sometimes subject to spending or taxing limits, and the federal government is considering a reduction in its role in education, along with block grants to states as a replacement for categorical funding. Each of these changes is likely to influence who gets what in K-12 education, even though motivations of efficiency and productivity are the dominant publicly expressed concerns. Whatever the public motivation, equity may turn out to be a more important issue in the 1980s than in the 1970s because major changes such as those just enumerated can bring about unintended and, at first glance, overlooked effects. And, even if improvements in equity are not a pressing public issue, preventing losses might be.

This book is about alternative ways to conceptualize and empirically measure equity in school finance. It emphasizes the different values inherent in alternative equity concepts. The intended audience includes policymakers who wish to understand their staff's analyses, analysts themselves, members

---

1. For example, between 1970-71 and 1979-80, the percent of state and local revenues funded from state sources rose from 44.3 percent to 51 percent; National Center for Education Statistics, *Revenues and Expenditures for Public Elementary and Secondary Education*, 1970-71 (Washington, D.C.: National Center for Education Statistics, 1972). and *Statistics of Public Elementary and Secondary School Systems, fall 1979* (Washington D.C.: National Center for Education Statistics, 1980).

of public interest groups, and in general anyone who wants to be able to critically evaluate levels, changes, or recommendations for changes in school-finance equity. Various chapters present a conceptual framework of equity, a review of recent equity studies, step-by-step procedures and examples showing how to implement the conceptual framework, and comprehensive examples of the framework using actual data from two states, Michigan and New York. In general, the book provides a useful framework for monitoring school finance systems as they respond to changes in types and levels of federal, state, and local funding.

In this chapter, we expand on the various ways that school-finance-equity analysis will be important in the years ahead, and we end with an outline of how the book is organized.

The many fiscal and intergovernmental changes witnessed in the 1980s will affect the nation's school finance systems. As the public-education pie fails to grow as quickly as in the past, or possibly even begins to shrink, equity may become more of an issue than ever before. When resources are expanding, most people receive somewhat more, and even though the distribution of increases may not be exactly what some might hope, there is unlikely to be as much distributional concern as when some people actually receive less than before. In addition, the methodology of equity measurement has, up until the present, been applied to growth situations. This book's methodology is appropriate for analysis of either growth or decline, which is not necessarily true for all methodologies.

The changes that are likely in the 1980s will affect equity in different ways. If the federal government should change the nature of its intergovernmental grant giving, emphasizing broader, untied block grants in lieu of more narrowly focused categorical funding, then what is described in this book as vertical equity is likely to be affected. Vertical equity in this book is defined as appropriately unequal treatment of unequals. Since 1965, federal funds for education have been largely restricted to specific purposes, viz compensatory education, aid to handicapped students, and aid for vocational education. When spent as intended, so that neither state nor local monies for these purposes are reduced and the funds are truly added onto existing funds, then students who fall into the targeted groups should benefit in relation to others. To the extent that the federal categories are considered legitimate candidates for unequal treatment, a switch away from funding that is targeted to them can be expected to harm them. This is not to say that if given more leeway over allocation decisions, states and localities will discontinue completely the programs in place for special students, but only that some of the federal monies are likely to find their way into other programs of higher priorities to the specific states or districts. Over the past few decades significant numbers of people have been working to improve vertical equity for special-needs students. A rearrangement of federal grant priorities that resulted in decreased funding for these students would clearly be seen as regressive, and there will be intense interest in tracking the actual effects.

The tax limitations instituted in several states in recent years have affected the ability of local school districts to raise property tax revenues. This change is most likely to affect what we will call wealth-related equal opportunity in this book. Wealth-related equal opportunity refers to the degree to which a child's schooling (its funding and quality) depends on the property wealth of the school district in which he or she resides. To the extent that schooling is positively related to property wealth, opportunity is less equal. If property-tax limits imposed at the state level significantly cut the ability of all districts in a state to raise local revenues, then the state may take over a good part of K–12 school funding, perhaps with positive effects on equal opportunity. On the other hand, if tax limits differentially affect districts' local revenue-raising potential, then equal opportunity could be made worse or better depending upon which districts are most restrained. The direction of change cannot be a priori predicted. However, because the tax limits mostly influence local (usually property-tax) revenue, they are likely to most directly influence wealth-related equal opportunity.

In many instances, changes at the state level of government will result from tighter fiscal environments, as well as from changes such as those just discussed at the federal and local levels. All of these changes could affect any of the equity concepts developed in this book, either from children's or from taxpayers' perspectives. Proposed changes in federal grants giving would allow states more leeway to follow their own policy preferences rather than those of Washington. This may mean less emphasis on vertical equity in some cases. On the other hand, revenue restrictions at local levels may force some states into financing larger shares of K–12 education and may influence equity in a positive direction. But this increased role for the states may coincide with a period of rising state budget deficits. One can develop fewer specific hypotheses concerning what states in general will do when given more responsibility than about what will happen if the federal government changes its grants or if local governments are more fiscally constrained. That no changes would result is, however, the most unlikely outcome. Thus, this book's methodology will be useful both in documenting what happens as states' shares and roles change and in generating hypotheses about how states behave.

In addition to federal grant changes, new tax limits, and increased states' roles, a fourth kind of change that could affect school-finance equity is the actions of state courts. While a great many states witnessed rulings during the 1970s by their highest courts on the equity of their finance systems, there are still a number of states that will have such cases resolved in the 1980s.[2] Two such states that are of particular importance are California and Colorado. Even if those in political power begin to swing more to the right compared to

---

2. States with yet-to-be resolved cases include Arkansas, California, Colorado, Connecticut, Maryland, Massachusetts, New Hampshire, New Jersey, Oklahoma, South Dakota, Washington, West Virginia, and Wisconsin; from "Box Score on Constitutional Challenges to School Finance Systems in the United States" (Normal, Ill.: Center for the Study of Educational Finance, Illinois State University, February 1982).

the 1970s, the rulings of the courts may continue to have an influence. David Long, a lawyer involved for the plaintiffs in numerous states, put it as follows: "The kind of disparities that were exposed in the suits have lost their legitimacy.... No longer do you hear it argued that there is some wellspring of innovation going on in the wealthy districts that justifies their having resources that others cannot have. They still do, but in the long run those disparities will disappear, if not by judicial then by legislative or administrative leadership."[3]

Finally, in general, as reducing the growth of public spending becomes increasingly necessary, the importance of comprehensive equity measurement will become more evident. For example, with slower-growing funding, it will help to more clearly specify the particular equity values important to a state rather than attempting to satisfy a whole variety of vaguely articulated values. In addition, adjustments of equity measures to include differential prices of inputs across regions in a state or differential "needs" of children should result in agreement upon a narrower definition of equity and permit better targeting of limited funds.

In addition to the relevance that this book has for policy issues, it also addresses methodological questions. During the 1970s, scholars took an active interest in the methodology of school-finance-equity measurement.[4] The various strands of these activities have never been integrated in one place; this book provides such an integration.

The book is written to serve readers at different levels of analytical sophistication. For those with little experience critiquing or performing equity analysis, chapters 3 and 4 provide step-by-step illustrations. For more experienced readers, these chapters can be omitted and the conceptual and empirical chapters read. In general, the book focuses on school finance and explains alternative equity conceptions, describes alternative procedures to measure these conceptions, and provides extensive empirical illustrations and examples.

The remainder of this book is divided into nine chapters. A framework that can be used to organize and clarify alternative conceptions of equity is presented in chapter 2. The framework is organized around the answers to the following four questions.

    1. Who? What is the makeup of the groups for which school finance systems should be equitable?

    2. What? What services, resources, or, more generally, objects should be distributed fairly among members of the groups?

    3. How? What principles should be used to determine whether a particular distribution is equitable?

---

3. David Long, quoted in the *New York Times*, Thursday, June 24, 1982, p. B7.
4. See chapter 5 for a comprehensive review of the literature.

4. How much? What quantitative measures should be used to assess the degree of equity?

Each question generates numerous answers, and the answers incorporate particular value judgments. The questions, answers, and associated value judgments are discussed extensively in chapter 2. Although the framework considers equity from the perspectives of both the children and the taxpayers, the remainder of the book is concerned almost exclusively with children's equity.

The next three chapters illustrate the implementation of the framework in various ways. Chapters 3 and 4 present detailed examples of how to use the previously developed framework to measure children's equity in school finance. Both these chapters include step-by-step instructions so that readers can manipulate the hypothetical data using hand calculators. The examples in chapter 3 focus on alternative units of analysis and objects, while chapter 4 stresses measures of the three children's equity principles: horizontal equity, equal opportunity, and vertical equity. Chapter 5 utilizes the methodological framework to review the major school-finance-equity studies carried out over the last decade. The literature review shows how the four questions that comprise the framework are useful in identifying and organizing the methodological diversity contained in the existing school-finance-equity literature.

In chapters 6 through 9, the equity framework is applied comprehensively to the school finance systems in Michigan and New York over nine and fourteen years respectively. The equity analyses of Michigan and New York in this book focus entirely on children's equity. Once the first question—Equity for whom?—has been answered with *children*, the second question—Equity of what?—must be addressed. This is done in chapter 6. The variety of input-based dollar, price-adjusted dollar, and resource objects utilized in Michigan and the input-based dollar and price-adjusted dollar objects analyzed in New York are defined in detail.

For the analyses of Michigan and New York, the answers to the third and fourth questions—What principles and what quantitative measures should be used to determine equity?—which comprise the heart of the assessments, are presented in chapters 7, 8, and 9. Each of these chapters examines numerous measures for one equity principle, using data from both Michigan and New York. Thus, horizontal equity is analyzed in chapter 7, equal opportunity in chapter 8, and vertical equity in chapter 9. In all three chapters, the effects of alternative objects and measures are examined from a methodological perspective, and the substantive results for Michigan and New York are reported and explained.

The concluding section, chapter 10, summarizes and synthesizes the findings in the book. Although the empirical chapters of the book demonstrate that trends in equity depend on the object, principle, and measures used, the concluding chapter makes some explicit choices (ones the readers need not agree with!) and then discusses what can be said about equity over time in Michigan and New York. The last chapter also highlights the way we think future research in the area of school-finance-equity analysis will proceed.

Until now, a book such as this one, which thoroughly explains the most up-to-date equity-measurement methodologies and shows how to carry out the equity analyses, did not exist. Yet decisions about equity are being made continually, and this book will help insure that the current methodologies are not concentrated in the hands of a small number of researchers. The decisions about equity are difficult enough, even when there is agreement on methodology; debate over methodology often masks more important decisions about value judgments. This book communicates the methodologies broadly, so that difficult social decisions can be informed by the best available research. At the same time, the book shows the limitations of the current state of the art of equity analysis and points the way to the lines of developments that could improve such assessments.

2

A FRAMEWORK FOR ORGANIZING ALTERNATIVE SCHOOL-FINANCE-EQUITY CONCEPTS

There are many ways to conceptualize equity in school finance. Therefore, empirical work, which requires unambiguous statements of equity standards, can proceed along a wide variety of paths. For the most part, we do not argue for the adoption of particular equity concepts. Rather, our goal is to provide a framework that will allow analysts and policymakers to easily identify the important dimensions of alternative concepts and to explore quantitatively those concepts that best represent their own values.

The framework developed here is organized around the answers to the four questions presented in the preceding chapter.

1. Who? What is the makeup of the groups for which school finance systems should be equitable?
2. What? What services, resources, or, more generally, objects should be distributed fairly among members of the groups?
3. How? What principles should be used to determine whether a particular distribution is equitable?
4. How much? What quantitative measures should be used to assess the degree of equity?

Answers to these four practical questions can lead to a surprisingly wide variety of different equity concepts. In order to understand the strengths of the four-question framework, we develop each question in some detail in the sections that follow.

EQUITY FOR WHOM?

Two groups have captured the attention of most equity scholars. These two groups are children, who receive education services, and taxpayers, some of whom receive education services for their children and all of whom pay for education services through taxes.

Why are children targets for equity? There are numerous reasons, but two are paramount. First, education is viewed as an investment in an individual child's future. In order to make the distribution of future life-status equitable, attention must be paid to the way current services are provided. A second rationale for the specification of children as a group depends, not on the effect that the quality of education has on future status, but rather on a concern for the experiences of children in the present. A large part of a child's day is spent in school; there is an argument for providing those educational experiences in an equitable manner.

The major reason to choose taxpayers as the equity target is that equity in school finance also applies to those who pay for education services. The taxpayer focus is useful also because it can be expanded to a household unit whereby equity concerns apply to education taxes paid by and education services received by the household. The household unit can be used to enlarge the scope of the equity conception even further by including all resources available in the household for education, not just for schooling.

The two answers to the question Equity for whom? naturally divide the rest of the conceptual framework. For the most part, this book concentrates on children. This is not because children are necessarily more important, although they are probably the more common target in school-finance studies. Rather, we focus on children because there is a much richer empirical data base with which to illustrate alternative children's concepts. Nevertheless, at the end of this chapter there is also a brief discussion of taxpayer equity.

Figure 2.1 illustrates the application of the four-question framework to the analysis of school-finance equity for children; the figure previews as well the upcoming discussion of the remaining three questions in the framework: What? How? and How much?

CHILDREN'S EQUITY CONCEPTS

The Choice of an Object for Children's Equity Concepts

There are numerous things that could be distributed equitably among school children. In fact, one of the most difficult and important decisions that must be made in assessing equity in school finance is the object or objects that a policymaker or analyst wants to have distributed fairly. One can divide objects related to children into three general categories: inputs, outputs, and outcomes. Each of the general categories represents different values and entails different measurement problems. In this section, we discuss the three general categories of objects, highlighting the various kinds of differences among them. The contrasts among the descriptions of the input, output, and outcome objects will enable the reader to understand how values change as particular objects are selected for analysis.

Figure 2.1 Alternative Concepts of School-Finance-Equity for Children

Component of Equity Concept	Alternative for Each Component		
Who? The group	*Children*		
What? The object	*Inputs* —Dollars —Price-adjusted dollars —Physical resources	*Outputs* —Student achievement —Behavioral output measures	*Outcomes* —Earning potential —Income —Satisfaction
How? The principle	*Horizontal Equity* —Equal treatment of equals: minimize spread in distribution	*Vertical Equity* —Unequal treatment of unequals: more of the object to the needier	*Equal Opportunity* —No discrimination on the basis of property wealth in school district or other categories: minimize undesirable systematic relationships
How much? The summary statistic		*Univariate Dispersion* —Range —Restricted range —Federal range ratio —Relative mean deviation —The McLoone index —Variance —Coefficient of variation —Standard deviation of logarithm —Gini coefficient —Atkinson's index —Theil's measure	*Relationship* —Simple Correlation —Simple Slope —Quadratic Slope —Cubic Slope —Simple Elasticity —Quadratic Elasticity —Cubic Elasticity —Constant Elasticity —Adjusted Relationship Measure from Simple Regression —Adjusted Relationship Measure from Quadratic Regression —Adjusted Relationship Measure from Cubic Regression —Implicit Weight —Averaged Implicit Weight

Children's Input Concerns. Inputs are the basic building blocks of education. They are the resources that are combined to educate children in schools, measured either in actual physical resources (e.g., books and teachers), in dollars, or in price-adjusted dollars. A concern for inputs implies one of two values. On the one hand, there is a concern that each child be permitted a current environment that is as stimulating, pleasant, and enriched as that of any other child. Alternatively, future outputs or outcomes may be the real concern, with the distribution of inputs seen as the way to influence those other two objects.

Dollars Measured by Revenues or Expenditures. Dollar measures are the most commonly used objects in school-finance analyses. They can be divided into revenues (the dollars received by the school district and eventually the child) and expenditures (the dollar value of resources that are purchased for the child). Revenues and expenditures yield different information because of the ways they can be subdivided. Revenues can be examined by source: local, state, and federal. These individual sources can be divided further by type of program, such as general and categorical at the state level or Title I and impact aid at the federal level. Expenditures, on the other hand, can be identified by purpose, such as current operating, debt-service, and capital expenditures. Current operating expenditures can be further subdivided into instruction, utilities and maintenance, transportation, food service, etc. Thus, the selection of a precise revenue or expenditure measure is not a trivial question, even if one decides to use dollars as an input.

Price-Adjusted Dollars. In any given state at a given point in time, school districts may pay different prices for the same resources, such as teachers or supplies. The different prices mean that dollars are an inaccurate measure of resource availability. Over the past several years, methodologies have been developed to construct school-district price indexes. This research on price indexes is in a developmental phase, and some definite problems exist. First it appears that a "market basket" approach to price-index construction is not appropriate. If an existing market-basket index, such as the Consumer Price Index, is utilized, it may not capture price variation in inputs for schooling. This leads to a second approach, an examination of the schooling inputs themselves. But in this case, the measurement of price variation is difficult, since this variation is caused by both supply and demand factors. Conceptually, only supply factors that are not controllable by the school district should be included in a price index. Interwoven in the supply-demand problem is the issue of input quality. A price index should compare inputs of identical quality, but this may be impossible if quality cannot be observed and measured. Most recent research on price indexes has utilized statistical econometric techniques to identify a supply function, and subsequently a price index, but there are still significant measurement problems.

In terms of reliability, there is a good chance that any particular index includes some measurement error, since the components of the model used to estimate the indexes are measured with error and the estimated regressions do not explain all the variance. A more serious problem of validity may be applicable to the econometric price indexes, since they are highly dependent on a priori assumptions that are very difficult to test. Certain of the recent research efforts have compared alternative specifications of indexes and found that the indexes can vary substantially.[1] Thus, one is faced with the

1. For a discussion of this issue, see W. Norton Grubb and James Hyman, "Constructing Teacher Cost Indices: Methodological Explorations with California Unified School Districts," in Esther O. Tron, ed., *Selected Papers in School Finance, 1975* (Washington, D.C.: Office of Education, 1975).

question of which index, among many, to choose and whether the chosen index is more valid than no adjustment at all. Although we believe that indexes estimated with "reasonable" assumptions and with adequate data take us closer to physical resource measures than unadjusted dollar measures do, we are not yet in a position to base these beliefs on existing research. Thus, the issues of validity and reliability raise difficult questions, but questions that will eventually be answered.

Physical Resource Levels. In addition to, or instead of, selecting a dollar figure for analysis of school-finance equity on the input side, measures of actual physical resources can be used. For example, pupil-teacher ratios or the number of certified professional staff per student are possible objects. This type of figure can be augmented by numbers of books per student and numbers of noncertified staff per student. It is also possible to subdivide the gross figure of total professional staff, with analysis being made of the number of classroom teachers, number of pupil-support staff, and number of administrators per student. Once the resources are identified, there are a variety of ways to measure them, including counting each one separately, counting separately and then converting them to a common measure, or counting separately and then adjusting for quality differences.

An advantage of using resources as objects is that resources are measured in real terms. Thus, they are not subject to intralocational or intertemporal price differences. A crucial disadvantage, however, is the absence of a valid procedure to add together different resources such as teachers, teacher's aides, and books. This problem is intensified by the difficulty of measuring quality differences among the resources. Resource measures solve one set of problems—price differences and changes—yet introduce another set of problems.

Children's Output Concerns. Some argue that the results of the schooling system are what should be distributed equitably among children. Results include achievement-test scores, mastery of competency levels in different subject areas, high school graduation, or numerous other measures of a student's behavior at the end of high school or other identified grade levels. Indeed, current litigation trends in some states indicate that the state has affirmative duties to insure student achievement, at least at minimum levels.

Equity in the distribution of outputs does not have to be defined as equal schooling outputs. While equal levels of schooling outputs is one definition of equity, at least two other possibilities exist. If a student's initial level of the output variable could be measured prior to entrance to the educational system, then equity could be defined as equal gains or increments for each student. Or, if the inputs or resources required to obtain equal gains vary considerably over the population of students, equity could be defined as equal gains per dollar of resource for each student. This last possibility is more of an efficiency than an equity goal, but nonetheless, equal gains per dollar of resource could conceivably be consistent with some people's equity conception.

The degree of difficulty encountered in measuring outputs will differ depending upon the specific choice of an output measure. Measures such as achievement-test scores are likely to be highly reliable and valid in measuring rather narrow objectives. They may be less valid as indicators of what the education system should produce, because of their narrowness. Broader behavioral measures, such as graduation rates, may also have validity problems both because graduation is a rather minimal output measure and because the quality represented by similar graduation rates in different districts may not be the same. In general, outputs are likely to encounter more measurement problems and are less controllable than inputs.

Children's Outcome Concerns. Some argue that the perspective should be longer term than just the immediate results of the schooling system, and that lifetime outcomes such as income, occupational status, personal satisfaction, ability to compete in the labor market, or status in life should be the object of interest. While such a perspective may be asking too much of the schooling process or the education financing system, it does raise the issue of how such lifetime outcomes, which reflect the ultimate position of a child in adult society, are affected by the public-education financing system.

Measurement of outcomes will invariably be more difficult than for outputs or inputs. First, many of the concepts, such as status or satisfaction, do not have one widely accepted quantitative representation. Thus, the analyst must construct as well as quantify such measures. Second, appropriate data generally are not collected by the school systems themselves, so a massive tracking procedure that relates data from various sources with elementary and secondary education of students would be necessary.

Frederick Mosteller and Daniel Moynihan claimed in 1972 that *Equality of Educational Opportunity* marked the turning point from the use of inputs to the use of outputs or outcomes in studies of educational equity.[2] In school-finance studies through the late 1970s and the early 1980s, this has not been true. Analysts and policymakers have no easy answers to the choice of objects for school-finance-equity studies. They must, instead, consider the values inherent in a choice of each type of object as well as measurement problems. There is no single answer to the question of what should be equitably distributed.

Children's Equity Principles

The discussion above indicates that there are numerous objects that can be considered in assessing whether the school financing system is fair to children. But when a particular object such as inputs per pupil is selected, one

---

2. Frederick Mosteller and Daniel P. Moynihan, "A Pathbreaking Report," in *On Equality of Educational Opportunity*, ed. Mosteller and Moynihan (New York: Random House, 1972). They refer to James S. Coleman et al., *Equality of Educational Opportunity* (Washington, D.C.: Office of Education, 1966).

must then apply an equity principle in order to draw conclusions on whether the object is distributed fairly. A wide diversity of potential equity principles exists. Education scholars emphasize equal opportunity; lawyers are very concerned with fiscal neutrality; and economists explore horizontal and vertical equity. We think that almost all of the definitions of equity for children can be encompassed under the three broad principles described below.

Equal Treatment of Equals: Horizontal Equity. This principle states that students who are alike should receive equal shares. Equity is assessed by measuring the dispersion, or inequality, in the distribution of objects; no dispersion indicates perfect equity. Very often in school finance for purposes of equity analysis, all students in a state are treated as being equal. When children are so treated, this principle requires (in terms of some of the objects considered above) equal expenditures or revenues per pupil, equal education resources for the basic education program, equal pupil-teacher ratios, equal mastery of basic competency levels, or equal contributions by schooling to long-term outcomes such as income or status in life.

This principle is a restatement of the public-finance criterion of horizontal equity. It is also the principle implicit in much of the work of economists such as Amartya Sen and Anthony Atkinson, who have explored the equity characteristics of dispersion statistics. The dispersion statistics are most often applied to income distributions and the implicit assumption is often that perfect equality of income, with each person considered equal to all others, is desirable.[3]

The problem with the horizontal-equity criterion in school finance is that in most instances the assumption that children are substantially equal is easily refuted. Thus, the horizontal-equity criterion rightfully should be applied only to subgroups, where equality among children can be agreed upon.

Unequal Treatment of Unequals: Vertical Equity. While the above principle is applicable when children are alike, the second principle recognizes that students are different and states the positive requirement that unequals receive appropriately unequal treatment. Both the identification of "legitimate" differences among children and the selection of the nature and extent of the appropriate unequal treatment must be made; these choices are based largely on values.

Identification of Differences among Children. Differences among children can be categorized as those due to characteristics of the individual child, those due to characteristics of the districts where children reside, or those due to school programs in which the children are enrolled. In addition, each of these differences can be classified as legitimate, and deserving of unequal treat-

---

3. For example, see Amartya Sen, *On Economic Inequality* (New York: W. W. Norton, 1973), and Anthony B. Atkinson, "On the Measurement of Inequality," *Journal of Economic Theory* 2 (1970): 244-63. Occasionally, however, these authors conceptualize equality of welfare, which when formulated with varying utility functions among individuals need not mean that perfect equality of income is desirable.

ment, or illegitimate, and not deserving of differential treatment. There is bound to be controversy over the classification of some characteristics as legitimate or illegitimate, but for a wide variety of other characteristics there is likely to be substantial agreement among policymakers, analysts, lawyers, and scholars concerning classification. In table 2.1 a matrix of characteristics by legitimate-illegitimate classification is presented. These classifications are our own perceptions of what is widely accepted, but of course individual readers may wish to make some shifts. The remainder of this section expands on these classifications.

1. *Child-Based Characteristics.* Children's characteristics frequently given special consideration in school-finance equity include learning disabilities, such as those that result when English is a second language; poor pre-school preparation that sometimes results from an impoverished upbringing; and health-related problems such as physical and severe mental handicaps. Most finance programs give recognition to the necessity for more educational resources in order to meet minimum output goals for these children. On the other hand, children's characteristics such as race, sex, and ethnicity are generally not considered legitimate differentiating characteristics. The child's age and grade level do not clearly fall into either the legitimate or the illegitimate category. Many people think that either younger or older children or children in different grade levels require differential treatment, but many others think it necessary or even discriminatory to classify by age. Furthermore, even if the legitimacy of grade differences is agreed upon, there is no universal agreement on whether the higher or the lower grades should be treated more favorably.

Table 2.1 Differences among Children by Characteristics and Their "Legitimacy"

Type of Characteristic	Difference Accepted as		
	Legitimate	Controversial	Illegitimate
Child-based	Learning disabilities Inadequate preschool preparation Severe physical or mental handicaps	Age Grade level	Sex Race Ethnicity
District-based	Technological (costs) Economies of scale (district size) Safety production Transportation	Municipal overburden Geography (urban/rural, upstate/downstate, etc.)	Fiscal capacity Property wealth Household income
Program-based	Student mandated Handicapped	Student chosen Vocational education College preparatory	

Note: Classifications of all characteristics contain some value judgments. The assignments in the table reflect the authors' judgments of currently widespread agreements.

2. *District-Based Characteristics.* Legitimate differences based on district characteristics generally result from a need to provide more resources in order to achieve a constant level of output because of technological factors. Technological factors include economies and diseconomies of scale due to district size, measured by the number of pupils in the district, and different resource requirements for the production of safety, of transportation, etc.

Probably the most often discussed factor in the category of technological characteristics is district size, measured by number of children. The question concerning district size can be posed as follows: Does an equivalent amount of expenditures or resources per child in districts of varying size produce different outputs? It may be that smaller districts have smaller classes, since they have fewer children per grade to allocate to classes; it would only be inferred that costs are higher for the small district if there were no commensurate benefits derived from smaller classes. Outside of the classroom there may be higher noninstructional costs for smaller districts due to an inability to take advantage of certain economies of scale and for larger districts due to higher coordination costs. Nevertheless, there is still the question of whether the services to the children vary as well.

If cost differences among districts of varying size reflect differences in quantity or quality of output, then size adjustments are not appropriate in equity measures: if cost differences among districts of varying size do not reflect these differences, then size adjustments are appropriate in equity measures. In reality the "truth" probably lies somewhere in between these two extreme positions, and existing research cannot give the precise adjustments. The question of an adjustment for size becomes, to some degree, a value judgment.

Sometimes the "urbanness" of a district is considered a legitimate differentiating characteristic. Often the arguments that urban districts require more resources per unit of output revert back to already-discussed characteristics of children (higher proportions of handicapped, bilingual, poorly prepared, etc.) or of the district (diseconomies of scale, more resources needed per unit of security, etc.), in which case urbanness is merely a proxy for these other differences. Some people think that in addition to the children and district characteristics, urban districts require more resources because of "municipal overburden." Municipal overburden is a measure of the "needs" of a district to finance services other than education. There is no clear-cut consensus on whether this is a legitimate or an illegitimate measure, in part because it represents a problem with revenues rather than with expenditures and in part because the problem may affect services other than education more than it affects education.

Property wealth of a district (and, alternatively, fiscal capacity or income) has received abundant attention inside and outside of the courts in the last decade. Most people now classify district wealth as an illegitimate characteristic.

3. *Program-Based Characteristics*. A final category of differentiating characteristics is based on the kind of program the child is enrolled in. For example, differences in resources for vocational education versus college-preparatory curriculums are often considered legitimate. The differences are usually justified on the basis of higher costs for vocational programs. The acceptance of this kind of difference as the basis of cost differentials is on fairly shaky ground conceptually, because costs are always a function of the quality and quantity of output produced. Vocational education programs need not be costlier per child if output levels are set lower. For example, class size or time spent on machines is a variable affecting cost and output. If predetermined output levels are established and anything else is considered inequitable, then costs would be a legitimate difference. The use of program differentials as legitimate characteristics also implies that children's *choices* as to program are acceptable reasons for varying resources to achieve equity. The previously considered differentials were outside the immediate control of the child (i.e., handicap) or the district (i.e., size), and thus program enrollment differentials have a different conceptual basis.

It should be reiterated that all the classifications of differentiating characteristics summarized in Table 2.1 and discussed above are to some extent value judgments, and the particular choices made reflect our judgments about currently acceptable classifications.

Assessing Appropriately Unequal Treatment. Although it is possible to identify differences among children, it is more difficult to determine the ways these differences should be handled in making assessments about the equity of the system. A more detailed discussion of how to *measure* the unequal treatment of unequals appears shortly. Here, we briefly outline some of the procedures in order to exemplify more concretely the meaning of the principle.

First, if there is good information on the program costs of extra services for the special pupil populations and some specifications of levels of achievement expected for the special population groups, a weight could be derived indicating the extra cost of a particular program in relation to the basic program. If each student is then weighted to reflect these program-cost differences, analyses could be done on revenues, expenditures, or services per weighted pupil. An analysis using weighted pupils, in effect, combines the equal treatment of equals and the unequal treatment of unequals principles into a single assessment of equity.

Alternatively, all expenditures or programs for these special purposes could hypothetically be eliminated and an analysis made of the equity of the distribution of just the basic education program. Of course, this solution skirts the issues of how much additional is required for the needier groups, whether the categorical funds are actually spent on special pupil populations, and whether districts spend noncategorical funds on special pupils. An analysis that eliminates the objects for special pupils, in effect eliminates any real assessment of the unequal treatment of unequals. Such elimination may, however, improve the assessment of the equal treatment of equals.

A third way to measure pupil differences is to calculate a relationship across a state's districts between the object per pupil and the percentage of pupils in a particular group that deserves additional amounts of the object. As we will discuss in detail in the next section on statistical measures, the interpretation of such a relationship measure is not always straightforward.

A final way to measure pupil differences is to calculate the statewide average revenues, expenditures, services, etc., per pupil for the special population group as well as for the nonspecial or regular group. Then the two averages can be compared. This is a direct way to judge the unequal treatment of unequals, but difficult judgments must be made about how large the differences in average spending between groups should be.

The unequal treatment of unequals is identical to the vertical-equity criterion used by public-finance economists in tax studies. It is also similar to the ideas expressed in the education literature by those such as Charles Benson who argue that equal opportunity of outputs and outcomes has no chance of success unless there is unequal treatment with respect to inputs. That is, children who "start the race behind" must be provided additional resources in order to catch up.

Equal Opportunity. The third equity principle incorporates one of many lines of thinking on equal opportunity. We label this third principle equal opportunity, but caution readers to study our definition closely because the words *equal opportunity* have taken on so many other meanings in the last twenty years. The principle can be formulated in a negative way: there should not be differences according to characteristics that are considered illegitimate, such as property wealth per pupil, household income, fiscal capacity, or sex. For example, this principle would require that there be no relationship between expenditures, resources, programs, outcomes, and per-pupil wealth or fiscal capacity. This example illustrates one way of implementing fiscal or wealth neutrality where the general fiscal or wealth neutrality concept states that education should not be a function of local wealth.

Children's Equity Measures

After choosing the objects of concern and the equity principles, the remaining step in the assessment of children's equity, based on our framework, is the selection of appropriate measures to quantify the degree of equity or inequity. Decisions about the equity measures are analogous to those already discussed in this chapter, because numerous measures are available and many of the alternatives can be differentiated by value judgments. The presentation of the equity measures in this part of the chapter is organized around the three equity principles. Measures of horizontal equity are discussed first; next, equal-opportunity measures are considered; and finally, an examination is presented of the vertical-equity measures. In each case, the measures are described, and then the differences among the alternatives are explained. Numerical examples that illustrate many of the concepts introduced in this part are presented in chapter 4.

Although the equity measures treated here can be used to answer many questions, it is assumed in this discussion that the issue of interest is the assessment of the equity of a state's school-finance system over time or the comparison of the equity of two or more states' school-finance systems at one or more points in time. When discussing children's equity measures in this context, it is helpful to briefly comment on the unit of analysis. Conceptually, data on per-pupil objects could be available at the individual-pupil level, i.e., actual revenues or expenditures on each individual pupil. On the practical side, data are usually available for the average level of a per-pupil object in each district. For example, a district's state and local revenues per pupil are computed by dividing the total state and local revenues in the district by the total number of pupils in the district. The implicit assumption in this calculation is that all pupils in the district receive the average level of per-pupil state and local revenues.

Even when intradistrict data on individual pupils are unavailable, a choice must be made between the district and the pupil units of analysis. The district unit of analysis views each state (in each year) as a distribution of districts. Therefore, the equity measures are computed with one observation for each district. The pupil unit of analysis views each state (in each year) as a distribution of pupils. Since only one observation is available for each district, the district average for variables such as per-pupil revenues is assigned to each pupil. This, in effect, weights each district by the number of pupils in the district. Basically, the pupil unit of analysis takes districts with more pupils into account more heavily than the district unit of analysis does.

The choice between the pupil and the district unit of analysis is a value judgment that can make a difference empirically. Nevertheless, the discussion of the equity measures is simplified considerably by using only one unit of analysis. This discussion utilizes the pupil of analysis, since it appears to be preferred by most school-finance analysts and because it is easier for a reader to translate from the pupil to the district unit of analysis than to do the reverse. A numerical example that shows how the equity measures are computed using both units of analysis and demonstrates that the choice of the unit of analysis can affect an equity assessment is presented in chapter 3.

Measures of Horizontal Equity. The horizontal-equity principle states that equals should be treated equally. Measures of this principle are statistics that capture the spread, or dispersion, in a distribution. Perfect equity would exist when every pupil in the distribution receives the same object, and the horizontal-equity measures assess how far the distribution is from perfect equality.

Horizontal-equity measures can be general statistical dispersion measures applied to school finance, such as the variance, or measures that have been developed through research in school finance or income inequality, such as the McLoone index or Atkinson's index respectively. Although no list of horizontal-equity measures is exhaustive, a rather complete list of the measures that could be used to assess horizontal equity and a brief explanation of each follows.

1. Range—the difference between the highest and the lowest per-pupil objects in the distribution.
2. Restricted range—the difference between the per-pupil object at the 95th and 5th percentiles of pupils arranged in ascending order of per-pupil objects.
3. Federal range ratio—the restricted range divided by the per-pupil object at the 5th percentile of pupils.
4. Relative mean deviation—the sum of the absolute value of the differences between each per-pupil object and the mean per-pupil object, as a proportion of total per-pupil objects in the distribution.
5. McLoone index—the ratio of the actual sum of per-pupil objects for pupils below the median to the sum of per-pupil objects that would exist if each pupil below the median were at the median per-pupil object.
6. Variance—the average of the squared deviations of each per-pupil object from the mean per-pupil object.
7. Coefficient of variation—the square root of the variance of per-pupil objects divided by the mean per-pupil object.
8. Standard deviation of logarithms—the square root of the variance of the natural logarithm of per-pupil objects.
9. Gini coefficient—shows how far the distribution of per-pupil objects is from providing each percentage of pupils (e.g., 5 percent of pupils) with an equal percentage of object (e.g., 5 percent of objects); based on the Lorenz curve.
10. Theil's measure—a measure of inequality based on the notion of entropy in information.
11. Atkinson's index—a measure of inequality based on the choice of an explicit social-welfare function.

More precise formulas for each horizontal-equity measure are presented in table 2.2. These formulas are specified using the pupil unit of analysis. If, in these formulas, the number of pupils in each district, P_i, is set equal to one, then the formulas would reflect the district unit of analysis.

Before describing a way to categorize the differences among these measures, a few comments on some of the more complex measures may be helpful. The Gini coefficient, which is used widely in the measurement of per-capita income inequality, can be employed to assess per-pupil object inequality. The Gini coefficient can be calculated by the formula presented in table 2.2, although this formula is not linked in an obvious way to the concept of a Lorenz curve upon which the Gini coefficient is based. The Lorenz curve

Table 2.2 Formulas for Revenue-Disparity Measures (Pupil Unit of Analysis)

Measure	Formula
1. The range	Highest X_i − lowest X_i.
2. The restricted range	X_i at or above which 5 percent of the pupils lie − X_i at or below which 5 percent of the pupils lie.
3. The federal range ratio	(restricted range)/(X_i at or below which 5 percent of the pupils lie).
4. The relative mean deviation	$\left(\sum_{i=1}^{N} P_i \mid \bar{X}_p - X_i \mid\right) / \left(\bar{X}_p \sum_{i=1}^{N} P_i\right)$
5. The McLoone index	$\left(\sum_{i=1}^{J} P_i X_i\right) / \left(M_p \sum_{i=1}^{J} P_i\right)$ where districts 1 through J are below M_p.
6. The variance	$\left(\sum_{i=1}^{N} P_i (\bar{X}_p - X_i)^2\right) / \left(\sum_{i=1}^{N} P_i\right)$
7. The coefficient of variation	$\sqrt{VAR} / \bar{X}_p$
8. The standard deviation of logarithms	$\left[\left(\sum_{i=1}^{N} P_i (Z - \log_e X_i)^2\right) / \left(\sum_{i=1}^{N} P_i\right)\right]^{1/2}$ where $Z = \left(\sum_{i=1}^{N} P_i (\log_e X_i)\right) / \left(\sum_{i=1}^{N} P_i\right)$.
9. The Gini coefficient	$\left(\sum_{i=1}^{N} \sum_{j=1}^{N} P_i P_j \mid X_i - X_j \mid\right) / \left[2 \left(\sum_{i=1}^{N} P_i\right)^2 \bar{X}_p\right]$
10. Theil's measure	$\left(\sum_{i=1}^{N} P_i (X_i \log_e X_i - \bar{X}_p \log_e \bar{X}_p)\right) / \left(\bar{X}_p \sum_{i=1}^{N} P_i\right)$ or $\frac{1}{N} \sum_{i=1}^{N} \left(P_i \left(\frac{X_i}{\bar{X}_p}\right)\right) \left(\log_e \frac{X_i}{\bar{X}_p}\right)$
11. Atkinson's index ($E > 0; E \neq 1$)	$\left[\left(\sum_{i=1}^{N} P_i (X_i / \bar{X}_p)^{1-E}\right) / \left(\sum_{i=1}^{N} P_i\right)\right]^{1/(1-E)}$

Note: The following symbols are used in the formulas above: P_i = number of pupils in district i; N = number of districts; X_i = average revenues (expenditures) per pupil in district i; $\bar{X}_p$ = mean revenues per pupil for all pupils; M_p = median revenues per pupil for all pupils.

can be plotted on a graph that has the percent of total objects in a state as the y-axis and the percent of pupils in a state as the x-axis, where both axes run from 0 to 100 percent. The Lorenz curve is a plot of the percentage of total objects received by increasing percentages of pupils calculated when pupils are placed in ascending order of per-pupil objects. When every pupil receives the same object, the Lorenz curve is the 45° line running from the lower left (0%, 0%) to the upper right (100%, 100%) corners of the graph, since 10 percent of the pupils receive 10 percent of the objects, 20 percent of the pupils receive 20 percent of the objects, and so on. But as long as there is some inequality, the Lorenz curve will lie below the 45° line, and the greater the inequality the farther below the 45° line the Lorenz curve will lie. The Gini coefficient is the ratio of the area between the 45° line and the Lorenz curve to the total area below the 45° line, and varies from 0 (perfect equality) to 1 (percent inequality). A detailed numerical example of the calculation of the Gini coefficient using the Lorenz curve and the formula will be presented in chapter 4.

Theil's measure of inequality is based on information theory, and the reader is referred to Theil's original work for a detailed explanation of the derivation of the measure, since the formula may not be very intuitive.[4] In essence, Theil shows how a measure that was originally designed to capture the information content of a set of probabilistic events can be used to measure the inequality of an income distribution. When an individual's share of total income is equated to the probability of an event (the sum of income shares, and thus of probabilities, equals one), the information-content measure becomes an inequality measure. By analogy, if per-pupil objects are viewed in the same way as per-capita income, then Theil's measure can be utilized to assess horizontal equity as well. Theil shows that, in addition to the measurement of inequality of a distribution, the measure can be used to calculate the inequality within and between subsets of the distribution.

Atkinson's index is a measure of income inequality that is derived from a specific utility function.[5] Again, by equating income inequality with per-pupil object inequality, Atkinson's index can assess horizontal equity in school finance. Without duplicating Atkinson's original derivation here, several characteristics of Atkinson's index are explained so that the measure can be better understood. As a measure of horizontal equity, Atkinson's index is based upon a function, analogous to a social-welfare function, that converts a distribution of per-pupil objects to a single number that theoretically measures the total welfare (or desirability) of the distribution. The so-called welfare function simultaneously takes into account how much of the object each pupil receives and the equity among pupils. Built into the welfare function is a trade-off between the levels of per-pupil objects and the equity of the per-pupil objects. That is, it is assumed that within some range people favor a lower level of the objects if more equity is achieved.

A social-welfare function that is commonly used by economists because of certain desirable properties is the following:

$$\text{Social Welfare} = \frac{1}{\sum_{i=1}^{N} P_i} \left(\sum_{i=1}^{N} P_i \left[A + B \left(\frac{X_i^{1-E}}{1-E} \right) \right] \right)$$

---

4. See Henri Theil, *Economics and Information Theory* (Chicago: Rand McNally, 1967), chap. 4.
5. Atkinson, "On the Measurement of Inequality."

where N is the number of districts in a state, P_i is the number of pupils in district i, X_i is the per-pupil objects in district i, A and B are constants, and E is a parameter that has a specific interpretation. The parameter E, which can vary from zero to infinity, explicitly incorporates the equity concerns into the social-welfare function and into the equity measure, as we will show shortly. The larger the value of E, the more concern is shown for the lower end of the distribution. Thus, an important advantage of this particular social-welfare function is that equity concerns can be expressed explicitly by specifying values of E.

When the social-welfare function is specified as above, the formula for Atkinson's index of equity, I is the following:

$$I = \left[\left(\sum_{i=1}^{N} P_i \left(\frac{X_i}{\overline{X}} \right)^{1-E} \right) \Big/ \left(\sum_{i=1}^{N} P_i \right) \right]^{1/(1-E)}$$

With this formulation, Atkinson's index equals 1 for perfect equity and 0 for complete inequity. Furthermore, the derivation leads to an appealing interpretation. For any distribution, the value of the index can be interpreted to mean that if per-pupil objects were equally distributed (i.e., perfect horizontal equity were achieved), then one would need the fraction I of total per-pupil objects to achieve the same level of welfare as in the actual distribution. When $I = .75$, for example, it means that the same level of welfare would be obtained if 75 percent of the total objects were redistributed equally among all pupils. But this distribution is more equitable and is preferred on equity grounds to one that has an index of .74, where the welfare in the actual distribution is the same as if all pupils receive 74 percent of the objects, and so on. Finally, note that the parameter E that was specified in the social-welfare function continues to play a critical role in the index of equity; higher values of E make the index more sensitive to pupils at the low end of the distribution.

Both the descriptions of the measures and the formulas for each suggest that there are some rather striking differences among the horizontal-equity measures. In order to differentiate among these horizontal-equity measures, the particular values that are incorporated in each measure can be examined. One way to enumerate these values is through a series of questions, and such a series is displayed in table 2.3. The way in which any particular measure answers these questions characterizes the value judgments embedded in the horizontal-equity measure. Once the meaning of the value judgments are understood, they can be used for many purposes, including to select a subset of measures that are consistent with a desired group of values or to better understand how to interpret a horizontal-equity assessment when there is disagreement among the measures. The value-judgment questions can be explained in more detail to give more meaning to the various values.

Question 1 asks whether all observations in the distribution are included in the measure. In some cases, people's values may prefer the exclusion of some

Table 2.3 Value Judgments Inherent in Eleven Horizontal-Equity Measures

Value-Judgment Questions	Restricted Range	Range	Federal Range Ratio	Relative Mean Deviation	McLoone Index	Variance	Coefficient of Variation	Standard Deviation of Logarithms	Gini Coefficient	Theil's Measure	Atkinson's Index ($E > 0$)
1. Are all children taken into account in the measure?	No	No	No	Yes	No	Yes	Yes	Yes	Yes	Yes	Yes
2. Does the measure always show an improvement when objects are transferred from one child to another lower in the distribution, without reversing the ranking of the children? (Such a transfer is often referred to as "mean preserving.")	No	No	No	No	No	Yes	Yes	Almost always*	Yes	Yes	Almost always**
3. Does the measure always change when the objects of each child are increased by a constant proportional amount? (Often referred to as degree of relative inequality aversion.)	Yes	Yes	No	No	No	Yes	No	No	No	No	No
4. Does the measure always change when the objects of each child are increased by a constant absolute amount? (Often referred to as degree of absolute inequality aversion.)	No	No	Yes	Yes	Yes	No	Yes	Yes	Yes	Yes	Yes
5. Does the measure record object changes at different levels of the distribution in the same way?	No	No	No	No	No	Yes	Yes	No	No	No	No
6. Is the mean used as a basis of comparison?	No	No	No	Yes	No	Yes	Yes	Yes	No	Yes	Yes
7. Is the median used as a basis of comparison?	No	No	No	No	Yes	No	No	No	No	No	No
8. Are all levels compared to one another as a basis for comparison?	No	No	No	No	No	No	No	No	Yes	No	No

Source: Berne and Stiefel, "Concepts of Equity and Their Relationship to State School Finance Plans," *Journal of Education Finance* 5 (fall 1979): 114–15.
*Not always true for transfers that are made within the high end of the distribution.
**Not true when $E = \infty$.

of the pupils. For example, a policymaker who prefers a minimum-foundation school-finance program may be concerned only with raising the bottom of the distribution (leveling up), in which case the McLoone index is a possible measure. Other policymakers may wish to have most of the pupils bunched fairly closely together without being overly concerned by either tail—the extremes—of the distribution. If so, the federal range ratio is useful. As a final example, a policymaker may want to see no more than a specific difference in objects between any two children, in which case the range would be an appropriate measure. Notice that seven of the eleven horizontal-equity measures in table 2.3 take all children into account in the measure. If the results from these seven differ systematically from the other four, then this value judgment may provide part of the explanation.

Question 2 is concerned with what happens to the measure when there is a transfer of objects from a child higher in the distribution to one lower in the distribution. Such a transfer does not affect the value of the mean, nor does it change the relative positions of children involved in the transfer. Many people think that such a transfer should increase the equity rating. Table 2.3 shows that about half of the measures do exhibit such an increase in equity, while half do not. In particular, the most commonly used measures in studies of income distribution—the variance, the coefficient of variation, and the Gini coefficient—all exhibit the increase in equity. Although in the case of the standard deviation of the logarithms and Atkinson's index, question 2 cannot be answered yes all of the time, the instances when the answer is no for these measures are quite limited. For the standard deviation of the logarithms, the answer may be no for some transfers at the very high end of the distribution, and a no answer for Atkinson's index occurs when E equals ∞. The answers to questions 1 and 2 are related, since question 2 must be answered no when question 1 is answered no.

Question 3 asks how the measure responds to equal percentage changes in the objects associated with each child. There are alternative views on how an equity measure should respond to such percentage changes. On the one hand, since there are more of the objects to be distributed, some may think that equity has diminished if the dispersion stays relatively the same. The range, the restricted-range, and the variance are the only three measures that show less equity after equal percentage increases. Others may think that because each child's level has increased by the same percent, each child is as well off in relation to every other child as before and that therefore the equity of the distribution has not changed. The eight remaining measures are all consistent with this second value judgment, because they do not change with equal percentage increases. When a state or group of states is being assessed over time and the object is measured in dollars such as revenues or expenditures, this value judgment has a particular interpretation. Since inflation in a state is likely to be partly uniform across districts, and because uniform inflation for a state is an equal proportional increase, the horizontal-equity measures that do not respond to equal proportional increases are, in a sense, inflation proof. Thus, in inflationary times, the measures that *are* sensitive to equal percentage increases produce misleading results when measuring equity longitudinally.

Question 4 asks if the measure changes when a constant amount of the object is added to each pupil. With a constant absolute increase for each pupil, the differences among the pupils may seem less important. All the measures except the range, the restricted range, and the variance show more equity when a constant absolute amount is added to each pupil. For any particular measure, the answers to questions 3 and 4 are always either yes-no or no-yes. As a result, if the performance of the range, the restricted range, and the variance is at odds with the other horizontal-equity measures, it may be useful to ask whether part of the difference is attributed to the value judgments captured by questions 3 and 4.

Question 5 is concerned with the way transfers of objects between one pupil and another are treated at various points in the distribution. It follows that a measure that answers no to question 1 must answer question 5 in the negative, since some transfers would be considered and others would not. But for certain measures, an answer of no does not fully characterize the nature of this value judgment. More specifically, the standard deviation of the logarithms, the McLoone index, and Atkinson's index (when E has larger values) place more weight on transfers at the lower end of the distribution, and this value judgment may be particularly relevant in school finance. The standard deviation of the logarithms places more weight at the low end due to the logarithmic transformation; the McLoone index only considers pupils below the median; and Atkinson's index can place more or less weight on the bottom of the distribution depending upon the specified value of E.

Finally questions 6, 7, and 8 describe the points of comparison used in the horizontal-equity measures. The mean is used as a basis of comparison by six of the eleven measures, while the median and all levels are used by one each. Questions 6, 7, and 8 are all answered no for the range, the restricted range, and the federal range ratio, since these use selected points in the distribution for comparisons.

Very few of the measures provide similar answers to all the value judgment questions, so that the questions do differentiate among the measures. However, based on the answers to certain questions, it is possible to view the measures in conceptual groups rather than as eleven individual measures. First, questions 3 and 4 isolate the range, the restricted range, and the variance into one group of measures that is sensitive to equal percentage increases and insensitive to equal additions. The McLoone index, the standard deviation of the logarithms, and Atkinson's index (with high values of E) all weight the low end of the distribution more heavily than the rest of the distribution and thus form the second group. Of the remaining measures, the relative mean deviation, the coefficient of variation, the Gini coefficient, Theil's measure, and Atkinson's index (with low values of E) are insensitive to equal percentage increases, include all the observations, and, therefore, can form the third group. This leaves the federal range ratio in a fourth group. If these conceptual groupings perform as groups in empirical research, then this will provide one way to select a subset of the measures. We will examine this question in the empirical chapters later in the book.

Measures of Equal Opportunity. The equal-opportunity principle incorporates the belief that a relationship should not exist between the objects in an education system and certain characteristics. Stated in this way, it is a negative principle; equal opportunity exists when there is an absence of a relationship between the objects and what were presented earlier in the chapter as illegitimate characteristics. Measures of the equal-opportunity principle, therefore, are essentially relationship measures where, in most cases, perfect equity is defined as the absence of a relationship. The specification of the equal-opportunity principle itself involves certain value-laden choices, particularly the selection of the illegitimate characteristics. In this part of the chapter we focus on the role that values play in the measurement of the principle, once it has been specified.

Although there are a diverse set of characteristics that could be considered illegitimate by some people, the presentation of the equal-opportunity measures can be simplified by selecting one particular characteristic to utilize throughout the discussion. In education finance, the obvious choice is the characteristic that receives the most attention—a measure of property wealth—and this is the characteristic used here as an example. In this part of the chapter it is assumed that property wealth in a state is measured in dollars or assessed value of property per pupil. Further, it is assumed that assessments are equalized within a state to some fraction of market value, although the fraction is not necessarily 1 (full market value). While per-pupil property wealth is the characteristic employed in the discussion, this should not be interpreted as an endorsement of this variable as a preferred measure of wealth compared to others such as income (per capita or per pupil), fiscal capacity, or a combined property-income measure. The major points addressed in this part revolve around the characteristics of the measures, and these are not generally affected by the selection of the illegitimate characteristic.

There are numerous equal-opportunity measures that could be employed to determine whether a relationship exists between the object and property wealth, but in school finance, as in many other areas, regression-based measures are the most common. Regression measures are popular not only because they are based on certain statistical principles, but also because there are several possible equal-opportunity measures that can be derived from regression analysis. As a result of their desirability and diversity, only regression-based measures are assessed in this part.[6] Also, the convention of only

---

6. The use of a grouping technique such as quintiles is illustrated in chapter 4.

using the pupil unit of analysis is continued. One additional point to keep in mind is that, as will be shown in the next part of this chapter, regression measures are also used to assess vertical equity. Therefore, much of the discussion here is applicable as well to measures of the vertical-equity principles.

Eleven regression-based relationship measures are evaluated in this part. The eleven measures represent different ways that regressions can be used to assess the relationship between two variables, where per-pupil objects are treated as the dependent variable, per-pupil property values as the independent variable, and all regressions are run on a pupil-weighted basis. A brief description of the eleven regression-based relationship measures is presented in table 2.4.

Among these eleven measures there are four types: correlation, slopes, elasticities, and adjusted relationship measures. All four groups of measures are based on a regression estimate of the relationship between a dependent variable (per-pupil objects) and an independent variable (per-pupil property values in this illustration), but each group captures a different aspect of this estimate. Two approaches are used here to explain the differences among the measures. First, the meanings and interpretations of the measures are explored, and second, the manner in which the measures incorporate value judgments, similar to those used in the previous part, are described.

The *correlation coefficient* measures the degree to which the two variables are related, or, in other words, the strength of the linear relationship. Using the symbols defined above, the formula for the pupil-weighted Pearson correlation coefficient is as follows:

$$\text{SIM CORR} = \frac{\sum_{i=1}^{N} P_i(X_i - \bar{X})(W_i - \bar{W})}{\sqrt{\sum_{i=1}^{N} P_i(X_i - \bar{X})^2} \sqrt{\sum_{i=1}^{N} P_i(W_i - \bar{W})^2}}.$$

The correlation coefficient ranges from -1 to 1. A value of 1 indicates a perfect positive linear relationship, and a value of -1 signifies a perfect negative linear relationship. A correlation coefficient of 0 means either that the objects and the independent variable do not move together linearly or that they are related in a nonlinear way. As a measure of equal opportunity, a correlation coefficient of 0 is indicative of perfect equity, and a value of 1 signifies the most inequitable case. Finally, another way of viewing the simple correlation is to note that the square of the simple correlation, the coefficient of determination, is the fraction of variation in the dependent variable that is explained by the regression line. While this interpretation is useful, the simple correla-

Table 2.4 Descriptions of Eleven Regression-Based Relationship Measures (Pupil Unit of Analysis)

Measure	Description
1. Correlation (SIM CORR)	The Pearson correlation coefficient between X_i (dependent variable) and W_i (independent variable).
2. Slope from the simple regression (SLOPE1)	b_1 from the pupil-weighted regression $X_i = a + b_1 W_i$.
3. Slope from the quadratic regression (SLOPE2)	$b_1 + 2b_2 \overline{W}$ from the pupil-weighted regression $X_i = a + b_1 W_i + b_2 W_i^2$, computed at $\overline{W}$.
4. Slope from the cubic regression (SLOPE3)	$b_1 + 2b_2 \overline{W} + 3b_3 \overline{W}^2$ from the pupil-weighted regression $X_i = a + b_1 W_i + b_2 W_i^2 + b_3 W_i^3$, computed at $\overline{W}$.
5. Elasticity from the simple regression (ELAST1)	(SLOPE1) $\times (\overline{W}/\overline{X})$, computed at $\overline{X}, \overline{W}$.
6. Elasticity from the quadratic regression (ELAST2)	(SLOPE2) $\times (\overline{W}/\overline{X})$, computed at $\overline{X}, \overline{W}$.
7. Elasticity from the cubic regression (ELAST3)	(SLOPE3) $\times (\overline{W}/\overline{X})$, computed at $\overline{X}, \overline{W}$.
8. Constant elasticity (ELASTC)	b_1 from the pupil-weighted regression $\log X_i = a + b_1 \log W_i$.
9. Adjusted relationship measure from the pupil-weighted simple regression (ARM1)	$(2 \times \text{SLOPE1} \times \sigma_w)/\overline{X}$.
10. Adjusted relationship measure from the pupil-weighted quadratic regression (ARM2)	$(2b_1 \sigma_w + 4b_2 \overline{W} \sigma_w)/\overline{X}$
11. Adjusted relationship measure from the pupil-weighted cubic regression (ARM3)	$(2b_1 \sigma_w + 4b_2 \sigma_w \overline{W} + 6b_3 \sigma_w \overline{W}^2 + 2b_3 \sigma_w^3)/\overline{X}$

Note: The following symbols are used in the descriptions above: X_i = per-pupil objects in district i; $\overline{X}$ = pupil-weighted mean per-pupil objects in the state; W_i = per-pupil property values in district i; $\overline{W}$ = pupil-weighted mean per-pupil property values in the state; σ_w = pupil-weighted standard deviation of per-pupil property wealth in the state.

tion is a preferred measure of equal opportunity because it records the direction of the relationship (positive or negative) as well as the strength. Usually only a relationship in a positive direction is considered inequitable, but this depends on the independent variable of concern.

While the correlation measures whether two variables move together linearly, the slopes and elasticities assess the magnitude of the relationship. The *slopes* show the size of the change in the dependent variable (per-pupil objects) associated with a one-unit change in the independent variable (per-pupil property values in the descriptions above). For example, with per-pupil objects measured in dollars and per-pupil property values measured in thousands of dollars, a slope of 5 indicates that every change in assessed value of $1,000 per pupil is associated with a five dollar per-pupil change in the object.

In an equal-opportunity context a slope of zero is equated with equity, and for positive slopes, the higher the value, the more inequitable the relationship. Three different functional forms, simple, quadratic, and cubic, are used to estimate the slopes in order to allow for nonlinear as well as linear relationships. In all cases, we follow the usual convention and calculate the slopes at the mean values of the dependent and independent variables. The formula used to compute the bivariate slope from the pupil-weighted bivariate regression is as follows:

$$\text{SLOPE1} = \frac{\sum_{i=1}^{N} P_i(X_i - \bar{X})(W_i - \bar{W})}{\sum_{i=1}^{N} P_i(W_i - \bar{W})^2}.$$

The formulas used to compute the values of b_1, b_2, and b_3 in SLOPE2 and SLOPE3 are complex algebraically and are not presented here. The reader interested in the formulas is referred to a standard statistics text.[7]

The *elasticity*, like the slope, measures the magnitude of the relationship, but in terms of percentage changes rather than in the absolute unit changes reflected in the slope. Suppose an elasticity of .3 exists, with per-pupil objects and per-pupil property values as the dependent and independent variables respectively. This means that a 1 percent change in per-pupil property values is associated with a .3 percent change in per-pupil objects. When used as an equal-opportunity measure, an elasticity of zero is equitable, and inequity increases as the elasticity increases. Elasticities are calculated from the same simple, quadratic, and cubic regressions utilized in the calculation of the slope, and the elasticities are computed at the mean values of the independent and dependent variables. In addition, a logarithmic functional form ($\log X_i = b_0 + b_1 \log W_i$) is used to obtain a fourth estimate of the elasticity.

Although the notions of strength of the relationship versus magnitude of the relationship differentiate between the correlation on the one hand and the slopes and elasticities on the other, the differences between these measures take on more meaning when they are illustrated graphically, as in figure 2.2. In part A there is a high simple correlation, since the points are tightly fitted to a line; but the line exhibits a low simple elasticity and simple slope. This might result for the following reason. Per-pupil property values may be an excellent explanatory variable for the variation that exists in per-pupil objects, thus resulting in a high simple correlation, indicating a good fit. However if the variation in per-pupil objects is low in relation to the variation in

---

7. For example, see Eric A. Hanushek and John E. Jackson, *Statistical Methods For Social Scientists* (New York: Academic Press, 1977).

Figure 2.2 Hypothetical Data Illustrating Two Different Combinations of Correlation and Bivariate Elasticity and Slope Measures

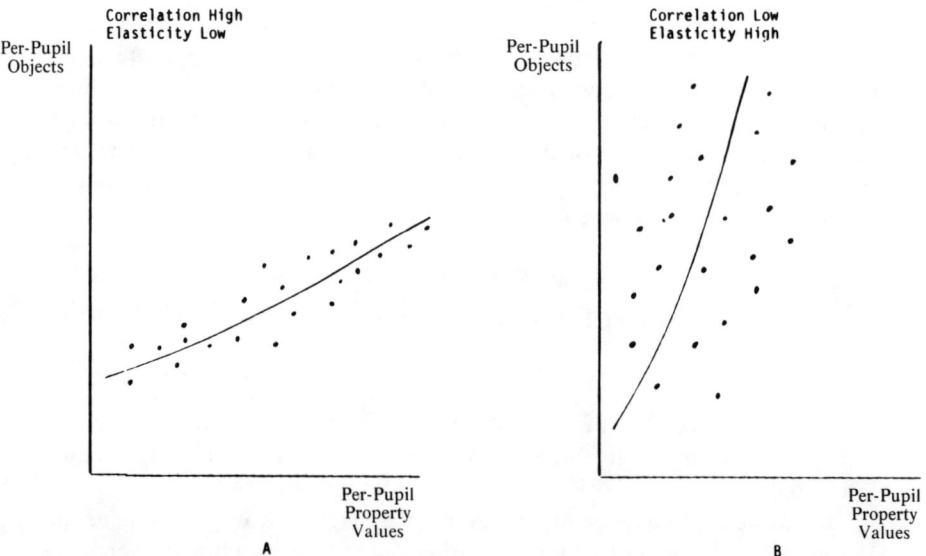

per-pupil property values, the magnitude of the effect of either a one-unit or a 1 percent change in per-pupil property values on per-pupil objects can be low. This leads to a relatively low simple slope and simple elasticity.[8]

Part B in figure 2.2 illustrates the situation in which the data exhibit a low simple correlation and a high simple slope and simple elasticity. The explanation for such a phenomenon is that while per-pupil property values explain some of the variation in per-pupil objects, there remains a large part of the variation that is not explained by per-pupil property values. The low simple correlation is describing a loose fit around the regression line, but the best estimate of the magnitude of the relationship between per-pupil objects and property values is still the estimated simple slope or simple elasticity, both of which are high.

Figure 2.2 shows that the choice between the correlation versus the slopes

---

8. The importance of the ratio of the variation in objects to the variation in property values can be seen in the algebra of the relationship between the correlation and the elasticity in the bivariate regression:

$$\text{ELAST1} = (\text{SIM CORR}) \left(\frac{\sigma_x}{\sigma_W}\right)\left(\frac{\bar{W}}{\bar{X}}\right),$$

with σ_x equal to the pupil-weighted standard deviation of the per-pupil object and the other symbols as defined in the text.

and elasticities depends on which aspect of the relationship is critical: the degree of interrelatedness (correlation) or the magnitude of the relationship (slope and elasticity). Some people may be able to focus on the slopes and elasticities, in part because they feel that situations such as the one displayed in part A are not inequitable.[9] Yet this does not appear to be a universally held value judgment, since the correlation is so widely used. Of course, there is no need to use only one measure, so that if the questions of existence and size of a relationship are both of concern, two or more measures could be used simultaneously.

This discussion of the relationship measures has focused on instances, such as those displayed in figure 2.2, when conclusions that result from the application of the measures are likely to conflict. Even when there is complete agreement among the simple correlation, simple slope, and simple elasticity, however, there is still an ignored aspect of the equal-opportunity concept that leads to the development of a different measure than those previously considered. When equal opportunity between per-pupil objects and per-pupil property values is being evaluated, it is not necessarily the relationship between the two variables that is inequitable. Instead, the inequity may hinge on the degree to which large disparities in per-pupil objects are associated with large values of relationship measures. Situations can exist where the simple correlation, slopes, and elasticities are high but where meaningful differences in per-pupil objects do not result, because the disparity in per-pupil property values is relatively low.

The graphs in figure 2.3 are constructed to illustrate this point. In states A and B the mean per-pupil objects and mean per-pupil property values are equal, and there are the same number of observations (pupils) in each state. Further, the two hypothetical states are constructed so that the simple correlation, simple slopes, and simple elasticities are equal, but the disparities in per-pupil objects and per-pupil property values are different. Despite the identical simple correlations, slopes, and elasticities in states A and B, the disparities in per-pupil objects that are associated with disparities in per-pupil property values are significantly less in state A than in state B. Since some (perhaps most) people would judge state A to be more equitable than state B on the equal-opportunity principle, there is a need for a measure that goes beyond the correlations, slopes, and elasticities.

The *adjusted relationship measures* are designed to incorporate the disparity in per-pupil objects that is associated with the relationship measure, and therefore, they differentiate between states A and B in terms of equal opportunity. The adjusted relationship measures are based on the same simple, quadratic, and cubic regressions used to estimate the slopes and correlation.

---

9. See Stephen Michelson, "What is a 'Just' System for Financing Schools? An Evaluation of Alternative Reforms," in Betsy Levin, ed., *Future Directions for School Finance Reform* (Lexington, Mass.: Lexington Books, 1974).

Figure 2.3 Hypothetical Relationship between Per-Pupil Objects and Property Values in Two States

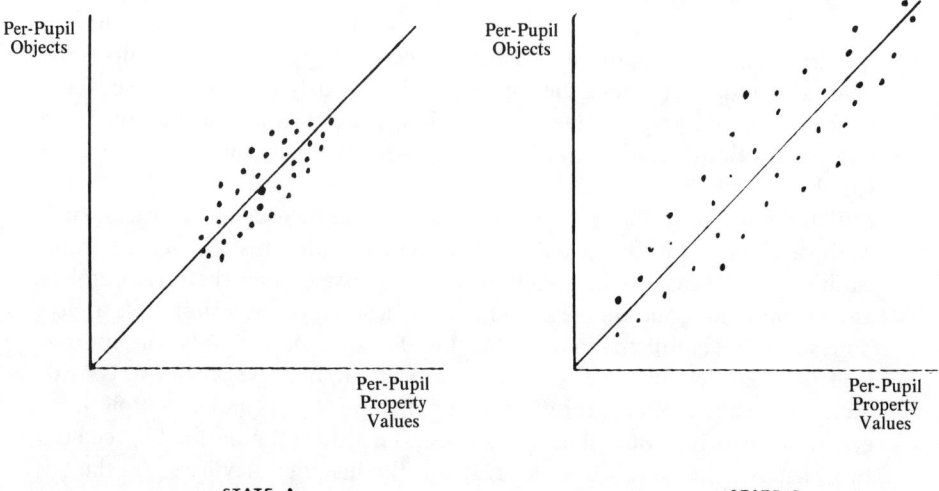

STATE A   STATE B

In order to estimate the measures, a range of per-pupil property values is defined by points that are one standard deviation of per-pupil property values above and below the mean per-pupil property value. The regressions then use these points to predict a difference in per-pupil objects, a difference that is thus based upon both the regression and the disparity in property values. Finally, the predicted difference in per-pupil objects is divided by the mean per-pupil objects, and the adjusted relationship measures' units are, therefore, fractions of mean per-pupil objects. In terms of equal opportunity, a value of zero for the adjusted relationship measures is equitable, with inequity increasing as the adjusted relationship measures increase.

For example, in the case of the simple regression, $X_i = b_0 + b_1 W_i$, the numerator of the adjusted relationship measure is $b_0 + b_1(\bar{W} + \sigma_w) - (b_0 + b_1(\bar{W} - \sigma_w))$, which reduces to $2b_1\sigma_w$, where σ_w is the standard deviation of per-pupil property values. The adjusted relationship measure from the simple regression (ARM1) is thus $(2b_1\sigma_w)/\bar{X}$. Returning one final time to figure 2.3, since b_1 and $\bar{X}$ are the same for states A and B, and because σ_w is smaller in state A than in state B, ARM1 is lower in state A. Therefore, using the bivariate adjusted relationship measure, state A is more equitable from an equal-opportunity perspective.

While the differences in the equal-opportunity measures explained thus far should help people choose one or more measures of equal opportunity, several additional aspects of the measures come to light when they are examined along with a series of value-judgment questions. These value judgment ques-

ORGANIZING ALTERNATIVE SCHOOL-FINANCE-EQUITY CONCEPTS   33

tions are analogous to the ones developed for the horizontal-equity measures except that they have been reformulated for a dependent variable (per-pupil objects) and an independent variable (per-pupil property values in the examples). The value-judgment questions and the answers are displayed for the eleven relationship measures in table 2.5.

The answers to question 1 show that each of the eleven regression-based relationship measures considered here includes all of the pupils in the measure. This question would not be answered yes for all conceivable relationship measures, particularly those that are based on comparisons between levels of per-pupil objects at specific points in the distribution of the per-pupil independent variable. Question 2 is the relationship analogue to the mean-preserving transfer discussed as question 2 under horizontal equity. As table 2.5 shows, only the bivariate slope, the bivariate elasticity, and the bivariate adjusted relationship measure always show an improvement when an object transfer takes place from a high property value–high-object pupil to a pupil who is lower on both variables. The other relationship measures may show an improvement under such conditions, but they will not always do so. Thus, this question may be useful in the selection of one functional form over another.

Questions 3 through 6 are aimed at showing how the relationship measures respond to changes in the dependent and independent variables. While we urge readers to think through how they believe a relationship measure should respond to each of these changes, question 5 takes on particular meaning in an equal-opportunity context when per-pupil property values are the independent variable. Since per-pupil property values are often measured as a fraction of market value (sometimes called "equalized values"), comparisons across states that equalize to a different fraction of market value, or comparisons over time in a state in which the fraction has been changed, can be considered comparisons that involve an equal percentage change in the independent variable. If it is desirable for the equal-opportunity measure to be unaffected by this equalization ratio, since it is somewhat artificial, then the slope measures are not appropriate. Note also that if per-pupil objects are measured in dollars and if inflation is uniform over time, then an answer of no to question 3 insures that the measure is "inflation-proof." For example, the slope measures change as a result of inflation in the dependent variable, holding all else constant. Therefore, the appropriateness of the slope as an equity measure in time-series analysis is questionable if inflation is present.

Based on both the meaning of the measures and the value judgments inherent in them, the relationship measures fall into four groups: correlation, slopes, elasticities, and adjusted relationship measures. Hopefully, by understanding these various measures, an informed selection of one or more of them for the assessment of equal opportunity can take place. At a conceptual level, there are differences among the relationship measures, and later chapters will document the extent of the differences in actual empirical results.

Table 2.5 Value Judgments Inherent in Eleven Relationship Measures

					Measures						
Value Judgment Questions	Simple Correlation (SIM CORR)	Simple Slope (SLOPE1)	Quadratic Slope (SLOPE2)	Cubic Slope (SLOPE3)	Simple Elasticity (ELAST1)	Quadratic Elasticity (ELAST2)	Cubic Elasticity (ELAST3)	Constant Elasticity (ELASTC)	Adjusted Relationship Measure From Simple Regression (ARM1)	Adjusted Relationship Measure From Quadratic Regression (ARM2)	Adjusted Relationship Measure From Cubic Regression (ARM3)
1. Are all children taken into account in the measure?	Yes	Yes	Yes	Yes	Yes	Yes	Yes	Yes	Yes	Yes	Yes
2. Does the measure always show an improvement in equity when objects (dependent variable) are transferred from one child to another with lower objects per child and lower independent variable per child without reversing the ranking of the children? (Such a transfer is often referred to as "mean preserving.")	Not necessarily	Yes	Not necessarily	Not necessarily	Yes	Not necessarily	Not necessarily	Not necessarily	Yes	Not necessarily	Not necessarily
3. Is the measure sensitive to equal percentage changes in objects per child (dependent variable)?	No	Yes	Yes	Yes	Yes	No	No	No	Yes	No	No
4. Is the measure sensitive to equal additions to objects per child (dependent variable)?	No	No	No	No	No	Yes	Yes	Yes	No	Yes	No
5. Is the measure sensitive to equal percentage increases in independent variable per child?	No	Yes	Yes	Yes	No	Yes	Yes	Yes	Yes	Yes	Yes
6. Is the measure sensitive to equal additions to independent variable per child?	No	No	No	No	Yes	No	No	Yes	No	No	No

Before doing that, however, various measures of the third equity principle, vertical equity, are examined.

Measures of Vertical Equity. As will be shown in this part, vertical equity is the most complex of the three principles to measure. Part of this complexity can be traced to the following three questions that must be answered if vertical equity, or the unequal treatment of unequals, is to be assessed:

1. What are the legitimate differences among children that define "unequal" groups of children?
2. Once groups with legitimate differences are defined, how should the educational objects vary over these groups?
3. After the appropriate groups and desired object differences are articulated, how should the equity of the actual situation in comparison with the desired one be measured?

In the discussion of vertical equity earlier in this chapter, the value judgments embodied in the first two questions above were discussed, and in this part the focus is on the third question. Thus, this section addresses technical characteristics of vertical-equity measures. These technical characteristics will be related to policy considerations in the empirical chapters of the book, especially chapter 9. For expositional purposes, it is assumed that there are two groups of pupils, handicapped and nonhandicapped, and there are no different types of handicaps within the former group. This simplifying assumption clarifies the presentation of the measurement issues without seriously reducing the generalizability of the findings. At the end of this part, however, the effects of a relaxation of this assumption are enumerated.

In many ways question 2 (How should educational objects vary over unequal groups?) is the most difficult, and the organization of this discussion of vertical equity measurement is based upon how question 2 is answered. Three sets of vertical-equity measures are considered; question 2 must be answered in detail for the first set, but need only be answered in a general way for the second and third sets. This creates a situation in which the first set of measures addresses a somewhat different question than the second and third sets. To summarize the differences, the first set of measures requires answers to all three questions, and these measures can straightforwardly rank states or assess progress over time in terms of vertical equity. The second and third sets of measures are based only on the identification of special groups of pupils (answer to question 1) and on a more general answer to question 2—whether these special groups should receive more or less of the objects, not on a precise estimate of the appropriate amounts. The second and third sets of measures are well designed to assess whether groups who should receive more actually do receive more, but are less well suited to the production of a precise vertical-equity ranking.

Before beginning to discuss the differences among the three sets of vertical-equity measures, a reminder of the assumptions regarding data availability is in order. Recall that data on the total number of pupils, the number of pupils in special groups, and the total objects are assumed to be available for every district in a state. The important point for the following discussion is that while a per-pupil object figure can be computed for every district in a state, nothing is known about the intra-district distribution of objects among pupils. This will be important in the discussion of the vertical-equity measures.

Weighted Dispersion Measures. The first set of vertical-equity measures, weighted dispersion measures, is based upon a modification of the horizontal-equity measures so that vertical-equity concerns are incorporated. Since the horizontal-equity measures are essentially dispersion measures and because the vertical-equity adjustment is a weighting procedure, these measures are called weighted dispersion measures. As noted above, to utilize weighted dispersion measures, question 2 must be answered precisely. This results in the specification of the appropriate object level for pupils in the special group, compared to those not in the special group. If, for example, in answering question 2 it is determined that handicapped pupils should receive twice as much of the object as nonhandicapped pupils, then handicapped pupils are weighted 2 compared to a weight of 1 for nonhandicapped pupils. With weights such as these, the total number of weighted pupils in every district is computed. Then, in each district, the total objects are divided by the number of weighted pupils to obtain the object per weighted pupil in each district. Finally, any or all of the horizontal-equity (dispersion) measures are computed with per-weighted-pupil objects and weighted pupils replacing per-pupil objects and pupils respectively.

The weighted dispersion measures are interpreted the same way as the horizontal-equity measures; zero dispersion is vertical equity, and inequity increases as the weighted dispersion increases. The same value judgment issues presented in table 2.3 for horizontal-equity measures, apply to weighted dispersion measures. For example, some weighted dispersion measures are insensitive to equal percentage changes, while others are not. Also, some weighted dispersion measures pay more attention to the bottom part of the distribution.

An overly simplistic two-district state can clarify how the weighted dispersion measures operate. Districts A and B have ten pupils each. In district A, however, five pupils are handicapped, while in district B no pupils are handicapped. The total objects in districts A and B are $30,000 and $20,000 respectively. If handicapped pupils are weighted 2, the weighted pupil count in district A becomes 15 (5 + (5 × 2)), while the count in district B remains 10. The per-weighted-pupil objects in both districts are equal ($30,000/15 = $20,000/10 = $2000), indicating that this simplified state is vertically equitable, since there is no dispersion.

There are two ways the weighted dispersion measures can be compared to the other two sets of vertical-equity measures. First, in the calculation of the weighted dispersion measures, each district gets credit for its special groups.

The vertical-equity measure is computed as though the district should receive additional objects for pupils in the special groups. Second, the weighted dispersion measures capture the dispersion that exists after the application of the weights. Thus, all the remaining dispersion is considered to be vertically inequitable.

To summarize, weighted dispersion measures are formulated with a precise answer to question 2, and they can rank a set of states or one state over time in terms of vertical equity. If the requirement of an exact answer to question 2 is too strenuous, then sensitivity analysis can be performed to see how conclusions regarding vertical equity are affected by a particular set of weights. If, however, the specification of a range of usable weights is not possible or preferable, then one of the other two sets of vertical-equity measures may be used.

Regression-based Relationship Measures. For many reasons—stemming perhaps from ideology, methodology, or political considerations—there may be a desire to measure vertical equity without specifying an answer to question 2. If there is only one special group (handicapped versus nonhandicapped, for example) or if each special group can be treated separately, then the regression-based relationship measures, described earlier under the equal-opportunity principle, can serve as vertical-equity measures.

Although the use of the regression-based relationship measure does not require the specification of weights for the special groups, a decision must be made on whether pupils in a special group should receive more or less of the objects than pupils who are not in the special groups, recognizing that this is often a value judgment. In our example, there may be agreement that handicapped pupils should receive more of the object than nonhandicapped pupils. With an agreement such as this, a regression with per-pupil objects as the dependent variable and percent handicapped as the independent variable can form the basis for the calculation of the correlation, the slopes, the elasticities, and the adjusted relationship measures. Any or all of these measures can be used to provide an answer to the question: Do groups who should receive more of the object actually do so? Positive values of the regression-based relationship measures in our example answer this question affirmatively, although due to the different functional forms (bivariate, quadratic, and cubic), all measures may not agree.

This assessment of vertical equity by the regression-based relationship measures is conceptually different from the assessment provided by the weighted dispersion measures. The latter can be used to rank states in terms of vertical equity, while the former only address the more general question concerning whether the more deserving groups actually receive more of the object. Although the regression-based relationship measures are well designed to assess vertical equity from this more general perspective, it is useful to ask whether there are any conditions under which the relationship measures can be used to rank states in terms of vertical equity. To use the regression-based relationship measures to rank states on vertical equity, the values of the measures must be interpreted in a particular way, and this turns out to be analogous to, and perhaps even more difficult than, providing a specific answer to question 2. The problem boils down to this: With correlations, slopes, elasticities, and adjusted relationship measures, is a higher number always more equitable? The answer to this question is no and can be illustrated with an oversimplified example.

Suppose there are two states, each with two districts comprised of one pupil each. In state A there is a district with a nonhandicapped pupil and an object of $2,000 and a district with a handicapped pupil and an object of $4,000. In state B the district with the nonhandicapped pupil has an object of $250 and the district with the handicapped pupil has an object of $5750. The elasticity (or slope) in state B greatly exceeds the elasticity (or slope) in state A, but is state B more vertically equitable? We believe some people would say no. For the regression-based relationship measures, it may be that increases in the measures suggest increases in vertical equity only up to some point. After this point, higher values of the relationship measures correspond to decreases in vertical equity. Even if this is true, however, the determination of the assessment point would not be simple or straightforward, given the formulations and meanings of the various relationship measures. What is the desired correlation, slope, elasticity, or adjusted relationship measure? This question appears to be considerably more difficult to answer than the determination of the appropriate weights for the weighted dispersion measures, which in itself may not be easy.

When the independent variable is a percentage of a group such as handicapped pupils, there is a regression-based relationship measure, not previously described, that should be considered. The new measure, the implicit weight, is based on the bivariate regression and is calculated by dividing the predicted per-pupil object when the independent variable is set to 100 percent (i.e., all handicapped pupils in a district) by the predicted per-pupil object when the independent variable is set to 0 percent (i.e., no handicapped pupils).

The implicit weight can be interpreted analogously to the weight applied in the weighted dispersion measures in the following sense. Assume every district in a state has total (aggregate) objects equal to the number of weighted pupils times the base amount for nonhandicapped pupils. Under these conditions a district with all handicapped pupils will have more *per-pupil* objects then a district with no handicapped pupils. Further, all observations will lie on a regression line such that the implicit weight, the ratio of the predicted per-pupil object for a district with 100 percent handicapped pupils to the predicted per-pupil object for a district with 0 handicapped pupils, equals the weight used in the pupil weighting scheme. Thus, the implicit weight can be viewed as the weight that is implied by the regression line estimated from the actual observations.

To conclude this section, we return to a basic point concerning all the regression-based relationship measures that contrasts them to the weighted dispersion measures. The regression-based relationship measures record the statistical association between the dependent and the independent variables. Thus, there can be significant disparities in object levels across districts, but if these are not related to the independent variables, they will not affect the regression-based relationship measures. This is different from the weighted dispersion measures, where any dispersion remaining after the weighting procedures affects the vertical-equity measure.

The strength of the regression-based relationship measures is their ability to evaluate an aspect of vertical equity in the absence of a specification of a set of desired weights. However, the regression-based relationship measures only assess whether those who should get more do indeed receive more, and they are not well suited to rank states in terms of vertical equity or to assess changes in vertical equity over time. The final vertical-equity measure considered in this section is conceptually similar to the regression-based relationship measures, but the regression method is not used to estimate the relationship.

Ratio Measures. There are techniques other than regression that can be relied upon to assess the differences in per-pupil objects between groups of pupils. Of course, since knowledge is not available about intradistrict distributions of objects, assumptions are necessary for any measure of this kind. If, for example, it is explicitly assumed that all pupils in any district receive the same object levels, then a measure such as the following can be computed:

> the ratio of the average value of per-pupil objects for pupils in the special group to the average value of per-pupil objects for pupils not in the special group.

This measure, called here the "averaged" implicit weight, is calculated in the following way. First, every pupil in a state is assigned the per-pupil object level from his or her district. Then, once the number of pupils in the special group in each district has been determined, an average level of per-pupil objects statewide can be computed for pupils who are in the special group and for those who are not. The measure is computed as the ratio of the average per-pupil object for this special group to the average per-pupil object for the group that is not special.

The averaged implicit weight is similar to the regression-based relationship measure. A specific answer to question 2 is not required to compute the averaged implicit weight. As a result, however, the averaged implicit weight answers only the general question: Do pupils in the special group, who should receive more of the object, actually receive more of the object? According to the measure, the answer to this question is yes if the averaged implicit weight is greater than one.

Summary. The presentation of an array of vertical-equity measures has shown that although an assessment of vertical equity is difficult, it is possible to draw conclusions about this important principle. Conceptually, the weighted dispersion measures differ from the regression-based relationship measures and the ratio measure. In chapter 9, the behavior of the measures will be analyzed to determine whether these conceptual differences affect empirical findings.

Throughout this part, vertical equity was examined with the assumption that there was only one special group of pupils. If this assumption is relaxed, how are each of the three sets of measures affected? The weighted dispersion measures can incorporate multiple groups in a straightforward way. As long as the number of pupils in each specific group in each district can be determined and weights for each group expressed in terms of pupils who are not in a special group, then several weighting procedures can be applied simultaneously. This will yield a grand total of weighted pupils, and the dispersion measures can be calculated with these.

In the case of the regression-based relationship measures, separate regressions using the different independent variables can be run to assess whether each of the special groups who deserve more of the object actually receives more. The ratio measures also can incorporate multiple groups by estimating measures (e.g., mean comparisons) separately for each group.

EQUITY FOR TAXPAYERS

Most of the conceptual and empirical work in this book is focused on equity for children. This is because the thinking on children's equity is more developed, and perhaps as a consequence, data with which to quantify alternative concepts are more easily obtained. In addition, preliminary explorations by us and others indicate that equity from the taxpayers' perspective is more complex than from the children's.

Despite these caveats, we briefly outline here certain characteristics of equity from the taxpayers' perspective. It should be remembered that the term *taxpayer* can be used in both a narrow and a broad sense. Narrowly, it refers to adults who bear the burden of taxation; broadly it encompasses the household unit, including children, and all the household activities that might affect the children's education.

Taxpayer Objects

There are numerous objects of concern for taxpayers, just as there were numerous objects for children. Here two kinds of taxpayer objects are considered. First, tax burdens on taxpayers are examined, and second, taxes paid and benefits received by the taxpayer are treated.

Tax burdens. Tax burdens can be defined as the taxes paid by taxpayers, usually stated as a percentage of the taxpayers' ability to pay. For example, taxes as a percentage of income is a common tax-burden measure. Despite this relatively straightforward definition of tax burdens, there are many complicated technical and conceptual issues related to this object. The first is whether tax burdens on school districts or on individuals should be the concern. The second is whether education taxes or taxes for all public services should be analyzed. Education taxes could be distributed fairly, while total taxes are not, and vice versa. The third is whether local taxes, or state taxes, or the combination of the two should be considered. Again, the choice would have important implications for assessments on the equity of the tax burden. A fourth concern is whether legal tax incidence or economic tax incidence should be analyzed. It is fairly straightforward to identify legal tax incidence, i.e., those who actually pay the tax to a government. But sometimes tax burdens can be shifted, i.e., a landlord can (under some circumstances) shift the real tax burden to a tenant in the form of a higher rent. Economic tax incidence accounts for such shifting, but the actual degree of shifting, as well as the group to whom the tax is shifted, is now debated for some taxes. Despite the increased difficulties of measuring economic rather than legal tax incidence, economic incidence is the more meaningful concept. Finally, if tax incidence is related to ability to pay, there are choices to be made on what ability-to-pay measure should be used: current or lifetime income or consumption; income from salaries and returns from investments; transfer payments, such as social security; or imputed income such as for work performed in the home.

While research can guide choices on each of these issues, many of the choices are value judgments where there is no right or wrong choice. Thus, on the taxpayer's as well as the children's side of equity, the choice of an object is neither straightforward nor value-free.

Taxes Paid and Education Received. One characteristic of using the tax burden as an object is that it ignores the education services that the taxes support. Since taxpayers themselves do not directly receive education services, the taxpayer group can be broadened to include the entire taxpaying unit, i.e., the household. With the household as the unit, the object can include education services received by the children in the household and taxes paid by the taxpayers in the household. Of course, the use of this object requires choices to be made both for children's objects and for tax-burden objects. Furthermore, the consideration of the household as the group raises the difficult question of how to treat households with varying numbers of children (including none).

Taxpayer Equity Principles

The choice of a taxpayer object is basically between a tax-only approach or a combination tax-and-education-service approach. In order to present examples of taxpayer equity principles, principles that apply to these two objects have been selected. First, tax-burden equity principles are discussed, followed by principles that combine taxes paid with services received.

Tax-Burden Equity Principles. With tax burden as the object, there are two equity principles that can be applied. The first is horizontal equity, expressed as equal tax burdens for taxpayers with equal ability to pay. If horizontal tax equity is assessed within a district, equity can be violated by inconsistencies in assessment (or equalization) practices. Horizontal tax burdens can also be examined for taxpayers with the same ability to pay who reside in different districts. Before this issue is addressed, however, the question of whether horizontal tax burdens among districts is an appropriate issue should be raised. Equal tax burdens for all taxpayers with the same ability to pay may not make sense across districts where education services for the taxpayers' children vary considerably.

The second tax-burden principle is vertical equity, which examines the relationship among tax burdens by varying levels of ability to pay. When tax burdens are assessed in this manner, they may be regressive, proportional, or progressive. The choice of the degree of regressivity or progressivity is another value judgment, although most people agree that a proportional or progressive tax burden is preferable. As was the case for horizontal equity, vertical equity can be examined within or among districts.

Equity Principles for Taxes Paid and Education Services Received. When the object for taxpayers is expanded to include taxes paid and education services received, a diverse set of principles can be articulated. For example, both the horizontal and the vertical equity principles can be reformulated with education received, net of taxes paid, as the object. In addition, in school finance there are other principles that apply to this object.

One principle that takes taxes paid and education received into account is the "equal yield for equal effort" principle. This principle is satisfied when increments in per-pupil education services (revenues, expenditures, resources, etc.) that result from an increment in the property tax rate are equal across districts. A different way of stating this principle is that when complete equal yield for equal effort prevails, school districts that tax themselves at the same rate receive equal amounts for each student. The equal-yield-for-equal-effort principle is a way of measuring fiscal or wealth neutrality. It is an *ex ante* fiscal or wealth neutrality principle, since it depends on how the formula is structured rather than on what districts actually spend.

A second equity principle that combines taxes paid and education received is similar to the equal-yield-for-equal-effort principle but is based on a broader measure of ability to pay than on just the property base. A statement of the principle is as follows: Equity is reached when the distribution of the object (education services) is determined solely by the preferences of the taxpayers for education, and not by their ability to pay, as measured by wealth, income, or some broader variable. The methodological and conceptual issues surrounding the measurement of ability to pay, and the separation of ability to pay from preferences, are not yet resolved to the point where this principle is commonly found in school-finance analyses, but it is a conceptually sound principle nevertheless.

CONCLUSIONS

The equity framework for school finance outlined in this chapter can be used to organize thoughts and policy goals related to school-finance equity. Choices must be made about the groups of concern—children or taxpayers—and about the legitimate and illegitimate distinctions among them, the objects of concern, the equity principles to be applied, and statistical measures of these principles. All these have to be addressed by governors, legislatures, educators, and analysts as school-finance policies are forged. Many choices are primarily value judgments, while others can be made based on careful research and analysis. Foremost among the choices that revolve around values is the selection of the equity goals. Research can inform these choices, but value-laden questions of goals are not appropriate concerns for researchers alone. What research can do is contribute to the ability of policymakers to measure the alternative equity goals with available data and to evaluate the movement toward or away from them.

3

HYPOTHETICAL ILLUSTRATIONS OF THE EQUITY-MEASUREMENT METHODOLOGY: ALTERNATIVE UNITS OF ANALYSIS AND OBJECTS

The conceptual framework that we presented in the last chapter is based upon diverse notions of equity. To the uninitiated, the empirical measurement of these alternative concepts of equity may appear formidable. For those readers who could profit from a bridge between conceptual ideas and the complexities of the empirical techniques, a series of hypothetical illustrations, focusing on how to operationalize the equity framework, is presented in this chapter and the next. The primary conceptual and empirical contributions of this book are in the area of children's, rather than taxpayers', equity, and therefore, only concepts of children's equity are illustrated in the hypothetical examples. The illustrations in these two chapters show how alternative objects, principles, and measures are incorporated in empirical assessments of children's equity. Since these chapters are written for the reader with little background in school finance and statistics, some readers may only need to skim the chapters, and certain readers may skip them altogether.

The first section of this chapter summarizes the advantages of hypothetical illustrations. The hypothetical illustrations should increase the understandability of the measurement methodology presented in this book and raise the probability that the approach can actually be implemented. The hypothetical illustrations are not as complex as actual distributions of school districts in states, and the second section explains how the simplified illustrations in this chapter and the next are structured. In addition, the second section presents a simple example that introduces the details of the hypothetical illustrations and the comparative nature of equity analysis. Several basic statistics such as the mean and median and the use of quintiles are presented as well.

The third and fourth sections of this chapter illustrate two aspects of the equity-measurement methodology. The most commonly employed units of analysis, the pupil unit of analysis and the district unit of analysis, are explained and compared in the third section. This is an important comparison, since only the pupil unit of analysis is used in the rest of the hypothetical examples. The fourth and final section of this chapter shows how alternative objects can be measured and incorporated within the equity-measurement methodology. The four sections of this chapter describe several significant aspects of the equity measurement methodology and set the stage for the measurement of the three equity principles that is presented in chapter 4.

THE ADVANTAGES OF HYPOTHETICAL ILLUSTRATIONS

What are the advantages of hypothetical illustrations? First, compared to analyses of actual school-finance systems, hypothetical illustrations can be followed more easily and understood in greater depth, since the complications that almost always accompany real data are absent. For example, the particular idiosyncrasies of each state as well as the inevitable data shortcomings, such as lack of comparability or incompleteness, can be put aside. Thus, the hypothetical illustration can present a clearer picture of the measurement issues. Second, if there is any validity to the idea that one can "learn" about the measurement methodology by "doing" the methodology, then this opportunity is lost with real data, since in most cases it must be processed by a computer. With the hypothetical illustrations in this chapter, the reader can work out most, if not all, of the equity measurements with a hand calculator, so that a sensitivity for the methodology can be obtained.

Hypothetical examples are also useful in clarifying the meaning of particular values in equity analysis. It is one thing to think abstractly about whether, for example, a horizontal-equity measure should show any changes when all the objects in the distribution are increased by a constant percent. But the meaning of issues such as this can be enhanced by examining distributions that are actually derived to highlight the single issue in question. Hypothetical illustrations are necessary, since two real distributions are not likely to allow for this comparison. Furthermore, the hypothetical distributions can simultaneously enhance one's self-awareness of preferences and values. Since, in some cases, two simple hypothetical distributions can be assessed directly by an individual to determine which one is more equitable, it can be inferred that the equity measures that yield similar conclusions reflect the individual's values. Also, because many of the values in the equity measures are not commonly thought about, an examination of hypothetical distributions can alter one's first impression of which values should be incorporated in an equity measure.

Finally, hypothetical illustrations can show the potential importance of different dimensions of the equity framework. By using hypothetical illustrations that are simplified but plausible representations of school-finance systems, the effect of alternative objects, principles, and measures on equity analyses can be demonstrated. While hypothetical illustrations are not the last word on a determination of which parts of the framework make a difference in real-world situations, they sensitize the analyst or researcher who performs more detailed empirical work by clearly illustrating where the roots of the differences may be found. An introduction to the hypothetical illustrations utilized in this book is the purpose of the next section.

THE STRUCTURE AND USE OF HYPOTHETICAL ILLUSTRATIONS

The nature of the hypothetical illustrations is explored in this section in two ways. The first part describes the key assumptions that guide the formation of all forthcoming hypothetical examples. The second part introduces the hypothetical examples by presenting a simple one. This first example is used to define and explain certain basic ideas and concepts that need to be understood before aspects of the equity-measurement methodology are examined. Statistics of central tendency, such as the median and the mean, and grouping techniques, such as quintiles, are defined and illustrated in this first example and used extensively in all the hypothetical examples presented in chapters 3 and 4.

The Assumptions Incorporated in the Hypothetical Illustrations

The illustrations presented in this chapter and the next, as well as the empirical examples in later chapters, are similar in structure to the most common empirical analyses in school finance, where the focus is on the assesment of a state's school-finance system, either over time or compared to another state. In chapters 3 and 4, when the equity of a hypothetical state's school-finance system for a particular year is under investigation, the following four assumptions are built into all the illustrations.

1. *The state is divided into local school districts for the provision of public primary and secondary education in the state.* No public primary or secondary education is provided by any facility that is not part of a local district, and local districts do not offer any prekindergarten or higher-education services. This assumption eliminates the empirical complications that might be introduced by state-administered schools or joint primary-secondary/community-college districts, where the separation of public primary and secondary objects or pupils within districts may be necessary.

2. *All local school districts provide education for kindergarten through grade twelve.* This assumption simplifies the illustrations, compared to the cases when districts provide education for different grade levels. In actuality, some states have K-12 districts, districts that include only the elementary grades, and districts that only include high schools. When all districts

do not serve the same grade levels, an equity analysis could examine each type of district separately, or combine the data of high school districts and their "feeder" elementary districts to form fictitious K-12 districts. Assumption number two makes this unnecessary in the hypothetical illustrations.

3. *Comparable data are available on the number of pupils in each district.* In the hypothetical examples, no attention is paid to different pupil counts such as membership versus attendance. It can be assumed that all examples in this chapter employ the same pupil count, such as membership, and that all students attend school for the full school day. Of course, if some pupils attend school for part of the day, as is the case in a half-day kindergarten, a weight (.5 or otherwise) could be used to obtain a full-time-equivalent pupil count, but this is not necessary in the hypothetical examples.

4. *Besides data on pupils, data on other characteristics of the district such as the objects (revenues, expenditures, teachers, etc.), property values, or number of handicapped pupils are available for all districts in comparably measured units.* This assumption implies that while comparable information is at hand regarding a district-level variable, no information is available on intradistrict distribution of the variable. For example, to compute per-pupil expenditures, total district expenditures must be divided by total pupils in the district, and within district per-pupil expenditure differences cannot be ascertained.

With these assumptions, an actual illustration can now be considered.

Getting Started: An Introductory Hypothetical Illustration

It is essential that the basic structure of the hypothetical illustrations and certain background statistics are fully understood before the hypothetical illustrations are used to clarify particular measurement issues. Therefore, this first example is not designed to highlight aspects of the equity-measurement framework, but instead should serve as an introduction to the substance and style of the hypothetical illustrations. All of the illustrations in this chapter and the next consist of two or more "states"; these sets of states can be thought of as different states at one point in time, or as the same state at various points in time. Each state is comprised of seven to ten local K-12 school districts. The number of pupils in each district and the total of one or more inputs are always available for every district in every state. The availability of data on other aspects of the districts in the hypothetical school-finance systems, such as percent of pupils who are handicapped or per-pupil property wealth, varies within each illustration.

Only two states are needed to raise the introductory points in this part. The data for the two hypothetical states, labeled A1 and A2, are displayed in table

3.1.[1] Both states A1 and A2 have seven local K–12 school districts, and there are 100 pupils in each district. Total inputs, measured in dollars that can be thought of as either revenues or expenditures, are available for each district. By dividing the district's total dollar inputs by the number of pupils in the district, per-pupil dollar-input figures can be calculated for each district, and these are shown in the last column of table 3.1.

Several concepts and statistics that are important in equity analysis can be explained using the data from states A1 and A2. The unit-of-analysis issue is considered in detail in the next section of this chapter. For this hypothetical illustration, however, the pupil unit of analysis is employed, meaning that the distribution of pupils is the focus of the analysis, and pupils are *assumed* to receive the average level of per-pupil dollar inputs in their district. Thus, states A1 and A2 each consists of a distribution of 700 pupils, and every pupil in a district receives the same per-pupil dollar input level in the district. Using this unit of analysis, two measures of central tendency that are utilized in the equity analyses, the mean and the median, can be illustrated.

The mean of a distribution is the sum of the values of the observations divided by their number. In this case, the mean of per-pupil dollar inputs in a state equals the total per-pupil dollar inputs for all pupils in a state divided by the total number of pupils in the state. If per-pupil dollar inputs in district i

Table 3.1 Basic Data for States A1 and A2

District Number	Number of Pupils in District	Total $ Inputs in District	Per-Pupil $ Inputs in District
		State A1	
1	100	$100,000	$1,000
2	100	140,000	1,400
3	100	160,000	1,600
4	100	180,000	1,800
5	100	220,000	2,200
6	100	280,000	2,800
7	100	350,000	3,500
		State A2	
1	100	$110,000	$1,100
2	100	150,000	1,500
3	100	170,000	1,700
4	100	190,000	1,900
5	100	220,000	2,200
6	100	280,000	2,800
7	100	350,000	3,500

1. In each of the hypothetical illustrations in chapters 3 and 4, the hypothetical states are labeled by a letter and a number. A new letter is used in each section of a chapter.

ALTERNATIVE UNITS OF ANALYSIS AND OBJECTS   49

are represented by X_i, the number of pupils in district i is represented by P_i, and the number of districts in the state is represented by N, then the mean per-pupil dollar inputs in a state, represented by the symbol $\bar{X}_p$, can be designated by the formula

$$\sum_{i=1}^{N} P_i X_i / \Sigma P_i.$$

For states A1 and A2 the numerator is the sum of 700 per-pupil dollar-input figures and the denominator is the total number of pupils in the state, 700. To show one example, mean per-pupil dollar inputs in state A1 can be calculated in the following manner:

$$\bar{X}_p = \frac{\begin{array}{c}(100 \times \$1,000) + (100 \times \$1,400) + (100 \times \$1,600) \\ + (100 \times \$1,800) + (100 \times \$2,200) + (100 \times \$2,800) \\ + (100 \times \$3,500)\end{array}}{100 + 100 + 100 + 100 + 100 + 100 + 100}$$

$$= \frac{(\$100,000 + \$140,000 + \$160,000 + \$180,000 + \$220,000 + \$280,000 + \$350,000)}{700}$$

$$= \frac{\$1,430,000}{700} = \$2042.86.$$

The mean per-pupil dollar inputs in state A2 can be calculated similarly and is $2100.00.

The median, represented by the symbol M_p, is defined as the value of the "middle most" item in a distribution when the distribution is ordered by size of the observations. When there are an odd number of observations in the distribution, the median is the value of the middle observation. When there are an even number of observations, the median can be defined by the average value of the two observations that form the two middle-most points. For example, states A1 and A2 are already displayed in increasing order of per-pupil dollar inputs in table 3.1, and both have an even number of pupils. With 700 pupils, the 350th and the 351st pupils each have 349 pupils below and above them, respectively, and thus form the middle points in our hypothetical distributions. Since it turns out that in states A1 and A2 these middle-point pupils both have the same per-pupil dollar inputs (they are both in district no. 4 in their respective states), the median is the value of the per-pupil dollar inputs for the 350th and 351st pupil in each state. Thus, the median per-pupil dollar input in state A1 and state A2 is $1800 and $1900, respectively.

Since there are relatively few districts in the hypothetical states, a display such as table 3.1 that shows a state's school finances, ordered by a particular variable such as per-pupil dollar inputs, conveys a fair amount of information on the distribution. For data from actual states, however, an ordered listing of all the districts is not as easy to digest, since there are usually tens or even hundreds of districts in the state. Furthermore, when comparing two different states or two states over time, the number of pupils in each district and the total number of pupils are likely to differ, making direct comparison between a list of districts more difficult. Therefore, a state's entire distribution is often ordered by a particular variable and displayed by groups, where each group includes a fixed percentage of the pupils in the state. Often there are five or ten groups displayed, and these are referred to as quintiles or deciles, respectively.

Table 3.2 shows states A1 and A2 grouped by quintiles, where the principle ordering variable is per-pupil dollar inputs. To form table 3.2, the distribution of pupils in each state is organized in increasing order of per-pupil dollar inputs, as shown in table 3.1. Then, each quintile is formed by including one-fifth of the pupils in the distribution, taken in order. In this case with 700 pupils, each quintile contains 140 pupils. Within each quintile the mean value of any characteristic of the group can be computed, but in this case the only known variable is per-pupil dollar inputs. For example, in state A1, the mean per-pupil dollar inputs of the lowest quintile is calculated by dividing the total per-pupil dollar inputs in the quintile [(100 × $1,000) + (40 × $1,400) = $100,000 + $56,000 = $156,000] by the number of pupils in the quintile (140) to yield $156,000/140 or $1,114.3.

In addition to an examination of the layout of the illustrations, the definitions of the mean and median, and the presentation of quintiles, this illustration can show the comparative nature of the subsequent examples. Each illus-

Table 3.2 Per-Pupil Dollar Inputs by Quintiles for States A1 and A2

Quintile	Number of Pupils	Lowest and Highest per-Pupil $ Inputs in Quintile	Mean Value of per-Pupil $ Inputs in Quintile
		State A1	
1	140	$1,000–$1,400	$1,114.3
2	140	1,400–1,600	1,514.3
3	140	1,600–2,200	1,828.6
4	140	2,200–2,800	2,457.1
5	140	2,800–3,500	3,300.0
		State A2	
1	140	$1,100–$1,500	$1,214.3
2	140	1,500–1,700	1,614.3
3	140	1,700–2,200	1,914.3
4	140	2,200–2,800	2,457.1
5	140	2,800–3,500	3,300.0

tration proceeds by presenting two or more distributions, such as states A1 and A2, and then shows how different decisions regarding components of the equity framework can lead to varying judgments about the hypothetical states. Although states A1 and A2 are not designed to highlight any specific difference in the framework, they can be used to provide an example of the equity assessments that are used in the illustrations that follow.

Assume that states A1 and A2 are identical in every respect except for the differences in inputs shown in table 3.1. With this assumption, the only equity differences between the two states that are considered here involve the horizontal-equity principle, the equal treatment of equals, since there are no differences upon which to base vertical-equity or equal-opportunity assessments. Before reading on, the reader may wish to see if she or he can decide which state, A1 or A2, is more equitable on the horizontal-equity principle. The judgment can be made by using both tables 3.1 and 3.2.

One way to summarize the differences between states A1 and A2 is to see that per-pupil dollar inputs are $100 higher in the lowest four districts in state A2 compared to state A1. Since all the pupils at the low end of the distribution receive more dollar inputs in A2 compared to A1, and nothing else is different, many people would conclude that state A2 is more equitable than state A1 on the horizontal-equity principle. Although the reader may have to take this assessment on faith before reading the rest of the examples, if you assessed state A2 as more equitable than state A1, then you are in agreement with all the horizontal-equity measures discussed in chapter 2. In other words, the relative horizontal equity of states A1 and A2 is not sensitive to the choice of a particular horizontal-equity measure. This perfect agreement will not be found in the illustrations that follow, because these illustrations are designed so that the assessment of one hypothetical state in comparison with another will show how differences in values translate to different judgments about equity. The first instance of this can be found in the next section, where the two alternative units of analysis are described.

THE UNIT OF ANALYSIS: PUPILS VERSUS DISTRICTS

The hypothetical illustration in the section above utilized the pupil unit of analysis by assuming that each state's school-finance system is comprised of a distribution of pupils. Although data on variables such as per-pupil dollar inputs were only available at the district level, each pupil was "assigned" the average per-pupil dollar input. There is an alternative to the pupil unit of analysis, namely, the district unit analysis. With the district unit of analysis, each state's school-finance system is assessed as a distribution of districts, rather than of pupils. By disregarding the relative size of each district, the district unit of analysis treats each district as if it had the same number of pupils. Thus, the difference between the units of analysis hinges on the way the data are analyzed, not on the availability of data.

Although the two units of analysis can yield very different conclusions, the choice of one unit over another often goes unmentioned in empirical equity studies. In this part, the operationalizations of the two units of analysis are illustrated, and some of the assumptions behind them are discussed.

The only case in which an equity analysis is unaffected by the choice of the unit of analysis is when all districts have the same number of pupils within every state under investigation. But since a state with districts of equal size in terms of the number of pupils is not to be found, there are always differences resulting from the selection of a unit of analysis. The key differences between the two units of analysis can be illustrated with a simple example. The basic data for states B1 and B2 are displayed in table 3.3. The two hypothetical states both have ten districts and 1,000 pupils. Furthermore, the average per-pupil dollar inputs in each of the ten districts in state B1 is the same as in each of the ten districts in state B2. The only difference between the states, then, is the number of pupils in districts one through six.

Since each unit of analysis views the state from a unique perspective, differences show up in the assessment of every characteristic of the state, including the mean and median of a distribution of observations. For the pupil unit of analysis, the calculation of the mean per-pupil dollar inputs utilizes the distri-

Table 3.3 Basic Data for States B1 and B2

District Number	Number of Pupils in District	Total $ Inputs in District	Per-Pupil $ Inputs in District
		State B1	
1	100	$ 90,000	$ 900
2	100	100,000	1,000
3	100	140,000	1,400
4	100	160,000	1,600
5	100	180,000	1,800
6	100	190,000	1,900
7	100	200,000	2,000
8	100	220,000	2,200
9	100	280,000	2,800
10	100	350,000	3,500
		State B2	
1	50	$ 45,000	$ 900
2	50	50,000	1,000
3	50	70,000	1,400
4	150	240,000	1,600
5	150	270,000	1,800
6	150	285,000	1,900
7	100	200,000	2,000
8	100	220,000	2,200
9	100	280,000	2,800
10	100	350,000	3,500

bution comprised of 1,000 pupils. Using state B2 and the same symbols introduced in the preceding section, the mean per-pupil dollar inputs with the pupil unit of analysis is $\bar{X}_p$, which equals

$$\frac{\sum_{i=1}^{N} P_i X_i}{\sum_i P_i},$$

or

$$\frac{\begin{array}{l}[(50 \times \$900) + (50 \times \$1,000) + (50 \times \$1,400) + (150 \times \$1,600) \\ + (150 \times \$1,800) + (150 \times \$1,900) + (100 \times \$2,000) \\ + (100 \times \$2,200) + (100 \times \$2,800) + (100 \times \$3,500)]\end{array}}{(50 + 50 + 50 + 150 + 150 + 150 + 100 + 100 + 100 + 100)}$$

$$= \frac{\begin{array}{l}[\$45,000 + \$50,000 + \$70,000 + \$240,000 + \$270,000 + \$285,000 \\ + \$200,000 + \$220,000 + \$280,000 + \$350,000]\end{array}}{1000}$$

$$= \frac{\$2,010,000}{1000} = \$2,010.$$

The district unit of analysis assesses the state as a distribution of districts. Thus, the distributions in states B1 and B2 are comprised of ten observations. The mean per-pupil dollar inputs in a state using the district unit of analysis, represented by the symbol $\bar{X}_d$, can be expressed by the formula

$$\frac{\sum_{i=1}^{N} X_i}{D},$$

where D equals the number of districts in the state. It follows, then, that for state B2, the mean per-pupil dollar inputs equals

$$\frac{[\$900 + \$1,000 + \$1,400 + \$1,600 + \$1,800 + \$1,900 + \$2,000 + \$2,200 + \$2,800 + \$3,500]}{10}$$

$$= \frac{\$19,100}{10} = \$1,910.$$

This example illustrates that, in state B2, the mean per-pupil dollar input differs depending upon the unit of analysis. This does not occur in state B1, since the number of pupils in each district in the state is the same. As an exercise, the reader should calculate the mean per-pupil dollar inputs for state B1 under the pupil and the district units of analysis and find them both to be $1,910.

The calculation of the median is also different for the pupil unit of analysis compared to the district unit. While the median using the pupil unit of analysis is the value of the observation for the middle-most pupil, the median using the district unit of analysis is the value of the observation for the middle-most district. Using state B2 as an example, the median with the pupil unit of analysis, M_p, equals the mean per-pupil dollar inputs for the 500th and 501st pupils. Since both the 500th and 501st pupils are in the sixth district and have the same per-pupil dollar inputs, the median with the pupil unit of analysis is $1,900. With the district unit of analysis, the fifth and sixth districts are the midpoints, since there are ten districts. The median for state B2 using the district unit of analysis is thus the mean per pupil dollar inputs in the fifth and sixth district, or ($1,800 + $1,900)/2, which equals $1,850. By this point the reader should be able to verify that the median under both units of analysis for state B1 is $1,850.

With just the mean and median, differences between the two units of analysis have been demonstrated. Is the mean (median) per-pupil dollar input the same in states B1 and B2? There is no difference using the district unit of analysis, but the mean (median) in state B2 exceeds the mean (median) in state B1 using the pupil unit of analysis. Thus, the judgment that the mean (or median) per-pupil dollar inputs in state B2 is greater than in state B1 is consistent with the pupil, but not the district, unit of analysis.

The presentation of state-finance data in a summary form such as quintiles or deciles is also affected by the choice of the unit of analysis. On the one hand, with the pupil unit of analysis, pupils are ranked on a particular variable, then grouped together where each group contains the same number of pupils, and mean values of the group are computed using a pupil unit of analysis. On the other hand, with the district unit of analysis, districts are ranked on a particular variable and then grouped together with the same number of districts in each group. Further, mean values of characteristics of the district-based groups are calculated using the district unit of analysis.

Since quintiles in state B1 are not affected by the unit of analysis because there are an equal number of pupils in each district, state B2 is used to illustrate the effect of the unit of analysis on the computation of quintiles. Table 3.4 shows state B2 in quintiles ordered by per-pupil dollar inputs using both the district and the pupil units of analysis. With the district unit of analysis, 20 percent of the districts are in each quintile. Furthermore, the calculation of the mean per-pupil dollar inputs in each quintile is carried out using the district unit of analysis, so that each district in the quintile is weighted equally. Using the district unit of analysis, therefore, each quintile in state B2 contains two districts, and the mean per-pupil dollar-input figure in each quintile is the value of the two observations divided by two. Utilizing the pupil unit of analysis, the quintiles each include 20 percent of the pupils, or 200 pupils, and the mean per-pupil input for the quintile is computed using a pupil unit of analysis. For state B2 the mean per-pupil dollar input in the first quintile is based on the fact that the quintile is composed of 50 pupils from districts 1, 2, 3, and 4. As a further exercise, utilizing the concepts presented in this and the previous sections, the reader should be able to verify the mean per-pupil dollar inputs for each quintile displayed in table 3.4.

Even without considering equity directly in the hypothetical states, the influence of the unit of analysis is apparent. Using the district unit of analysis the mean, median, and values of the quintiles are identical for per-pupil dollar inputs in states B1 and B2.[2] Using the pupil unit of analysis, however, the mean and median per-pupil dollar inputs are higher in state B2 than in B1. Furthermore, with the pupil unit of analysis, the values of per-pupil dollar inputs in the lowest three quintiles are also higher in B2 compared to B1. Although particular equity measures have not yet been introduced, the treatment of the unit of analysis would be incomplete without including an illustration of the effect of the unit of analysis on at least one equity measure.

If it is assumed that all the districts in states B1 and B2 are alike in all respects (same wealth per pupil, same percent minority, same prices for inputs, etc.) except for the variation in per-pupil inputs displayed in table 3.3, then there are grounds for comparing the horizontal equity of the two states without considering vertical equity or equal opportunity. Although the con-

Table 3.4 Per-Pupil Dollar Inputs by Quintiles for State B2
(District and Pupil Units of Analysis)

Quintile	Number of Districts	Lowest and Highest per-Pupil $ Inputs in Quintile	Mean Value of per-Pupil $ Inputs in Quintile
		District Unit of Analysis	
1	2	$ 900–$1,000	$ 950
2	2	1,400–1,600	1,500
3	2	1,800–1,900	1,850
4	2	2,000–2,200	2,100
5	2	2,800–3,500	3,150
		Pupil Unit of Analysis	
1	200	$ 900–$1,600	$1,225
2	200	1,600–1,800	1,700
3	200	1,800–1,900	1,875
4	200	2,000–2,200	2,100
5	200	2,800–3,500	3,150

2. The calculations of the mean and median for state B1 were left as exercises for the reader. The mean is $1,910 for both the pupil and the district unit of analysis and the median is $1,850 for both units of analysis. The quintiles for B1 are identical to those for the district unit of analysis in B2.

ceptual framework includes numerous measures of horizontal equity, only one measure, the coefficient of variation, is utilized here, since the purpose of the illustration is to show the effect of the units of analysis rather than to assess equity comprehensively. The selection of the coefficient of variation is not an expression of the authors' values.

The definition of the coefficient of variation is the square root of the variance divided by the mean, and both the numerator and denominator are affected by the unit of analysis. As in each case examined thus far, the key difference between the coefficient of variation computed using the pupil versus district unit of analysis is the assumption in the former that the state is a distribution of pupils and in the latter that the state is a distribution of districts. With X_i and P_i representing per-pupil dollar inputs in district i and number of pupils in district i respectively, the coefficient of variation of per-pupil dollar inputs under the pupil unit of analysis can be represented as

$$\frac{\sqrt{\frac{\sum_i P_i(\bar{X}_p - X_i)^2}{\sum_i P_i}}}{\bar{X}_p},$$

where $\bar{X}_p$ equals the mean calculated with the pupil unit of analysis and $\Sigma_i P_i$ is the number of pupils in the state.[3]

The coefficient of variation of per-pupil dollar inputs using the district unit of analysis can be represented by

$$\frac{\sqrt{\frac{\sum_i (\bar{X}_d - X_i)^2}{D}}}{\bar{X}_d},$$

where $\bar{X}_d$ is the mean using the district unit of analysis and D is the number of districts in the state. Notice that when it is assumed that there is only one pupil in every district in the state, the formulas for the coefficient of variation using the pupil unit of analysis and the district unit of analysis are identical. This is important, since it turns out to be true for all equity measures.

The coefficient of variation is not affected by the unit of analysis in state B1, so that state B2 is again used as an empirical illustration. Table 3.5 illustrates in considerable detail the calculation of the coefficient of variation of per-pupil dollar inputs for state B2, using the pupil unit of analysis. First, in each district the squared deviations of per-pupil dollar inputs from the mean

---

3. From this point forward, the index on the summation sign will be represented as Σ_i instead of $\Sigma_{i=1}^{N}$. The reader should understand that the summations run over all N districts and that Σ_i is a commonly used shorthand representation.

Table 3.5 Calculation of Coefficient of Variation for State B2 (Pupil Unit of Analysis)

District	X_i	P_i	$\bar{X}_p - X_i$	$(\bar{X}_p - X_i)^2$	$P_i(\bar{X}_p - X_i)^2$
1	$ 900	50	−1,110	1,232,100	61,605,000
2	1,000	50	−1,010	1,020,100	51,005,000
3	1,400	50	−610	372,190	18,605,000
4	1,600	150	−410	168,100	25,215,000
5	1,800	150	−210	44,100	6,615,000
6	1,900	150	−110	12,100	1,815,000
7	2,000	100	−10	100	10,000
8	2,200	100	190	36,100	3,610,000
9	2,800	100	790	624,100	62,410,000
10	3,500	100	1,490	2,220,100	222,010,000

$$\sum_i P_i(\bar{X}_p - X_i)^2 = 452,900,000$$

$$\frac{\sum_i P_i(\bar{X}_p - X_i)^2}{\sum_i P_i} = \frac{452,900,000}{1000} = 452,900$$

$$\sqrt{\frac{\sum_i P_i(\bar{X}_p - X_i)^2}{\sum_i P_i}} = \sqrt{452,900} = 672.98$$

$$\text{Coefficient of variation} = \frac{\sqrt{\dfrac{\sum_i P_i(\bar{X}_p - X_i)^2}{\sum_i P_i}}}{\bar{X}_p} = \frac{672.98}{2010} = .3348$$

are multiplied by the number of pupils in the district, and then these are summed for the entire state

$$\left(\sum_i P_i(\bar{X}_p - X_i)^2\right).$$

Next, this sum is divided by the number of pupils in the state

$$\left(\frac{\sum_i P_i(\bar{X}_p - X_i)^2}{\sum_i P_i}\right),$$

and the square root of this results in the numerator of the coefficient of variation

$$\left(\sqrt{\frac{\sum\limits_i P_i (\bar{X}_p - X_i)^2}{\sum\limits_i P_i}} \right).$$

Finally, by dividing the numerator by the mean per-pupil dollar inputs, the coefficient of variation is determined to be .3348. An analogous series of calculations are shown in table 3.6 for the coefficient of variation of per-pupil dollar inputs in state B2 utilizing the district unit of analysis, where the coefficient of variation turns out to be .3928.

These calculations using state B2 demonstrate that a measure of equity can be affected by the unit of analysis. Since using either unit of analysis in state B1 the coefficient of variation of per-pupil dollar inputs equals .3928, this shows how two states can be judged to be the same on one measure of horizon-

Table 3.6 Calculation of Coefficient of Variation for State B2 (District Unit of Analysis)

District	X_i	$\bar{X}_d - X_i$	$(\bar{X}_d - X_i)^2$
1	$ 900	−1,110	1,020,100
2	1,000	−910	828,100
3	1,400	−510	260,100
4	1,600	−310	96,100
5	1,800	−110	12,100
6	1,900	−10	100
7	2,000	90	8,100
8	2,200	290	84,100
9	2,800	890	792,100
10	3,500	1,590	2,528,100

$$\sum_i (\bar{X}_d - X_i)^2 = 5,629,000$$

$$\frac{\sum\limits_i (\bar{X}_d - X_i)^2}{D} = \frac{5,629,000}{10} = 562,900$$

$$\sqrt{\frac{\sum\limits_i (\bar{X}_d - X_i)^2}{D}} = \sqrt{562,900} = 750.27$$

$$\text{Coefficient of variation} = \frac{\sqrt{\dfrac{\sum\limits_i (\bar{X}_d - X_i)^2}{D}}}{\bar{X}_d} = \frac{750.27}{1910} = .3928$$

tal equity using one (district) unit of analysis and to be different on the other (pupil) unit of analysis. Roughly speaking, for state B2 the district unit of analysis ignores the fact that the three lowest per-pupil dollar input districts have the fewest pupils.

There is no question that each unit of analysis embodies different values about what is important in equity analysis. The pupil unit of analysis focuses on the pupils in a state; thus, districts that have greater numbers of pupils have a greater influence on the equity assessment compared to smaller districts. Basically, each pupil receives equal weight in the pupil unit of analysis. The district unit of analysis ignores district size and gives equal weight to each district in the state. This implies that each pupil in the larger districts has a relatively smaller influence on the equity assessment than each pupil in the smaller districts.

Since it would be unwieldly to present each empirical illustration and equity assessment using both units of analysis, the illustrations, examples, and analyses in the remainder of the book utilize the pupil unit of analysis. Once it was decided that a choice had to be made, the pupil unit of analysis was adopted for several reasons. First, for the remaining hypothetical examples in this chapter, the illustrations using the pupil unit of analysis can be translated to the district unit of analysis by the reader in a fairly straightforward manner. For each example the number of pupils in each district needs to be set equal to one to yield the district unit of analysis. If the hypothetical illustrations utilized the district unit of analysis, the translation to the pupil unit of analysis would be much more difficult than the translation in the other direction. Second, while both units of analysis are currently utilized in actual empirical assessments of equity, the pupil unit of analysis predominates. Third, although this book presents a methodology that incorporates a wide range of values that goes well beyond our own, in this case, since a choice was necessary, the choice was made in accordance with our values. Since children's equity is concerned with pupils, it seems to us that each pupil should receive equal weight regardless of the size of the district in which she or he is enrolled. Finally, in some cases the use of the district unit of analysis may be seen as a way to overcome the influence of an unusually large district, such as New York City, Chicago, or Detroit. However, there are alternative procedures for treating a state with an especially large district, such as performing the analyses with and without the unusually large district while maintaining the pupil unit of analysis.

ALTERNATIVE OBJECTS: DOLLAR INPUTS, PRICE-ADJUSTED DOLLAR INPUTS, AND ACTUAL INPUTS

The second component of the equity measurement framework is built around the question, "Equity of what?" In this hypothetical illustration the operationalization of three alternative objects is presented to show how variations in this component of the framework can be accommodated. Actually, the most difficult problem surrounding the different objects is, not how to incorporate them into the framework once they are measured, but how to measure them in the first place. This is especially true for objects in the output or outcome areas, but there are significant measurement problems for inputs as well. The conceptual and empirical questions surrounding the measurement of alternative objects are addressed in the preceeding chapter and in the chapters containing the empirical analyses later in the book, and as a result, the illustration in this section can be more narrowly focused on how to incorporate the alternative objects in the framework once they are measured.

This illustration and the actual empirical analyses in later chapters are limited to objects in the input category. Objects in the output and outcome categories, which are subject to cardinal measurement, can be treated in a similar manner. Within the input category of objects, there is one alternative that is commonly employed in almost all school-finance assessments, although there are two other input-based objects that warrant attention. The predominant object in equity analyses is one that measures inputs in dollars. Not only do dollars reflect the quantity and quality of inputs utilized by a school district but, in addition, inputs measured in dollars capture the prices that districts must pay for their inputs. When the equity analyses focus on a state, and the districts face different prices for the same quantity of inputs of identical quality, a strong argument can be made to develop a method to adjust the dollar inputs for these price variations. Since unadjusted dollars incorporate price differences and the empirical estimation of education price indexes is not universally accepted, there may be a preference for the utilization of measures of actual physical resources, such as teachers and books, in equity assessments.

Without judging which input category should be used, the employment of dollar inputs, price-adjusted dollar inputs, and physical resources can be illustrated with an example. Table 3.7 displays three input measures for two states, C1 and C2. The total dollar inputs for each district are displayed, and in addition, a price-of-education index and the number of teachers in each district are shown. The price-of-education index measures price differences across the districts in each state. Districts with lower price indexes pay lower prices for inputs of similar quality compared to districts with higher price indexes. Price-adjusted dollar inputs can be derived by dividing the dollar inputs by the price index. The price index can be used to adjust either total dollar inputs or per-pupil dollar inputs, and it is the latter that is displayed in table 3.7.

By comparing per-pupil dollar inputs with per-pupil price-adjusted dollar inputs, the effect of the price index can be seen. For example, districts 1 and 2 in state C1 face lower than average prices for educational inputs. As a result, when the per-pupil dollar inputs ($1,000 and $1,400, respectively) are divided by the district's price index (.85 and .93, respectively), the price-adjusted dollar inputs ($1,000/.85 = $1,176 and $1,400/.93 = $1,505) are higher than

Table 3.7 Basic Data for States C1 and C2

District	$ Inputs	Education Price Index	Teachers	Pupils	Per-Pupil $ Inputs	Per-Pupil Price-Adjusted $ Inputs	Teachers per 1000 Pupils
			State C1				
1	$100,000	.85	7	100	$1,000	$1,176	70
2	140,000	.93	8	100	1,400	1,505	80
3	160,000	1.01	8	100	1,600	1,584	80
4	180,000	1.04	8	100	1,800	1,731	80
5	220,000	.93	10	100	2,200	2,366	100
6	280,000	1.17	11	100	2,800	2,393	110
7	350,000	1.07	13	100	3,500	3,271	130
			State C2				
1	$110,000	.96	6	100	$1,100	$1,146	60
2	150,000	1.10	8	100	1,500	1,364	80
3	170,000	.90	8	100	1,700	1,889	80
4	190,000	1.03	9	100	1,900	1,845	90
5	220,000	1.07	10	100	2,200	2,056	100
6	280,000	.98	12	100	2,800	2,857	120
7	350,000	1.04	13	100	3,500	3,365	130

the unadjusted dollars in both cases. On the other hand, districts 6 and 7 in state C1 face higher than average prices, and their price-adjusted dollar inputs ($2,800/1.17 = $2,393 and $3,500/1.07 = $3,271, respectively) are lower than the unadjusted dollar inputs in both cases.

The total number of teachers for each district in states C1 and C2 are displayed in table 3.7 as a representation of a physical-resource measure. Teachers per pupil are often displayed in terms of teachers per 1,000 pupils, and that is the convention used in this example. Teachers per pupil is more consistent with the other input measures than its inverse, pupils per teacher (or class size), since higher values of teachers per pupil signify more inputs. Class size could be used instead, however, as long as this difference is recognized.

The hypothetical examples are constructed to show how the alternative input measures might affect the assessment of equity. To illustrate the point, only differences in horizontal equity measured with the coefficient of variation are examined.

Table 3.8 presents the mean, the median, and the coefficient of variation for per-pupil dollar inputs, per-pupil price-adjusted dollar inputs, and teachers per 1,000 pupils in states C1 and C2. If the coefficient of variation is used to asses horizontal equity in the two states, state C2 is more equitable than state C1 when per-pupil dollar inputs are the object. When the dollar inputs are adjusted by the price indexes in both states, however, state C1 has a lower coefficient of variation than state C2 and is therefore more equitable. Thus, this simple illustration shows how the price index can potentially change the

Table 3.8 Mean, Median, and Coefficient of Variation in States C1 and C2 Using Alternative Input-Based Objects

	Per-Pupil $ Inputs	Per-Pupil Price-Adjusted $ Inputs	Teachers per 1000 Pupils
	State C1		
Mean	$2,043	$2,004	92.9
Median	$1,800	$1,731	80
Coefficient of variation	.3915	.3307	.2132
	State C2		
Mean	$2,100	$2,075	94.3
Median	$1,900	$1,889	90
Coefficient of variation	.3609	.3520	.2396

results of an interstate comparison if C1 and C2 are viewed as two different states, or of an intertemporal analysis if C1 and C2 represent one state at two points in time. Notice that, for this example, the equity comparison using teachers per 1,000 pupils is the same for per-pupil price-adjusted dollar inputs. This is intended solely as an illustration, however, since empirical generalities of this kind based on real data from several states cannot yet be made. A comprehensive assessment of one state, Michigan, over a significant time period using dollar inputs, price-adjusted dollar inputs, and teachers per 1,000 pupils is presented in chapters 7, 8, and 9.

In this chapter the notion of hypothetical illustrations has been justified, introduced, and utilized to show the differences between the pupil and district units of analysis and the potential effects of alternative input-based objects. In the next chapter, hypothetical illustrations are again employed to explain alternative measures of the three equity principles. In order to highlight the effects of different measures, only one unit of analysis, the pupil unit of analysis, and only one object, per-pupil dollar inputs, are incorporated in the hypothetical illustrations presented in chapter 4.

4

HYPOTHETICAL ILLUSTRATIONS OF THE EQUITY-MEASUREMENT METHODOLOGY: ALTERNATIVE MEASURES OF THE EQUITY PRINCIPLES

The third and fourth questions in the equity-measurement framework ask which principles should be used to judge equity and how these principles should be measured. The framework includes three equity principles with diverse measures of each principle. The presentation in chapter 2 showed how choices among the principles and measures can be viewed as an expression of particular values. It is difficult to gain a full understanding of the principles, the measures, and the values incorporated in each solely through a conceptual discussion. This chapter is designed to further explain the equity principles and measures by presenting a series of hypothetical illustrations that demonstrate, first, how the principles and measures are operationalized, second, how conflicts can arise from this process, and third, how knowledge of the measures can be used to resolve some of the conflicts.

Each of the first three sections of this chapter focuses on a different equity principle. The first section contains illustrations of the alternative measures of horizontal equity, the second treats the equal-opportunity principle, and the third explores the diverse measures of vertical equity. The hypothetical illustrations are similar in structure to those presented in chapter 3, except only the pupil unit of analysis is utilized and per-pupil dollar inputs are the only object considered. The final section of this chapter summarizes the important points that can be drawn from the range of hypothetical illustrations included in chapters 3 and 4. This final section addresses the issues of the appropriate guidance for actual empirical analysis that can be inferred from the hypothetical illustrations.

ALTERNATIVE MEASURES OF HORIZONTAL EQUITY

In chapter 2, where the equity-measurement framework is first presented, numerous measures of the horizontal-equity principle are described. Although each measure assesses the unequal treatment of equals, or the inequality in a distribution, this multiplicity of measures is problematic because the measures may disagree in their comparative assessments of different distributions. Further, it was suggested that the reasons for the varying assessments could be based, in part, on the different values that are incorporated into each measure. The simple numerical examples presented in this section are designed to highlight how these values can affect horizontal-equity assessments, so that a more concrete understanding of the interactions among the values and the measures can be obtained.

All the horizontal-equity measures are not presented in this section, but the six measures that are included reasonably represent the diversity of value judgments that are incorporated in horizontal-equity measures. The measures that are examined include the range, the restricted range, the federal range ratio, the McLoone index, the coefficient of variation, and the Gini coefficient. The basic data for the four states that are used to show the differences among the measures are displayed in table 4.1. All four states are comprised of seven districts, and all districts contain 100 pupils. The six horizontal-equity measures, along with the mean and the median for each state, are shown in table 4.2, and the four states, arranged by quintiles of per-pupil dollar inputs, are presented in table 4.3.

Before examining the different equity assessments, the calculations of the

Table 4.1 Basic Data for States D1, D2, D3, and D4

District Number	Number of Pupils in District	Per-Pupil $ Inputs	District Number	Number of Pupils in District	Per-Pupil $ Inputs
	State D1			*State D2*	
1	100	$1,000	1	100	$1,100
2	100	1,400	2	100	1,540
3	100	1,600	3	100	1,760
4	100	1,800	4	100	1,980
5	100	2,200	5	100	2,420
6	100	2,800	6	100	3,080
7	100	3,500	7	100	3,850
	State D3			*State D4*	
1	100	$1,120	1	100	$1,120
2	100	1,568	2	100	1,540
3	100	1,760	3	100	1,760
4	100	1,980	4	100	1,980
5	100	2,420	5	100	2,420
6	100	3,080	6	100	3,080
7	100	3,920	7	100	3,850

Table 4.2 Horizontal-Equity Measures for States D1, D2, D3, and D4 (Pupil Unit of Analysis)

	State			
	D1	D2	D3	D4
Mean	$2,043	$2,247	$2,264	$2,250
Median	$1,800	$1,980	$1,980	$1,980
Range	$2,500	$2,750	$2,800	$2,730
Restricted range	$2,500	$2,750	$2,800	$2,730
Federal range ratio	2.5000	2.5000	2.5000	2.4375
McLoone index	.7778	.7778	.7847	.7807
Coefficient of variation	.3915	.3915	.3937	.3893
Gini coefficient	.2178	.2178	.2179	.2164

Table 4.3 Quintiles of Per-Pupil Dollar Inputs for States D1, D2, D3, and D4

Quintile	Number of Pupils in Quintile	Mean Per-Pupil $ Inputs in Quintile			
		D1	D2	D3	D4
1	140	$1,114	$1,226	$1,248	$1,240
2	140	1,514	1,666	1,678	1,666
3	140	1,829	2,011	2,011	2,011
4	140	2,457	2,703	2,703	2,703
5	140	3,300	3,630	3,680	3,630

five horizontal-equity measures not previously discussed in chapter 3 are described to provide more insight into the measures themselves. State D1 is used as the example in each of these calculations. The range is defined quite simply as the difference between the highest and the lowest per-pupil dollar inputs in the state. Since $3,500 and $1,000 are the highest and lowest values of per-pupil dollar inputs in state D1, the range is $2,500, or the difference between $3,500 and $1,000.

Conceptually the restricted range is a range-type measure that ignores the upper and lower tails of the distribution. More specifically, the restricted range is defined as the difference between the per-pupil dollar inputs at or above which 5 percent of the pupils fall (X_{95}) and the per-pupil dollar inputs at or below which 5 percent of the pupils fall (X_5). In state D1, since 14.3 percent of the pupils are in each of the districts with the highest and lowest per-pupil dollar inputs, the restricted range ($X_{95} - X_5$) is identical to the range and is equal to $3,500 less $1,000, or $2,500. If the two points, X_{95} and X_5, had different values than the highest and lowest points in the distribution respectively, the range and the restricted range would differ.

The federal range ratio is computed by dividing the restricted range ($X_{95} - X_5$) by the per-pupil dollar inputs at or below which 5 percent of the pupils fall (X_5). For state D1 the restricted range $[(X_{95} - X_5)/X_5]$ is equal to 2.5, or ($3,500 - $1,000)/$1,000.

The McLoone index is defined as the ratio of the total dollar inputs for pupils below the median to the dollar inputs that would be required if all pupils below the median were receiving the per-pupil dollar amount at the median. The median per-pupil dollar inputs in state D1 is $1,800. If all pupils below the median in state D1 were receiving $1,800, then the total dollar inputs below the median would be 350 times $1,800, or $630,000, and this forms the denominator of the McLoone index. The numerator of the McLoone index is the total dollar inputs below the median, which in state D1 can be calculated as follows:

$[(100 \times \$1,000) + (100 \times \$1,400) + (100 \times \$1,600) + (50 \times \$1,800)]$

$= [\$100,000 + \$140,000 + \$160,000 + \$90,000]$

$= \$490,000.$

Thus, the McLoone index in state D1 is $490,000/$630,000, or .7778. Note that the McLoone index varies between zero and one and gets larger as equity increases. All of the other horizontal-equity measures examined in this section become smaller as equity increases.

The Gini coefficient can be calculated from a formula, but it is more appropriate to first show its meaning graphically. Assume that a distribution is arranged in ascending order by per-pupil dollar inputs, as in table 4.1. If a distribution is perfectly equal (all pupils receive the same per pupil dollar inputs), then any cumulative percentage of the pupils would be receiving the same cumulative percentage of dollar inputs. If the distribution is not perfectly equal, then at some cumulative percentages, the cumulative percentage of pupils would be receiving less than their cumulative percentage of dollar inputs. State D1 is not perfectly equal and can serve as an example. There are 700 pupils in state D1, and total dollar inputs in the state are $1,430,000. The first 100 pupils comprise 14.3 percent of the distribution of pupils but receive only $100,000/$1,430,000, or 7.0 percent, of the dollar inputs. Similar findings occur for all cumulative percentages of pupils in state D1.

Given any distribution, this relationship can be plotted on a graph that has the cumulative percent of pupils as the x-axis and the cumulative percent of dollar inputs as the y-axis. For a perfectly equal distribution, the graph would be the 45° line running diagonally from the lower-left corner of the graph (0%, 0%) to the upper-right corner of the graph (100%, 100%). Any distribution that is not perfectly equal would be graphed as a curve below the 45° line, and the more unequal the distribution, the further below the 45° line the curve would lie. This curve is referred to as the Lorenz curve. The Gini coefficient is defined as the area between the Lorenz curve and the 45° line, expressed as a fraction of the total area below the 45° line.

Table 4.4 shows the cumulative percentages and the actual plot of the Lorenz curve for state D1. The upper part of the table shows the cumulative percentages when each district is added in ascending order of per-pupil dollar inputs. The lower part of table 4.4 shows the Lorenz curve. The Gini coefficient is calculated by dividing the area between the Lorenz curve and the 45° line (area a in table 4.4) by the total area on the graph below the 45° line (areas a plus b). Areas a plus b equal 1250 units on the graph ($\frac{1}{2} \times 50 \times 50$), and area a alone is 272.25 units, resulting in a Gini coefficient of 272.25/1,250, or .2178.

Although the Gini coefficient is easily explained graphically, it would be difficult to compute directly from the graph. Fortunately, there is an exact formula for the Gini coefficient equal to the following:

$$\frac{\left(\sum_{i=1}^{N} \sum_{j=1}^{N} P_i P_j |X_i - X_j|\right)}{2\left(\sum_{i=1}^{N} P_i\right)^2 \bar{X}_p},$$

where X_i (X_j) represents per-pupil dollar inputs in district i (j); P_i (P_j) represents the number of pupils in district i (j); $\bar{X}_p$ is the mean of per-pupil dollar inputs in the state; and N equals the number of districts in the state.

Table 4.5 shows the calculation of the Gini coefficient of per-pupil dollar inputs for state D1 using this formula. Since each district in state D1 contains 100 pupils, the numerator in the Gini coefficient formula for state D1 can be rewritten as $(100)(100) \sum_{i}^{N} \sum_{j}^{N} |X_i - X_j|$. The upper part of table 4.5 calcu-

Table 4.4 Graph of Lorenz Curve for State D1

Cumulative Percent of Pupils	Cumulative Percent of $ Inputs
14.3%	7.0%
28.6	16.8
42.9	28.0
57.1	40.6
71.4	55.9
85.7	75.5
100.0	100.0

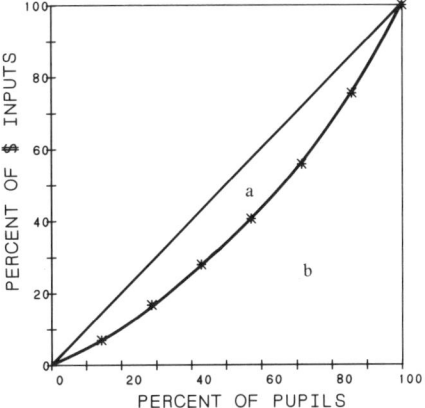

Table 4.5 Calculation of Gini Coefficient for State D1

				$\|X_i - X_j\|$				
				X_j				
X_i	$1,000	$1,400	$1,600	$1,800	$2,200	$2,800	$3,500	$\sum_{j=1}^{N} \|X_i - X_j\|$
$1,000	0	400	600	800	1,200	1,800	2,500	7,300
1,400	400	0	200	400	800	1,400	2,100	5,300
1,600	600	200	0	200	600	1,200	1,900	4,700
1,800	800	400	200	0	400	1,000	1,700	4,500
2,200	1,200	800	600	400	0	600	1,300	4,900
2,800	1,800	1,400	1,200	1,000	600	0	700	6,700
3,500	2,500	2,100	1,900	1,700	1,300	700	0	10,200

$$\sum_{i=1}^{N}\sum_{j=1}^{N} |X_i - X_j| = \$43,600$$

$$\sum_{i=1}^{N}\sum_{j=1}^{N} P_i P_j |X_i - X_j| = (100)(100) \sum_{i}^{N}\sum_{j}^{N} |X_i - X_j| = 10,000(\$43,600) = \$436,000,000.$$

$$2(\sum_{i} P_i)^2 \bar{X}_p = 2(700)^2 (\$2,042.86) = \$2,002,002,800.$$

$$\text{Gini coefficient} = \frac{\$436,000,000}{\$2,002,002,800} = .2178.$$

lates the sum of the absolute values of the differences between all the pairs of per-pupil dollar inputs in the distribution, and this equals $43,600. The numerator of the Gini coefficient thus equals (100)(100)($43,600) or $436,000,000. The denominator of the Gini coefficient for state D1 is $2(\Sigma_i^N P_i)^2 \bar{X}_p$, or $2(700)^2(\$2,042.86)$, which equals $2,002,002,800. Therefore, the Gini coefficient equals $436,000,000/$2,002,002,800, or .2178.

Once the mechanics of the calculations of the six horizontal-equity measures are understood, we can return to the original question of how the value judgments embedded in each measure affect the way in which horizontal equity is assessed. The four hypothetical states in this part are constructed so that when the horizontal equity of the states is compared two states at a time, several differences in values are highlighted.

State D2 is constructed by increasing per-pupil dollar inputs in all districts in state D1 by 10 percent. The evaluation of horizontal equity in response to an equal proportional increase distinguishes the two range-type measures from the other four measures. Table 4.2 shows that the restricted range and the range assess state D2 as less equitable than state D1, since both measures are higher for state D2. The other four measures—the federal range ratio, the McLoone index, the coefficient of variation, and the Gini coefficient—are insensitive to equal proportional changes, and as a result, states D1 and D2 are not different in terms of horizontal equity using these four measures. This difference is a critical one among the measures, and judging by the fact that a significant number of school-finance investigations utilize range-type measures, opinions appear to be divided over which value is preferred. When one state is evaluated over time and inflation is significant, the treatment of proportional increases is not just a conceptual exercise. If, for example, states D1 and D2 are the identical state at two points in time when inflation is 10 percent over the period, the distribution of real resources is equivalent in D1 and D2. Therefore, the measures that show different levels of equity for D1 and D2, the range and the restricted range in this case, are inappropriate horizontal-equity measures under these circumstances.

State D3 is formed by increasing per-pupil dollar inputs in districts 1, 2, and 7 in state D1 by 12 percent, and by increasing per-pupil dollar inputs in districts 3, 4, 5, and 6 in state D1 by 10 percent. Thus, state D3 differs from state D2 in districts 1, 2, and 7 only. Compared to state D2, state D3 can be viewed as a state that has higher per-pupil dollar inputs at the extremes. The introduction of state D3, particularly when compared to state D2, helps to show that the horizontal-equity measures treat changes at various levels in the distribution differently, in part because some of the measure only include some of the pupils. For example, the federal range ratio only includes the pupils at the 5th and 95th percentiles. Since, compared to state D2, the particular pupils in state D3 are 2 percent higher at both the 5th and 95th percentiles, the federal range ratio views this as an equal proportional increase, and states D2 and D3 (and D1 for that matter) are assessed as equal in terms of horizontal equity.

The McLoone index is also based on a subset of the pupils, since it only considers the half of the distribution at the median level and below. In states D2 and D3 the median levels of per-pupil dollar inputs are identical. Yet districts 1 and 2 in state D3 have higher per-pupil dollar inputs than districts 1 and 2 in state D2, while the other two districts at or below the median in states D2 and D3, districts 3 and 4, have the same per-pupil dollar inputs. Therefore, state D3 has a higher McLoone index than state D2 and is judged to be more horizontally equitable. When the McLoone index is used to compare states D2 and D3, the different level of per-pupil dollar inputs in district 7 in the two states does not affect the comparison.

The coefficient of variation and the Gini coefficient are both horizontal-equity measures that include all pupils in the measure. When D3 is constructed from D2, note that per-pupil dollar inputs in districts 1, 2, and 7 in state D3 are higher than their counterparts in state D2, but the mean per-pupil dollar inputs is also higher in state D3 than state D2. The result is that districts 1, 2, 5, and 6 are closer to the mean in state D3 than their counterparts in state D2, while districts 3, 4, and 7 are closer to the mean in state D2 than their counterparts in state D3. These differences tend to balance out somewhat, but the differences are not exactly offsetting, and the coefficient of variation assesses state D3 as being less horizontally equitable than state D2.

According to the Gini coefficient, state D3 is also less horizontally equitable than state D2. Again, the changes to districts 1, 2, and 7 as well as the change in the mean in state D3 compared to state D2 cause offsetting differences that do not completely balance out. From the formula for the Gini coefficient it could be shown that the changes from state D2 to state D3 produce an increase in the numerator and denominator that results in a slight increase in the Gini coefficient for state D3.

Finally, note that the range and the restricted range indicate that state D3 is less horizontally equitable than state D2. Thus, four of the six measures indicate that state D3 is less horizontally equitable than state D2 (range, restricted range, coefficient of variation, and Gini coefficient), one shows no difference (federal range ratio), and one assesses state D3 as more horizontally equitable than state D2 (McLoone index).

The final state, D4, is constructed from state D1 by increasing district 1 by 12 percent and all the other districts by 10 percent. Again, the behavior of the measures in this situation where the bottom is brought up more than the rest of the distribution can be seen by comparing states D2 and D4. Because of the differential growth in only the lowest district in state D4 compared to state D2, and since the pupil at the 5th percentile in state D4 is in this lowest district, state D4 is judged to be more horizontally equitable than state D2 by all six horizontal-equity measures. Thus, there can be instances when all the measures agree, yet the slight differences among states D2, D3, and D4, and the significant variation in the relative rankings that result, suggest that in real empirical analyses, complete agreement among the measures may not occur all of the time. Furthermore, the different rankings are related to values such as whether the measure includes all of the pupils, whether the measure focuses on the lower part of the distribution, and how the measure responds to equal percentage increases.

A summary of how each measure ranks the four states is presented in table 4.6. Although for these hypothetical states the range and the restricted range always agree in rankings and the coefficients of variation and the Gini coefficient always agree in rankings, the overall differences among the six measures are still rather substantial.[1] All states except D4 are ranked as the least equitable by at least one measure and all states except D2 are ranked as the most equitable by at least one measure. Yet by knowing the value judgments embedded in each measure, some of the reasons for the different rankings can be analyzed and discussed. Each individual measure incorporates explicit assumptions and ranks the states in precise ways. This outcome can be contrasted with the use of a grouping technique, such as quintiles, to assess eq-

1. Hypothetical examples could, of course, be constructed to show differences in these measures also.

Table 4.6 Ranking of States D1, D2, D3, and D4 by the Six Horizontal-Equity Measures

Range	Restricted Range	Federal Range Ratio	McLoone Index	Coefficient of Variation	Gini Coefficient
D1	D1	D4	D3	D4	D4
D4	D4	D1	D4	D1	D1
D2	D2	D2*	D1	D2*	D2*
D3	D3	D3*	D2*	D3	D3

*Tied with state above it in list.

uity. From our perspective, however, the use of measures is preferable for two reasons. First, it is not clear whether anyone can rank the four states in terms of horizontal equity by examining the quintile distributions from table 4.3 in isolation. Second, if the four states can be ranked using the quintiles, is it likely that different "rankers" would agree? If disagreement results (and we believe it would), there is not a sound basis upon which the sources of the disagreement can be unraveled. The use of multiple measures of horizontal equity may not lead to consensus, but may bring forth a discussion of the sources of disagreement.

ALTERNATIVE MEASURES OF EQUAL OPPORTUNITY

The equal-opportunity principle is assessed by measuring the relationship between two characteristics of a school-finance system, and equity exists when there is no relationship between the two characteristics. In order to operationalize this principle, the two characteristics must be chosen and quantified, and the extent of the relationship must be measured. In this section of the chapter, attention is focused on this latter issue, the alternative ways that a relationship between two variables can be assessed. As was the case in the previous section on horizontal equity, the assessment of the equal-opportunity principle can be affected by the selection of a particular measure, and the example presented in this part is constructed to show how these differences can arise and be interpreted.

In order to concentrate on the differences among the measures of equal opportunity, only a limited number of variables in each hypothetical state are examined. Because the existence of a relationship between spending and wealth is an important issue in school finance, all the examples utilize per-pupil dollar inputs as the dependent variable and per-pupil property values as the independent variable. The questions of measurement that are addressed, however, apply to the assessment of the relationship between any two variables. In fact, since the measures discussed in this part can also be used to assess vertical equity, the measures are referred to simply as relationship measures, rather than measures of equal opportunity. Although similar measures can be used to examine both principles, their interpretation depends upon the principle under investigation. In the examples in this section, the measures assess the relationship between per-pupil dollar inputs and property values and are interpreted as equal-opportunity measures where the absence of a relationship is considered perfect equity.

Only a subset of the relationship measures are illustrated in this part, but the measures are selected to represent the range of values that can be incorporated in the measures. All of the four measures that are examined are based on a *simple* regression where per-pupil dollar inputs and per-pupil property values are the dependent and independent variables, respectively. The four measures include the correlation, the simple slope, the simple elasticity, and the simple adjusted relationship measure. Five hypothetical states, E1, E2, E3, E4, and E5, are used to show the differences among the relationship measures. The basic data for the five states are displayed in table 4.7, and the

Table 4.7 Basic Data for States E1, E2, E3, E4, and E5

District Number	Number of Pupils in District	Per-Pupil Property Values (thousands of $)	Per-Pupil $ Inputs	District Number	Number of Pupils in District	Per-Pupil Property Values (thousands of $)	Per-Pupil $ Inputs
		State E1				State E2	
1	100	$ 8	$ 900	1	100	$ 30	$ 900
2	100	10	800	2	100	75	800
3	100	70	1,700	3	100	80	1,500
4	100	80	1,800	4	100	80	1,800
5	100	90	1,900	5	100	80	2,100
6	100	150	2,800	6	100	85	2,800
7	100	152	2,700	7	100	130	2,700
		State E3				State E4	
1	100	$ 30	$ 900	1	100	$ 60	$1,100
2	100	55	800	2	100	70	1,300
3	100	60	1,700	3	100	70	1,700
4	100	80	1,800	4	100	80	1,800
5	100	100	1,900	5	100	90	1,900
6	100	105	2,800	6	100	90	2,300
7	100	130	2,700	7	100	100	2,500
		State E5					
1	100	$15.0	$ 900				
2	100	37.5	800				
3	100	40.0	1,500				
4	100	40.0	1,800				
5	100	40.0	2,100				
6	100	42.5	2,800				
7	100	65.0	2,700				

relationship measures are shown in table 4.8. The per-pupil property values are assumed to be assessed at the same percent of market value for all districts within any state. The percent of market value may vary among states and may be less than 100 percent.

Although in actual school-finance analyses the calculation of the measures would be carried out with the help of a computer, some knowledge of the measures can be gained by working through the actual computations. Therefore, before the discussion of the differences among the measures begins, the calculations of the four measures for one state, E1, are presented. The use of the pupil unit of analysis is continued throughout this part.

With per-pupil dollar inputs (X_i) and per-pupil property values (W_i) expressed as deviations from their mean values ($x_i = X_i - \bar{X}$; $w_i = W_i - \bar{W}$), the correlation (r) can be represented by the formula

$$r = \frac{\sum_i P_i x_i w_i}{\sqrt{\sum_i P_i x_i^2} \sqrt{\sum_i P_i w_i^2}},$$

where P_i represents the number of pupils in each district. The actual computation of the correlation for state E1 is shown to be .9975 in table 4.9. (Note that the computation is simplified somewhat because there are equal numbers of pupils in every district.) The square of the correlation multiplied times 100 is the percent of the variation in per-pupil dollar inputs that is explained by per-pupil property values. Using this latter interpretation, we can see that state E1 shows a rather high correlation; it is very close to its maximum value of one. When the correlation is presented with this formula, the reader should be able to verify, either through algebra or with adjustments to the hypothetical data in state E1, that neither a constant amount added to all X_i's or W_i's

Table 4.8 Equal-Opportunity Measures with Per-Pupil Dollar Inputs as Dependent Variable and Per-Pupil Property Value as Independent Variable for States E1, E2, E3, E4, and E5

	States				
	E1	E2	E3	E4	E5
Mean per-pupil $ inputs	$1800	$1800	$1800	$1800	$1800
Mean per-pupil property values (thousands of $)	$80	$80	$80	$80	$40
Correlation	.9975	.7219	.8989	.9428	.7219
Simple slope	13.33	19.80	20.43	33.33	39.60
Simple elasticity	.5927	.8801	.9078	1.4815	.8801
Simple adjusted relationship measure	.7998	.5914	.7208	.4853	.5914

nor the multiplication of all X_i's or W_i's by a constant percentage changes the correlation.

Using the same notation as above, the simple slope, b, can be represented by the formula

$$b = \frac{\sum_i P_i x_i w_i}{\sum_i P_i w_i^2}.$$

Taking advantage of the fact that there are the same number of pupils (P) in all districts in state E1, the simple slope for E1 can be computed as

$$\frac{P \sum_i x_i w_i}{P \sum_i w_i^2} = \frac{\sum_i x_i w_i}{\sum_i w_i^2} = \frac{271{,}600}{20{,}368} = 13.33.$$

This can be interpreted to mean the linear regression predicts that every additional thousand dollars of per-pupil property values will be associated with an additional \$13.33 of per-pupil dollar inputs. The fact that the simple slope changes as a result of constant percentage changes in the independent and dependent variables but does not respond to equal additions to the independent and dependent variables can be verified from the formula or with modifications to the numerical example.

The formula for the simple elasticity, calculated at the mean values of the variables, based on the simple regression is the following:

$$e = b \left(\frac{\bar{W}_p}{\bar{X}_p} \right),$$

where $\bar{W}_p$ and $\bar{X}_p$ are the means (pupil unit of analysis) of per-pupil property values and per-pupil dollar inputs respectively. The simple elasticity for state E1 is equal to the following:

$$b \left(\frac{\bar{W}_p}{\bar{X}_p} \right) = 13.33464 \left(\frac{80}{1800} \right) = .59265.$$

This can be interpreted to mean that a 1 percent change in per-pupil property values is associated with a .59265 percent change in per-pupil dollar inputs, at the mean level of per-pupil property values and per-pupil dollar inputs. Since the elasticity is the slope multiplied by the ratio of means, the elasticity is unaffected by percentage changes in the independent and dependent variables but does change as a result of constant additions to the independent and dependent variables.

Finally, the adjusted relationship measure from the simple regression can be represented by the formula

$$ARM = \frac{2 b \sigma_w}{\bar{X}_p},$$

Table 4.9 Calculation of Simple Correlation between Per-Pupil Dollar Inputs and Per-Pupil Property Value for State E1

District	Per-Pupil $ Inputs (X_i)	Per-Pupil Property Value (thousands of $) ($W_i$)	$X_i - \bar{X}$ (x_i)	$W_i - \bar{W}$ (w_i)	$x_i w_i$	x_i^2	w_i^2
1	$ 900	$ 8	−900	−72	64,800	810,000	5,184
2	800	10	−1,000	−70	70,000	1,000,000	4,900
3	1,700	70	−100	−10	1,000	10,000	100
4	1,800	80	0	0	0	0	0
5	1,900	90	100	10	1,000	10,000	100
6	2,800	150	1,000	70	70,000	1,000,000	4,900
7	2,700	152	900	72	64,800	810,000	5,184
					$\sum_i x_i w_i = 271{,}600$	$\sum_i x_i^2 = 3{,}640{,}000$	$\sum_i w_i^2 = 20{,}368$

$$r = \frac{\sum_i P_i x_i w_i}{\sqrt{\sum_i P_i x_i^2}\sqrt{\sum_i P_i w_i^2}}.$$

When $P_i = P_j$ for all i and j,

$$r = \frac{P\sum_i x_i w_i}{\sqrt{P\sum_i x_i^2}\sqrt{P\sum_i w_i^2}} = \frac{100\sum_i x_i w_i}{\sqrt{100\sum_i x_i^2}\sqrt{100\sum_i w_i^2}} = \frac{100(271{,}600)}{\sqrt{364{,}000{,}000}\sqrt{2{,}036{,}800}}$$

$$= \frac{27{,}160{,}000}{(19{,}078.784)(1427.165)} = \frac{27{,}160{,}000}{27{,}228.573} = .9975$$

where b is the slope from the simple regression, σ_w is the standard deviation of per-pupil property values, and $\bar{X}_p$ is the mean of per-pupil dollar inputs. The formula[2] for the standard deviation of per-pupil property values, σ_w, using the pupil unit of analysis is

$$\sqrt{\frac{\sum_i P_i w_i^2}{\sum_i P_i - 1}}.$$

For state E1, σ_w is equal to the following:

$$\sigma_w = \sqrt{\frac{2{,}036{,}800}{700 - 1}} = \sqrt{2913.877} = 53.98.$$

Therefore, the simple adjusted relationship measure for state E1 equals

$$\frac{2b\sigma_w}{\bar{X}_p} = \frac{2(13.33464)(53.98)}{1800} = .7998.$$

This means that in state E1, a movement of two standard deviations of per-pupil property values along the regression line is associated with a difference in per-pupil dollar inputs equal to 79.98 percent of the mean per-pupil dollar inputs. Or in other words, pupils who differ by two standard deviations of property values can be expected to differ in per-pupil dollar inputs by roughly 80 percent of the mean value of per-pupil dollar inputs. The simple adjusted relationship measure is only affected by equal additions to the dependent variable, as this would leave the numerator unchanged and would increase the denominator by the equal addition.

In addition to measures such as the four just computed, the relationship between an independent and a dependent variable is sometimes displayed with a grouping technique such as quintiles. The pupils are arranged in ascending order of the independent variables and grouped to form quintiles (or deciles or any number of equal-sized groups). Once this grouping is accomplished, the mean value of the dependent variable is computed for each group to show whether a relationship exists between the independent and dependent variables.

The values of per-pupil dollar inputs for quintiles of pupils, arranged by per-pupil property values, are shown in table 4.10. While in each state the display of quintiles shows that per-pupil dollar inputs and per-pupil property values are related, it is unclear whether more precise judgments about the relative equal opportunity of the five states can be made using the table of

---

2. The formula for the standard deviation uses P_i in the denominator for the population statistic and P_i-1 in the denominator for the sample statistic. We use one or the other depending on how computer programs are written for the various measures. When working with real data, the choice of a formula is irrelevant because the total numbers of pupils are so large.

quintiles alone. As an exercise, the reader may find it useful to try to rank the states on the equal-opportunity principle using table 4.10. Since our experience leads us to believe that the formation of rankings from tables of quintiles is rarely humanly possible, the measures of equal opportunity must be relied upon. This conclusion emphasizes that an understanding of the measures and the differences among them is essential, and it is to this point that we now turn.

A comparison of the equity in the five hypothetical states shows some, but not all, of the important differences among the relationship measures that were discussed in the earlier chapter. One key distinction among the measures concerns whether the relationship is assessed in terms of "goodness of fit" or of the magnitude of the relationship. The correlation is a measure in the former category, while the simple slope and the simple elasticity are in the latter. States E1 and E2 are constructed to highlight the difference between these two types of relationship measures. Table 4.8 shows that state E1 is more equitable according to the simple slope and simple elasticity, while state E2 is more equitable according to the correlation. The essence of the differences can be

Table 4.10 Per-Pupil Dollar Inputs by Quintiles Ordered by Per-Pupil Property Values for States E1, E2, E3, E4, and E5

Quintile	Number of Pupils in Quintile	Mean Per-Pupil Property Value (thousands of $)	Mean Per-Pupil $ Inputs	Quintile	Number of Pupils in Quintile	Mean Per-Pupil Property Value (thousands of $)	Mean Per-Pupil $ Inputs
		State E1				State E2	
1	140	$ 8.6	$ 871.4	1	140	$ 42.9	$ 871.4
2	140	44.3	1,314.3	2	140	77.9	1,200.0
3	140	80.0	1,800.0	3	140	80.0	1,800.0
4	140	115.7	2,285.7	4	140	82.1	2,400.0
5	140	151.4	2,728.6	5	140	117.1	2,728.6
		State E3				State E4	
1	140	$ 37.1	$ 871.4	1	140	$ 62.9	$1,157.1
2	140	57.9	1,314.3	2	140	70.0	1,528.6
3	140	80.0	1,800.0	3	140	80.0	1,800.0
4	140	102.1	2,285.7	4	140	90.0	2,071.4
5	140	122.9	2,728.6	5	140	97.1	2,442.9
		State E5					
1	140	$ 21.4	$ 871.4				
2	140	38.9	1,200.0				
3	140	40.0	1,800.0				
4	140	41.1	2,400.0				
5	140	58.6	2,728.6				

Figure 4.1 Relationship between Per-Pupil Dollar Inputs and Per-Pupil Property Values, State E1

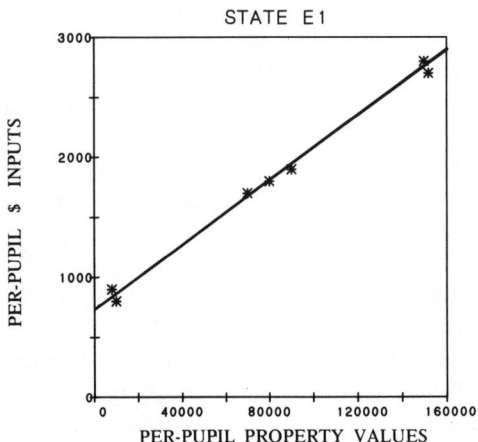

illustrated most clearly with a graph. Figures 4.1 and 4.2 show the districts in states E1 and E2 respectively, plotted with per-pupil dollar inputs on the y-axis and per-pupil property values (wealth) in the x-axis, along with the estimated regression line. The higher correlation in state E1 compared to state E2 is due to the fact that the districts lie closer to the regression line in state E1 than in state E2. The higher simple slope and simple elasticity in state E2 compared to state E1 reflects the fact that, in state E2, the regression line shows greater changes in per-pupil dollar inputs associated with comparable changes in per-pupil property values regardless of whether the changes are measured in absolute units (simple slope) or percentages (simple elasticity).[3]

If the reader can decide whether state E1 is more or less equitable than state E2, then at an individual level, a preference for the goodness-of-fit type measure versus the magnitude-of-the-relationship measure may be emerging. While we believe that many people's preferences are more in line with the magnitude-of-the-relationship measures as opposed to the goodness-of-fit measures, the extensive use of the correlation suggests that agreement on this point is far from complete. This example shows that different meanings of the measures can result in contradictory empirical findings, and as a result, analysts may have to use several measures if they intend to capture a reasonable range of values.

---

3. The simple slopes and simple elasticities based on the simple regression in states E1 and E2 yield identical conclusions, since the mean values of the independent and dependent variables are the same in state E1 as they are in state E2. An example that shows how the simple slope and simple elasticity can vary will be considered shortly.

Figure 4.2 Relationship between Per-Pupil Dollar Inputs and Per-Pupil Property Values, State E2

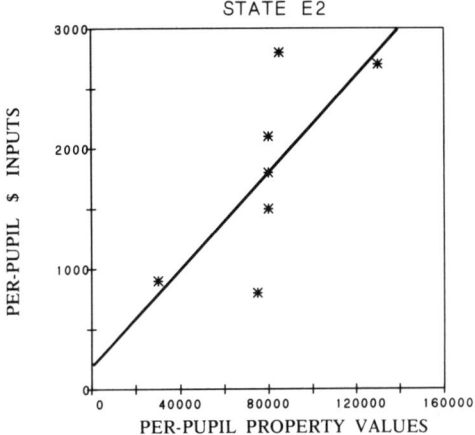

While the differences between the correlation and the simple elasticity or simple slope are important, even when the decision is made to use a measure that captures the magnitude of the relationship, the question is, Which measure? In fact, there is a real difference between the slope and the elasticity that has an important meaning when they are used as equal-opportunity measures, particularly with property values as the independent variable. Recall that the slope is affected by equal proportional changes in the independent variable and the elasticity is not. When the independent variable is per-pupil property values, differences in the statewide ratio of assessed value to market value across states or across time can be viewed as an equal proportional difference. We think most people would prefer a measure that is not affected by an artificial factor such as the assessment ratio, and if this is the case, the elasticity would be preferable to the slope. In addition, when assessing equity over time, uniform inflation in property values (as well as in dependent variables) will affect the slope measures but not the elasticities. Thus, in the presence of inflation, the slopes are inappropriate measures because they will show a change in equity when the real, inflation-adjusted values of the variables have not changed.

State E5 can illustrate the property-valuation point, since it is identical to state E2, except that the per-pupil property values in state E2 are multiplied by .5 to obtain the per-pupil values in state E5. As we have seen in table 4.8, with this change—which is analogous to a change in the assessment ratio—the simple slope is twice as large in state E5 as in state E2, while the simple elasticities are identical. Since, due to inflation, it may be desirable for a measure to be unaffected by equal proportional changes in the independent and

Figure 4.3 Relationship between Per-Pupil Dollar Inputs and Per-Pupil Property Values, State E3

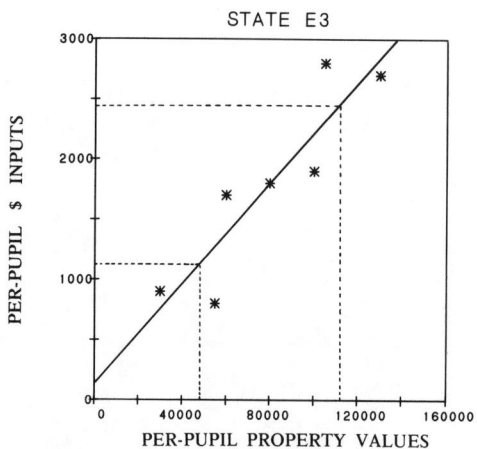

dependent variables, there is another reason to favor the elasticity over the slope.

When assessing the relationship between two variables, there is an additional aspect that is not captured by either the correlation or the simple elasticity. For example, in chapter 2 it was argued that when the actual dispersion in the dependent variable is relatively low, a high correlation and simple elasticity may not be as inequitable as the case where the correlation and simple elasticity are lower but the dispersion in the dependent variable is higher. Due to this possibility, the adjusted relationship measure was introduced, and states E3 and E4 are constructed to show how this measure differs from the correlation and the simple elasticity.[4] Table 4.8 shows that state E4 has a somewhat higher correlation and considerably higher elasticity compared to state E3, and this pattern can be observed in figure 4.3 (state E3) and figure 4.4 (state E4) as well. (Ignore the dashed lines on figures 4.3 and 4.4 for the moment.) In figure 4.4, the regression line is steeper and the points are clustered closer to the regression line compared to the display in figure 4.3. Thus, the correlation and the simple elasticity both assess state E4 as less equitable than state E3 on the equal-opportunity principle with property values as the independent variable.

The simple adjusted relationship measure is not only concerned with the relationship between the two variables, per-pupil dollar inputs and property

---

4. The simple adjusted relationship measure differs from the simple slope as well, but since we believe that most people find the simple elasticity preferable to the simple slope, this discussion is simplified by comparing only the correlation and the simple elasticity to the simple adjusted relationship measure.

Figure 4.4 Relationship between Per-Pupil Dollar Inputs and Per-Pupil Property Values, State E4

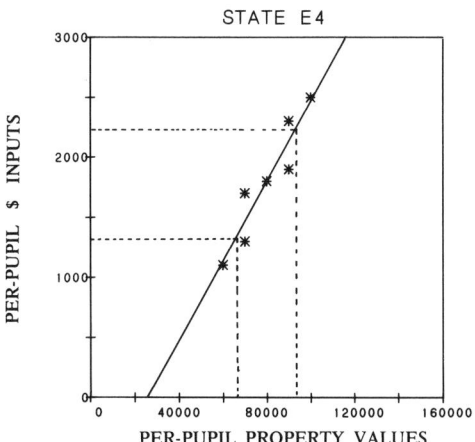

values, but it also assesses the size of the differences in per-pupil dollar inputs that is predicted by the actual differences in per-pupil property values. In figures 4.3 and 4.4, one standard deviation of per-pupil property values above and below the mean is marked off with dashed vertical lines that run beneath the simple regression line. The difference in per-pupil dollar inputs that is predicted by this two-standard-deviation span in per-pupil property values is marked off with dashed horizontal lines that run to the left of the simple regression line. The simple adjusted relationship measure expresses this predicted difference in per-pupil dollar inputs as a percentage of the mean. Since states E3 and E4 have the same mean per-pupil dollar inputs, a direct comparison of the differences in per-pupil dollar inputs traced out by the horizontal dashed lines in figures 4.3 and 4.4 illustrates graphically that the simple adjusted relationship measure predicts a greater difference in per-pupil dollar inputs in state E3 than in state E4. Although on the equal-opportunity principle, state E3 is more equitable than E4 when the correlation and simple elasticity are used as the equity measures, this conclusion is reversed with the simple adjusted relationship measure. This is confirmed by the data in table 4.8.

The five hypothetical states introduced in this part demonstrated that, in the assessment of equal opportunity, the correlation could disagree with the simple slope and simple elasticity, the simple elasticity could disagree with the simple slope, and the simple elasticity and the correlation could agree—but both could differ from the simple adjusted relationship measure. In other words, the various relationship measures focus on somewhat different aspects of the relationship and, as a result, can potentially yield conflicting assessments of equal opportunity. Table 4.11 summarizes the rankings of the five

Table 4.11 Ranking of States E1, E2, E3, E4, and E5 by the Four Equal-Opportunity Measures

Correlation	Simple Slope	Simple Elasticity	Simple Adjusted Relationship Measure
E2	E1	E1	E4
E5*	E2	E2	E2
E3	E3	E5*	E5*
E4	E4	E3	E3
E1	E5	E4	E1

*Tied with state above it in list.

states that are produced by the four relationship measures considered in this part, and the potential for conflicts is confirmed. Since it is unlikely that various analysts and decision makers agree on what is *the* appropriate relationship measure, more than one relationship measure is called for in school-finance analyses of the equal-opportunity principle.

ALTERNATIVE MEASURES OF VERTICAL EQUITY

Vertical equity can be defined as the unequal treatment of unequals, but several major decisions must be made before this principle can be operationalized and measured. These include choices about the characteristics that are used to classify "unequals," the differences in objects that each class of unequals should receive, and the measurement of the equity of the actual distribution of objects compared to the desired one. In keeping with the spirit of this chapter, the latter issue—that of measurement—is focused on in this section. Hypothetical examples are used to show how vertical equity can be measured and to emphasize the point that different measures may alter the conclusions of an assessment of vertical equity. Due to the nature of vertical-equity measurement, however, some attention is also paid to the determination of the appropriate distribution of objects among different classes of pupils.

In the examples presented in this section, the particular characteristic that defines unequals and the object do not vary, so that the measures of vertical equity can be placed at center stage. As in previous examples, the object is per-pupil dollar inputs. In the illustrations in this section the characteristic used to differentiate among pupils who should receive more or less dollar inputs is the presence or absence of "handicapping" conditions. Vertical equity is usually assumed to exist when handicapped pupils receive more dollar inputs than nonhandicapped pupils—although this assumption can be problematic, as we will see later in this section. For simplicity, it is assumed that guidelines exist to determine which students have physical or learning handicaps and which ones do not. In addition, differences among types of handicaps are ignored; a student is either handicapped or nonhandicapped. While

ALTERNATIVE MEASURES OF THE EQUITY PRINCIPLES 83

these assumptions regarding the identification of children with handicaps and the differentiation of handicapping conditions by type are oversimplications, they permit a more straightforward assessment of the characteristics of the vertical-equity measures.

Three types of vertical-equity measures are presented in this section. The first type utilizes what are essentially dispersion measures with modifications through weightings to adjust for vertical-equity considerations. The second type consists of the regression-based relationship measures described previously, though the interpretation of these measures changes when they are used to measure vertical equity rather than equal opportunity. The third type of vertical-equity measure is also a relationship measure, but is based on an averaging procedure that is different from the regression-based relationship measures. The modified dispersion measures are presented first, followed by an examination of the regression-based relationship measures. Next, these two types of measures are compared, and then the third type of vertical-equity measure is discussed. The section concludes with an assessment of the strengths and weaknesses of the measures of vertical equity.

If a decision can be made regarding the appropriate differences in objects that unequal groups of pupils should receive, then the dispersion measures used earlier to assess horizontal equity can be reformulated to incorporate the vertical-equity dimension. Because the horizontal-equity measures are basically dispersion measures, and since the reformulation consists of a weighting procedure, the reformulated horizontal-equity measures are referred to as weighted dispersion measures. The calculation of these weighted dispersion measures can be described as follows. First, for each different group of pupils identified for vertical-equity considerations, a weight must be established that expresses the amount of the object that the group of pupils should receive compared to a baseline group. After this weighting scheme is established, the number of pupils times their assigned weights is computed for each district. Next, the total dollar inputs in each district is divided by the number of *weighted* pupils in the district to obtain the dollar inputs per weighted pupil in each district. Finally, the dispersion measures are computed using the dollar inputs per weighted pupil as the object and the weighted-pupil count as the number of pupils in the district. Any of the measures discussed in the first section of this chapter can be reformulated in this way.

This procedure can be clarified with a numerical example. The first three columns in the upper part of table 4.12 present the district number, the total number of unweighted pupils (including handicapped pupils), and the number of handicapped pupils in the seven districts in state F1. For this example, handicapped pupils are assigned a weight of two; that is, each handicapped pupil is weighted as two pupils. This weight may be based on an assessment that handicapped pupils should receive twice the level of dollar inputs, or that handicapped pupils "cost" twice as much as nonhandicapped pupils. The fourth column displays the number of weighted pupils in each district when

Table 4.12 Calculation of Coefficient of Variation Using Unweighted and Weighted Pupils in State F1

District	Total Number of Unweighted Pupils (P_i)	Number of Handicapped Pupils	Total Number of Weighted Pupils (P_i^*)	Total $ Inputs	Per-Pupil $ Inputs (X_i)	Per-Weighted-Pupil $ Inputs (X_i^*)
1	100	5	105	120,000	1,200	1,142.9
2	100	8	108	130,000	1,300	1,203.7
3	100	8	108	160,000	1,600	1,481.5
4	100	7	107	180,000	1,800	1,682.2
5	100	8	108	200,000	2,000	1,851.9
6	100	10	110	230,000	2,300	2,090.9
7	100	8	108	240,000	2,400	2,222.2

$$\bar{X}_p = \frac{\sum_i P_i X_i}{\sum_i P_i} = \frac{1{,}260{,}000}{700} = 1800.0$$

$$\bar{X}_p^* = \frac{\sum_i P_i X_i}{\sum_i P_i^*} = \frac{1{,}260{.}000}{754} = 1671.09$$

Unweighted-Pupil Coefficient of Variation			Weighted-Pupil Coefficient of Variation		
$\bar{X}_p - X_i$	$(\bar{X}_p - X_i)^2$	$P_i(\bar{X}_p - X_i)^2$	$\bar{X}_p^* - X_i^*$	$(\bar{X}_p^* - X_i^*)^2$	$P_i^*(\bar{X}_p^* - X_i^*)^2$
600	360,000	36,000,000	528.2	278,982.1	29,293,117
500	250,000	25,000,000	467.4	218,451.1	23,592,719
200	40,000	4,000,000	189.6	35,943.4	3,881,891
0	0	0	−11.1	123.5	13,213
−200	40,000	4,000,000	−180.8	32,693.1	3,530,860
−500	250,000	25,000,000	−419.8	176,242.5	19,386,676
−600	360,000	36,000,000	−551.1	303,725.0	32,802,295

$$\sum P_i(\bar{X}_p - X_i)^2 = 130{,}000{,}000 \qquad \sum P_i^*(\bar{X}_p^* - X_i^*)^2 = 112{,}500{,}770$$

Unweighted-Pupil coefficient of variation $= \dfrac{\sqrt{\dfrac{\sum P_i(\bar{X}_p - X_i)^2}{\sum P_i}}}{\bar{X}_p}$

Weighted-Pupil coefficient of variation $= \dfrac{\sqrt{\dfrac{\sum P_i^*(\bar{X}_p^* - X_i^*)^2}{\sum P_i^*}}}{\bar{X}_p^*}$

$$= \frac{\sqrt{\dfrac{130{,}000{,}000}{700}}}{1800} = \frac{430.946}{1800} = .2394$$

$$= \frac{\sqrt{\dfrac{112{,}500{,}770}{754}}}{1671.09} = \frac{386.271}{1671.09} = .2311$$

Note: Variables calculated with weighted pupils are noted with an asterisk. Handicapped pupils receive a weight of 2.

handicapped pupils are assigned a weight of two. The number of weighted pupils in district 1, for example, is 95 nonhandicapped pupils plus 5 times 2, or 10, weighted handicapped pupils, which equals 105 weighted pupils. The last three columns at the top of table 4.12 show that total dollar inputs in each district, the per-pupil dollar inputs on an unweighted-pupil basis, and the per-weighted-pupil dollar inputs. Per-unweighted-pupil dollar inputs (which are referred to simply as per-pupil dollar inputs for the remainder of this section) are derived by dividing total dollar inputs by the number of unweighted pupils, and this equals $120,000 divided by 100, or $1,200, for district 1. Per-weighted-pupil dollar inputs are calculated by dividing total dollar inputs by the number of weighted pupils, and for district 1 this is $120,000 divided by 105, or $1142.90.

The lower part of table 4.12 shows the calculation of one dispersion measure, the coefficient of variation, using unweighted pupils and weighted pupils. The unweighted-pupil coefficient of variation is one of the horizontal-equity measures presented in the first section of this chapter and is calculated identically as before. The weighted coefficient of variation, which is the vertical-equity measure, uses the weighted-pupil count, from the fourth column at the top, and the per-weighted-pupil dollar inputs in the last column, but the essential formula for the measure is unchanged. For the weighted measure, the total number of pupils in the state and the mean per-weighted-pupil dollar inputs are different from their unweighted counterparts. All of the horizontal-equity measures presented in the first section can be calculated on a weighted-pupil basis in a similar fashion using the weighted-pupil count (the fourth column) and the per-weighted-pupil dollar inputs (the last column) as the pupil and object data respectively.

The use of weighted dispersion measures incorporates a particular perspective that deserves attention. The measures basically address the question, What is the dispersion in a state after adjusting for the differences in certain vertical-equity characteristics in a prescribed way? But notice that data are only available on a district (not a pupil) basis, and therefore, there is no way of knowing whether any specific pupil actually receives the prescribed differential object levels. Pupils may receive more or less than the weighting implies, but this is not known. In a sense, the weighted dispersion measures give each district credit for having a special category, but the credit is determined by weighting the pupils without any knowledge of the actual distribution of inputs.

When interpreting the weighted dispersion measures, it is assumed that the dispersion that remains after all the legitimate weightings have been applied is unrelated to the particular characteristics considered in the vertical-equity principle and is, therefore, inequitable. Although only one characteristic is used in this example, the assessment of vertical equity can be carried out with several different categories (simultaneously, if desired), such as handicapping conditions, school size, or district size. Furthermore, if there is disagreement on the appropriate weights, sensitivity analysis (the use of different weightings) can be used to determine how conclusions are affected by particular weights. Examples of sensitivity analyses appear in chapter 9, where empirical assessments of actual states are presented.

The computation of unweighted and weighted measures for two states can illustrate how conclusions can change once vertical-equity considerations are introduced. Table 4.13 presents the basic data for states F1 and F2, and table 4.14 shows the values for several weighted and unweighted dispersion measures. When the two states are compared on the horizontal-equity principle using the unweighted dispersion measures, state F1 is judged to be more equitable than state F2 according to the six unweighted dispersion measures shown in table 4.14. This conclusion does not hold up, however, when the weighted dispersion measures are used to compare the two states. On all the weighted dispersion measures except the federal range ratio, state F2 is more equitable than state F1, a general reversal of the findings for the unweighted measures. This example demonstrates that the utilization of the weighting procedure, which can be viewed as a way of shifting from horizontal to vertical equity, has the potential to change the conclusion of an equity assessment. In addition, the example highlights a central theme in this chapter; the comparison between weighted and unweighted measures is affected by the choice of the particular measure.

A second approach to the measurement of vertical equity is to employ the relationship measures. These measures can quantify the relationship between

Table 4.13 Basic Data for States F1 and F2

District	Total Number of Unweighted Pupils	Total Number of Handicapped Pupils	Total Number of Weighted Pupils	Per-Pupil $ Inputs	Per-Weighted-Pupil $ Inputs
		State F1			
1	100	5	105	$1,200	$1,142.9
2	100	8	108	1,300	1,203.7
3	100	8	108	1,600	1,481.5
4	100	7	107	1,800	1,682.2
5	100	8	108	2,000	1,851.9
6	100	10	110	2,300	2,090.9
7	100	8	108	2,400	2,222.2
		State F2			
1	100	0	100	$1,100	$1,100.0
2	100	5	105	1,300	1,238.1
3	100	3	103	1,600	1,553.4
4	100	5	105	1,800	1,714.3
5	100	11	111	2,000	1,801.8
6	100	12	112	2,300	2,053.6
7	100	15	115	2,500	2,173.9

Note: Handicapped pupils are weighted by a factor of two.

Table 4.14 Unweighted and Weighted Dispersion Measures for States F1 and F2

	Unweighted Measures		Weighted Measures	
	F1	F2	F1	F2
Mean	$1,800	$1,800	$1,671.1	$1,677.8
Median	$1,800	$1,800	$1,682.2	$1,714.3
Range	$1,200	$1,400	$1,079.3	$1,073.9
Restricted range	$1,200	$1,400	$1,079.3	$1,073.9
Federal range ratio	1.0000	1.2727	.9444	.9763
McLoone index	.7937	.7778	.7950	.8009
Coefficient of variation	.2394	.2623	.2311	.2188
Gini coefficient	.1361	.1497	.1314	.1239

the level of objects in districts on the one hand and the number of pupils in the legitimate special categories in each district on the other. If, as was assumed earlier, vertical equity requires that more of the objects should be present in districts with greater numbers of pupils in the special categories, then the relationship measures can be used to assess whether this is the case. Recall that the use of the weighted dispersion measures requires an explicit decision regarding the appropriate weight for pupils in each special group. One advantage sometimes claimed for the relationship measure is that the computation of the measure itself does not require this explicit decision. While this is true, the advantage in certain situations is short-lived, since the interpretation of the relationship measures requires a similar judgment. An example of the assessment of vertical equity with the relationship measures is presented to explore this issue.

The basic data for states F3 and F4 are displayed in table 4.15. To compute the relationship measures of vertical equity where the special group is handicapped pupils, per- (unweighted-) pupil dollar inputs are the object, or dependent variable, and the percent of handicapped pupils in the district is the independent variable. The percent of handicapped pupils is a more useful independent variable than the number of handicapped pupils, since the percent is not sensitive to the total number of pupils in the district. Relationship measures based on the simple regression, with per-pupil dollar inputs and percent handicapped pupils as the dependent and the independent variables respectively, are displayed in table 4.16. In addition to the four relationship measures discussed in the previous section, the implicit weight, a measure that has particular meaning for vertical-equity measurement, is shown. The implicit weight is the following ratio: the predicted per-pupil dollar inputs for a district with 100 percent handicapped pupils divided by the predicted per-pupil dollar inputs for a district with no handicapped pupils, where the prediction is based on the simple regression. For state F3, the predicted regression is the following: per-pupil dollar inputs = 1696 + (15.44 × percent handicapped). Thus, the predicted per-pupil dollar inputs in state F3 at 0

Table 4.15 Basic Data for States F3 and F4

District	Total Number of Unweighted Pupils	Total Number of Handicapped Pupils	Total Number of Weighted Pupils	Per-Pupil $ Inputs	Per-Weighted-Pupil $ Inputs
			State F3		
1	100	2	102	$1,700	$1,666.7
2	100	3	103	1,750	1,699.0
3	100	6	106	1,750	1,650.9
4	100	8	108	1,800	1,666.7
5	100	5	105	1,850	1,761.9
6	100	11	111	1,850	1,666.7
7	100	12	112	1,900	1,696.4
			State F4		
1	100	2	102	$1,750	$1,715.7
2	100	3	103	1,850	1,796.1
3	100	6	106	1,800	1,698.1
4	100	8	108	1,800	1,666.7
5	100	5	105	1,850	1,761.9
6	100	11	111	1,850	1,666.7
7	100	12	112	1,900	1,696.4

Note: Handicapped pupils are weighted by a factor of two.

percent and 100 percent handicapped equals $1,696 and $3,240, respectively. The implicit weight is $3,240 divided by $1,696, or 1.9102. The implicit weight can be interpreted to mean that the simple regression estimates that per-pupil dollar inputs of a district with all handicapped pupils would be 1.9102 times those of a district with no handicapped pupils.

The interpretation of the measures presented in table 4.16 can be guided by two questions. First, do the measures indicate that districts with higher percentages of handicapped pupils have higher per-pupil dollar inputs? Second, can the measures be utilized to assess which state is more equitable? The answer to the first question can be obtained from the sign of the relationship measures. If the estimated regression line has a positive slope, then the correlation, simple elasticity, and simple adjusted relationship measure will be positive as well. When this is the case, the regression can be interpreted to

Table 4.16 Relationship Measures of Vertical Equity for States F3 and F4

	F3	F4
Correlation	.8336	.6328
Simple slope	15.4412	8.0882
Simple elasticity	.0576	.0297
Simple adjusted relationship measure	.0607	.0313
Implicit weight ($\hat{Y}_{100}/\hat{Y}_0$)	1.9102	1.4556

indicate that districts with higher percentages of handicapped pupils have higher per-pupil dollar inputs. The positive relationship measures for states F3 and F4 answer the first question and indicate that, for these two hypothetical states, inputs are distributed in a vertically equitable direction.

This type of evaluation is less precise than the usual conclusions drawn from equity measures for which the second question is answered and some states are assessed as more or less equitable than others. In order to use the relationship measures to rank states on vertical equity, however, a judgment must be made to determine whether one relationship is more equitable than another. This judgment is complicated by the fact that vertical equity may mean that the special class should receive more of the object, but this may hold only up to a point, after which a stronger relationship may not be representative of vertical equity. At an extreme, handicapped pupils receiving fifty times as much as nonhandicapped pupils may be less vertically equitable than handicapped pupils receiving four times as much. Returning to table 4.16, is state F3 more equitable than state F4, or vice versa? While any of the relationship measures could be used to help make this evaluation, the implicit weight measure may be preferable for vertical equity with percent handicapped as the group of concern. It is somewhat easier to interpret, since the value of the measure has an understandable meaning; it is analogous to the weighting scheme explicitly chosen for the pupil-weighted dispersion measures. In the hypothetical example, if handicapped pupils are weighted at two, then state F3, with an implicit weight of 1.9102, would be closer to this desired point than state F4, with an implicit weight of 1.4556, and therefore, F3 could be assessed as more vertically equitable.

Although in this particular example the relationship measures, especially the implicit weight, can be used to assess vertical equity, two important points deserve attention. First, although a decision regarding the differential amount of the object that the special groups should receive is not required in order to compute the measures, this decision (or assumption) is necessary for the interpretation of the measures. Therefore, except for the cases where distinctions are drawn only among states that have positive versus negative relationships, the utilization of the relationship measures to assess vertical equity requires the same judgments that are necessary to use the weighted dispersion measures.

The second important point focuses on the way in which differences in the object are related to the special classes. Recall that for the weighted dispersion measures, any differences that existed after the application of the weighting procedure are judged to be inequitable. For the relationship measures, the association between the districts' objects and the size of the special class in the districts is not established by an explicit weight, but is determined instead by the statistical association between the dependent and the independent variables in a regression. In other words, any variation in the object that is associated with the special class is captured by the relationship measure, and any variation in the object that is not associated with the special class is not captured by the measure. This feature of the relationship measures helps explain why a judgment on the desired relationship is not necessary to compute the measure, but such a judgment is still required to interpret the measure.

This characteristic of the relationship measures may lead to the difficulties in interpretation hinted at above. Stated simply, how would two states be ranked in terms of vertical equity when the relationship measures in both states exceed the desired relationship? Is the state with the greater relationship (i.e., higher relationship measure) necessarily more equitable? We do not know how the districts use the objects, and therefore, this information is not available to answer the question. It turns out to be very difficult to evaluate vertical equity when the measured relationship is greater than desired. An example of this situation will be presented shortly.

States F1, F2, F3, and F4 can be examined further to show cases where there is agreement and disagreement between the weighted dispersion measures and the regression-based relationship measures of vertical equity. Taking states F3 and F4 first, the weighted dispersion measures can be computed from the number of weighted pupils and the per-weighted-pupil dollar inputs displayed in table 4.15. These weighted dispersion measures, computed with handicapped pupils weighted at two, are shown in table 4.17, and all the weighted dispersion measures show that state F3 is more equitable than state F4. This is completely consistent with the conclusions from the relationship measures for states F3 and F4 shown in table 4.16, when it is assumed that the weight of two is desirable, since the relationship measures are higher for state F3 than for state F4 and the implicit weights suggest that the desired relationship has not yet been reached by either state. This example is designed to show that agreement can occur among all measures; however, it should not be inferred that agreement among all the measures is a likely occurrence. This type of assessment must be made with actual empirical studies rather than with hypothetical examples, and these assessments will be presented in chapter 9.

While either the relationship measures or the weighted dispersion mea-

Table 4.17 Weighted Dispersion Measures of Vertical Equity for States F3 and F4

	F3	F4
Mean	$1,686.7	$1,713.5
Median	$1,666.7	$1,698.1
Range	$ 111.0	$ 129.4
Restricted range	$ 111.0	$ 129.4
Federal range ratio	.0672	.0776
McLoone index	.9973	.9888
Coefficient of variation	.0204	.0260
Gini coefficient	.0103	.0141

sures could be employed to assess state F3 as vertically more equitable than state F4, an example of the contradictions that can arise between the two sets of measures appears when states F1 and F2 are examined. The basic data for those two states and the weighted dispersion measures were displayed in tables 4.13 and 4.14, respectively. The relationship measures with per-pupil dollar inputs as the dependent variable and percent of pupils that are handicapped as the independent variable are shown in table 4.18. Recall that all the weighted dispersion measures presented in table 4.14 except the federal range ratio assessed state F2 to be more vertically equitable than state F1. The picture that emerges from the relationship measures that appear in table 4.18 is considerably less clear. On the one hand, the correlation and the simple adjusted relationship measure are higher in state F2. The simple slope and the simple elasticity, on the other hand, are higher in state F1. Finally, the implicit weight in state F1 is over ten times as large as the implicit weight in state F2.

The application of the various vertical-equity measures to states F1 and F2 highlights several potential problems. There may be cases where the different relationship measures disagree in the way they rank two (or more) states. Perhaps the value judgments incorporated in the measures or the way in which they describe the relationship (magnitude versus association) can be used to focus on a single measure or a subset of measures to reduce such disagreement. But even if this is possible, can the relationship measures be interpreted when they show a "stronger" relationship than desired? Furthermore, the relationship measure—if interpreted simply by assuming that more of the object for the special class is more vertically equitable—can disagree with the weighted dispersion measures. This is precisely the situation in states F1 and F2, where an implicit weight of 110 or even 8.6 may be much larger than any desired weight, and the state with the larger implicit weight has the less-equitable weighted dispersion measures.

Given the different assumptions built into the weighted dispersion measures in comparison with the relationship measures, the added interpretational problem of overly positive relationship measures, and the possibility of empirical disagreements (as shown by the preceding example), the use of a single vertical-equity measure is not advisable. Instead, when vertical equity

Table 4.18 Relationship Measures of Vertical Equity for States F1 and F2

	F1	F2
Correlation	.67105	.9377
Simple slope	208.51	87.93
Simple elasticity	.8936	.3359
Simple adjusted relationship measure	.3211	.4922
Implicit weight ($\hat{Y}_{100}/\hat{Y}_0$)	109.88	8.58

in Michigan and New York is analyzed in chapter 9, the two sets of measures are presented simultaneously. The relationship measures are used to assess whether the object and the special group are related in a positive or a negative way. The weighted dispersion measures are compared to the unweighted measures and are utilized to detect trends in the weighted dispersion over time.

This section of the chapter would be incomplete without describing a third type of vertical-equity measure that is a relationship measure, but not a regression-based relationship measure. Instead of relying on a least-squares technique to estimate the relationship between per-pupil objects and the percent handicapped, a ratio measure can be constructed that relies on the differences in the average level of per-pupil objects across different groups. The example of this approach, which was discussed in chapter 2, is here based on a ratio of two averages: the average per-pupil object for handicapped pupils and the average per-pupil object for nonhandicapped pupils. This third vertical-equity measure, the averaged implicit weight, is calculated by dividing the average per-pupil object for handicapped pupils by the average per-pupil object for nonhandicapped pupils, and vertical equity requires the averaged implicit weight to be greater than one.

In order to calculate the average per-pupil object and the averaged implicit weight for specific categories of pupils, such as handicapped and nonhandicapped, several steps and related assumptions are necessary. First, it is assumed that all pupils in a district, regardless of their category, receive the average per-pupil object in the district. With this assumption, pupils in each category can be assigned the average per-pupil object in their district. Next, all pupils in a category can be grouped together to calculate the average (or mean) per-pupil object level in that category, and finally, these averages can be compared across categories to determine the averaged implicit weights.

The upper part of table 4.19 shows how this implicit weight is calculated for state F1. Assuming every pupil receives the average dollar inputs in the district, the distributions of nonhandicapped and handicapped pupils are used to estimate the total dollar inputs for nonhandicapped and handicapped pupils. These totals are divided by the number of pupils in each category to determine the average values. For state F1, the average per-pupil dollar inputs for handicapped pupils is $1,851.85 and the average per-pupil dollar inputs for nonhandicapped pupils is $1,795.67. The averaged implicit weight for state F1 is the ratio of the two averages, which equals $1,851.85/ $1,795.67, or 1.0313. In the lower part of table 4.19 the averaged implicit weights for states F2, F3, and F4 are displayed.

The averaged implicit weight incorporates vertical-equity concerns differently than either the weighted dispersion measures or the regression-based relationship measures, and this is illustrated in table 4.20, where it can be seen that the ranking obtained from the implicit weight disagrees with all of the other vertical-equity measures. Although all of the averaged implicit weights are greater than one, indicating that handicapped pupils receive

ALTERNATIVE MEASURES OF THE EQUITY PRINCIPLES

Table 4.19 Calculation of Averaged Implicit Weight for State F1 and Values of Averaged Implicit Weight for States F2, F3, and F4

	Calculation of Averaged Implicit Weight for State F1						
	Nonhandicapped Pupils				Handicapped Pupils		
District	Number of Pupils	Per-Pupil $ Inputs	Total $ Inputs	District	Number of Pupils	Per-Pupil $ Inputs	Total $ Inputs
1	95	$1,200	$ 114,000	1	5	$1,200	$ 6,000
2	92	1,300	119,600	2	8	1,300	10,400
3	92	1,600	147,200	3	8	1,600	12,800
4	93	1,800	167,400	4	7	1,800	12,600
5	92	2,000	184,000	5	8	2,000	16,000
6	90	2,300	207,000	6	10	2,300	23,000
7	92	2,400	220,800	7	8	2,400	19,200
	Total 646		Total $1,160,000		Total 54		Total $100,000

Average per-pupil $ Inputs for Nonhandicapped Pupils

$$\frac{\$1{,}160{,}000}{646} = \$1{,}795.67$$

Average Per-Pupil $ Inputs for Handicapped Pupils

$$\frac{\$100{,}000}{54} = \$1{,}851.85$$

$$\text{Averaged implicit weight for state F1} = \frac{\$1{,}851.85}{\$1{,}795.67} = 1.0313$$

Averaged implicit weights for States F2, F3, and F4

F2	F3	F4
1.1858	1.0171	1.0083

Table 4.20 Ranking of States F1, F2, F3, and F4 by Four Vertical-Equity Measures

Weighted Coefficient of Variation (weight of two)[a]	Weighted Gini Coefficient (weight of two)[a]	Regression-Based Implicit Weight[b]	Averaged Implicit Weight[b]
F3	F3	F1	F2
F4	F4	F2	F1
F2	F2	F3	F3
F1	F1	F4	F4

[a]The smaller the weighted measure, the greater the equity
[b]The larger the implicit measure, the greater the equity

more of the object than nonhandicapped pupils, the use of the averaged implicit weight to rank the states raises the same problems that exist for the regression-based relationship measures. There are, in fact, some similarities between the averaged implicit weight and the regression-based relationship measures, and these are discussed next, in the final portion of this section.

A significant characteristic of vertical equity is the specificity that is required for its definition. Legitimate groups of concern must be identified, and a decision must be made on how unequal these groups should be. If we consider the weighted dispersion measures as one group of vertical-equity measures (called the dispersion group) and the regression-based relationship measures and the averaged implicit weight as a second group (called the relationship group) then we can show that the operationalization of the two groups differ.

To operationalize the measures in the dispersion group, legitimate special classes must be identified and specific weights decided upon. Although there may be disagreements among different dispersion measures, the computation of any single measure for a series of states can be used to rank the states in terms of vertical equity. The dispersion measures do not, however, answer the less specific question discussed earlier: namely, do the districts that contain more pupils in the special classes have higher object levels than the districts with fewer pupils in the special classes. The specificity of the weighted-dispersion measures enables them to rank states, or to assess progress over time, but precludes them from answering the more general question.

The relationship measures require only that the special classes be identified; the measures can be computed without specifying the levels of the objects that are desired for each class. If no other decisions are made, however, the measures in the relationship group only answer the general question that was not answered by the weighted dispersion measures. If the simple regression-based relationship measures are greater than zero and if the averaged implicit weight is greater than one (they should agree most of the time), then, on the average, districts with a higher percent of pupils in the special class have higher object levels than districts with a smaller percent of pupils in the special class. Although the relationship group can answer this general question, the empirical examples in this part demonstrated how difficult it is to answer the more specific question (How are a set of states ranked?) with the relationship measures.

Since the dispersion group's assets are the relationship group's liabilities, and vice versa, we think that a case can be made to select vertical-equity measures from both groups. Vertical equity is the most difficult of the principles to operationalize, but by focusing on the two groups of measures and their comparative advantages, measurement can be accomplished even with the complexity of the task.

WHAT CAN BE LEARNED FROM HYPOTHETICAL ILLUSTRATIONS

The examples presented in chapters 3 and 4 clearly show that the way in which children's equity is measured has the potential to significantly influence the results of an equity assessment. The illustrations presented alternative operationalizations of the objects, principles, and measures not only to show

how to implement the equity framework empirically but, equally important, to elaborate the role that values and preferences play in differentiating among the choices that an equity evaluation must face, explicitly or implicitly.

After digesting the material presented in the first four chapters of this book, an individual faced with the task of assessing the equity in one state over time or of comparing the equity of a set of states could react in one of several ways.

One reaction could be to ignore the description of the multidimensional nature of equity presented here. Many, and perhaps even most, evaluations of school-finance equity employ only a small subset of the concepts and measures presented here, and the analyst can follow this path by selecting one or two measures to evaluate equity. We hope this reaction will only occur in a small fraction of the cases. While it is helpful to deal with complexity through simplification, oversimplification can be detrimental or even wrong. The hypothetical illustrations demonstrate that conclusions about equity can be exactly opposite from one approach to the next, so that a random or uninformed selection of one or two measures has the potential to be misleading. After some empirical experience with the equity-measurement methodology is gained, it may turn out that some of the alternatives can be eliminated because they never or rarely change the conclusions drawn from a smaller set of measures. Yet until the empirical evidence is accumulated, the analyst who ignores the multiplicity of measures runs the risk of being just plain wrong.

The first four chapters of this book could cause a different reaction if the analyst becomes overloaded with the alternative ways of measuring equity that have been introduced. This could lead to the use of undifferentiated presentation of every conceivable measure in an equity assessment, rendering it almost incomprehensible. Again we hope this is not a common occurrence. In a sense, an analyst who follows this route has received the message that alternative measures may matter, but has not understood the way in which the framework and the use of values can shape and give meaning to alternative measurement approaches.

These first two reactions leave plenty of room for a middle course that we will illustrate with real empirical examples later in the book. Essentially, this middle course combines the structure of the framework, the values inherent in the equity measures, and the use of sensitivity analysis to evaluate equity comprehensively and to present the results so they can be understood. In practice, this may mean that every single measure may not be necessary in every analysis. An analyst may choose some approaches and reject others because the parameters of the evaluation indicate that certain alternatives within the framework are inappropriate. An explanation of these choices will help those who desire to evaluate the evaluation. Or it may be that data availability precludes certain analyses, but at least future decision makers can be helped in their assessment of whether the data should be gathered by knowing what equity concepts will be better measured.

Analysts may also narrow the set of equity measures if they can determine which values the consumers of the assessment favor. While this may be difficult and risky, it may be possible in certain instances. In cases where a set of measures capture what are, for the most part, identical values, then only one or two measures in the set may be necessary.

Finally, the actual empirical assessment can employ sensitivity analysis to determine which parts of the framework do make a difference. Those aspects that affect the conclusions can be emphasized, and areas where alternatives do not alter the conclusions can be simplified. Chapters 7 through 10 can be used to assess whether we can practice what we preach.

5

REVIEW OF METHODOLOGIES OF RECENT SCHOOL-FINANCE-EQUITY LITERATURE

Over the past decade, there have been numerous studies of equity in school finance. These studies have varied greatly with respect to their methodological approaches, and no one of them has presented a comprehensive assessment of equity along the lines attempted here in subsequent chapters for Michigan and New York. In order to put the analyses in this book in context, this chapter presents a review of the major studies of school-finance equity. This review will document some of the shortcomings as well as the strengths of the most recent literature. Both children's and taxpayers' equity studies are reviewed, although children's studies are more numerous.

The chapter is organized around a series of issues, most of which are derived from the framework presented in chapter 2. Thus for the group of studies reviewed, we assess the frequency of use of different groups, objects, principles, and measures. In addition, we look at the frequency with which various fiscal capacity measures and units of analysis are employed. Altogether, fifty-five studies are reviewed. They are listed in the bibliography at the end of the chapter and are grouped as single-state, multistate, fifty-state, and methodological studies. The studies numbered 1 through 32 are single-state studies; multistate studies are numbered 33 through 41; fifty-state studies are numbered 42 through 50, and methodological studies are 51 to 55. While many studies contain methodological contributions, the latter group is distinct because these studies include only methodological analyses.

WHO IS THE GROUP OF CONCERN? CHILDREN? TAXPAYERS? BOTH?

The first aspect of the four-party equity framework presented in chapter 2 is the group: From whose perspective is equity assessed? Every study in our data base examines children's equity—either alone or in combination with taxpayers' equity. Moreover, the frequency of coverage of taxpayers' equity varies across the categories of studies, with the highest relative frequency among the single-state studies and the lowest among the fifty-state studies. Thus, the single-state studies contain a broader set of perspectives for the assessment of school-finance equity, since they are more likely to focus on both children's and taxpayers' equity. While the fifty-state studies taken together underemphasize the taxpayer perspective, the two fifty-state studies that measure equity in 1970 and 1977 (nos. 43 and 46) include an assessment of both children's and taxpayers' equity. In general, however, the higher the number of states included in the study, the greater the data-gathering tasks and the comparability problems and the less likely it is that the taxpayer perspective will be included—perhaps because the concepts of taxpayer-equity measurement are relatively underdeveloped.

WHICH CHILDREN'S OBJECTS ARE UTILIZED IN THE STUDIES?

After selecting the group, the second issue raised by the equity framework is the object, or the answer to the question: Equity of what? This will first be addressed from the children's perspective, then the taxpayers'.

Table 5.1 displays the frequency with which the various children's objects are employed by the four categories of studies. The objects are grouped by expenditures, revenues, and inputs. Furthermore, within these broad groupings are subgroupings that reflect commonalities among certain objects. The objects are listed in table 5.1 as they are defined in the studies, and no attempt was made to determine whether objects that are labeled differently are actually the same. For example, "Total expenditures" may be the same as "Expenditures," but research that goes beyond the studies themselves would be required to draw that conclusion. Therefore, some of the diversity portrayed by table 5.1 may be overstated, but we are rather confident our findings would not be affected.

Several conclusions can be drawn from table 5.1. First, judging from the number of objects and their frequency, there is considerable diversity in the selection of the children's object. Across all studies, objects based on expenditures are the most common; revenue objects, the next frequent; and input-based objects, the least common. But even within the expenditure, revenue, and input groupings, there is substantial variation in the children's objects.

Second, judging by the frequencies in relation to the number of studies in the single-state, multistate, and fifty-state categories, there is more diversity among the single-state studies than among the multistate and fifty-state studies. The lack of diversity among the fifty-state studies and, to a more limited degree, the multistate studies stems, in part, from the utilization of the same data base in several studies.

Table 5.1. Frequency of Children's Equity Objects in School-Finance Studies

Object	Single State	Multi-state	Fifty State	Methodological Only
Expenditures				
Total expenditures				
1. Total expenditures	6	0	1	1
2. Expenditures	3	0	2	0
3. Total expenditures less Title I	0	1	0	0
4. Expenditures less state and federal categoricals	1	0	0	0
Current expenditures				
5. Current expenditures	5	4	0	0
6. Current expenditures, cost adjusted	1	0	0	0
7. Current expenditures less transportation	1	0	2	0
8. Current expenditures less state and federal block grants	1	0	0	0
9. Current expenditures less federal ESEA act aid	1	0	0	0
10. Core current expenditures less food service and transportation	0	0	1	0
11. Core current expenditures excluding transportation and interest	0	0	1	0
12. Core current expenditures adjusted for cost of living	0	0	1	0
13. Current expenditures with salary controlled by degree level	0	0	1	0
14. Current expenditures with salary adjusted by degree level and quality	0	0	1	0
15. Current expenditures less transportation, lunches, community services, tuition payments, capital outlay, and debt service	0	0	1	0
Operating expenditures				
16. Operating expenditures	3	1	0	0
17. Approved operating expenditures	1	0	0	0
18. Operating expenditures less transportation costs	0	1	0	0
19. Price-adjusted operating expenditures less transportation	0	1	0	0
20. Current operating expenditures	1	0	0	0
21. Current operating expenditures from nonfederal sources	1	0	2	0
Instructional expenditures				
22. Instructional expenditures	2	1	0	0
Costs				
23. Net operating costs	1	0	0	0
24. Total costs of operations	1	0	0	0

Table 5.1. (*cont.*)

Object	Single State	Multi-state	Fifty State	Methodological Only
Other				
25. State and local expenditures	2	0	0	0
26. Locally financed expenditures	0	0	0	1
Revenues				
State and local revenues				
27. Total state and local revenues	1	3	2	0
28. Local revenues plus direct state aid	1	0	0	0
29. Local plus intermediate plus state noncategorical revenues	0	1	0	0
30. State and local current revenue	0	1	0	0
31. Local plus state general revenues	0	1	0	0
32. Authorized revenue base (local taxes plus general state aid with certain growth constraints)	1	0	0	0
33. Revenue for current operating purposes from state and local sources	0	1	0	2
State, local and federal revenues				
34. Total revenues	1	2	0	1
35. Total current revenues	0	1	0	0
36. Revenues for current operations	0	1	0	0
37. Local plus state plus federal general revenues	0	1	0	0
38. General fund revenues	2	0	0	0
39. Adjusted revenues (local current plus state except transportation and debt service plus Title I and impact aid)	1	0	0	0
40. Local, intermediate, and state noncategorical and federal impact aid revenue	0	1	0	0
Other				
41. State aid	1	0	0	0
42. Local revenues	0	1	0	1
43. Local plus federal revenues	0	1	0	0
Inputs				
Personnel				
44. Professionals per 1000 pupils	1	0	0	0
45. Teachers per 1000 pupils	1	0	0	0
46. Classroom teachers	0	0	3	0
47. Instructional staff weighted by degree level	0	0	1	0
48. Paraprofessionals per 1000 pupils	1	0	0	0
Other				
49. Educational attainment of teachers	1	0	0	0
50. Teacher experience	2	0	0	0
51. Median teacher salary	1	0	0	0
52. Average teacher salary	1	0	0	0
53. Average teacher salary per pupil	1	0	0	0
54. Measures of school services	1	0	0	0

Third, despite the diversity among the expenditure, revenue, and input objects, there are particular objects that are used relatively more frequently. These include total expenditures, expenditures, current expenditures, current expenditures less transportation, operating expenditures, current operating expenditures from nonfederal sources, and instructional expenditures, within the expenditure grouping; total state and local revenues, revenues for current operating purposes from state and local sources, and total revenues, within the revenue grouping; and classroom teachers, within the input grouping. When the more-frequent revenue and expenditure objects are examined, many of them represent either a measure of total resources (with or without minor exceptions) or a measure of resources from state and local sources. This is true for single state, multistate, and fifty-state studies. But we doubt that many of the objects that appear to be similar could be equated across the single-state and multistate studies. In addition, note that the fifty-state studies that assess multiple recent years (including nos. 43 and 46) utilize one or more of the frequently used objects.

Fourth and finally, cost adjustments have not, as yet, become an accepted component of school-finance-equity assessments, despite the research on these adjustments in the literature.[1] Furthermore, almost all of the cost adjustments used in the studies were not representative of the econometric cost of education indexes that represent the state of the art.

WHICH TAXPAYERS' OBJECTS ARE UTILIZED IN THE STUDIES?

The taxpayer objects and the frequency of their use in the four categories of studies are displayed in table 5.2. Due to more limited use and development of taxpayer-equity concepts and the findings from the assessment of children's objects just completed, we have focused this analysis on the generic types of taxpayer objects. It must be recognized, however, that the more frequently employed objects, especially "expenditures or revenues and tax rates" and "tax rates," are not exactly comparable across studies.

Table 5.2 shows these two types of taxpayer objects are used quite extensively. Although the relationship is not perfect, tax rates as an object is usually related to the principle of inequality in tax rates; expenditures or revenues and tax rates is often the object for the equal-yield-for-equal-effort principle.

Table 5.2 also further documents the absence of taxpayer concerns in multistate and fifty-state studies. In particular, the expenditures-or-revenues-and-tax-rates object is used in only two multistate studies and in no

---

1. See Leanna Stiefel and Robert Berne, "Price Indexes for Teachers in Michigan: A Replication and Extension" in Esther O. Tron, ed., *Selected Papers in School Finance, 1981* (Washington, D.C.: U.S. Department of Education, National Institute of Education, March 1981), pp. 159–211, and the references therein.

Table 5.2. Frequency of Taxpayer Objects in School-Finance Studies

	Single State	Multi-state	Fifty State	Methodological Only
1. Expenditures or revenues and tax rates*	11	2	0	0
2. Need-adjusted revenues or expenditures and tax rates	1	0	0	0
3. Expenditures or revenues and taxes as a percent of income	1	0	0	0
4. Tax rates	12	3	2	0
5. Taxes as a percent of income	0	0	1	0
6. Tax burdens	2	1	0	0
7. Reimbursement ratio and wealth	1	0	0	0
8. Tax price	0	0	0	1
9. Education benefits, net of taxes paid, and income	0	0	0	1
10. State and local revenues	0	0	0	1

*Definitions of expenditures and revenues may vary across studies. For more details, see table 5.1.

fifty-state studies. Viewed another way, from multistate and fifty-state studies where the years and objects are likely to be somewhat more comparable, expenditure-or-revenue-and-tax-rate objects are available for only eight states (in studies 36 and 37).

Finally, another possible indicator of the relative underdevelopment of taxpayer equity compared to children's equity is the fact that three taxpayer objects have been utilized only in methodological studies (not in state-by-state assessments) within our universe of studies. The use of objects in just methodological studies occurred only once in table 5.1 for children's objects.

WHICH CHILDREN'S EQUITY PRINCIPLES ARE EMPLOYED BY THE STUDIES?

The third component of the equity framework is the principle used to assess the fairness of the distribution of objects to the group. The analysis of the principles is carried out in this section for children and in the next for taxpayers.

The frequency of the utilization of the various children's equity principles is documented in table 5.3. Recall that in chapter 2, three children's equity principles were articulated, and almost all of the principles used in the studies are classified as either horizontal equity, vertical equity, or equal opportunity. Of the three principles, horizontal equity is the most frequently utilized, since it is assessed in three-quarters of the single-state studies, eight of the nine multistate studies, and all nine of the fifty-state studies.

Table 5.3. Frequency of Various Children's Equity Principles in Studies

Principle	Single State	Multi-state	Fifty State	Methodological Only
Horizontal equity	24	8	9	3
Vertical equity				
Special education needs*	3	1	0	0
Low achieving or compensatory education	1	0	0	0
Costs	0	1	0	0
District size	1	1	0	0
Equal opportunity with respect to				
Property wealth	24	6	5	4
Income	12	3	0	1
Ability to pay	0	0	1	0
Minorities or race	3	3	1	0
Poverty	5	1	0	0
SES	2	0	0	0
District type	3	0	2	0
District size	0	1	1	0
Adequacy	0	1	0	0
Sufficiency	1	0	0	1
Other	1	0	0	1

Note: Studies may add to greater than total number in group because many use more than one principle.
*Special education needs refers primarily to students with handicapping conditions.

The least frequently examined principle is vertical equity. Vertical equity is the most methodologically demanding principle to assess, since unequal pupils must be identified, the appropriate unequal treatment for unequal pupils determined, and the distribution of unequal objects to pupils measured. While this may account for the lack of attention to it in the universe of studies, it is nevertheless a legitimate and important concern in school-finance equity. Furthermore, given the overall societal concern for groups such as the handicapped, federal intervention on their behalf in the education system, and the expanding role being played by the courts, there is a good chance that vertical equity will become a more important concern in the future. It is probably safe to say that the absence of vertical-equity measurement is the most serious flaw in the literature. No fifty-state studies, one multistate study, and only a handful of single-state studies assess vertical equity.

Equal opportunity is actually a group of principles, each formulated with reference to a different independent variable. Table 5.3 shows that the principle of equal opportunity with respect to property wealth is assessed almost as frequently as horizontal equity. The only category where there are considerably fewer assessments of equal opportunity with respect to property wealth than of horizontal equity is in the fifty-state studies. Given the other advantages of these studies, this is a serious problem. Specifically, one recent multiyear fifty-state study (no. 43) does not measure equal opportunity with respect to wealth, while another (no. 46) reports that equalized property values are only available for thirty-six states.

Equal opportunity with respect to income is the only other equal-opportunity principle that appears in more than ten studies. However, this principle was unmeasured in the fifty-state studies and appears in about one-third of the single-state and the multistate studies. Other equal-opportunity principles that appear several times include equal opportunity with respect to race and equal opportunity with respect to poverty; however, they do not appear in the vast majority of studies.

Thus, only horizontal equity is well covered in all the studies, including the fifty-state studies. Of the equal-opportunity principles, only equal opportunity with respect to property wealth is examined by more than a majority of the studies, including five of the nine fifty-state studies. Other equal-opportunity principles—for example, with respect to race and to income—receive some, but far from universal, coverage, and they are largely absent from the fifty-state studies. Vertical equity, although recognized by many equity scholars as being important, is almost completely ignored in these studies.

WHICH TAXPAYERS' EQUITY PRINCIPLES ARE EMPLOYED BY THE STUDIES?

From the taxpayers' perspective, there are two frequently utilized school-finance-equity principles, namely, equal-yield-for-equal-effort and inequality-in-tax rates. Table 5.4 shows the distribution of the use of all taxpayers' equity principles across the four categories of studies, and the relative underattention to taxpayer principles in all but the single-state studies is reaffirmed.

Table 5.4. Frequency of Various Taxpayer Equity Principles in Studies

Principle	Single State	Multi-state	Fifty State	Methodological Only
Equal-yield-for-equal-effort	15	2	0	1
Inequality-in-tax-rates	11	2	2	0
Incidence of taxes	2	1	0	0
Districts with identical preferences but different wealth tax themselves at identical tax rates	1	0	0	0
Inequality in tax prices	0	0	0	1
Social welfare function	0	0	0	1

Note: Studies may add to greater than total number in group because many use more than one principle.

Specifically, there is no measurement of equal-yield-for-equal-effort in the fifty-state studies at all. Since a considerable part of the school-finance community treats equal-yield-for-equal-effort as an important taxpayers' equity principle, its absence from the fifty-state studies must be viewed as an important shortcoming. Like the children's vertical-equity principle, equal-yield-for-equal-effort is not a straightforward principle to measure, and the data requirements are more demanding than for most other principles. Thus, this may account for the underattention in the fifty-state studies. The inequality-in-tax-rates principle is better represented in the fifty-state studies, yet it appears to us to be less central than the equal-yield-for-equal effort principle in most people's school-finance-equity considerations. There are also a few other taxpayers' principles that have been measured in one or two studies or proposed in methodological analyses.

WHICH CHILDREN'S EQUITY MEASURES ARE USED IN THE STUDIES?

The final component in the four-part equity framework is the measure of equity. Explicitly or implicitly, the use of a certain measure corresponds to a particular group, object, and principle. The analysis proceeds from the children's perspective first, followed by the taxpayers'.

The various children's equity measures and their frequency of use by children's equity principle and category of study are reported in table 5.5. One focus of the school-finance-equity literature has been the alternative equity measures, and the value judgments that are incorporated into each alternative; table 5.5 reflects the array of alternatives. Since for every principle and every category of study the number of measures exceeds the number of studies, multiple measurement of the same principle is common.

For the horizontal-equity and equal-opportunity principles, there are particular measures that appear more frequently in the single-state, multistate, and fifty-state studies. These include the coefficient of variation, the Gini coefficient, and the federal range ratio for horizontal equity, and the correlation (Pearson), the elasticity, and the means or medians by percentiles for equal opportunity. At the same time, there are equity measures commonly found in the single-state and multistate studies that are found infrequently in the fifty-state studies. Such measures that are not often found in the fifty-state studies are the range, the restricted range, the McLoone index, and the standard deviation for horizontal equity, and the wealth-related Gini for equal opportunity. While methodological criticisms or specific value judgments are available to justify the exclusion of some of these measures, they are not often dealt with in an explicit manner in the fifty-state studies. In several cases, though, the alternative measures are presented and compared in the fifty-state studies.

In general, the use of multiple measures of the horizontal-equity and equal-

Table 5.5. Frequency of Various Equity Measures in Children's Studies, Cross-Tabulated by Principle

Measure	Single State	Multi-state	Fifty State	Methodological Only
Horizontal equity				
Range	10	2	0	1
Restricted range	8	3	0	1
Coefficient of variation	9	7	7	2
Gini coefficient	7	3	5	2
McLoone index	5	2	1	1
Standard deviation	4	2	0	1
Federal range ratio	7	4	5	1
Relative mean deviation	1	1	1	2
Standard deviation of logarithms	1	0	0	1
Theil coefficient	0	0	2	0
Means or medians ordered by percentiles	1	1	1	0
Other*	8	2	5	1
Vertical equity				
Restricted range	1	1	0	0
Federal range ratio	1	1	0	0
Coefficient of variation	0	1	0	0
McLoone index	0	1	0	0
Expenditures (etc.) by percentiles of second variable	1	0	0	0
Regression coefficients	1	1	0	0
Other*	1	0	0	0
Equal Opportunity				
Pearson correlation	12	4	2	3
Elasticity	6	4	2	4
Rank correlation	1	0	0	0
Slope	0	2	1	2
Wealth-related Gini	1	3	0	0
Regression coefficients	2	1	0	0
Means or medians ordered by percentile of second variable	9	3	2	1
Other*	6	1	2	1
Other				
Hypothetical examples	1	0	0	0
Regression statistics	1	0	0	0
Cost related	0	0	0	1

*Other includes a diversity of different measures.

opportunity principles is fairly well accepted in all categories of studies, although certain measures are not often available in the fifty-state studies. Of course, the absence of vertical-equity measures in the fifty-state studies and in nearly all the multistate and single-state studies is consistent with the earlier findings on the principles.

WHICH TAXPAYERS' EQUITY MEASURES ARE USED IN THE STUDIES?

The frequency of utilization of the various taxpayers' equity measures is displayed in table 5.6 by principle and category of study. While there were certain children's equity measures that were used more than others for horizontal equity and equal opportunity, the taxpayers' equity measures are not dominated by a subset of measures. This is due, in part, to the lack of conceptual development of taxpayers' equity, compared to children's equity.

The measures of equal yield for equal effort include dispersion and regression measures, bivariate tables and graphs, and several others, including displays of hypothetical examples. In almost every case, the measures are trying to capture the relationship between taxing and revenues (or expenditures), with a "perfect" relationship being indicative of equal-yield-for-equal-effort.

Table 5.6. Frequency of Various Equity Measures in Taxpayer Studies, Cross-Tabulated by Principle

	Single State	Multi-state	Fifty State	Methodological Only
Equal-yield-for-equal-effort				
Coefficient of variation	3	0	0	0
Correlation	3	1	0	0
Change in R^2	0	1	0	0
Graphs by second variable	1	0	0	0
Tables by second variable	3	0	0	0
Hypothetical examples	3	0	0	0
Other*	5	0	0	1
Inequality-in-tax-rates				
Coefficient of variation	2	2	1	0
Range	5	1	0	0
Restricted range	1	1	0	0
Standard deviation	2	1	0	0
Federal range ratio	2	1	1	0
Relative mean deviation	2	1	0	0
Gini coefficient	0	1	0	0
Theil coefficient	0	0	1	0
Percentiles	0	1	0	0
Frequency distributions	2	0	0	0
Other*	6	0	0	0
Incidence of Taxes				
Tables by income class	1	1	0	0
Tables by percentiles of second variable	1	0	0	0
Other				
Hypothetical examples	1	0	0	1
Atkinson's index	0	0	0	1

*Other includes a diversity of measures.

The inequality-of-tax-rate principle is measured by essentially the same set of dispersion measures used in conjunction with children's horizontal equity.

Over the universe of studies, there are a diversity of taxpayer's equity measures presented in the single-state studies, yet only three tax-rate dispersion measures can be found in the fifty-state studies. With the exception noted above, the measurement of taxpayers' equity in the fifty states is rather incomplete.

WHICH FISCAL CAPACITY MEASURES ARE UTILIZED IN THE STUDIES?

An important component of school-finance equity is the way in which a school district's or pupil's ability to pay, or fiscal capacity, is assessed. Historically—due to the reliance by school districts on the property tax—property wealth, usually expressed in per-pupil terms, was the dominant fiscal-capacity measure. More recent research and policies in school finance have altered the traditional dominance of per-pupil property values, with income now being treated more seriously as a measure of fiscal capacity. Furthermore, this trend is apparent in the public finance arena as well.

Table 5.7 displays the use of fiscal-capacity measures in the four categories of studies, and the dominance of wealth is documented. Although income (or income combined with wealth) appears about one-third as often as wealth in the single-state and multistate studies, income is never utilized in the fifty-state studies.

For the fiscal-capacity measures based on property wealth, there is the question of whether the values are equalized across districts, and if they are equalized, whether they represent an estimate of full market value. If the wealth data are not equalized, then any measurement based upon them must be viewed with suspicion, since the wealth values may not be comparable. When the wealth data are equalized, then comparisons can potentially be made across states and over time. But since the states, and perhaps even the

Table 5.7. Frequency of Alternative Fiscal-Capacity Measures in Studies

	Single State	Multi-state	Fifty State	Methodological Only
Property wealth				
Assessed only	0	1	2	0
Equalized*	24	5	3	3
Not specified	0	1	2	1
Income	8	3	0	1
Combination wealth and income	1	0	0	0

*For one study, residential wealth, not total wealth, is used.

years, are likely to be equalized to different fractions of full market value, it is important to utilize equity measures that are unaffected by the equalization ratio. Note that when measuring equal opportunity with respect to wealth, the elasticity and the correlation fulfill this criterion while the slope does not.

The problem of comparable wealth data across states is not just a conceptual issue. For example, in one of the more recent and complete multiyear fifty-states studies (no. 46), wealth data are equalized for thirty-six states, assessed but not equalized for thirteen, and unavailable for one.

Although it will not be pursued in depth here, there are also serious questions surrounding the measurement of income. These include both the definition of income (money, census, state income tax, etc.) and the issue of the unit for the measure of income (population, pupils, households, etc). Thus, as income becomes more commonly used as a fiscal-capacity measure in school-finance studies, the question of comparability across states must be addressed.

WHICH UNIT OF ANALYSIS IS EMPLOYED BY THE STUDIES?

The final methodological issue concerns the unit of analysis, where the key distinction is between the pupil and the district units of analysis. Although the district unit of analysis is used in the majority of single-state studies, the pupil unit of analysis is more dominant in the multistate and fifty-state studies. In most cases the unit of analysis could be determined implicitly or explicitly from the studies, but there were several instances in which the choice of a unit of analysis was not clear. In a few studies the unit of analysis varied from one equity measure to another, without any apparent theoretical justification.

Finally, an issue that is related to the unit of analysis is the question of district organization. More specifically, in states where there is some combination of districts that provide education from kindergarten through high school, elementary grades only, or high school grades only, how are the data organized for the presentation and calculation of the equity measures? In a number of single-state and multistate studies, equity analyses are carried out and presented separately for each district type (for example, studies that include Illinois often do this). But in many of the fifty-state studies, a single equity measure is presented for each state, so that some assumptions must be made. For example, in one multiyear fifty-state study (no. 46), only data for the K–12 districts are presented.

CONCLUSIONS

Our major findings for each component of the conceptual framework, the fiscal-capacity measure, and the unit of analysis are summarized in table 5.8 for the single-state, multistate, and fifty-state studies. This table shows that

Table 5.8. Summary of Methodological Findings for Single-State, Multistate and Fifty-State Studies

Issue	Single State	Multistate	Fifty State
1. Group: children, taxpayers, or both	All studies use children; 21 of 33 use taxpayers.	All studies use children; 4 of 9 use taxpayers.	All studies use children; 2 of 9 use taxpayers.
2. Children's objects	Extreme diversity; examples of expenditures, revenues, inputs. Cost adjustments rarely used.	Less diversity than single-state studies; examples of expenditures, revenues, inputs. Cost adjustments rarely used.	Less diversity than single-state studies; examples of expenditures, revenues, inputs. Cost adjustments rarely used. Good comparability across states.
3. Taxpayers' objects	Expenditures or revenues and tax rates, and tax rates each used in about one-third of studies.	Expenditures or revenues and tax rates used in 2 of 9; tax rates used in 3 of 9.	Tax rates used in 2 of 9 studies.
4. Children's equity principles	Horizontal equity and equal opportunity with respect to property wealth in over two-thirds of studies; equal opportunity with respect to income in one-third of studies; only three studies with vertical equity.	Horizontal equity in 8 of 9 studies, equal opportunity with respect to property wealth in 6 of 9 studies; equal opportunity with respect to income in 3 of 9 studies; vertical equity in 1 study.	Horizontal equity in all 9 studies, equal opportunity with respect to property wealth in 5 of 9 studies; equal opportunity with respect to income in no studies; vertical equity in no studies.

5. Taxpayers' equity principles	Equal yield for equal effort in 15 of 33 studies; inequality in tax rates in 11 of 33 studies.	Equal yield for equal effort in 2 of 9 studies; inequality in tax rates in 2 of 9 studies.	Equal yield for equal effort in no studies; inequality in tax rates in 2 of 9 studies.
6. Children's equity measures	Multiple measures often used for each principle; no single measure used in more than 10 of 33 studies.	Multiple measures often used for each principle; no single measure used in all studies, but coefficient of variation (horizontal equity) used in 7 of 9 studies.	Multiple measures often used for each principle; no single measure used in all studies, but coefficient of variation (horizontal equity) used in 7 of 9 studies. McLoone index used in only 1 study.
7. Taxpayer's equity measures	Various measures of equal yield for equal effort, but no measure dominant; diverse dispersion measures used for inequality of tax rates	Different measures of equal yield for equal effort in the studies; coefficient of variation used to measure inequality of tax rates in 2 studies.	Different measures of inequality of tax rates in different studies.
8. Fiscal capacity measures	Equalized property wealth in 24 of 33 studies; income in 8 of 33; combined income and wealth in 1.	Property wealth in 7 of 9 studies; income in 3 of 9 studies.	Property wealth in 7 of 9 studies; income in no studies.
9. Unit of analysis	Pupil unit of analysis used in 16 of 33 studies.	Pupil unit of analysis used in 6 of 9 studies.	Pupil unit of analysis used in 4 of 9 studies.

there are differences among the study types. For example, taxpayer equity is most frequently examined in the single-state studies and is rarely analyzed in the fifty-state studies. The greater diversity of children's equity measures in the single-state studies compared to the other two types is another difference. However, it is not the comparisons among the study types but the shortcomings of the studies' taken in their entirety that are the most serious.

First, taxpayer equity is studied much less than children's equity. This may be because taxpayer-equity conceptions are less well developed. If this is the case, then additional research is needed. Second, the dominant object for children's equity is dollars. This is problematic, because in most states there are price differences across locations, so that a dollar does not purchase comparable inputs across the state. Solutions to this problem, such as the use of education price indexes or resource objects, now exist and should be more widely used. Third, the assessment of equal opportunity is often limited to equal opportunity with respect to property wealth. Other important concerns such as equal opportunity with respect to income, race, and region are often ignored. Finally, vertical equity is analyzed in only four of the fifty-five studies in the sample. Since, in most states, recognition of certain legitimate differences across pupils is desirable, this shortcoming is critical.

In the assessment of children's equity in Michigan and New York, presented in the remainder of the book, we show how the problems caused by the absence of price-adjusted and resource objects, by narrow conceptions of equal opportunity, and by the failure to analyze vertical equity can be overcome.

BIBLIOGRAPHY

Single-State Studies

1. Aronson, J. Richard, and John L. Hilley. "Taxpayer Equity in the Financing of Public Schools." In *Selected Papers in School Finance, 1981*, edited by Esther Tron. Washington, D.C.: U.S. Department of Education, National Institute of Education, March 1981.
2. Atkinson, Glen, and Thomas Sears. "School Finance and Tax Reform in Nevada." In *Selected Papers in School Finance, 1981*, edited by Esther Tron. Washington, D.C.: U.S. Department of Education, National Institute of Education, March 1981.
3. Augenblick, John. "An Analysis of the School Finance System in Delaware: Changes in Fiscal Equity between 1975-76 and 1978-79." Prepared for the School Finance Study Committee of the Delaware State Board of Education, Education Finance Center, Education Commission of the States, February 1980.
4. Augenblick, John, and Kathleen Adams. "An Analysis of Changes in the Funding of Elementary/Secondary Education in Texas: 1974/75 to 1977/78." Draft report, prepared for the Texas Legislative Commission on Public School Finance, Education Finance Center, Education Commission of the States, February 1979.

5. Black, David, Kenneth Lewis, and Charles Link. "Wealth Neutrality and the Demand for Education." *National Tax Journal* 32, no. 2 (June 1979): 157-64.
6. Brazer, Harvey, and Ann Anderson. "Michigan's School District Equalization Act of 1973: Its Background, Structure, and Effects." In *Selected Papers in School Finance, 1976*, edited by Esther Tron. Washington, D.C.: HEW, 1976.
7. Brown, Calvin. "The Adequate Program for Education in Georgia." *Journal of Education Finance* 4, no. 3 (spring 1978): 402-11.
8. Colorado Legislative Council, Committee on School Finance. *Recommendations for 1981, Committee on School Finance*. Denver, Col.: Colorado Legislative Council, December 1980.
9. Daicoff, Darwin. "An Analysis of the Kansas School District Equalization Act of 1973." In *Selected Papers in School Finance, 1976*, edited by Esther Tron. Washington, D.C.: HEW, 1976.
10. Education Finance Center, Education Commission of the States. "An Analysis of the Equity of the New York State Education Finance System: 1974-75 and 1977-78." Report to New York State Task Force on Equity and Excellence in Education, June 19, 1979.
11. Feldstein, Martin. "Wealth Neutrality and Local Choice in Public Education." *American Economic Review* 65, no. 1 (March 1975): 75-89.
12. Friedman, Lee S., and Michael Wiseman. "Toward Understanding the Equity Consequences of School Finance Reform." In *Education Finance and Organization: Research Perspectives for the Future*, compiled by Charles Benson, et al. Washington, D.C.: U.S. Department of Education, National Institute of Education, January 1980.
13. Gatti, James, Leonard Tashman, and Jonathan Sweet. "The Wealth Neutrality of District Power Equalizing Grants in Public School Financing: Additional Evidence." *Journal of Education Finance* 4, no. 2 (fall 1978): 213-24.
14. Ginsburg, Alan, Jay Moskowitz, and Alvin Rosenthal. "A School Based Analysis of Inter- and Intradistrict Resource Allocation." *Journal of Education Finance* 6, no. 4 (spring 1981): 440-55.
15. Goertz, Margaret E. *Where Did the 400 Million Dollars Go? The Impact of the New Jersey Public School Education Act of 1975.* Princeton, N.J.: Educational Policy Research Institute, Education Testing Service, March 1978.
16. Goertz, Margaret, Daniel Sullivan, Jay Moskowitz, and Joel Berke. *Evaluating Vermont's System of Financing Education and Recommendations for Equalizing State and Local Education Finance Programs, final report*. Princeton, N.J.: Educational Policy Research Institute, Education Testing Service, March 1977.
17. Goertz, Margaret, Dana Paige, Richard Coley, and Jay Moskowitz. "Evaluating Connecticut's System of School Finance, draft report no. 1." Princeton, N.J.: Educational Policy Research Institute, Education Testing Service, n.d.
18. Gutherie, James, George Kleindorfer, Henry Levin, and Robert Stout. *Schools and Inequality*. Cambridge, Mass.: MIT Press, 1971.
19. Hansen, W. Lee, and F. Howard Nelson. "Impact of the 1973 Wisconsin School Finance Reform." In *Selected Papers in School Finance, 1978*, edited by Esther Tron. Washington, D.C.: HEW, 1978.
20. Harris, Russell. "Act 59 and the Prospects For Reforming School Finance in Pennsylvania." *Journal of Education Finance* 4, no. 3 (spring 1978): 487-501.

21. Harrison, William, Jr., and Arlene Richman. "The Distributional Effects of Various Guarantees under S.B. 59 on State Aid to Ohio Public School Districts, FY80." Staff Report to the Education Review Committee, Ohio General Assembly, January 10, 1980.
22. Knickman, James, and Andrew Reshovsky. "The Implementation of School Finance Reform." *Policy Sciences* 12, no. 3 (October 1980): 301-14.
23. Ladd, Helen. "State-Wide Taxation of Commercial and Industrial Property for Education." *National Tax Journal* 29, no. 2 (June 1976): 143-53.
24. McMaster, Donald, and Judy Sinkin. *Money and Education: A Guide to Illinois School Finance.* Washington, D.C.: HEW, National Institute of Education, September 1979.
25. McMaster, Donald, Judy Sinkin, and Dana Paige. *Money and Education: A Guide to Rhode Island School Finance.* Washington, D.C.: HEW, National Institute of Education, September 1979.
26. McMaster, Donald, Judy Sinkin, Dana Paige, and Mark Kutner. *Money and Education: A Guide to Pennsylvania School Finance.* Washington, D.C.: National Institute of Education, September 1979.
27. Mockler, John, and Gerald Hayward. "School Finance in California: Pre *Serrano* to the Present." *Journal of Education Finance* 4, no. 3 (spring 1978): 386-401.
28. Nelson, F. Howard. "The Distribution Equity of an Income Factor in the State Aid Formula." *Journal of Education Finance* 6, no. 2 (fall 1980): 201-25.
29. Odden, Alan. "Missouri's New School Finance Structure." *Journal of Education Finance* 4 no. 3 (spring 1978): 465-75.
30. Salmon, Richard, and Ralph Shotwell. "Virginia School Finance Reform: Status Quo Maintained." *Journal of Education Finance* 4, no. 3 (spring 1978): 524-35.
31. Sherman, Joel. "An Evaluation of the Current Structure of School Finance in Ohio." Lawyers' Committee for Civil Rights Under Law, Washington, D.C., March 1978.
32. Ward, Cynthia. "State Support for Rhode Island Public School Operations: An Explanation and Critique." *Journal of Education Finance* 4, no. 3 (spring 1978): 502-14.

Multistate Studies

33. Beck, John. "Effects of Power Equalizing School Aid Formulas With an Income Factor." *Journal of Education Finance* 5, no. 1 (summer 1979): 55-74.
34. Berne, Robert, Allan Odden, and Leanna Stiefel. *Equity in School Finance.* Denver, Col.: Education Commission of the States, October 1979.
35. Brischetto, Robert, and David Vaughan. *Minorities, the Poor, and School Finance Reform: An Impact Study of Six States.* San Antonio, Tex.: Intercultural Development Research Association, 1977.
36. Carroll, Stephen J., Millicent Cox, and William Lisowski. *The Search for Equity in School Finance: Results from Five States.* Santa Monica, Cal.: Rand, March 1979.
37. Garms, Walter. "Measuring the Equity of School Finance Systems." *Journal of Education Finance* 4, no. 4 (spring 1979): 415-35.
38. Ginsburg, Alan, Jay Moskowitz, and Alvin Rosenthal. "Sources of Change in

School Finance Revenue Equality, 1970 to 1977." Washington, D.C.: AUI Policy Research, July 25, 1980.
39. Grubb, W. Norton, and Stephen Michelson. *States and Schools*. Lexington, Mass.: Lexington Books, 1974.
40. Hickrod, G. Alan, Ramesh Chaudhari, Ben C. Hubbard, and Virginia Lundeen. *Equity Measurement in School Finance, Indiana, Iowa, and Illinois*. Normal, Ill.: Center for the Study of Educational Finance, May 1980.
41. Sherman, Joel, and Pamela Tomlinson. "The Impact of School Finance on Minorities: A Study of Seven Southern States." *Journal of Law and Education* 9, no. 3 (July 1980): 353-67.

Fifty-State Studies

42. Brown, Lawrence, III, Alan Ginsburg, J. Neil Killalea, Richard Rosthal, and Esther Tron. *School Finance Reform in the Seventies: Achievements and Failures*. Washington, D.C.: HEW, Office of the Assistant Secretary for Planning and Evaluation, September 30, 1977.
43. McLoone, Eugene, and Warren Dahlstrom. "Resource Disparity in Elementary/Secondary Education." In Nancy Dearman and Valena White Plisko, *The Condition of Education*. Washington, D.C.: NCES, 1980.
44. Harrison, Russell. *Equality in Public School Finance*. Lexington, Mass.: Lexington Books, 1976.
45. National Center for Education Statistics. *Profiles in School Support, 1969-1970*. Washington, D.C.: National Center for Education Statistics, 1972.
46. National Center for Education Statistics. *School Finance Equity: A Profile of the States, 1976-77*. Draft review copy. Washington, D.C.: National Center for Education Statistics, December 1979.
47. Odden, Allan, and John Augenblick. *School Finance Reform in the States: 1981*. Denver, Col.: Education Commission of the States, January 1981.
48. President's Commission on School Finance. *Review of Existing State Programs*, volume II, Documentation of Disparities in the Financing of Public Elementary and Secondary School Systems—By State. Washington, D.C.: President's Commission on School Finance, 1972.
49. Pugh, George E., J. Neil Killalea, and Bruce Loatman. "Educational Opportunity: The Concept, Its Measurement, and Resource Disparities in 1970." A report to National Center for Education Statistics. McLean, Va.: General Research Corp., September 1976.
50. Stiefel, Leanna, and Robert Berne. "The Equity Effects of State School Finance Reforms: A Methodological Critique and New Evidence." *Policy Sciences* 13, no. 1 (February 1981): 75-98.

Methodological Studies

51. Adams, E. Kathleen. *Fiscal Response and School Finance Simulations: A Policy Perspective*. Denver, Col.: Education Commission of the States, December 1980.
52. Berne, Robert, and Leanna Stiefel. "Taxpayer Equity in School Finance Reform." *Journal of Education Finance* 5, no. 1 (summer 1979): 36-54.

53. Berne, Robert, and Leanna Stiefel. "Measuring the Equity of School Finance Policies: A Conceptual and Empirical Analysis." *Policy Analysis* 7, no. 1 (winter 1981): 47–69.
54. Berne, Robert, and Leanna Stiefel. "Alternative Measures of Wealth Neutrality." *Educational Evaluation and Policy Analysis* 4, no. 1 (spring 1982): 5–20.
55. Johns, Thomas, and Dexter Magers. "Measuring the Equity of State School Finance Programs." *Journal of Education Finance* 3, no. 4 (spring 1978): 373–85.

6

CHILDREN'S OBJECTS IN MICHIGAN AND NEW YORK

In this and subsequent chapters of the book, time-series data from the states of Michigan and New York are used to demonsrate how empirical equity analyses that highlight alternative value judgments can be performed. Our choice of New York and Michigan as the states with which to perform the analyses is based on a number of factors. Michigan is a state with excellent time-series data, allowing us to demonstrate a wide variety of different equity concepts and their behavior over time. The condition of Michigan's data is due, in large part, to the efforts of James Phelps, currently Associate Superintendent of Education, and to the Michigan legislature's continuing interest in having thorough projections of the effects of school-finance changes.[1]

The reasons for choosing New York are somewhat different. Comparable machine-readable data were unavailable, so that state comptroller's reports were keypunched. These data are consistent over time, but there are appreciably fewer variables available than for Michigan. The effort for New York seemed warranted, however, because the state has been shown in numerous recent studies to be one of the most inequitable according to a variety of standards and yet to spend at or near the top among the fifty states in average per-pupil amounts. Finally, New York State recently concluded a court case that has ruled in favor of the state (against the plaintiffs) by the state's highest court, The Court of Appeals, thus reversing two lower-court decisions. The governor and the Board of regents appointed a task force to study ways to meet the court's requirements, had the ruling been upheld by the Court of Appeals. The task force research staff, directed by Allan Odden at the Educa-

---

1. Dr. Phelps has not only kept the school finance data base up-to-date, but he has actively pursued and written about numerous research questions. Because he has remained in Michigan throughout his career, first as special assistant to Governor Milliken for school finance in the early 1970s and currently in the associate superintendent post, there is a consistent quality and richness to the Michigan time-series data that is rare across the fifty states.

tion Commission of the States, gathered and produced much good data for recent years, and these data are available to us to combine with the time series from the state comptroller's office. Thus, New York was chosen despite data difficulties because of its inherent interest and because the recent work of the task force compensates somewhat for data deficiencies.

The empirical analyses of children's equity in Michigan and New York are presented in this chapter and the three that follow. In this chapter we answer the question, Equity of what? by describing the objects that we utilize in our research. Then, each of the equity principles is measured in a separate chapter: horizontal equity in chapter 7, equal opportunity in chapter 8, and vertical equity in chapter 9.

In the education area, there are three general groups of objects that can be distributed among children: inputs, outputs, and outcomes.

Inputs are the actual physical resources that are used to educate students. They include such things as teachers, administrators, buildings, textbooks, and equipment. Inputs can be measured in physical units, in dollar values, or in dollar values adjusted for input prices to reflect purchasing power. The analyses in this book use a wide variety of inputs to assess educational equity in Michigan. Two inputs are available for New York. Shortly, each of the Michigan and the New York inputs will be described.

Outputs are a second group of children's objects. They are directly connected (and, most times, at least partially attributable to) the educational process. Outputs include cognitive skills measures (e.g., scores on standard achievement exams) and behavioral measures (e.g., graduation or attendance rates). The data for Michigan and New York do not include output measures.

The third group of children's objects is outcomes. Outcomes are indirectly related to a child's elementary and secondary education. Education is but one influence, sometimes major and sometimes not, on outcomes such as earning potential or actual income and the quality of adult life. As with outputs, the Michigan and New York data bases do not contain measures of outcomes.

Thus, only inputs are measured here. Their distribution is important because of the integral part they play in children's educational experiences and because of subjective ideas about their effects on outputs and outcomes. Although inputs are only one of three broad groups of objects, within the input group there are a wide variety of different specific measures. The measures available in the Michigan and New York data bases are described next.

For Michigan, fourteen input measures are analyzed. Two of the fourteen are physical resources, and six others are dollar measures. The six dollar measures are subsequently price-adjusted to more accurately reflect differential purchasing power across individual school districts. For New York, one dollar measure is available. In addition, a price index for New York school districts has been estimated by the Education Commission of the States to take price differences across locations into account, and this index is used to convert the dollar measure to a price-adjusted dollar measure. Thus, altogether, two measures will be analyzed for New York, one dollar and one price-adjusted dollar.

Next, the two physical-resource and the six dollar measures for Michigan are described. Then the conceptual basis for the Michigan price index, used to adjust the dollar measures to purchasing power, is explained. The chapter concludes with a description of the New York dollar variable.

MICHIGAN VARIABLES

Physical-Resource Measures in Michigan

As most past and present students will attest, teachers are a most important educational resource. The research on education production functions has not yet successfully identified which aspects of teachers are most efficient in producing student learning, or if teachers matter at all. In particular, the controversy about the effect of the number of teachers per child (or class size) on student outcomes continues. While a number of studies have found no differences in student learning when class size is varied within the normally small ranges observed in most schools, many researchers, teachers, parents, and students continue to use class size as one proxy for school quality.[2] Consistent with the observed practice, we use two definitions of teachers-per-student as resource measures. Without delving into the research results produced by the education production function studies, we feel confident that if one physical-resource measure is chosen to represent educational quality, teachers would be most people's choice rather than alternatives such as administrators, supplies, equipment, or building characteristics.

The two teacher measures employed are kindergarten through twelfth grade (K–12) teachers per 1,000 pupils and all classroom teachers per 1,000 pupils. K–12 teachers per 1,000 pupils include regular K–12 classroom teachers plus compensatory-education teachers. The compensatory-education teachers usually supplement regular classroom instruction and are generally funded from federal funds (Title I of the Elementary and Secondary Education Act) and from state compensatory-education funds.

All classroom teachers per 1,000 pupils are composed of all the K–12 teachers (defined above) as well as special education teachers (primarily for handicapped students), vocational education teachers, and other teachers such as those involved in adult education or teaching homebound students.

The teacher-pupil ratios are averages for a district. Each district will usually contain more than one school and many classrooms. The mean value of

---

2. For a study using "meta-analysis" that did find that small class size had a significant effect on student learning, see Gene V. Glass and Mary Lee Smith, "Meta-Analysis of Research on the Relationship of Class-Size and Achievement," Far West Labatory for Educational Research and Development, University of Colorado, September 1978.

the pupil-weighted teacher-pupil measures from the data base used in this book's analyses are displayed in table 6.1. The use of a pupil-weighted measure means that the average for each district is assigned to each pupil in the district, and then the average for all pupils in the state is calculated.[3] The averages range from thirty-nine to forty-six, depending on the year and the measure used. A teacher-pupil ratio of forty teachers per 1,000 pupils translates to an average class size of twenty-five.

Dollar Measures in Michigan

The characteristics and the differences among the six dollar measures are described below. Table 6.2 displays the state pupil-weighted mean value for each measure. This table will be referred to as each measure is discussed.

Instructional Expenditures. This is one of three expenditure numbers used in the analyses and is identical to the Michigan Department of Education category with the same name. It covers the expenditures for activities directly related to teaching of students, administering teaching, or supporting teaching. The expenditures include instruction (excluding employee benefits for instruction); pupil support services (excluding attendance and health services); instructional-staff support services; and school-administrative support services. Instructional expenditures cover a wider variety of costs than teacher salaries, and thus the category is broader than the dollar value of either of the teacher measures described previously.

Current Operating Expenditures. This is a broad category that covers all major non-capital-related spending (i.e., debt service and capital outlays are excluded). It includes expenditures for instruction; all administration; all pupil, staff, and administrative support; employee benefits; transportation; and operation and maintenance of plant. Items such as student bookstores,

Table 6.1. Michigan Teachers per 1,000 Pupils in K-12 Districts (Pupil-Weighted Statewide Analyses)

Year	K-12 Teachers Per 1000 Pupils	All Classroom Teachers Per 1000 Pupils
1972-73	38.96	43.92
1973-74	39.47	45.26
1974-75	41.32	45.10
1975-76	39.46	45.96
1976-77	38.98	45.65
1977-78	38.52	45.80

Source: Data base constructed by authors from Michigan Department of Education sources for over-time equity analyses. Hereafter labeled Michigan Equity Data Base.

3. See chapter 3 for a full description of pupil weighting and how it differs from district weighting.

Table 6.2. Michigan Per-Pupil Expenditure and Revenue Variables in K-12 Districts (Pupil-Weighted Statewide Averages)

Year	Instructional Expenditures per Pupil	Current Operating Expenditures per Pupil	Current Operating Expenditures Less Transportation per Pupil	Local Plus State Membership Revenue per Pupil	Local Plus Total State Revenue per Pupil	Local Plus Total State Plus Total Federal Revenue per Pupil
1969-70	$ 552	$ 728		$ 718	$ 759	$ 789
1970-71	625	822		793	832	869
1971-72	660	875		849	890	936
1972-73	718	958	$ 922	907	962	1,013
1973-74	785	1,060	1,018	1,024	1,097	1,151
1974-75	870	1,200	1,150	1,125	1,216	1,284
1975-76	933	1,313	1,257	1,227	1,322	1,398
1976-77	969	1,410	1,348	1,343	1,449	1,543
1977-78	1,069	1,587	1,515	1,502	1,631	1,753
Percent change 1969-70 to 1977-78	93.7	118.0	64.3 (1972-73 to 1977-78)	109.2	114.9	122.2

Source: Michigan Equity Data Base.

lunches, and community services are excluded. The figures in table 6.2 show that per-pupil current operating expenditures grew faster from 1969-70 to 1977-78 (118 percent) than did per-pupil instructional expenditures (94 percent). This means that some combination of items such as pupil health and attendance services, general administration, employee benefits, transportation, and plant maintenance and operation have grown more over the period than have instructional expenditures, which are part of current operating expenditures.

Current Operating Expenditures Less Transportation. Of all the components of current operating expenditures, the variation in transportation expenditures relates least directly to a child's educational experience. Transportation costs will depend to a large extent on the size of the school district and the density of the pupils within the district. In order to remove the effect of this clearly non-education-based expenditure, the third expenditure variable subtracts out transportation costs. As can be calculated from table 6.2, for the years when such a subtraction was possible, transportation accounts for between 4 percent and 5 percent of statewide average current operating expenditures per pupil.

Local Plus State Membership Revenue. Three revenue variables are analyzed, and all exclude revenues for capital and debt service. A primary difference between expenditure and revenue variables is that expenditures can be broken down by use or function (e.g., instruction, administration) and revenues can be broken down by source (i.e., local, state, federal). The differences among the revenue variables are based on the sources of revenue included in each.

Local plus total state membership is the sum of local revenues (primarily property taxes), revenue from intermediate sources (e.g., county), and state general aid (general formula aid, grandfather aid, municipal overburden aid, and the revenue guarantee). This variable does not include state categorical revenues.

Local Plus Total State Revenue. This revenue variable includes local revenue, intermediate revenue, and total state revenue. The difference between this variable and the previous one is that state categorical funds are included here. State categoricals are primarily comprised of revenues for compensatory education, special education, and transportation.

Local Plus Total State Plus Total Federal Revenue. The sixth dollar variable is the sum of local revenue, intermediate revenue, all state revenue, and all federal revenue. Federal revenue is primarily derived from Title I of the Elementary and Secondary Education Act of 1965 (compensatory education). Other federal revenue, of lesser dollar significance, is also for categorical purposes such as school lunches, vocational education, emergency school assistance (desegregation), headstart, and impact aid. The last of these, impact aid, is granted to districts heavily affected by the presence of federal employees or installations within their boundaries. Per-pupil local plus total state plus total federal revenues grew 122 percent between 1969-70 and 1977-78; this is faster than either of the two preceeding revenue variables. Thus federal revenues have grown faster than either general state or categorical state revenues.

Price Index Used to Adjust the Michigan Dollar Measures

The prices that school districts must pay to purchase equivalent education resources such as teachers or supplies are not the same for all districts. Therefore, at one point in time, two districts that have available identical dollar amounts of revenues or expenditures per pupil will not necessarily be able to provide identical quantities and qualities of school resources for pupils. One way to take intrastate price differences into account in an equity analysis is to adjust all dollar variables by a price-of-education index. Such an index should reflect differences in prices that are beyond a school district's control and those that do not reflect differences in the quality of resources. The desire to account only for uncontrollable price differences means that a district's revenues and expenditures will not be deflated for those elements of resource price that are caused by the decisions made by the school districts where they have free choice, such as hiring more male teachers who must be paid more than female teachers. Uncontrollable price differences such as the need to pay teachers more to work in schools with high proportions of learning disabled and handicapped children would be included in the price index. In addition, price differences that are related to quality differences, such as paying more for experienced or highly educated personnel (assuming these characteristics represent quality), would not be included in the price index.

Conceptually, the idea of a price index based only on uncontrollable price differences, is appealing. The problem is finding a way to construct such an index. Recently, researchers have developed two approaches to the problem. One approach uses econometrics to estimate the market-supply schedule for resources across districts. The other approach econometrically estimates individually based relationships of the employment decision. We will first discuss the district-supply-schedule approach.

The supply schedule is an equation that relates the prices of inputs to all the various factors, both controllable and uncontrollable, associated with the price. The estimated coefficients on the uncontrollable factors are then used to construct a price index that reflects the uncontrollable elements in each district's prices. A simplified example may help to explain the methodology.

Suppose we concentrate on only two districts in a hypothetical state, districts X and Y. For the moment, imagine that we are interested in a price index for teachers' services alone. For simplicity, assume that teachers' salaries are determined by two variables, the years of teaching experience and the percent of learning-disabled pupils in the district. For each additional year of teaching experience, teachers receive 300 extra dollars, and for each increase of one percentage point in the number of learning disabled, they receive 80 extra dollars. The supply schedule, with an arbitrarily set base salary of $12,000 would look as follows:

Salary = $12,000 + $300 (years of experience) + $80 (percent of learning disabled).

If the average years of experience statewide is four and the average percentage of learning disabled students is ten, then the statewide average teacher's salary will be $14,000:

Average Salary = $12,000 + $300 (4) + $80 (10) = $14,000.

In the simplified salary schedule, years of experience is a controllable variable and percent of learning disabled is uncontrollable.

In order to calculate the price index for districts X and Y, we must know the value of the uncontrollable variable, percentage of learning disabled, in each district. Suppose this variable is equal to twenty for district X and five for district Y. The price index will then involve two calculations. First, each district's salary is predicted from the supply equation, where the controllable variable (years of experience) is equal to the state average of four and the uncontrollable variable (percent of learning disabled) is equal to the actual district value. Then the predicted salary is divided by the state average salary of $14,000 to yield the index.

The calculations for districts X and Y would be as follows:

District X
Predicted salary = $12,000 + $300 (4) + $80 (20) = $14,800
Price index = $\frac{\$14,800}{\$14,000}$ = 1.06

District Y
Predicted salary = $12,000 + $300 (4) + $80 (5) = $13,600
Price index = $\frac{\$13,600}{\$14,000}$ = .97

These price indexes of 1.06 and .97 would be divided into the dollar measures in districts X and Y to adjust them for price differences.

An actual price index can combine indexes calculated for teachers, administrators, support staff, transportation, etc., by weighting each individual index by the share of the state (or district) budget devoted to each expenditure group. For Michigan this is not done, due to lack of appropriate data. Instead, the price index uses teachers salaries only, which are by far the largest expenditure category. The construction of the Michigan price index is based on the methodology just described. District data are used to estimate a supply schedule for the districts, and this schedule is used to construct the index.

Two price indexes, labeled Index 1 and Index 2, are used in the next three chapters to adjust dollar objects in Michigan for intrastate price variation.

The methodology and data used to estimate these price indexes are described in detail elsewhere; however, a few comments on their derivation are in order.[4] Each price index is based on a supply curve determined from a simultaneous estimate of supply and demand functions using district-level data. The major differences between the indexes stem from slightly different specifications and different assumptions regarding which variables are uncontrollable.

Index I includes the following as uncontrollable variables in the price index: average years of teaching experience, percent of teachers holding masters degrees or higher, the logarithm of the number of pupils, a basic skills composite score for fourth graders, dummy variables representing central city, rural, and suburban census areas, population per square mile, median yearly earnings of all male civilian employees age sixteen and over (in county), and percent of adults with one or more years of college. Index 2 includes the following as uncontrollable variables in the price index: dummy variables representing regions in the state (Upper Peninsula, Detroit Standard Metropolitan Statistical Area (SMSA), and northern part of lower peninsula), median yearly earnings of male civilian employees age sixteen and over (in county), percent of population that is black or Negro or has a Spanish surname, number of pupils, number of pupils squared, proportion of pupils who are in special education, and number of districts per square mile (in county).

Although many of the variables needed to estimate the price index are only available for one year (usually 1970), some of the variables are available on a yearly basis. Therefore, each index is estimated twice; once for the 1970 to 1974 period and again for 1975 through 1978. In both cases the original index and its update are very highly correlated, .964 and .978 for Index 1 and Index 2, respectively.

The two indexes themselves are also relatively highly correlated, .788 for Index 1 and Index 2 covering the 1970 to 1974 period and .826 for the two indexes for the 1975 to 1978 period. Despite this high correlation, the indexes can, of course, vary for particular districts. The values of the two indexes (covering the 1970 to 1974 period) for selected districts, along with the mean, standard deviation, and highest and lowest values for the entire sample of districts are displayed in table 6.3.

Detroit and one of its suburbs, Birmingham, are consistently above the mean on both indexes. The medium-sized city of Kalamazoo, in southwestern Michigan, is somewhat above the mean on both indexes, and Kingsley Area, a rural district in the northwestern part of the lower peninsula, is below the mean on both indexes. Finally, Marquette, in the Upper Peninsula, and Cheboygan, in the upper part of the lower peninsula, are above the mean on In-

4. See Leanna Stiefel and Robert Berne, "Price Indexes for Teachers in Michigan: A Replication and Extension," in Esther O. Tron, ed., *Selected Papers in School Finance, 1981* (Washington, D.C.: U.S. Department of Education, National Institute of Education, March 1981), pp. 159–211.

Table 6.3. Michigan Price Indexes for Selected Districts

District	Index 1	Index 2
Detroit	1.383	1.103
Birmingham	1.255	1.166
Kalamazoo	1.174	1.066
Cheboygan	1.004	.953
Marquette	1.053	.961
Kingsley area	.850	.966
Mean for all districts	1.000	1.000
Highest value for all districts	1.383	1.259
Lowest value for all districts	.798	.890
Standard deviation for all districts	.095	.068

dex 1 and below the mean on Index 2. Notice also that the range and the standard deviation for Index 1 are larger than for Index 2, primarily because average years of teachers experience and the percent of the teachers with masters degrees is treated as uncontrollable (and thus in the price index) in Index 1 and as controllable in Index 2.

The data analyses presented in chapters 7, 8, and 9 for Michigan use the two price indexes to adjust three dollar objects: instructional expenditures per pupil, local plus total state revenue per pupil, and local plus state plus total federal revenue per pupil. Table 6.4 displays the pupil-weighted statewide average value for each dollar object when adjusted by the two price indexes. Notice that while the first price index (Index 1) results in consistently lower levels for each variable than does the second price index (Index 2), the growth rate in each variable is almost identical across indexes. Finally, remember that all the price indexes used in the book adjust for differences across the state at one point in time, not for year-to-year price variations.

The methodology just described for constructing a price index relies on district data for estimation (i.e., the district is the unit of analysis). A second approach recently developed by researchers uses *individual* personnel data, thus making the individual teacher, administrator, etc., the unit of analysis. Such an approach has been employed for New York State by the Education Commission of the States in its role as staff to the New York State Special Task Force on Equity and Excellence in Education.[5] The conceptual basis of the individual-based index is somewhat different from that for the district-based one. The reader is referred to articles and papers by Wayne Wendling and Jay Chambers for a full explanation of the second approach.[6] The price

---

5. Wayne Wendling, "Cost of Education Indices," discussion paper prepared for the New York State Special Task Force on Equity and Excellence in Education, Education Commission of the States, Denver, Col., October 25, 1979.
6. Ibid., and Jay G. Chambers, "Educational Cost Differentials and the Allocation of State Aid for Elementary/Secondary Education," *Journal of Human Resources* 13 (fall 1978): 459-81.

Table 6.4. Michigan Price-Adjusted Per-Pupil Expenditures and Revenue Variables in K-12 Districts (Statewide Averages)

Year	Instructional Expenditures		Local Plus Total State Revenue		Local Plus Total State Plus Total Federal Revenue	
	Index 1	Index 2	Index 1	Index 2	Index 1	Index 2
1969–70	490	514	677	707	702	735
1970–71	555	581	743	776	775	811
1971–72	587	614	798	831	838	874
1972–73	641	668	866	899	911	947
1973–74	703	732	986	1,025	1,034	1,075
1974–75	774	806	1,089	1,130	1,147	1,192
1975–76	832	864	1,186	1,230	1,253	1,299
1976–77	866	899	1,304	1,350	1,387	1,437
1977–78	955	991	1,466	1,517	1,572	1,629
Percent change						
1969–70 to 1977–78	95%	93%	117%	115%	124%	122%

Source: Michigan Equity Data Base.

index estimated for New York by the Education Commission of the States is used in this report to adjust the New York dollar measure.

NEW YORK DOLLAR MEASURE

The dollar measure used in the New York analysis is general expenditures for current operations. It is almost exactly comparable to Michigan's current operating expenditures. Included are expenditures for all purposes except capital outlay, debt service, and operation of school lunches and student bookstores. School-district expenditures for public libraries sponsored by a district are included, and this differs from the Michigan definition, but such sponsored public libraries are likely to be rare. The New York data are taken from tables published annually by New York's Department of Audit and Control in a publication titled *Financial Data for School Districts*. Table 6.5 displays the pupil-weighted per-pupil value of current operating expenditures for all kindergarten through twelfth grade districts included in our data base. Expenditures have grown 235 percent over the period 1964–65 to 1977–78. Over a time period comparable to the Michigan data, 1969–70 to 1977–78, expenditures grew 100 percent in New York, as contrasted to 118 percent for the similarly defined variable in Michigan. Also included in table 6.5 are price-adjusted current operating expenditures. The levels are lower, but the growth rates are the same because the price index is calculated for one year only and then applied to the expenditures in all years.

Table 6.5. New York Current Operating Expenditures per Pupil in K-12 Districts

Year	Per-Pupil Current Operating Expenditures	Price-Adjusted Per-Pupil Current Operating Expenditures
1964–65	$ 718	$ 691
1965–66	784	754
1966–67	894	860
1967–68	969	932
1968–69	1,097	1,055
1969–70	1,201	1,153
1970–71	1,360	1,303
1971–72	1,450	1,390
1972–73	1,520	1,459
1973–74	1,749	1,672
1974–75	1,956	1,870
1975–76	2,076	1,988
1976–77	2,151	2,063
1977–78	2,404	2,304
Percent change		
1964–65 to 1977–78	235%	233%
1969–70 to 1977–78	100%	100%

Source: Data base constructed by authors from *Financial Data for School Districts*, State of New York, Department of Audit and Control, Division of Municipal Affiars, 1964-65 through 1977-78. Hereafter labeled New York Equity Data Base.

CONCLUSIONS

Clearly Michigan has a wider variety of input measures available for analysis than does New York. In particular, Michigan has physical resources, revenues, and expenditures, as well as a price index, all of which will enable us to perform a comprehensive sensitivity analysis of the dependence of equity trends on the definition of the input measure. New York has only a dollar-expenditure measure and a price index. Without revenues, the effect of local, state, and federal sources cannot be assessed, and without physical resources, the price index will have to be relied upon to remove the effects of geographic price differences.

7

HORIZONTAL EQUITY IN MICHIGAN AND NEW YORK

Once school-finance-equity measures are developed, they can be utilized to answer diverse questions including how one state's equity compares to another's, how equity has been affected by changes in state-finance schemes, or even how "noneducation" policies such as tax limits or assessment practices impact equity. While some of these questions are discussed in the final chapter, this chapter, along with the next two, illustrates in considerable depth how our equity framework can be used to answer what may be the most often asked question concerning a state's equity—Has equity become better or worse over time?

This analysis of equity over time is limited to only one of the groups of concern, namely children. In terms of the other three components of the framework, however, numerous alternatives are examined using data that were described in chapter 6 from Michigan and New York over nine and fourteen years respectively. The three chapters are organized around the three equity principles; horizontal equity is focused on in this chapter, equal opportunity in chapter 8, and vertical equity in chapter 9. Within each of these chapters different objects of the education system and different measures of the equity principles are analyzed, primarily, but not exclusively, from a methodological perspective.

Before specifically setting out the objectives of this examination of horizontal equity over time, it is important to understand the question that is being addressed, as well as the questions that are not. The purpose of this chapter is to show how to comprehensively assess the trends in children's horizontal equity in one state over time. Has equity improved, worsened, or stayed the same over a specified time period? Since this is such an important question, it is being examined separately from other critical questions such as, Why has equity changed over time? or, How does the level of equity that exists compare with what would have occurred if other policy options had been pursued? The question of how to measure changes in equity over time must be answered before these latter issues are addressed, and for this reason, we focus on the measurement of time-series trends in equity.

In this chapter, the assessment of time-series trends in children's horizontal equity is organized around the following methodological questions:

1. Are there differences in the trends in horizontal equity due to alternative measures? Do the measures form empirical groupings that are identical or similar to the conceptual groupings identified in chapter 2?

2. One measure of children's horizontal equity, Atkinson's index, includes a parameter that can be varied to alter the values incorporated in the measure. Do changes in the parameter in Atkinson's index cause differences in the trends in horizontal equity, holding the object constant? Do variations in the parameter in Atkinson's index create a diverse set of results that encompass the trends that emerge from some or all of the other ten horizontal equity measures?

3. Are there differences either in the trends or in the levels of horizontal equity due to alternative input-based dollar objects such as local plus total state revenues versus instructional expenditures, holding the equity measure constant?

4. How does the adjustment of input-based dollar objects by price indexes affect the trends in horizontal equity, holding the measure constant? Does the price index alter the trends in equity, the absolute levels of equity, or both?

5. How do the trends in and the levels of horizontal equity differ with input-based resource objects compared to input-based objects measured in dollars and price-adjusted dollars, holding the measure constant?

All five of these questions are initially addressed in the first section of this chapter using data from Michigan, followed, in the second section, by an assessment of New York, where data availability limits the analysis to questions 1, 2, and 4. The third section provides conclusions for the chapter.

An important prerequisite for the assessment of equity trends is a brief explanation of our method of presentation. What is the output of the equity-measurement framework in one state using a particular group, principle, object, and measure over a specified set of years? The upper part of figure 7.1 shows the output for one choice of the components of the framework, where horizontal equity for children is measured by the coefficient of variation of current operating expenditures per pupil in Michigan for 1969–70 through 1977–78. For any one group, principle, object, and measure, a table such as this is probably the most useful display. However, in this chapter and the next two, where numerous time series of measures are presented in order to compare trends and levels, it would be cumbersome to examine data in tabular form. The lower part of figure 7.1 illustrates in graphical form the same data displayed in the upper part. We believe that this method of presentation is a more useful way to assess and compare many equity measures, and therefore, in most cases graphs are the primary way the data are presented in chapters 7, 8, and 9.

Whenever graphs are used to compare data, the determination of the scales of the axes is important. For the horizontal axis of the graphs used in these chapters, the choice of a scale is straightforward; the horizontal axis is scaled in years, since all data are time series. Each year is represented by the *last* year in the school year. Thus, 1969-70 is designated "70" on the graph. The choice of a vertical axis is more complex, since alternative equity measures cover different ranges of absolute values, and in addition, different objects with identical measures may encompass very different levels. There is no "correct" choice of a vertical axis scale, but the scale should be chosen to accomplish the analytical task at hand. Since one of the primary purposes of this assessment is the comparison of trends, each graph has a vertical axis that reflects the full range of points on the graph. For example, in the graph in figure 7.1, the highest value, .1817, is close to the upper bound of the graph (.1850) and the lowest value, .1562, is close to the lower bound of the graph (.1550). This is true for all the graphs in this chapter and those in chapters 8 and 9.

Figure 7.1 Table and Graph of the Coefficient of Variation of Current Operating Expenditures in Michigan, 1969-70 to 1977-78

	Year				
	1969-70	1970-71	1971-72	1972-73	1973-74
Coefficient of Variation	.1685	.1644	.1630	.1817	.1771
	1974-75	1975-76	1976-77	1977-78	
Coefficient of Variation	.1736	.1795	.1562	.1591	

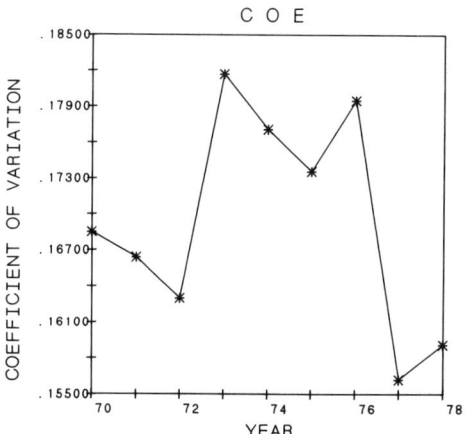

When the vertical axis is scaled in this manner, comparisons across dimensions other than the shape of the plot must be made by carefully examining the actual values of the vertical axes of the graphs under investigation. In particular, in order to determine whether one object is consistently more or less equitable than another object for the same horizontal-equity measure, the vertical axes of the two graphs must be consulted for each point on each graph. Due to the scaling conventions, the levels *and* the incremental units on the two graphs are likely to differ. Also, if the absolute amount of change between two points is being assessed for two or more graphs, the vertical axes need to be examined carefully, since the incremental units on the graphs are probably different. If the vertical-axis scaling procedure is kept in mind, comparisons among graphs are unlikely to be misinterpreted. That is, shapes of graphs can be easily compared, but levels, slopes, and rates of change between points cannot.

One final introductory point is a reminder that all analyses carried out in chapters 7 through 9 utilize the *pupil* unit of analysis. Each state is assumed to be comprised of a distribution of pupils even though data are only available at the district level.

AN ASSESSMENT OF HORIZONTAL EQUITY IN MICHIGAN

In this section, data from Michigan covering the nine-year period from 1969-70 to 1977-78 are utilized to answer the five methodological questions raised at the beginning of the chapter. Each of the next five parts treats one of these questions. Over the nine-year period more than 99 percent of Michigan's pupils attended schools in districts that offer education in kindergarten through the twelfth grade and only these K-12 districts are used in the analyses. In five years, all of the K-12 districts and pupils are included, but in the other years, data on a small number of pupils and K-12 districts are missing.[1]

Are There Differences in the Trends Due to Alternative Measures? Do the Measures Form Empirical Groupings?

In chapter 2, ten measures of horizontal equity, in addition to Atkinson's index, were presented. In this part these ten measures of horizontal equity are analyzed to determine whether the empirical trend that results from each measure is distinctive, or whether empirical groupings emerge. Simply stated, if we are examining trends in horizontal equity, does the measure make a difference? Since Atkinson's index is actually a set of measures, it is examined separately in the next part of this section.

---

1. For example, for current operating expenditures, all districts are included in 1972, 1973, 1974, 1975, and 1976. Data for two districts are missing in 1970 and 1971, for three districts in 1977, and for six districts in 1978. In all cases these are small districts in terms of numbers of pupils.

The analysis of the value judgments incorporated in the ten horizontal-equity measures in chapter 2 suggested that there were four conceptual groups of measures. The three measures that are sensitive to equal percentage increases and thus change simply as a result of inflation—the range, the restricted range, and the variance—form one group. The McLoone index and the standard deviation of logarithms comprise a second group, since they both place relatively more emphasis on the low part of the distribution. Four remaining measures that are insensitive to equal percentage increases and include all the children—namely, the Gini coefficient, the coefficient of variation, Theil's measure, and the relative mean deviation, are a third group, and the federal range ratio is alone in a fourth group. These conceptual groupings are used as a starting point, and three different input-based dollar objects are examined to determine if these groupings can be empirically validated. Although conceptually dollars are less preferred as an object than price-adjusted dollars or resources, they are used here because most readers are familiar with their meaning and because the emphasis here is on differences among *measures* not objects.

Instructional expenditures per pupil are examined first, and the ten horizontal-equity measures for the nine-year period in Michigan are displayed in table 7.1 and graphed in figures 7.2 and 7.3. Since this is the first display of these horizontal-equity measures in Michigan, a table is included that shows the number of districts and pupils in each year, along with the values of the mean and the median per-pupil instructional expenditures. Figure 7.2 includes the graphs of the range, the restricted range, the variance, the federal range ratio, and the McLoone index and figure 7.3 displays the graphs for the coefficient of variation, the Gini coefficient, Theil's measure, the standard deviation of logarithms, and the relative mean deviation.

There are definitely some similarities between the conceptual groupings and the empirical results for per-pupil instructional expenditures, but empirical and conceptual groupings are not identical. First, the range, the restricted range, and the variance do stand apart from the other seven measures. These three measures generally show an increase over the nine-year period, although only the restricted range is monotonic—that is, always increasing. Despite the variations in certain years, at this point these three measures seem to fall into one empirical group.

The differences and similarities among the remaining seven measures are more subtle. First, the coefficient of variation, Theil's measure, and the Gini coefficient produce very similar trends. Since the pattern formed by these three measures will appear repeatedly in Michigan, it will be referred to, with some artistic license, as the "inverted W" pattern. In addition, the standard deviation of logarithms also belongs with these three measures, since it too forms an inverted W. Apparently the qualities that the standard deviation of logarithms shares with these other three measures (such as inclusion of all pupils, insensitivity to equal percentage increases) empirically override the

Table 7.1. Michigan: Horizontal-Equity Measures for Instructional Expenditures per Pupil

	1970	1971	1972	1973	1974	1975	1976	1977	1978
Number of districts	525	525	529	530	530	530	530	526	523
Total pupils	2,150,084	2,165,537	2,206,408	2,187,818	2,153,216	2,132,846	2,124,221	2,074,223	2,008,180
Mean	552	625	660	718	785	870	933	969	1,069
Median	565	633	655	710	786	857	929	955	1,050
Range	710	710	760	1,236	1,089	1,253	1,328	1,224	1,212
Restricted range	302	343	361	443	472	491	499	521	603
Federal range ratio	0.7327	0.7357	0.7324	0.8309	0.8130	0.7626	0.7222	0.7181	0.7505
Relative mean deviation	0.1395	0.1445	0.1451	0.1483	0.1469	0.1504	0.1494	0.1404	0.1461
McLoone index	0.8424	0.8440	0.8609	0.8606	0.8523	0.8628	0.8538	0.8724	0.8688
Variance	9,332	11,766	13,010	19,889	22,733	28,356	34,826	27,281	36,246
Coefficient of variation	0.1749	0.1737	0.1729	0.1965	0.1920	0.1935	0.2001	0.1704	0.1782
Standard deviation of logarithms	0.1730	0.1731	0.1728	0.1855	0.1827	0.1851	0.1879	0.1697	0.1754
Gini coefficient	0.0971	0.0972	0.0973	0.1047	0.1029	0.1040	0.1055	0.0957	0.0993
Theil's measure	0.0151	0.0150	0.0148	0.0183	0.0176	0.0179	0.0189	0.0144	0.0156

Figure 7.2 Michigan: Range, Restricted Range, Variance, Federal Range Ratio, and McLoone Index for Instructional Expenditures per Pupil

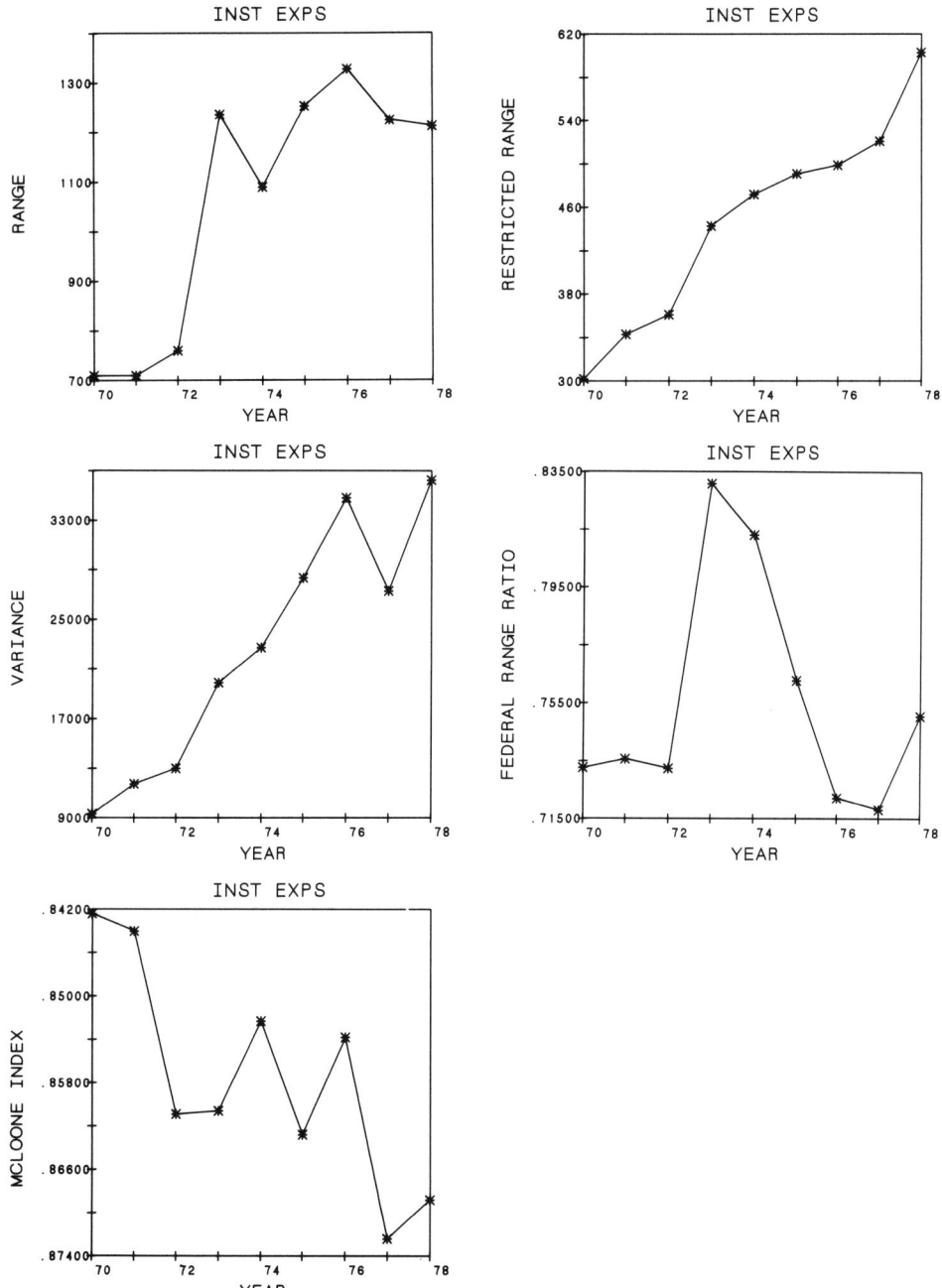

Figure 7.3 Michigan: Coefficient of Variation, Gini Coefficient, Theil's Measure, Standard Deviation of Logarithms, and Relative Mean Deviation for Instructional Expenditures per Pupil

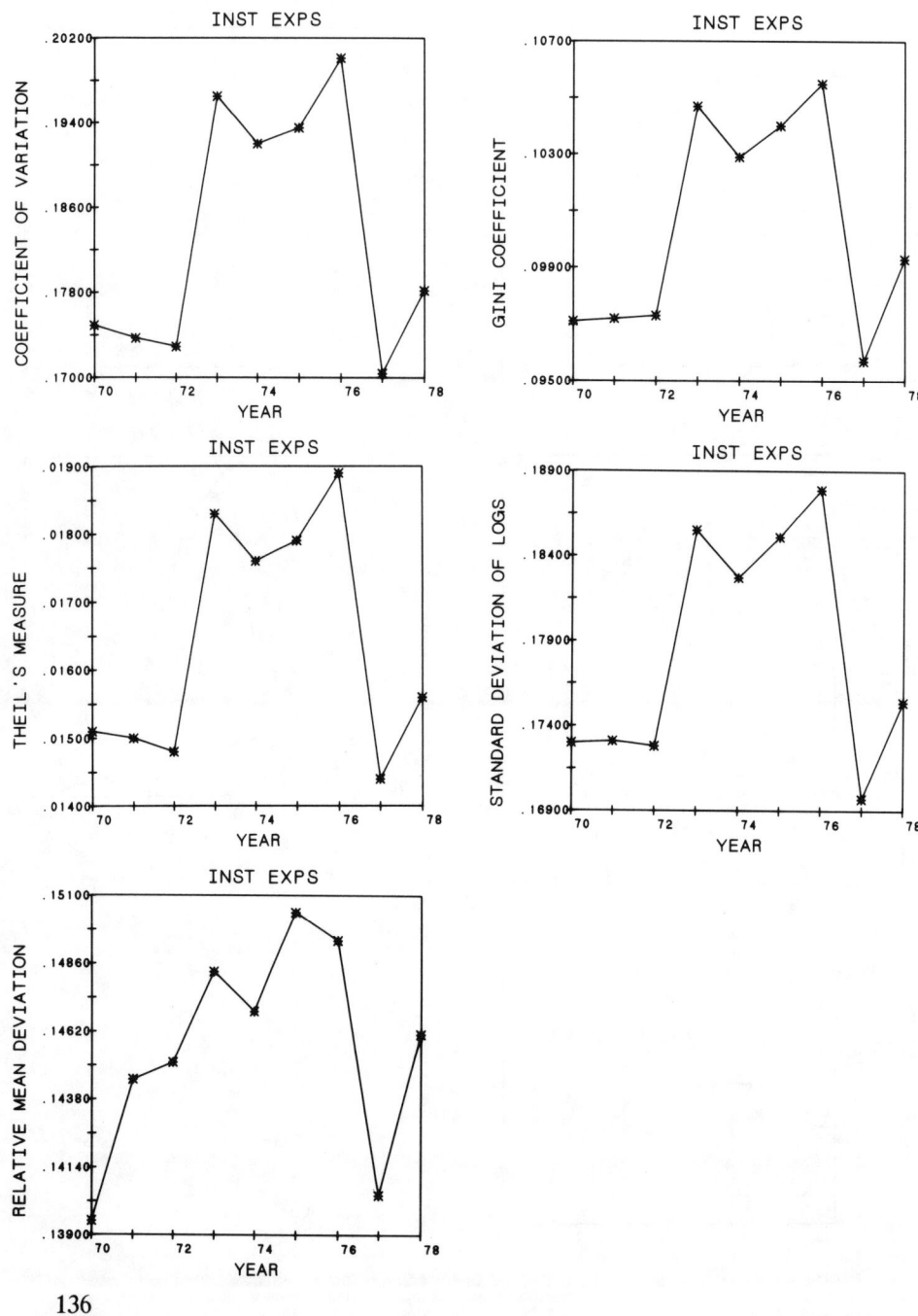

heavier weighting of the lower end of the distribution for instructional expenditures. The relative mean deviation, which was originally grouped with the coefficient of variation, the Gini coefficient, and Theil's measure does not form an exact inverted W, but there are still similarities with these three measures and the standard deviation of logarithms. At this point we conclude that the coefficient of variation, the Gini coefficient, Theil's measure, and the standard deviation of logarithms form a second group that could also potentially include the relative mean deviation.

Once the standard deviation of logarithms is separated from the McLoone index, the McLoone index stands in a group by itself. Although the McLoone index is not totally different from the inverted-W shape, particularly in the later years, the differences are noticeable enough for the McLoone index to be considered alone in a third empirical group. Finally, the federal range ratio is not that different from the inverted W, but enough so that it too will be placed in a fourth group by itself.

Judging only by instructional expenditures per pupil, we conclude that there are four empirical groupings, assuming that the relative mean deviation fits in with the other four inverted-W measures. But these results are based only on one object. Do they hold up for other objects? The answer is basically yes. First, using total revenues per pupil, the four empirical groups identified for instructional expenditures are replicated, and therefore, the graphs for total revenues are not shown here. In addition, a third object—local plus total state revenues (total revenues less federal revenues)—shows only minor differences in groupings. The range, the restricted range, and the variance show several small discrepancies, but the increasing trend over the period is still pronounced. For local plus total state revenues, these three measures can be treated as an empirical group when viewing the trend over the nine years. The treatment of the federal range ratio as a separate group is arguable for this object. The McLoone index resembles in some ways the trends for the group that includes the coefficient of variation. Finally, while the coefficient of variation, Theil's measure, and the standard deviation of logarithms are very similar, there are some differences between these measures and the Gini coefficient and the relative mean deviation, particularly between 1973 and 1974.

Judging by the results from the three input-based dollar objects, two conclusions can be drawn. First, in most instances there are four empirical groups comprised of the following:

1. range, restricted range, and variance;
2. coefficient of variation, Gini coefficient, Theil's measure, standard deviation of logarithms, and relative mean deviation;
3. federal range ratio;
4. McLoone index.

The most questionable element of these groups is the inclusion of the relative mean deviation in group two; an argument could be presented that it belongs in a separate group. Note that the major difference between these empirical groups and the conceptual groups is the inclusion of the standard deviation of logarithms in group two instead of group four. It can be concluded that, even if a wide variety of values are desirable, the use of ten measures may be unnecessary in time-series horizontal-equity analyses if four or five measures are chosen to represent the four groups. In addition, if the time period over which equity is assessed is one of high inflation, the range, the restricted range, and the variance should be omitted, because they will show a worsening solely as a result of the inflation.

The second conclusion is a qualification of the first. While these four empirical groups appear quite regularly, they are not absolute. Looking across the three input-based dollar objects, there are some instances when the four groups are well defined and distinctive and other instances when small variations cause the group boundaries to blur somewhat. The findings on the measures may be characterized by a fair degree of consistency, but not perfect agreement all the time.

What Are the Trends in Atkinson's Index?

Atkinson's index is a horizontal-equity measure developed from a specific welfare function. Utilizing the social welfare function presented in chapter 2, Atkinson's index can be expressed as the following:

$$\text{Atkinson's index} = \left[\left(\sum_{i=1}^{N} P_i \left(\frac{X_i}{\bar{X}_p} \right)^{1-E} \right) \Big/ \left(\sum_{i=1}^{N} P_i \right) \right]^{1/(1-E)},$$

where there are N districts in the state, P_i is the number of pupils in district i, X_i is the per-pupil object in district i, $\bar{X}_p$ is the pupil-weighted mean per-pupil object in the state, and E is a parameter that can be varied over positive values. Atkinson's index, therefore, is not one measure, but a set of measures; each measure in the set has a unique value of the parameter, E. Furthermore, the specification of the levels of E is an expression of a particular preference. Increases in E correspond to a heavier emphasis on the lower part of the distribution of per-pupil objects.

Before examining horizontal equity in Michigan using Atkinson's index, it is useful to review the value judgments incorporated in the measure. For *low* values of the parameter, E, seven of the eight value-judgment questions in table 2.3 are answered identically for the Gini coefficient, the coefficient of variation, and Atkinson's index. This suggests that, conceptually, Atkinson's index with low values of E may belong to the group that includes the Gini coefficient and the coefficient of variation. For *high* values of E, Atkinson's index may resemble the measures that place more weight on the lower part of the distribution. Recall, however, that the empirical analysis for the other ten measures showed that the standard deviation of the logarithms, a measure that emphasizes the low end of the distribution, belongs in the empirical group with the coefficient of variation. This raises the possibility that changes in E may not affect the empirical behavior of Atkinson's index.

The values of Atkinson's index for instructional expenditures per pupil in Michigan from 1970 through 1978, with varying levels of E, are displayed in table 7.2. Atkinson's indexes are shown for values of E ranging from 0.2 to 175. In 1973, when E equals 175 or higher, the index could not be computed, since the combination of a small exponent ($1 - E = -174$) and a relatively small value of $X_i/\bar{X}$ exceeded the computer's capacity. Before examining the trends, note that as E increases in any single year, the value of Atkinson's index declines. Since higher values of Atkinson's index are more equitable, this shows that for every year in Michigan, the state is more horizontally equitable with lower values of E. This is not surprising, since lower values of E decrease the weight that the measure places on the lowest observations in the distribution.

In order to examine the trends in horizontal equity produced by Atkinson's index, graphs of the index using four values of E are presented in figure 7.4. The graphs show that the pattern of horizontal equity over time is affected by changes in the value of E. Graphs of all the measures included in table 7.2 (not shown) indicate that the general trend in horizontal equity does not change appreciably when E ranges from 0.2 to 8. Figure 7.4 documents the change in the pattern that occurs as E changes from 8 to 16. The comparison of the graphs when E changes from 16 to 150 suggests that over this range of E's, the graphs are quite similar in most, but not all, respects. Thus, Atkinson's indexes with various levels of E are empirically different horizontal-equity measures.

The hypothesis that Atkinson's index with low values of E belongs in the empirical group with the coefficient of variation and the Gini coefficient is supported by the graphs in the upper part of figure 7.4. The pattern that results from Atkinson's index when E varies from 0.2 to 8 is quite similar to the inverted W shape that was observed for instructional expenditures per pupil in figure 7.3 for the group containing four (or five) measures, including the coefficient of variation and the Gini coefficient. Although the pattern of Atkinson's index when E is 16 or greater differs from the pattern when E is 8 or less, it still does not resemble the pattern of the McLoone index for instructional expenditures per pupil, as shown in figure 7.2.

Two of the three ideas concerning Atkinson's index have been supported with data over nine years in Michigan.

First, Atkinson's index is not one single measure; rather, by changing the parameter, E, Atkinson's index can become at least two measures. Further, the changes in the value of E lead to empirical differences in both the levels of equity and the trends in equity.

Second, the trend in horizontal equity in Michigan yielded by Atkinson's index with low values of E is very similar to the trend exhibited by the measures in the group with the coefficient of variation and the Gini coefficient. Although not shown here, this finding is replicated for the other two input-based dollar objects examined in the preceding part of this section.

Third and finally, based on instructional expenditures per pupil in Michi-

Table 7.2. Michigan: Atkinson's Indexes for Instructional Expenditures per Pupil

	1970	1971	1972	1973	1974	1975	1976	1977	1978
Number of districts	525	525	529	530	530	530	530	526	523
Total pupils	2,150,084	2,165,537	2,206,408	2,187,818	2,153,216	2,132,846	2,124,221	2,074,223	2,008,180
Mean per-pupil inst. exp.	552	625	660	718	785	870	933	969	1,069
Atkinson's (E = 0.20)	0.9970	0.9970	0.9970	0.9963	0.9965	0.9964	0.9962	0.9971	0.9969
Atkinson's (E = 0.50)	0.9925	0.9925	0.9925	0.9910	0.9913	0.9911	0.9907	0.9928	0.9922
Atkinson's (E = 0.95)	0.9849	0.9850	0.9850	0.9823	0.9830	0.9826	0.9819	0.9855	0.9845
Atkinson's (E = 2.50)	0.9634	0.9634	0.9635	0.9584	0.9595	0.9585	0.9574	0.9647	0.9625
Atkinson's (E = 8.00)	0.8933	0.8935	0.8933	0.8840	0.8876	0.8836	0.8827	0.8946	0.8931
Atkinson's (E = 16.00)	0.8235	0.8285	0.8261	0.7354	0.8148	0.7985	0.7875	0.8153	0.8246
Atkinson's (E = 50.00)	0.6319	0.7255	0.7076	0.4795	0.6676	0.6015	0.5784	0.6226	0.6841
Atkinson's (E = 100.00)	0.5679	0.6865	0.6658	0.4343	0.6326	0.5537	0.5329	0.5687	0.6254
Atkinson's (E = 125.00)	0.5560	0.6781	0.6572	0.4259	0.6236	0.5447	0.5244	0.5586	0.6139
Atkinson's (E = 150.00)	0.5482	0.6722	0.6513	0.4204	0.6174	0.5388	0.5188	0.5520	0.6064
Atkinson's (E = 175.00)	0.5428	0.6679	0.6471	*	0.6129	0.5347	0.5148	0.5473	0.6011

*Could not be computed.

Figure 7.4 Michigan: Atkinson's Index for Instructional Expenditures per Pupil (E = 0.2, 8, 16, 150)

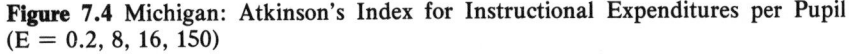

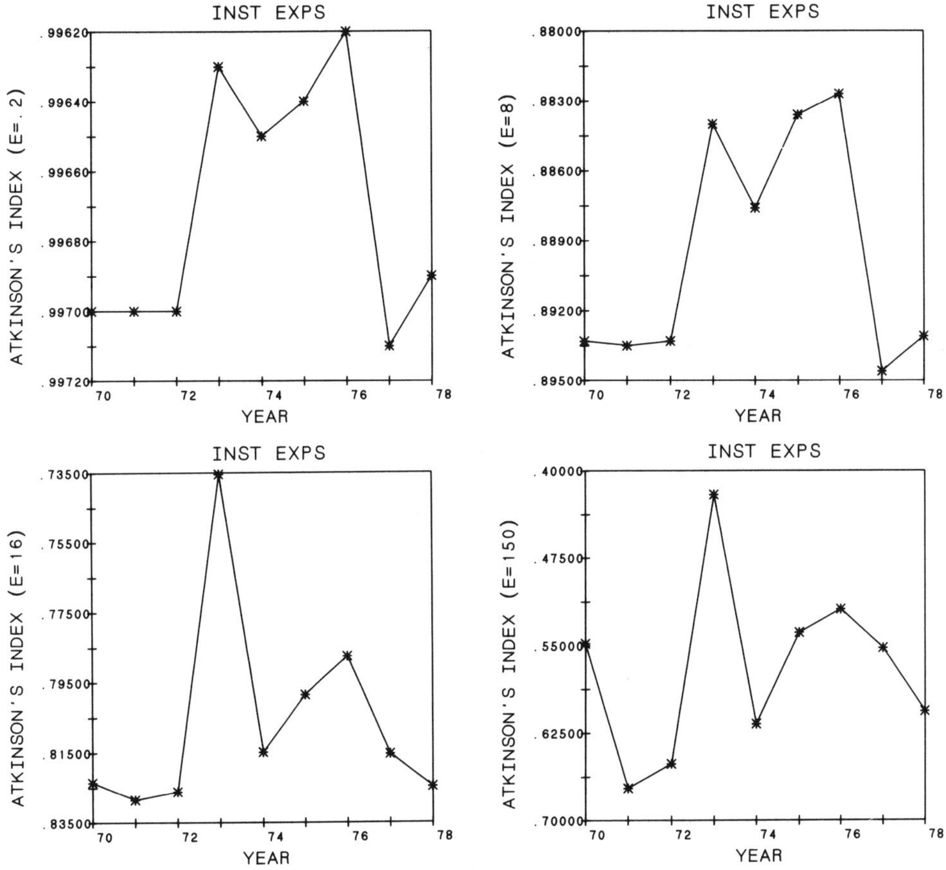

gan, while Atkinson's index with high values of E weights the low end of the distribution more heavily than most other horizontal-equity measures, it does not belong in the same group with the McLoone index. If confirmed by the results in New York, Atkinson's index with high values of E may comprise a fifth empirical group.

Are There Differences Either in the Trends or in the Levels Due to Alternative Input-Based Dollar Objects?

Having completed the examination of horizontal-equity measures in Michigan, we can now focus on the empirical differences among alternative objects. As stated at the beginning of the chapter, only input-based objects are analyzed, and in this part, the differences among six dollar objects are assessed.

Again, we begin with dollars because they are familiar to readers and are used in all of the studies of school-finance equity that we reviewed in chapter 5. Price-adjusted dollars or resources are conceptually preferred as objects, however. The next part of this section includes a comparison among dollar and price-adjusted dollar objects, and the differences between dollar and resource objects are treated in the part that follows.

The question of concern in this part is: Do differences in the input-based dollar object affect horizontal-equity conclusions when one state is examined over time, holding the measure constant? There are reasons to expect differences among the input-based dollar objects. Expenditure objects often include dollars from local, state, and federal sources, and many expenditure objects, such as instructional expenditures, only include a subset of total expenditures. Revenue measures may only include dollars from specific sources, and since some revenues address differences among unequals, or vertical equity—particularly state and federal categoricals—they may significantly affect horizontal-equity conclusions. Although there are reasons to expect differences among the dollar objects, it is important to know whether these affect empirical assessments of equity over time. If there are differences, then comparisons among two or more states that do not use the same dollar object may be suspect, and analysts examining one state may have to either obtain agreement on the object of concern, or examine several objects.

Six input-based dollar objects are the focus of attention in this part. Three objects—instructional expenditures (INST EXPS), current operating expenditures (COE), and current operating expenditures less transportation (COE − TRANS)—are based on the expenditure side. The other three—local plus state membership revenue (LOC + STATE MEMB REV), local plus total state revenue (LOC + ALL STATE REV), and local plus total state plus total federal revenue (ALL REV)—are from the revenue side. Note that nine observations are available for all of the objects except current operating expenditures less transportation, where data were available for only the last six years. Differences among the six objects are examined using three horizontal-equity measures. Rather than including all horizontal-equity measures, one measure each from three of the empirical groups identified in the first part of this section is utilized, since these are representative of the empirical behavior of all the measures in these groups. The horizontal-equity measures examined are, in turn, the federal range ratio, the McLoone index, and the coefficient variation. The group of measures including the range is not examined graphically because there are no differences in trends to be shown across objects. The range-type measures show a pattern of decreasing horizontal equity over time for all objects. This pattern is probably due to the effect of inflation on the measures and illustrates why range-type measures are conceptually inferior in times of high inflation.

The first horizontal-equity measure used to compare the objects is the federal range ratio, and the graphs of each of the six objects using this measure appear in figure 7.5. The shapes of the time-series observations vary among the objects, and the overall variation in the measures differs as well. For an example of the differences in shapes, compare instructional expenditures, current operating expenditures, and local plus total state revenues. Instructional expenditures are least horizontally equitable during the middle three years, 1973 through 1975, while for current operating expenditures, the last four years are more equitable than the first five years. Neither of these patterns can be observed for local plus total state revenues, since the last four years are not more equitable than the first five years nor are the years 1973 through 1975 the least equitable. Despite these differences (along with others that could be pointed out), there are some signs of the inverted W in the graphs of several of the objects, but not enough to change the conclusion that the patterns are different.

Although they are difficult to observe from the graphs because of our scaling conventions, considerable differences also exist in the overall variation in the federal range ratio across objects and in the two-year intervals when relatively large changes take place. The most striking example of the former point is the relatively small variation that occurs for local plus total state revenues in comparison with all the other objects except local plus total state plus total federal revenues. On the latter point, note that relatively large changes in equity occur between 1970 and 1971, 1972 and 1973, 1974 and 1975, and 1976 and 1977, depending on which object is under study. This also supports the conclusion that there are differences in patterns among the objects.

There are not consistent differences in levels among the three revenue objects, but current operating expenditures less transportation is consistently less equitable than current operating expenditures. It seems fairly safe to conclude that the object does matter when examining horizontal equity over time using the federal range ratio, especially for the trend.

The McLoone index is the second of the measures used to compare objects, and the six graphs of the McLoone index are displayed in figure 7.6. These graphs make it unnecessary to present a lengthy elaboration of the striking differences across objects. There is little similarity among the six objects; various patterns are evident, including a general increase in equity over all years except the last (current operating expenditures), a middle period of relative inequity (local plus total state revenues), and a highly variable pattern over the entire period (local plus state membership revenues). The trend in current operating expenditures from 1973 to 1978 does resemble the trend in current operating expenditures less transportation over the same period, but this is the only real similarity. Conclusions regarding large year-to-year changes, inequitable years, and equitable years are different depending on which object is examined, thus supporting the conclusion that the selection of the object affects the trends in horizontal equity yielded by the McLoone index.

The final measure analyzed in this part is the coefficient of variation, and the six objects are graphed using that measure in figure 7.7. The patterns that

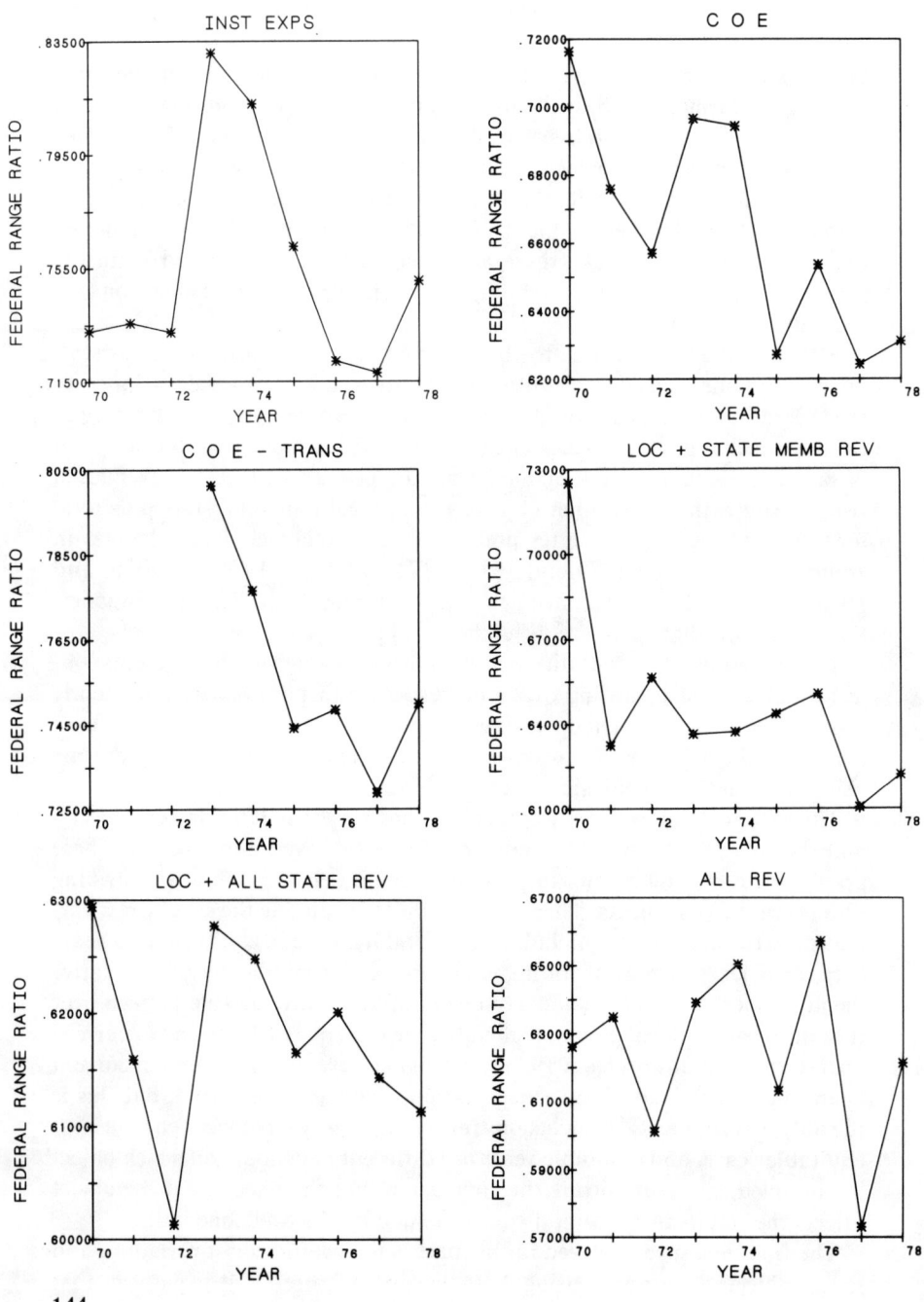

Figure 7.5 Michigan: Comparisons among Six Input-Based Dollar Objects Using the Federal Range Ratio as the Horizontal-Equity Measure

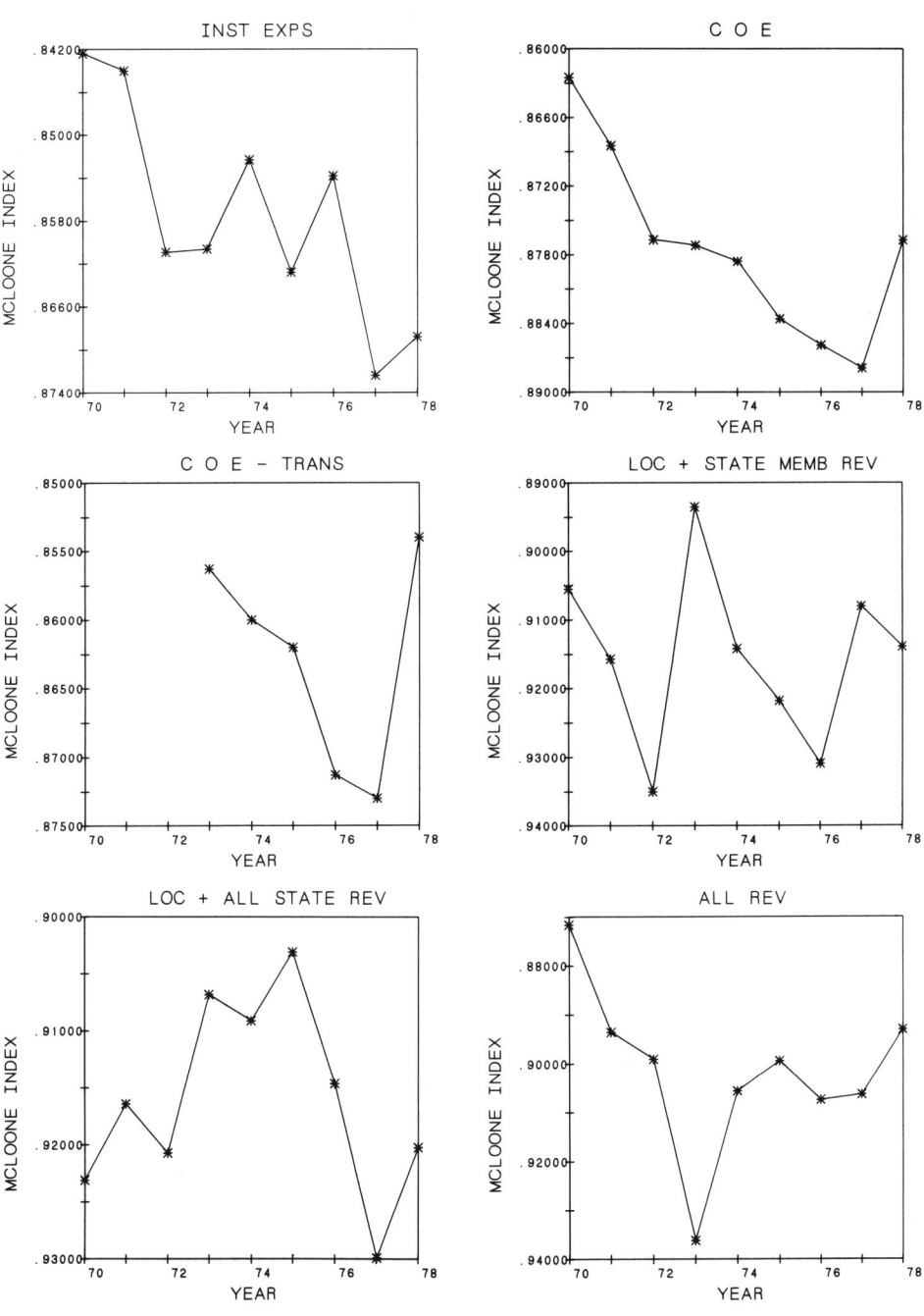

Figure 7.6 Michigan: Comparisons among Six Input-Based Dollar Objects Using the McLoone Index as the Horizontal-Equity Measure

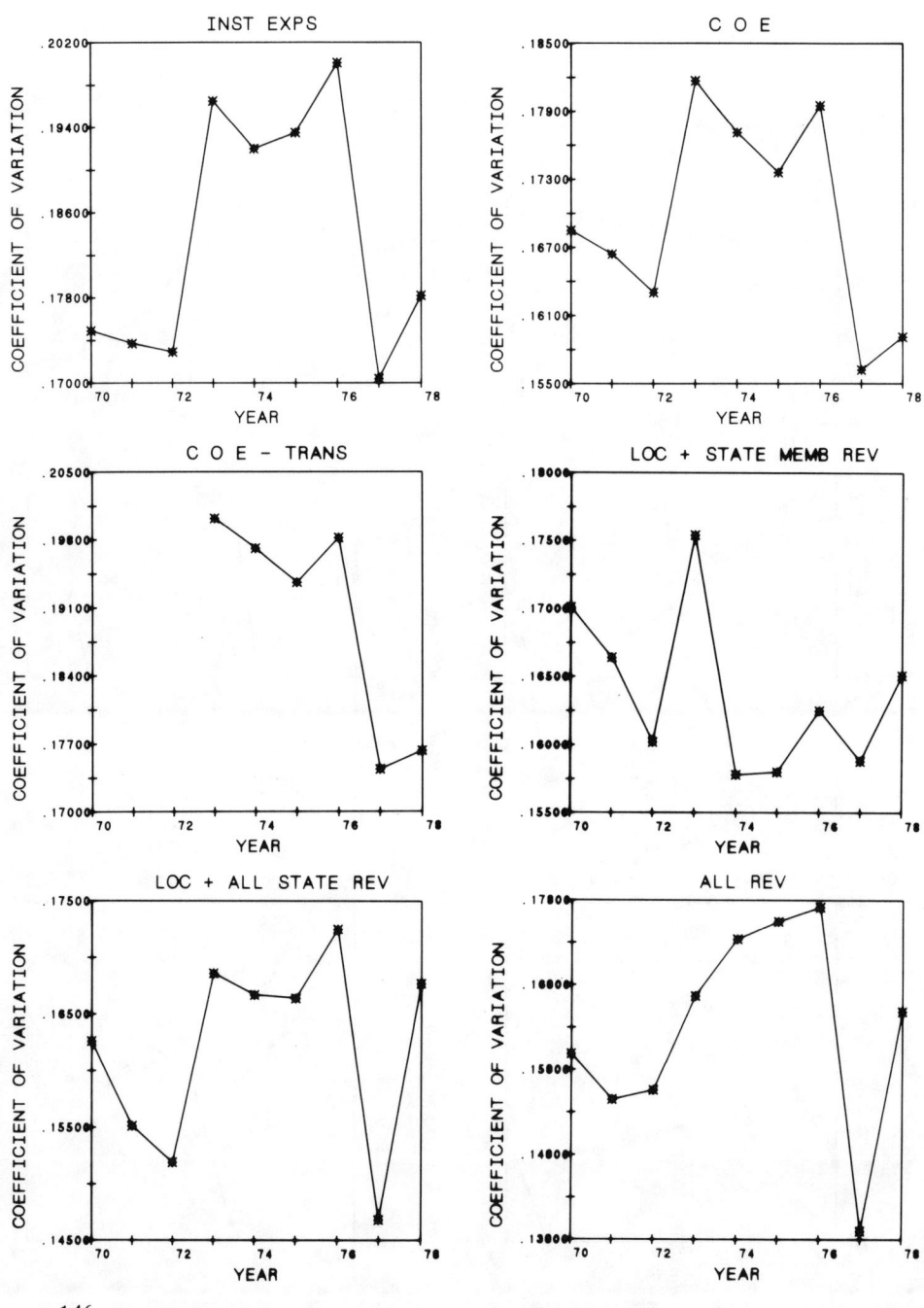

Figure 7.7 Michigan: Comparisons among Six Input-Based Dollar Objects Using the Coefficient of Variation as the Horizontal-Equity Measure

result when the coefficient of variation is the horizontal-equity measure are rather similar, and in four of the six cases the pattern matches the inverted-W shape identified in the first two parts of this section. In fact, it is only one year for local plus total state plus total federal revenues (1973) and three years for local plus state membership revenues (1974 to 1976) that prevent these two objects from forming the same inverted-W pattern. The agreement among the objects over the nine-year period is not as complete as was the case for the range-type measures, but there is relatively more consistency than for the federal range ratio or the McLoone index.

In terms of levels, current operating expenditures less transportation is less equitable than current operating expenditures, as was the case for the federal range ratio and the McLoone index. Furthermore, instructional expenditures and current operating expenditures less transportation are consistently less equitable than current operating expenditures and the three revenue objects.

Does the choice of an input-based dollar object matter? In general, yes, although in Michigan the differences among objects depend, in part, on the horizontal-equity measure being utilized. The effect of the object can be seen by the different patterns that emerge from the alternative objects, most clearly in the case of the federal range ratio and the McLoone index, and less so for the coefficient of variation and the range-type measures. As pointed out previously, the consistency in trends across objects observed for the range-type measures is probably due to the fact that these measures are sensitive to equal percentage changes, and thus increases in the measures are caused, in part, by inflation. The relative variation in the patterns formed by the objects when the federal range ratio and the McLoone index are used, compared to the patterns for the coefficient of variation, may be due to the inclusion of all the pupils in the latter measure, but not in the other two. The federal range ratio focuses on two points in the distribution, while the McLoone index only examines the pupils at the median level and below.

Not only does the selection of a dollar object influence the trends over time, but in addition, the levels of horizontal equity are affected by the alternative objects. Any absolute assessment of horizontal equity must be made with an awareness of the levels that are relevant for a particular object. Comparisons over time in one state must utilize consistently defined and measured objects, because a change in the object could result in a change that is a relatively large year-to-year variation. Finally, although we do not examine equity across states, the need for comparable objects in interstate studies is also supported by our results.

How Does the Adjustment of the Input-Based Dollar Objects by Price Indexes Affect the Trends in and Levels of Horizontal Equity?

A major problem with all input-based dollar objects is their failure to incorporate intrastate price variation. As explained in previous chapters, one way to adjust dollar objects for intrastate price variation is with price-of-education indexes. In this part, price indexes developed for Michigan are utilized to assess horizontal equity in Michigan with input-based price-adjusted dollar objects, and these are compared to unadjusted dollar objects. Thus, the question of concern in this part is: How does the adjustment of dollar inputs by price indexes affect the trends in horizontal equity, holding the measure constant?

Two price indexes, Index 1 and Index 2, are utilized in this chapter; both indexes are described in chapter 6. While both Index 1 and Index 2 are estimated using a supply-demand framework with district-level data, each has a somewhat different specification. The other major distinction between the two indexes is that average years of experience and percent of teachers with masters degrees are treated as uncontrollable in Index 1 and as controllable in Index 2. Actually, each index was originally estimated using data for 1973 and reestimated using data from 1976. The original index is used to price-adjust dollar inputs from 1970 to 1974, and the updated index is used to price-adjust dollar inputs from 1975 to 1978.

Price-adjusted dollar inputs are compared to dollar inputs with two dollar objects and three horizontal-equity measures using graphs. The objects are instructional expenditures and local plus total state revenues. The three horizontal-equity measures are the same ones that were used in the preceding part of this section, i.e., the federal range ratio, the McLoone index, and the coefficient of variation. First, one range-type measure, the restricted range, is briefly discussed, as well, but is not graphed. Differences in trends and levels between the dollar and price-adjusted dollar inputs are examined for each of the horizontal-equity measures.

The comparison of dollar and price-adjusted dollar objects begins with the restricted range. Both dollar objects display an increasing trend toward greater horizontal inequity over time, and the four price-adjusted dollar objects are consistent with this trend at a general level. Even with this similarity, however, there are some differences in patterns between the dollar and price-adjusted dollar objects for the two objects. The price adjustment tends to alter the magnitude of the change from year to year in certain instances, and this is exemplified by the greater frequency of downturns in the price-adjusted dollar objects compared to the dollar objects, especially with Index 1.

In addition, the price indexes affect the level of horizontal equity for each of the objects. For both objects, the price-adjusted restricted ranges are smaller, and thus more equitable, than the dollar restricted ranges. If some of the inequity that is captured by the dollar objects is due to intrastate price differences, then this is the expected result. One price index does not uniformly produce a level of horizontal equity that is more equitable than the other price index for both objects. For instructional expenditures, however, the adjustment with Index 1 (PRICE ADJ1) produces a more equitable level of horizontal equity at all points than with Index 2 (PRICE ADJ2) while in the case of local plus total state revenues, neither price index produces a level that is consistently more equitable than the other.

The second measure used to compare dollar and price-adjusted dollar inputs is the federal range ratio and the six objects are graphed with this measure in figure 7.8. For instructional expenditures and local plus total state revenues, the application of the price index changes the pattern of horizontal equity over time, although the degree of change varies across objects. Dramatic differences exist for the revenue object between the respective unadjusted dollar and price-adjusted dollar objects, and some differences can be seen for instructional expenditures as well. When the dollar objects are price-adjusted, changes occur in the most and least equitable years, the two-year intervals with relatively large changes, and the difference between the first and the last years in the time series.

For instructional expenditures, both price-adjusted objects are more equitable than the unadjusted object, and instructional expenditures adjusted by Index 1 is generally more equitable than instructional expenditures adjusted by Index 2. But these relationships are not consistently repeated with the revenue object. In some cases, the price-adjusted objects on the revenue side are more equitable than the unadjusted dollar objects; however the dollar object adjusted with Index 1 is not uniformly the most equitable.

Thus, the price-index adjustments with the federal range ratio as the horizontal-equity measure affect the patterns of equity quite substantially. Furthermore, the levels of equity are influenced by the price indexes, but the effects for the federal range ratio are not as consistent as they were with the restricted range in terms of which index produces the most equitable level.

The third horizontal-equity measure utilized to assess the effects of price indexes is the McLoone index, and the graphs of the objects over time are displayed in figure 7.9. When trends in the unadjusted dollar objects are compared to the trends in the price-adjusted dollar objects, there are meaningful differences for instructural expenditures and local plus total state revenues. The changes in certain cases are quite dramatic, such as the adjustment of instructional expenditures by Index 2. In no case do the price adjustments leave the trend unaltered.

The effect of the price index on the levels of horizontal equity for instructional expenditures that occurred with the restricted range and the federal range ratio is repeated for the McLoone index. The adjustment of instructional expenditures by Index 1 yields the most equitable level, and the unadjusted instructional expenditures are the least horizontally equitable. For local plus total state revenue, the adjustment by Index 2 generally produces the most equitable level, and the adjustment by Index 1 is the least equitable.

The conclusions for the McLoone index parallel those drawn for the federal range ratio. First, the adjustment of the input-based dollar objects by the price indexes changes the pattern of horizontal equity over time as measured

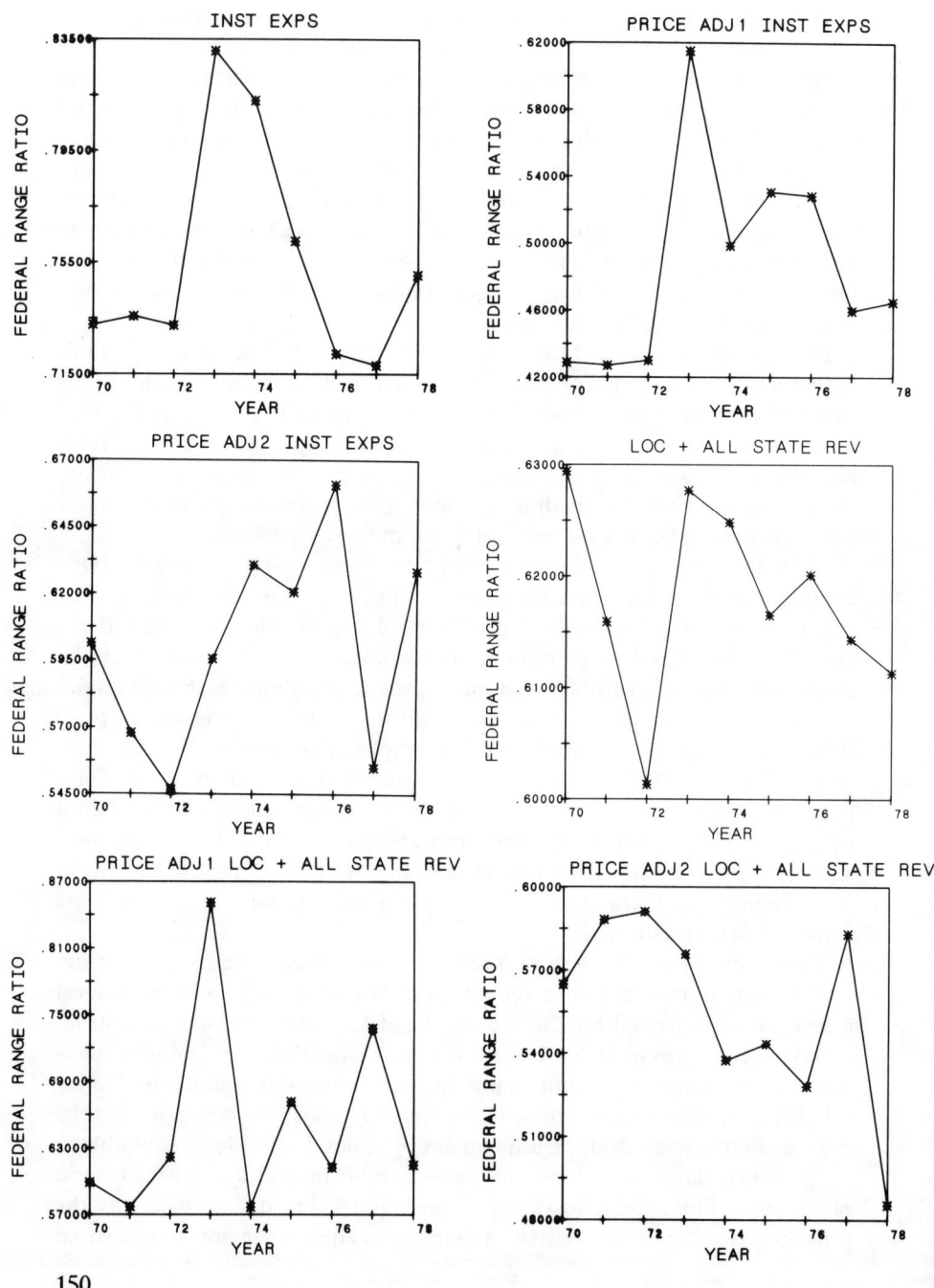

Figure 7.8 Michigan: Comparisons among Input-Based Dollar and Price-Adjusted Dollar Objects Using the Federal Range Ratio as the Horizontal-Equity Measure

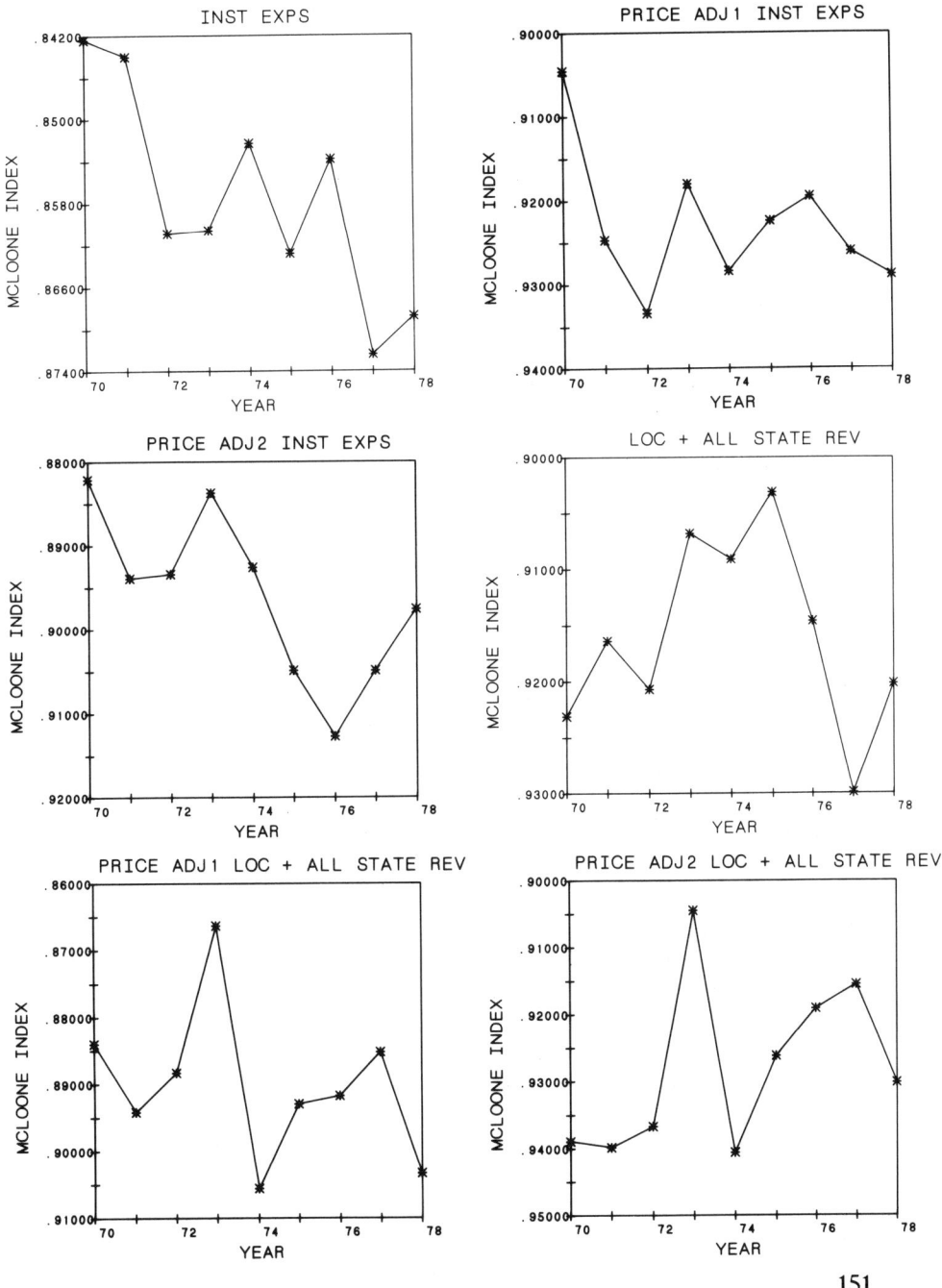

Figure 7.9 Michigan: Comparisons among Input-Based Dollar and Price-Adjusted Dollar Objects Using the McLoone Index as the Horizontal-Equity Measure

by the McLoone index. Second, in the majority of cases the levels of price-adjusted objects are more equitable than the unadjusted objects. Finally, neither price index always produces the most equitable level of the object; Index 1 yields the most equitable level for instructional expenditures, but not for the other revenue object.

The fourth and last horizontal-equity measure utilized to show the effects of price adjustments is the coefficient of variation, displayed in figure 7.10. The changes in the trends caused by the price indexes are small here compared to those for the federal range ratio and the McLoone index. The inverted-W shape that appears with unadjusted instructional expenditures is not affected in any substantial way by the application of the price indexes. For the revenue object, the only major change is the movement away from the inverted-W shape when the dollar object is adjusted by Index 1.

The graphs in figure 7.10 add further support to the finding that price-adjusted objects are more horizontally equitable than objects that are not price adjusted. Again, for instructional expenditures, the adjustment by Index 1 produces the most equitable level of horizontal equity, but the relative equity of the price-adjusted revenue objects does not indicate that one index always produces a more equitable level.

The price adjustments cause small changes in the horizontal-equity trends when measured by the coefficient of variation. In addition, the price adjustments usually increase the horizontal equity measured by the coefficient of variation, although one index does not always produce the most equitable trend. With these findings for the coefficient of variation, we can summarize our conclusions on the effects of price indexes for all four horizontal-equity measures.

Three conclusions can be drawn from this comparison of price-adjusted dollar and unadjusted dollar objects. First, price adjustments do alter the pattern of horizontal equity in Michigan over the nine-year period. Only small changes in trends occur when the restricted range is used as the horizontal-equity measure, and the altered patterns are not generally large for the coefficient of variation either. In the case of the federal range ratio and the McLoone index, however, the changes caused by the adjustment of dollar objects by price indexes are quite substantial. Note that for three horizontal-equity measures (excluding the restricted range), the price-index adjustment often changes the conclusions drawn for horizontal equity in Michigan when the last year of the time series is compared to the first.

Second, as a general rule, price-adjusted dollar objects are more horizontally equitable than dollar objects. Apparently, some of the horizontal inequity in the dollar measures is due to lower prices faced by the low spending districts and higher prices faced by high spending districts, so that the price adjustment produces a lower level of horizontal inequity. However, since the price-adjusted objects are not always more equitable than the unadjusted objects and because only a fraction of the inequity is removed by the adjustment,

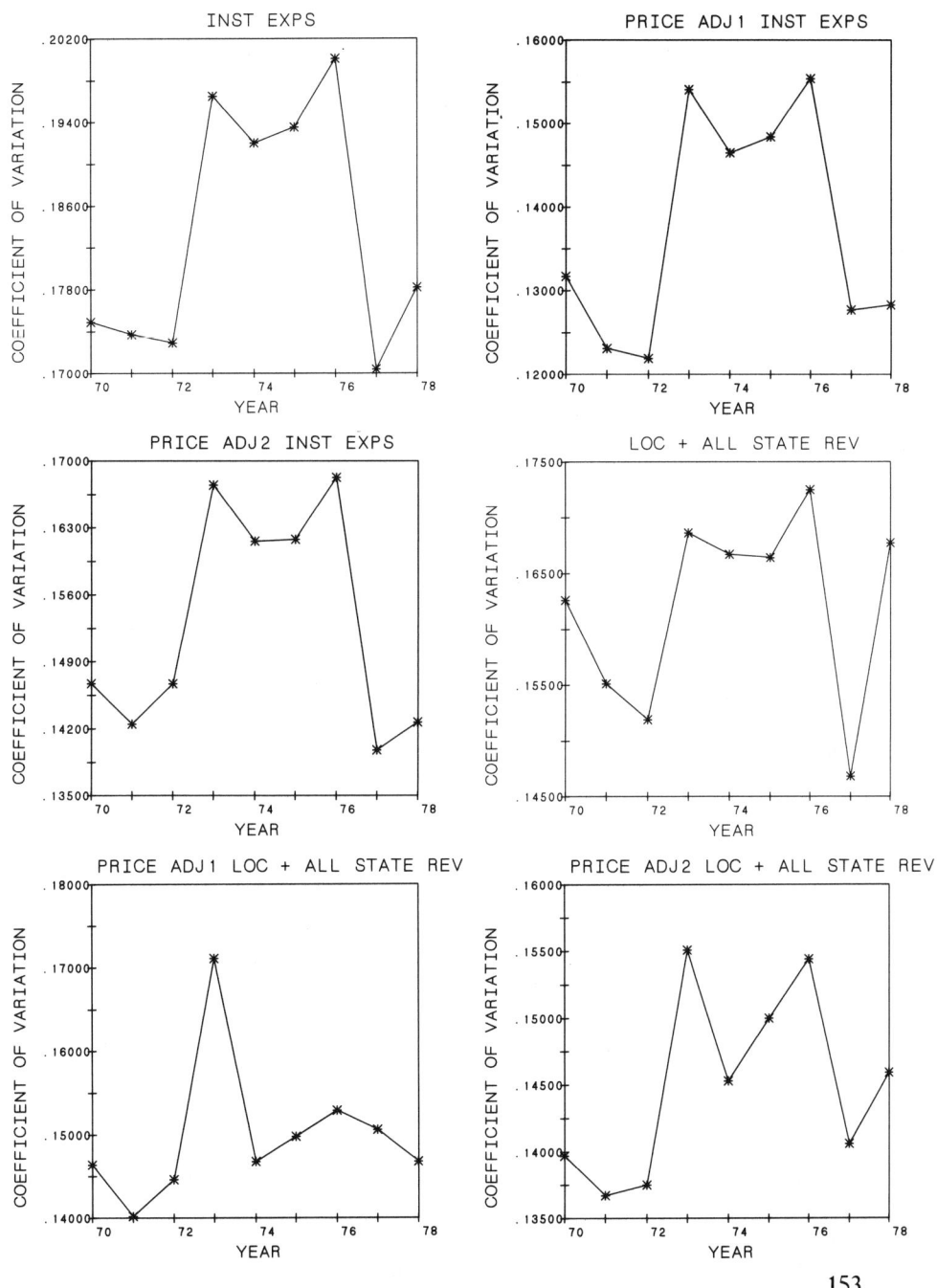

Figure 7.10 Michigan: Comparisons among Input-Based Dollar and Price-Adjusted Dollar Objects Using the Coefficient of Variation as the Horizontal-Equity Measure

153

intrastate price differences as captured by the price indexes are not the sole nor the major contributor to the horizontal-inequity measured by unadjusted dollars.

Third, although the two price indexes, Index 1 and Index 2, are formulated from somewhat different econometric specifications and incorporate different assumptions regarding the controllability of teachers' experience and education, one index does not always produce greater horizontal equity than the other. The only exception is for instructional expenditures, where Index 1 is consistently more equitable than Index 2.

Do Trends or Levels Differ for Resource Objects Compared to Dollar and Price-Adjusted Dollar Objects?

Resources comprise the final type of input-based objects examined in this part, and the strategy of analysis is similar to those utilized in the two preceding parts. Both resource measures are teacher-pupil ratios. One measure, K-12 teachers per 1,000 pupils (K-12 TEACH), is a subset of the second measure, all classroom teachers per 1,000 pupils (ALL CLASSRM TEACH); special education and vocational education teachers are included only in the latter measure. The resource measures are available for a six-year period, 1973 to 1978. In this part, the two resource measures are compared to each other and to instructional expenditures and price-adjusted (Index 1) instructional expenditures. Instructional expenditures is used in the comparisons because, of all the dollar objects, the inputs purchased with instructional expenditures most closely resemble the teachers included in the resource measures compared to the other dollar objects.

The dollar, price-adjusted dollar, and resource measures are examined using an approach that parallels those in the previous two parts. But, since the findings in this part are not greatly affected by the horizontal-equity measure, the graphs for only two measures are presented. Figures 7.11 and 7.12 compare the six-year horizontal-equity trends with unadjusted and price-adjusted instructional expenditures and K-12 and all classroom teachers per 1,000 pupils as the objects, using the McLoone index and the coefficient of variation respectively as the horizontal-equity measures.

A comparison of the trends in horizontal equity between the two resource objects, displayed in the lower parts of figures 7.11 and 7.12, leads to two conclusions. First, holding the measure constant, the differences between the two resource objects are small in terms of the levels and patterns of horizontal equity. For any measure of horizontal equity, including the ones not displayed here, there is greater consistency between the resource objects than there was for most pairs of dollars or price-adjusted dollars. Given the small differences between the two resource-based objects, this may not be surprising.

The second conclusion, that the trends in horizontal equity of the two resource objects are not affected by the measure of horizontal equity, is more

Figure 7.11 Michigan: Comparisons among Input-Based Dollar, Price Adjusted Dollar, and Resource Objects Using the McLoone Index as the Horizontal-Equity Measure

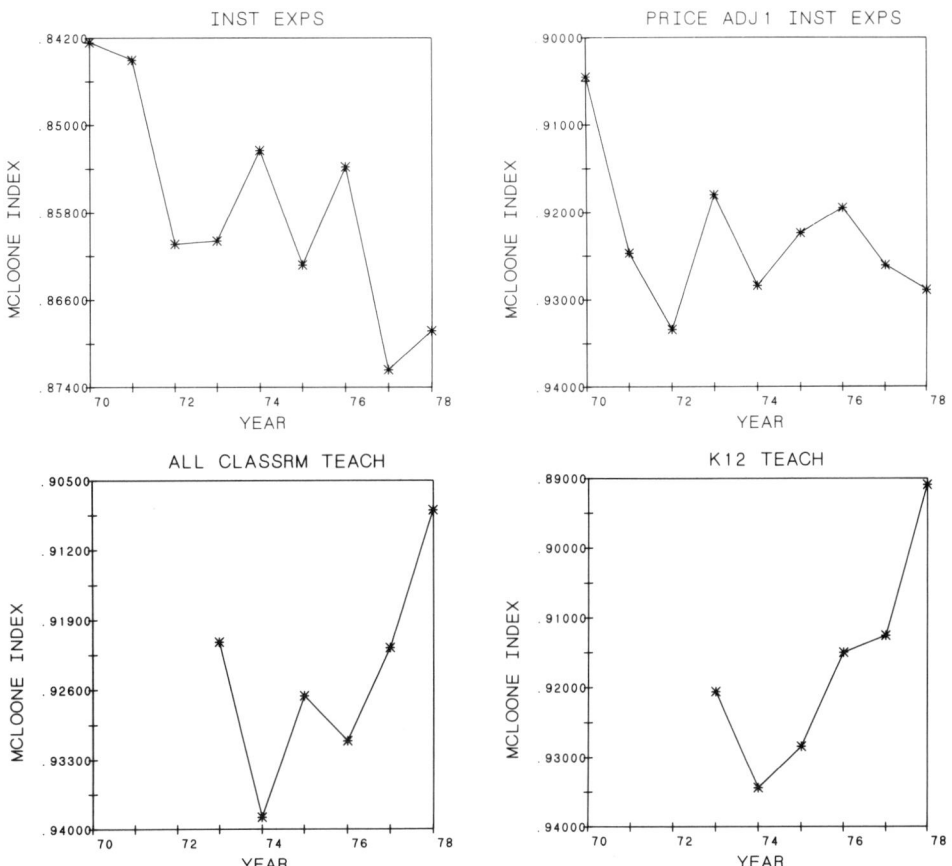

surprising, given the influence of the measure when dollars and price-adjusted dollars are employed. With both horizontal-equity measures, the trends of the two resource objects are J shaped where the second year (1974) is the most equitable and the last year (1978) is the least equitable. This holds for other measures, including the restricted range and the federal range ratio, as well. Although research to determine why the measures affect some objects but not others has not yet been carried out, it could, if successful, provide guidance to analysts who need to know when multiple measures are likely to produce different patterns. The fact that resource objects are measured in real terms, eliminating the effects of price differences across time and locations, may begin to account for the similarity across measures.

Figure 7.12 Michigan: Comparisons among Input-Based Dollar, Price-Adjusted Dollar, and Resource Objects Using the Coefficient of Variation as the Horizontal-Equity Measure

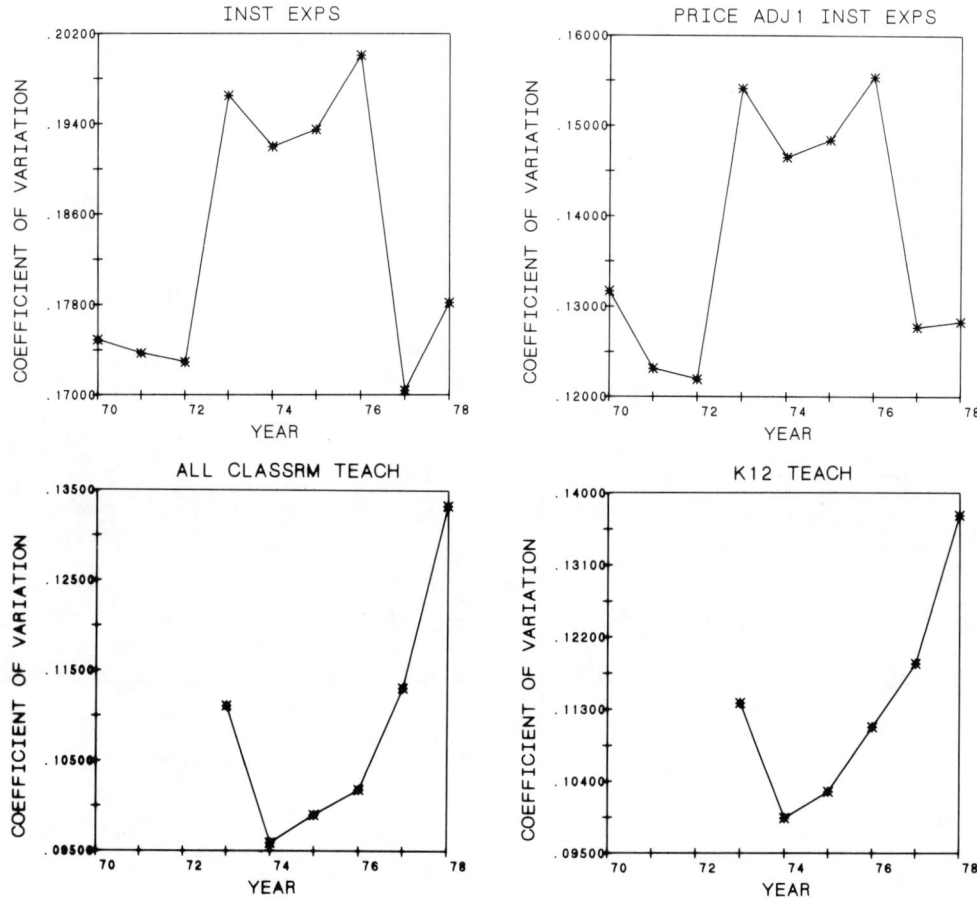

Two additional conclusions can be drawn when the levels and patterns of horizontal equity of the resource objects are compared with the levels and patterns of the dollar and price-adjusted dollar objects. In terms of the patterns, the two figures show quite clearly that the horizontal-equity trends of the resource objects are extremely different from the horizontal-equity trends of the dollar and price-adjusted dollar objects. None of the dollar and price-adjusted dollar objects exhibit the J-shaped pattern formed by the resource objects. Second, although because of the opposite trends it is not easy to compare the levels of the objects, in most cases the levels of horizontal equity of the resource objects are similar to the levels of the price-adjusted dollar objects and more equitable then the unadjusted dollar objects. This is consistent with the purpose of the price index, which is to remove input price differences from the objects. However, the different patterns reinforce the point that the values and assumptions incorporated in the price indexes are different from those that are required to measure resources directly. Resource and price-adjusted objects each remove the effects of intrastate price variation in different ways.

AN ASSESSMENT OF HORIZONTAL EQUITY IN NEW YORK

In this section of the chapter, we address the same basic question for New York that we did for Michigan in the preceding section—has horizontal equity become better or worse over time? Whereas the assessment of Michigan's horizontal equity trends was organized around five questions, for New York the availability of only one dollar object, current operating expenditures (COE), reduces the questions to the following three of the five raised at the beginning of the chapter.

1. Do the measures form empirical groupings that are similar to those observed for Michigan?
2. Do changes in the parameter in Atkinson's index cause differences in horizontal-equity trends? If so, do the changes in the trends occur at the same parameter value ($E = 16$) as was observed for Michigan?
3. Does the adjustment of the New York dollar object by a price index affect the trends and/or absolute level of horizontal equity, holding the measure constant?

In addition to the differences in numbers of questions addressed for New York and for Michigan, there is also a difference in the way school districts are defined over time. The New York time series is six years longer than that for Michigan and includes years in the 1960s when many consolidations of districts were taking place. In the first year of the New York time series (1965) there were 996 districts, and by the end of the series (1978) there were only 754.[2] A significant difference in the number of districts could have an effect of its own on equity trends. This is true even though all analyses are for pupil-weighted district objects. To avoid such an outcome, we have imposed the 1978 district pattern on the time series.[3] Also, the small number of non-K-12

2. Both numbers include non-K-12 districts.
3. The 1978 district pattern was achieved by assuming that districts that consolidated between 1965 and 1978 had made the consolidation in 1965. All financial, student, and other data are combined from 1965 on. In addition, throughout the time series, three high school districts in Nassau County and one in Erie County received students from thirteen elementary districts. These elementary districts were combined with their respective high school districts to form four K-12 districts all through the time series. Where possible, and with few exceptions, non-K-12 districts that never became K-12 (i.e., were still non-K-12 in 1978) were eliminated.

districts still in existence in 1978 were eliminated in almost all cases. The first line of table 7.3 shows the number of actual districts for each year. The second line shows the number of consolidated K-12 districts. The number of districts in the second line is the number used in all New York analyses in the book.[4] Thus, all numbers displayed in the bottom twelve rows in table 7.3 are calculated from the consolidated K-12 district data, using the pupil unit of analysis.

Are There Differences in Trends Due to Alternative Measures? Do the Measures Form Empirical Groupings?

Table 7.3 displays the mean and the median plus ten measures of horizontal equity. As was the case in the Michigan analyses, the trends presented in tabular form are difficult to assess except when there are fairly monotonic patterns. For example, the mean and the median current operating expenditures clearly show upward trends. In addition, the range, the restricted range, and the variance all move consistently upward with minor exceptions, empirically forming a group of measures, as they did in Michigan.

For all the other horizontal-equity measures, the trends are more easily assessed when the data are presented graphically. The New York graphs should be read the same way as the ones for Michigan were. The only difference is in the markings for the years. For New York every hash mark on the year axis represents two years rather than one. The graphs reveal nearly the same groupings of measures as were apparent for Michigan. As mentioned above, the range, the restricted range, and the variance are clearly similar to one another in table 7.3 and do not need to be displayed graphically. In figure 7.13, the coefficient of variation, the Gini coefficient, Theil's measure (not shown on graph), and the standard deviation of logarithms show the same patterns. In addition, in figure 7.13, the federal range ratio and to some extent the relative mean deviation are closely related to the second grouping, which includes the coefficient of variation. Once again, as in Michigan, the relative mean deviation is the most difficult to group. Except for a dip in 1973, it seems to follow the basic pattern set by the coefficient of variation for current operating expenditures. Finally, this figure shows that the McLoone index is in a group of its own and shows a particularly volatile pattern of ups and downs over the years. Thus, except that the federal range ratio no longer exhibits a unique pattern, the empirical groupings are the same as they were for Michigan.

What Are the Trends in Atkinson's Index?

As was the case in Michigan, two types of patterns emerge from Atkinson's index as the E parameter is changed from low to high values. Parameter val-

---

4. In future chapters, data in some districts are missing for needed variables, causing the number of consolidated districts to vary slightly from the numbers shown in table 7.3.

Table 7.3. New York: Basic Statistics and Horizontal-Equity Measures for Current Operating Expenditures per Pupil

	1964–65	1965–66	1966–67	1967–68	1968–69	1969–70
Number of actual districts (including non-K–12)*	996	986	934	848	819	762
Number of consolidated K–12 districts in data set	675	675	676	677	677	677
Total pupils	3,116,440	3,171,165	3,243,136	3,319,805	3,390,904	3,436,764
Mean per-pupil current operating expenditures	718	784	894	969	1,097	1,201
Median per-pupil current operating expenditures	739	834	929	993	1,124	1,256
Range	1,045	848	1,035	1,191	1,425	1,506
Restricted range	347	387	400	407	434	576
Federal range ratio	0.6164	0.6470	0.5581	0.5127	0.5428	0.6144
Relative mean deviation	0.1041	0.1159	0.0999	0.0931	0.0934	0.1206
McLoone index	0.8732	0.8350	0.8687	0.8874	0.8876	0.8430
Variance	12,085	13,932	15,127	16,724	21,992	34,508
Coefficient of variation	0.1531	0.1505	0.1376	0.1335	0.1352	0.1547
Standard deviation of logarithms	0.1457	0.1482	0.1322	0.1262	0.1275	0.1488
Gini coefficient	0.0772	0.0793	0.0712	0.0680	0.0685	0.0813
Theil's measure	0.0112	0.0111	0.0092	0.0085	0.0087	0.0116

Financial Data for School Districts (State of New York, Division of Municipal Affairs, Department of Audit and Control, various years), table B.

Table 7.3. (cont.)

1970–71	1971–72	1972–73	1973–74	1974–75	1975–76	1976–77	1977–78
754	753	755	751	748	745	743	742
677	677	678	678	680	681	681	681
3,483,010	3,497,321	3,467,782	3,420,843	3,394,994	3,376,051	3,301,632	3,183,607
1,360	1,450	1,520	1,749	1,956	2,076	2,151	2,404
1,428	1,523	1,542	1,794	2,008	2,185	2,162	2,512
1,810	2,044	2,720	3,334	3,458	3,890	5,522	4,742
696	780	889	1,021	1,120	1,183	1,326	1,474
0.6743	0.7104	0.7674	0.8236	0.8027	0.7703	0.8212	0.8342
0.1287	0.1279	0.1180	0.1622	0.1562	0.1378	0.1213	0.1365
0.8324	0.8345	0.8713	0.8178	0.8235	0.8211	0.8748	0.8310
50,352	62,713	74,706	117,564	140,545	143,232	167,881	212,212
0.1650	0.1727	0.1798	0.1961	0.1917	0.1823	0.1905	0.1916
0.1595	0.1639	0.1660	0.1955	0.1910	0.1758	0.1754	0.1822
0.0870	0.0892	0.0902	0.1060	0.1031	0.0953	0.0951	0.0985
0.0132	0.0142	0.0151	0.0189	0.0181	0.0160	0.0169	0.0175

Figure 7.13 New York: Coefficient of Variation, Gini Coefficient, McLoone Index, Standard Deviation of Logarithms, Federal Range Ratio, and Relative Mean Deviation for Current Operating Expenditures per Pupil

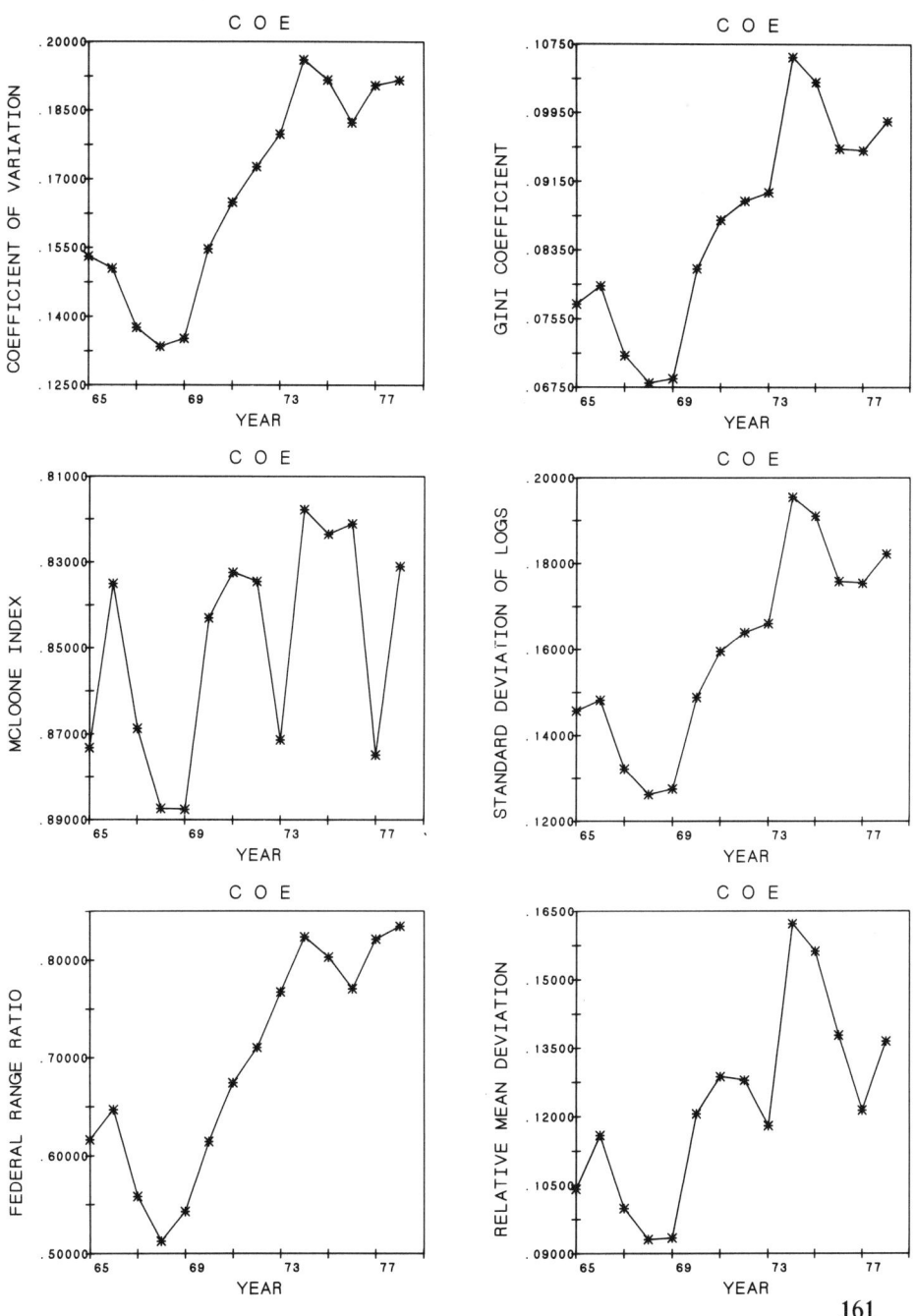

162 THE MEASUREMENT OF EQUITY IN SCHOOL FINANCE

ues of $E = .2$, $E = 50$, $E = 100$, and $E = 200$ are displayed in figure 7.14. The pattern for low values of E ($E = 50$ and below) is that of the coefficient of variation and associated measures. For parameter values of E greater than 50, the pattern begins to switch up and down, more like that of the McLoone index. This characteristic of Atkinson's index that allows it to move through a series of patterns similar to other measures as the parameter E changes was observed in Michigan as well.

The graphs also reveal that higher values of E for any given year's current operating expenditures reduce the overall level of equity. Whereas at $E = .2$, Atkinson's index shows nearly perfect equity (.9963 or above), by the time E has moved to 200, Atkinson's index has fallen to .73 or lower. At $E = 200$, an

Figure 7.14 New York: Atkinson's Index with E = .2, 50, 100, and 200 for Current Operating Expenditures per Pupil

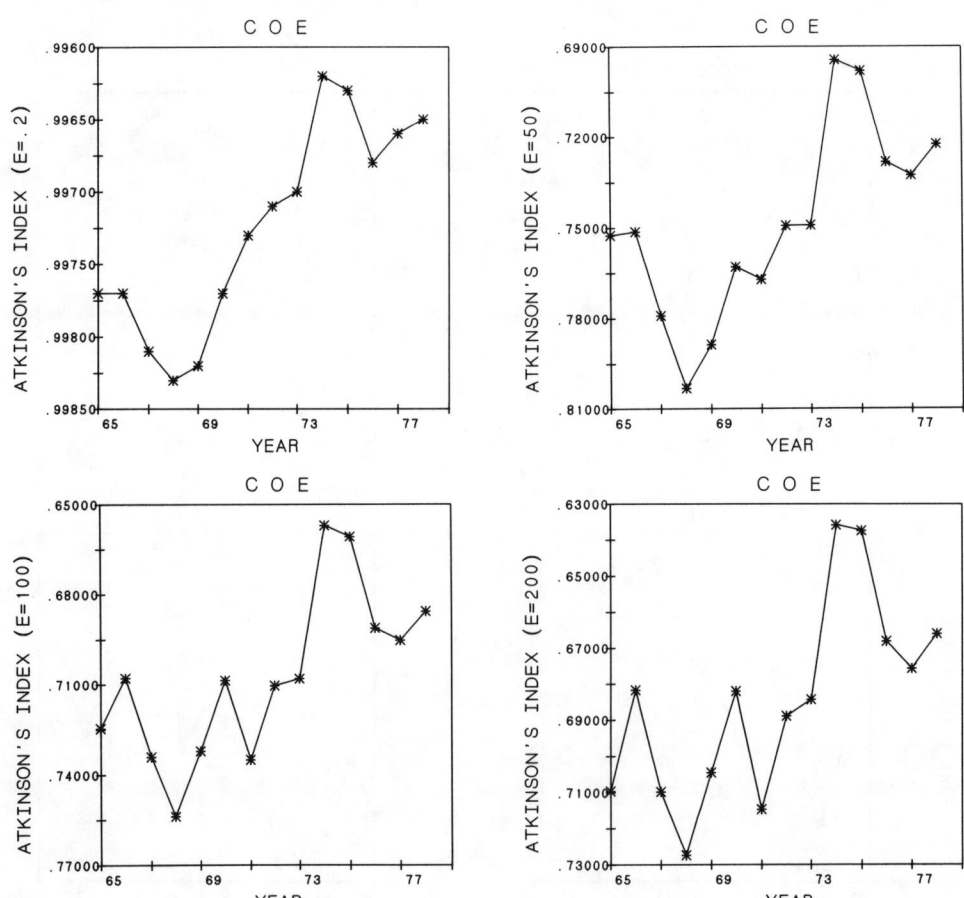

Atkinson's index this low means that if equally distributed, only 73 percent of total current operating expenditures for the state would be required in order to achieve the same level of equity as the actual distribution of current operating expenditures. The Michigan data showed the same lowering of the index, for a given year, as E was increased.

How Does the Adjustment of the Input-Based Dollar Object by the Price Index Affect the Trends in and Levels of Horizontal Equity?

The groupings of measures for price-adjusted current operating expenditures stay essentially the same as they were for current operating expenditures. In addition, within each group, the patterns, and thus the trends, are nearly the same as they were for current operating expenditures. Although not shown here, the range, the restricted range, and the variance all show their usual upward trend. In figure 7.15, the coefficient of variation, the Gini coefficient, the standard deviation of logarithms, and the federal range ratio are shown. The patterns of these four measures (as well as Theil's measure, not shown) are similar to one another, as they were for current operating expenditures in figure 7.13. The differences with the current operating expenditures pattern are that the last year of the series becomes more equitable for most of the measures using price-adjusted current operating expenditures. From 1971 on, the relative mean deviation shows a pattern comparable to the other five measures mentioned above. In the 1960s, it starts the same as the others (with an increase in equity), but then shows a worsening. A comparison of relative mean deviation for current operating expenditures in figure 7.13 and price-adjusted current operating expenditures in figure 7.15 reveals difference in the years in which peaks and valleys occur. The relative mean deviation does not clearly fall within the group containing the coefficient of variation, and as with Michigan, it could as easily be classified in a group of its own. Finally, the McLoone index for price-adjusted current operating expenditures, shown in figure 7.15, is similar to the McLoone index for current operating expenditures and different from the other measures in that figure. The empirical patterns of groupings of measures hold up for both New York current operating expenditures and price-adjusted current operating expenditures.

The most outstanding conclusion from the price-adjusted current operating expenditures patterns is that the level of equity for all the years is significantly increased due to the price adjustment. The McLoone index is especially noteworthy because it approaches perfect equity (1.0) when the price adjustment is made (especially 1969, 1973, 1977). Except for the McLoone index, all the price-adjusted measures show that equity is worse in the 1970s than the 1960s even though the levels are better for all years when current operating expenditures is price-adjusted.

Figure 7.15 New York: Coefficient of Variation, Gini Coefficient, McLoone Index, Standard Deviation of Logarithms, Federal Range Ratio, and Relative Mean Deviation for Price-Adjusted Current Operating Expenditures per Pupil

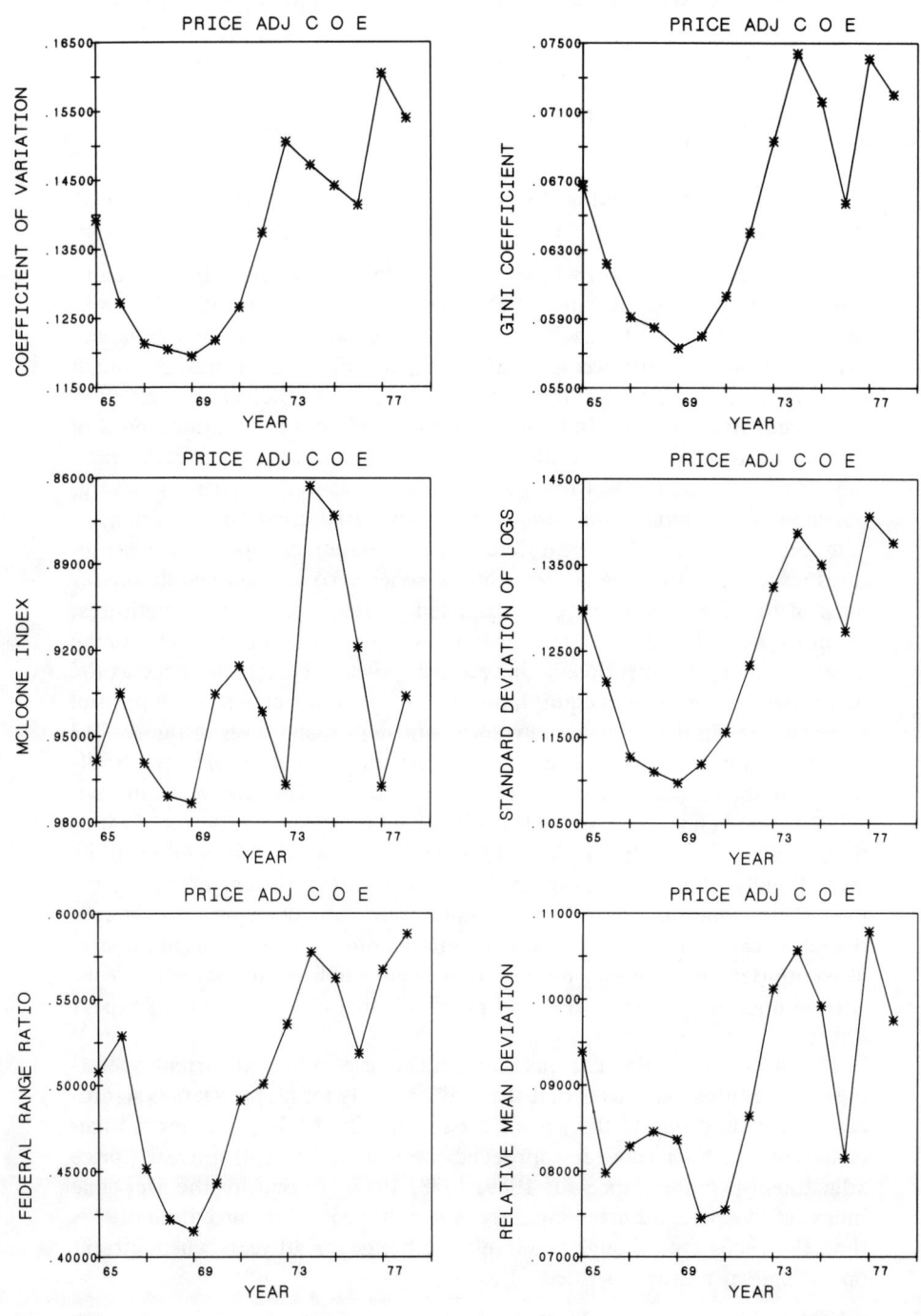

OVERALL CHAPTER CONCLUSIONS

The conclusions discussed in this section are based on the Michigan and New York analyses combined. They are meant to highlight the results that those who are performing horizontal-equity analyses in other states will find helpful. These conclusions also serve as a summary for all readers of the in-depth analyses that have preceded. The conclusions are divided into two parts. First, generalizations concerning methodology, such as behavior of alternative measures and objects, are made. Second, substantive conclusions about actual trends in horizontal equity in each state are reviewed.

Conclusions On Methodology

Two major methodological conclusions emerge, one on the empirical trends revealed by the measures, holding constant the object, and the other on the trends depicted by the objects, holding constant the measures. Put another way, the research helps answer questions on whether the measures and the objects make a difference when assessing trends in horizontal equity.

Does the measure make a difference when assessing horizontal-equity over time? The answer is clearly yes, with the qualification that not every measure is unique. Combining results for Michigan and New York, four clear-cut groups emerge, while two other measures sometimes require their own unique group and sometimes do not. One group is composed of the range, the restricted range, and the variance. These three measures consistently show a worsening of equity over time, although year to year deviations from this pattern are very occasionally observed. The severe influence of inflation on these measures should cause researchers and analysts to turn to alternative measures to assess horizontal equity. A second group includes the coefficient of variation, the Gini coefficient, Theil's measure, the standard deviation of logarithms, and Atkinson's index with low values of E. A third group is reserved for the McLoone index alone, and a fourth group for Atkinson's index with high values of E. Both the McLoone index and Atkinson's index weight the low end of the distribution more heavily, but in ways that are different enough that the trends over time are not similar, at least for the states of Michigan and New York as we have examined them. In Michigan, the federal range ratio forms a fifth group, but in New York this measure shows the same pattern as the measures in the second group (coefficient of variation, etc.). Because groupings in New York could only be observed for one object, we are more inclined to give credence to the Michigan findings and to put the federal range ratio in its own group. In addition, the federal range ratio is consistent with different value judgments than the measures in the second group, particularly in its failure to include all observations in the distribution. Finally, the relative mean deviation often shows the same pattern as the measures in group two, but occasionally it does not. Thus, a sixth group could be formed for this measure. Until further research is done for other states, or over longer time periods, we are willing to put the relative mean deviation in group two, on the basis of the most common empirical results and on the basis of the similarity in value judgments with group-two measures. In summary, then, the empirical findings, combined with some decisions supported by innate values contained in the measures, yield the following five distinct groups of measures:

1. Range, restricted range, variance;
2. Coefficient of variation, Gini coefficient, Theil's measure, standard deviation of logarithms, Atkinson's index at low values of E, relative mean deviation;
3. McLoone index;
4. Atkinson's index at high values of E;
5. Federal range ratio.

These groupings imply that analysts should either choose specific measures based on the values inherent in them or, if this is not possible, alternative measures from different groups should then be used, so that sensitivity analyses can be performed. Some choices are possible a priori, however. In particular, group one can be eliminated due to the effects of inflation. Alternative strategies in which analysts choose measures solely from one group without a clear-cut adoption of the implied values run the risk of finding esoteric results that would not hold up with a more complete analysis.

Does the object make a difference when assessing horizontal-equity over time? The answer here is also yes. Most of the evidence comes from the Michigan analyses, because in New York only one dollar object and one price-adjusted dollar object are available.

Based on Michigan data, there are quite clearly differences in both trends and levels of equity, depending on the choice of input-based dollar objects. The significance of these differences for analysts is noted here. First, analysts need to establish which objects are of particular importance in their study. If, for example, the effect of federal categoricals are of interest, then the use of an object such as local plus total state revenues may result in erroneous conclusions. If a specific object cannot be chosen a priori, then several different ones should be used to assess the robustness of results.

Second, intertemporal and interstate comparisons must pay particular attention to the objects used. Misleading results could be obtained if the horizontal-equity comparisons across states or over time did not standardize the object. In addition, since alternative objects may have different relationships to one another depending on the state, it is probably wise to use several different objects (and thus several different comparisons).

Finally, the Michigan data do not yield any readily observable logical relationships among the patterns of the various objects. For example, even though instructional expenditures and local plus total state plus total federal revenue both include federal categorical revenue, these two objects do not show similar patterns. The reasons for the relationships (or lack thereof) among objects is a question for further research.

The Michigan analysis also showed that teacher resource objects are very different in trend and level from input-based dollar objects. This is true even when the comparison is with the dollar objects that one would think are most closely related to resources (e.g., instructional expenditures). Interestingly enough, the patterns of equity displayed by the resource objects is the same (J shaped) for all measures, even the group-one measures (range, etc.), because the resources are not affected by inflation. Analysts interested in resources must move beyond dollar objects.

Finally, when the dollar objects are price adjusted, the trends and levels of equity are affected in Michigan, and the levels are affected in New York. In Michigan, the trends reveal a new pattern when the dollar object is price adjusted. Also, results of comparisons between equity in the first and last years of the time series are sometimes reversed when an object is price adjusted.

For both states the level of equity generally improves after price adjustments are made. This result, in combination with the possibility of a changing pattern and the lack of similarity in patterns and levels between resources and price-adjusted dollars, means that estimation of a price index may be an important part of a horizontal-equity analysis in a state over time.

Conclusions on Horizontal-Equity Trends in Each State

It is easier to describe the trends that do not emerge in Michigan than those that do. We did not find that equity consistently worsened, improved, or stayed as it was over the time period. Equity often begins and ends the nine-year period at comparable levels, although various trends are in evidence in between. The group-one measures are the only exceptions, but these measures have the undesirable property of being affected by inflation. The first section of this chapter described the details of these trends in Michigan by measure and object; here we will summarize the findings at a more general level.

Two distinctly different patterns are found in Michigan. A number of measures and objects show an inverted-W pattern, where the equity levels at the beginning (1970) and the end (1978) of the time series are quite similar, but the middle years show less horizontal equity. When the beginning and end levels are not quite the same, it is more common for the last year to be slightly more equitable than the first. The middle years are never the most equitable for this pattern.

Another fairly common pattern, seen for the resource objects, is a J-shaped trend, where the end year (1978) is clearly more inequitable than the beginning year (1973) and the most equitable year is 1974. Because resource data are only available back to 1973, we do not know what shape the earlier years would display.

Occasionally a measure or an object does not fit into any of the above patterns, but seems unique unto itself. The patterns that do distinctly emerge in this way are not similar, but by and large they do not show consistent improvement or worsening. We do not know the reasons for this result but note that horizontal equity has not been a major goal of the Michigan system, and the 1974 reform paid little attention to it.

By contrast to Michigan, the New York data do show a trend for both dollar and price-adjusted dollars and for all measures except the McLoone index and Atkinson's index at high E values. That trend is a worsening of horizontal equity from the 1960s to the 1970s. The trend is not monotonic; nevertheless, it is unmistakable. We cannot be sure that revenue and resource objects would yield the same results. On the other hand, a price adjustment does not change the trend in New York, as it often does in Michigan.

8

EQUAL OPPORTUNITY IN MICHIGAN AND NEW YORK

The equal opportunity principle is a negative principle; a relationship between the education object and a particular characteristic of the pupil or district should *not* exist. In this chapter, the measurement of equal opportunity over time in a state is illustrated and analyzed with the continuing examples of Michigan and New York. The issue of how to determine whether a state's equal opportunity has improved or worsened is addressed, and as a by-product, conclusions are drawn for Michigan and New York.

The organization and strategy of analysis of this chapter resemble chapter 7 in one important respect, but are different in another. Similar to the analysis of horizontal equity, this investigation of equal opportunity is structured around questions of whether the measure of equal opportunity and the education object employed in the assessment affect conclusions about trends in equal opportunity over time. More specifically, where data permit, the following four questions are addressed:

1. Are there differences in the trends in equal opportunity due to the alternative measures? Do the measures form empirical groupings that are identical or similar to the conceptual groupings identified in chapter 2?

2. Are there differences either in the trends or in the levels of equal opportunity due to alternative input-based dollar objects such as local plus total state revenues versus instructional expenditures, holding the equity measure constant?

3. How does the adjustment of input-based dollar objects by price indexes affect the trends in equal opportunity, holding the measure constant? Does the price index alter the trends in equity, the absolute levels of equity, or both?

4. How do the trends in and levels of equal opportunity differ with input-based resource objects compared to input-based objects measured in dollars and price-adjusted dollars, holding the measure constant?

The important difference between this analysis of equal opportunity and the previous chapter's assessment of horizontal equity is that the equal-opportunity principle requires the specification of an independent variable as well as an education object. That is, the question, Equal opportunity with respect to what? must be answered before equal opportunity can be measured. Four different independent variables are utilized in this chapter, including property wealth per pupil, income per capita or per return, region of the state, and minority percent by district. Besides being the most common independent variables included in assessments of equal opportunity, they represent a range of variables from a measurement perspective because income and property wealth are measured in dollars per capita or per pupil, regions are discrete areas in the state, and minority is a percentage for each district.

In the first section of this chapter, data from Michigan are used to answer all four methodological questions for all four independent variables. The analysis of New York, presented in the second section, is more limited due to data availability, and only questions 1 and 3 can be answered using only property wealth, income, and region. Methodological conclusions, along with a summary of the findings for both states, comprise the third section. One final introductory point is a reminder that all analyses carried out in this chapter utilize the pupil unit of analysis. Therefore, when regression is employed as part of the equal-opportunity measures, the regressions are pupil weighted.

AN ASSESSMENT OF EQUAL OPPORTUNITY IN MICHIGAN

Michigan is examined over the nine-year period from 1970 to 1978 to answer the four methodological questions for equal opportunity. The first four parts of this section focus on equal opportunity in relation to per-pupil property wealth, per-capita income, region, and minority composition of districts in Michigan respectively, and all four of the methodological questions are addressed in each part. Again, as in chapter 7, only the K–12 districts are included in the Michigan data set.

Equal Opportunity with Respect to Property Wealth

As a result of scholarly development of the concept of equal opportunity in school finance and the role played by the state courts over the past fifteen years, property wealth is the most commonly studied independent variable for equal-opportunity concerns. In this part, the effects of alternative measures and objects on the measurement of equal opportunity with respect to wealth are examined, but this should not be interpreted to mean that per-pupil property wealth is, in any way, *the* correct measure of a school district's wealth. Other possible wealth measures such as per-capita property wealth, per-pupil or per-capita income, or fiscal capacity have been employed to assess equity, and the use of per-pupil wealth in this part and per-capita income in the next should be viewed as examples, albeit popular ones.

The definition of property wealth utilized in the analyses is per-pupil state-equalized assessed value of real estate and personal property. For the remainder of this part, the wealth measure is referred to more simply as per-pupil property wealth. Per-pupil property wealth (pupil weighted) was $16,240 and $29,340 in 1970 and 1978 respectively, thus increasing by 81 percent over the study period.

In the four subparts to follow, each of the methodological questions is answered for equal opportunity with respect to property wealth in Michigan, and we begin with an assessment of the differences among the measures.

Are There Differences in Trends Due to Alternative Measures? Do the Measures Form Empirical Groupings? Conceptual differences among four groups of regression-based equal-opportunity measures were discussed in chapter 2. The groups are comprised of the correlation, three slopes, four elasticities, and three adjusted relationship measures. In chapter 4, hypothetical examples were employed to show that conflicts among the measures can arise. In this subpart, nine years of data in Michigan are examined to find out whether there are differences in the trends in equal opportunity among these eleven regression-based measures when one state is assessed over time. The measures are analyzed using instructional expenditures as the object, but our research has shown that the conclusions on the measures drawn for this dollar object hold for the other objects as well.

The eleven equal-opportunity measures computed from regressions are displayed in figures 8.1 and 8.2. Note that the practice of graphical presentations that was begun in chapter 7 is continued in this chapter. Figures 8.1 and 8.2 include graphs of the eleven equal-opportunity measures, with the correlation and the elasticities in figure 8.1 and the slopes and the adjusted relationship measures in figure 8.2. If our concern is focused on trends in equal-opportunity, then for instructional expenditures with respect to wealth in Michigan, the overall patterns displayed by all eleven measures are very similar. In every case, either 1970 or 1971 is the least equitable year, 1978 is the most equitable year, and equity increases from 1973 to 1978. There are some minor differences in the trends over the first four years, but these differences are overshadowed by the similarities.

Are There Differences Either in the Trends or in the Levels Due to Alternative Input-Based Dollar Objects? The second question of concern for equal opportunity with respect to wealth is whether the trends over time are influenced by the choice of an input-based dollar object. Given the consistency among the measures of equal opportunity with respect to wealth in Michigan, only four of the equal-opportunity measures are discussed in the comparison of dollar objects, and only two are shown graphically. The measures examined in this subpart include the correlation, the simple slope, the simple elasticity, and the simple adjusted relationship measure. The six objects are the same ones

Figure 8.1 Michigan: Equal-Opportunity Measures for Instructional Expenditures with Respect to Wealth—Correlation and Elasticities

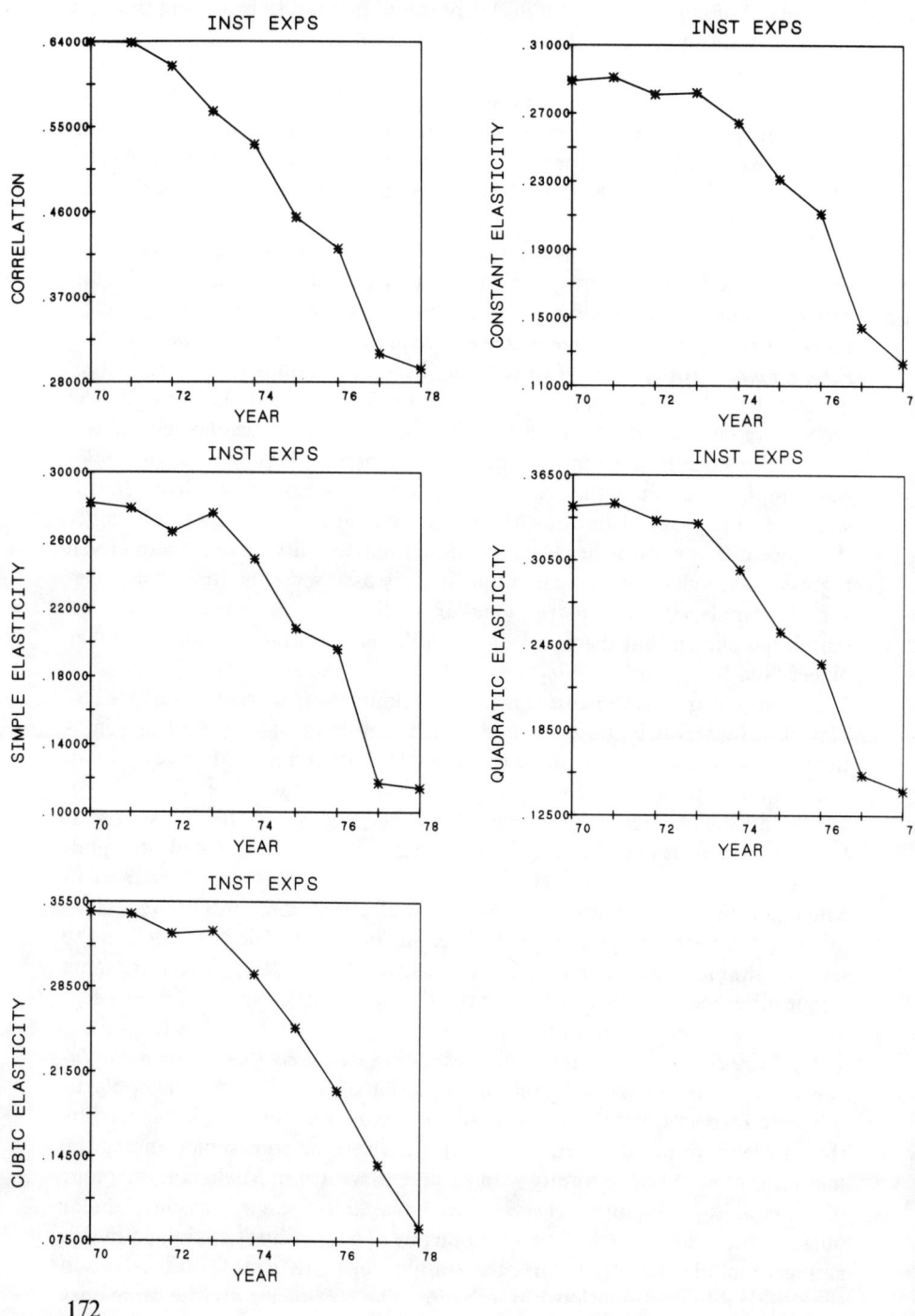

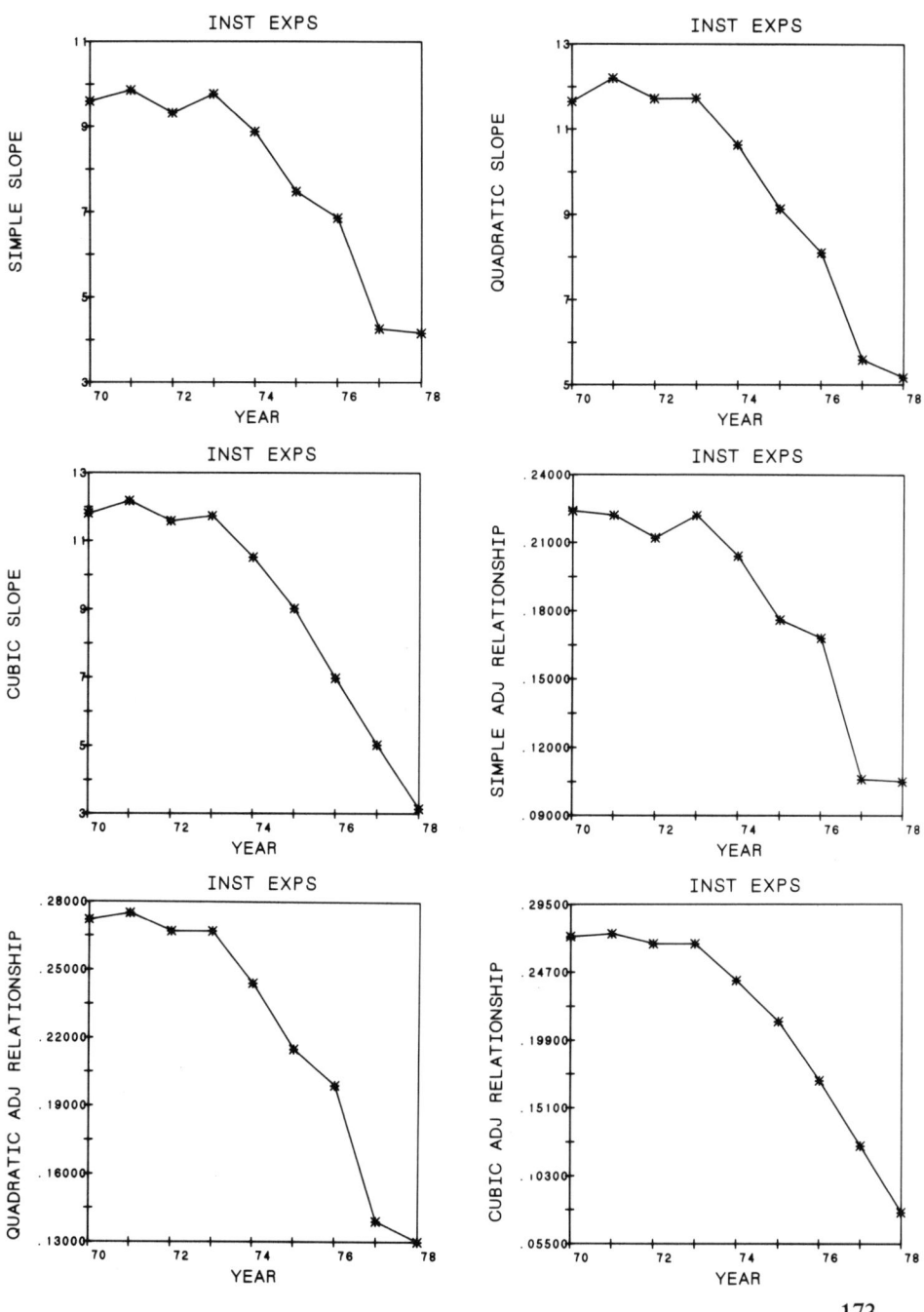

Figure 8.2 Michigan: Equal-Opportunity Measures for Instructional Expenditures with Respect to Wealth—Slopes and Adjusted Relationship Measures

examined in chapter 7 and include instructional expenditures (INST EXPS), current operating expenditures (COE), current operating expenditures less transportation (COE − TRANS), local plus state membership revenue (LOC + STATE MEMB REV), local plus total state revenue (LOC + ALL STATE REV), and local plus total state plus total federal revenue (ALL REV). The measures are available for nine years, except for current expenditures less transportation, where the measures are computed for the last six years of the study period.

Are the trends similar across all six input-based dollar objects? Similar, yes; identical, no. From a broad perspective, all objects and all measures show a general improvement in equal opportunity with respect to wealth in Michigan over the nine-year period. Regardless of the measure or the object, Michigan's relationship between dollar objects and wealth is consistently less at the end of the period than it was at the beginning, and one of the last few years is always the most equitable. Furthermore, equal opportunity almost always improves from one year to the next; the instances when equal opportunity worsens constitute a small minority of the year-to-year intervals. Figures 8.3 and 8.4 document these points for the correlation and the simple elasticity respectively.

Although the general patterns are similar across measures and objects, there are certain consistent differences across objects. In terms of the pattern of equal opportunity over time, all are subtle differences related to whether the object is expenditure based or revenue based. The pattern for the expenditure objects usually shows relatively small changes from 1970 through 1973 or 1974, with relatively larger changes after that. For revenue objects, the relatively flat pattern at the beginning of the period does not hold, and in fact, for local plus state membership revenues there are relatively smaller changes at the end of the nine-year period.

A comparison of the levels of equal opportunity across objects leads to some pronounced differences among the objects. For each measure, the improvement in equal opportunity over the period is greater for the expenditure objects than for the revenue objects. Furthermore, among the revenue objects, local plus total state plus total federal revenue is the most equitable revenue object at the end of the study period, and local plus state membership revenue is the least equitable revenue object at the end of the period. Viewing the differences in levels among objects in another way, all objects begin the period at the same level, for each measure, but there are consistent differences in where the objects end the period.

The differences in the trends that result from the six input-based dollar objects in Michigan are rather small. Regardless of which object is chosen, Michigan shows consistent improvement in equal opportunity with respect to wealth over the period 1970 to 1978. Where the object matters is not so much in the trend but in the actual level of equal opportunity with respect to wealth at any one time. There are consistent differences between the revenue-based

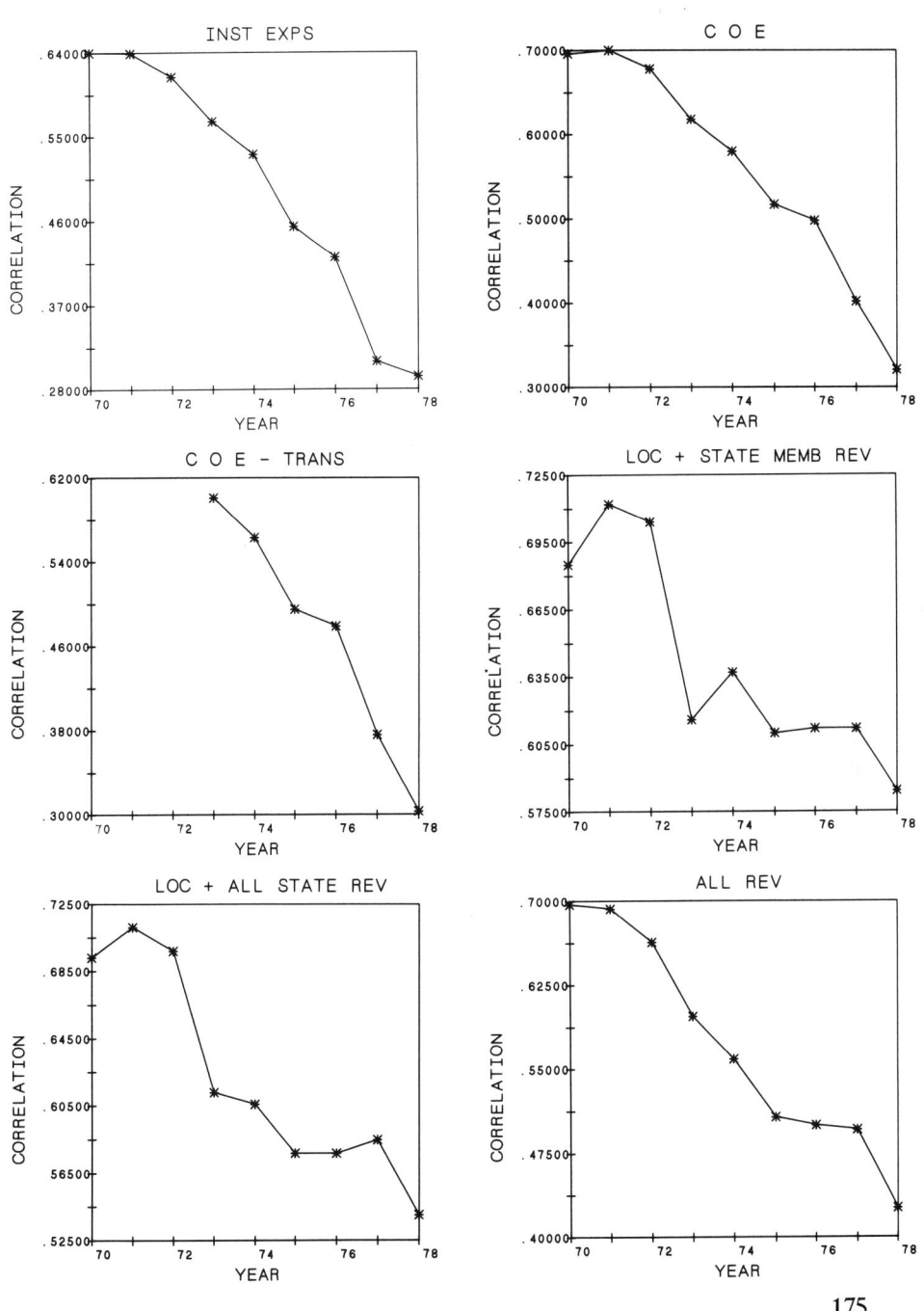

Figure 8.3 Michigan: Comparisons among Six Input-Based Dollar Objects Using the Correlation as the Equal-Opportunity Measure with Respect to Wealth

Figure 8.4 Michigan: Comparisons among Six Input-Based Dollar Objects Using the Simple Elasticity as the Equal-Opportunity Measure with Respect to Wealth

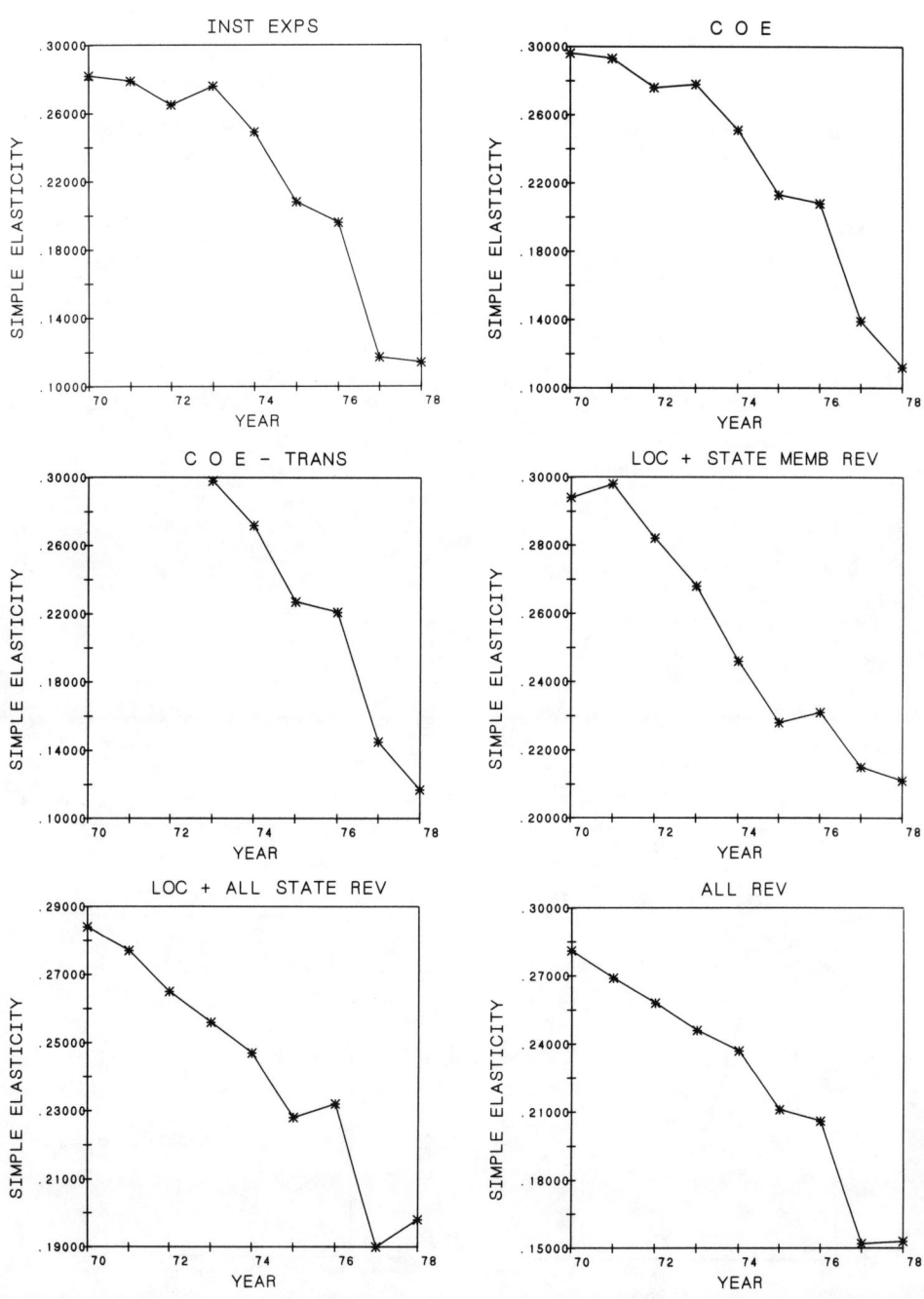

and the expenditure-based objects, and within the revenue-based objects as well.

How Does the Adjustment of the Input-Based Dollar Objects by Price Indexes Affect the Trends in and Levels of Equal Opportunity? Throughout the book, price indexes are employed to remove the variation in dollar objects caused by price-level differences within a state at one point in time. In this subpart, equal-opportunity measures with respect to property wealth computed with dollar objects are compared to the same measures computed with price-adjusted dollar objects to determine whether price indexes cause changes in the trends and levels of equal opportunity.

Two price indexes were used in chapter 7 to show their effects on the measurement of horizontal equity. Since the general conclusions in chapter 7 were essentially identical for both price indexes, and because the overall conclusions in this subpart are consistent across price indexes, only objects adjusted by one price index, Index 1 (ADJ1), are presented.

Price-adjusted dollar inputs are compared to dollar inputs using three objects and four measures of equal opportunity with respect to wealth. The three per-pupil objects are those that were included in a similar analysis in chapter 7: instructional expenditures, local plus total state revenues, and local plus total state plus total federal revenues. The four equal-opportunity measures incorporate a range of value judgments and include the simple correlation, the simple slope, the simple elasticity, and the simple adjusted relationship measure. The trends in equal opportunity over the nine-year period are displayed in figures 8.5 and 8.6, where each figure shows the three dollar and the three price-adjusted dollar objects, using the correlation and the simple elasticity, respectively. Since the conclusions can be drawn from these two measures, the other two graphs are not presented.

Does the adjustment of input-based dollar objects by a price index alter the trend of equal opportunity over time? The answer is yes, since for two of the three objects the trends over the nine-year period are almost reversed!

The pattern of equal opportunity over time for dollar objects is one of fairly consistent improvement over the nine-year period. After instructional expenditures are price adjusted, the general pattern is still one of improvement in equal opportunity over the nine-year period. The dramatic differences occur between the dollar and the price-adjusted dollar inputs for the two dollar-revenue objects: local plus total state revenues and local plus total state plus total federal revenues. While the dollar-revenue objects show improvement over time, the price-adjusted dollar-revenue objects are U shaped, with improvement at the beginning of the period and deterioration at the end. In fact, three of the four trends for the price-adjusted revenue objects end the nine-year period with equal opportunity at a lower level than when the period began.

Not only does the price adjustment affect the trends in equal opportunity, but the levels of equal opportunity are different when the dollar objects are

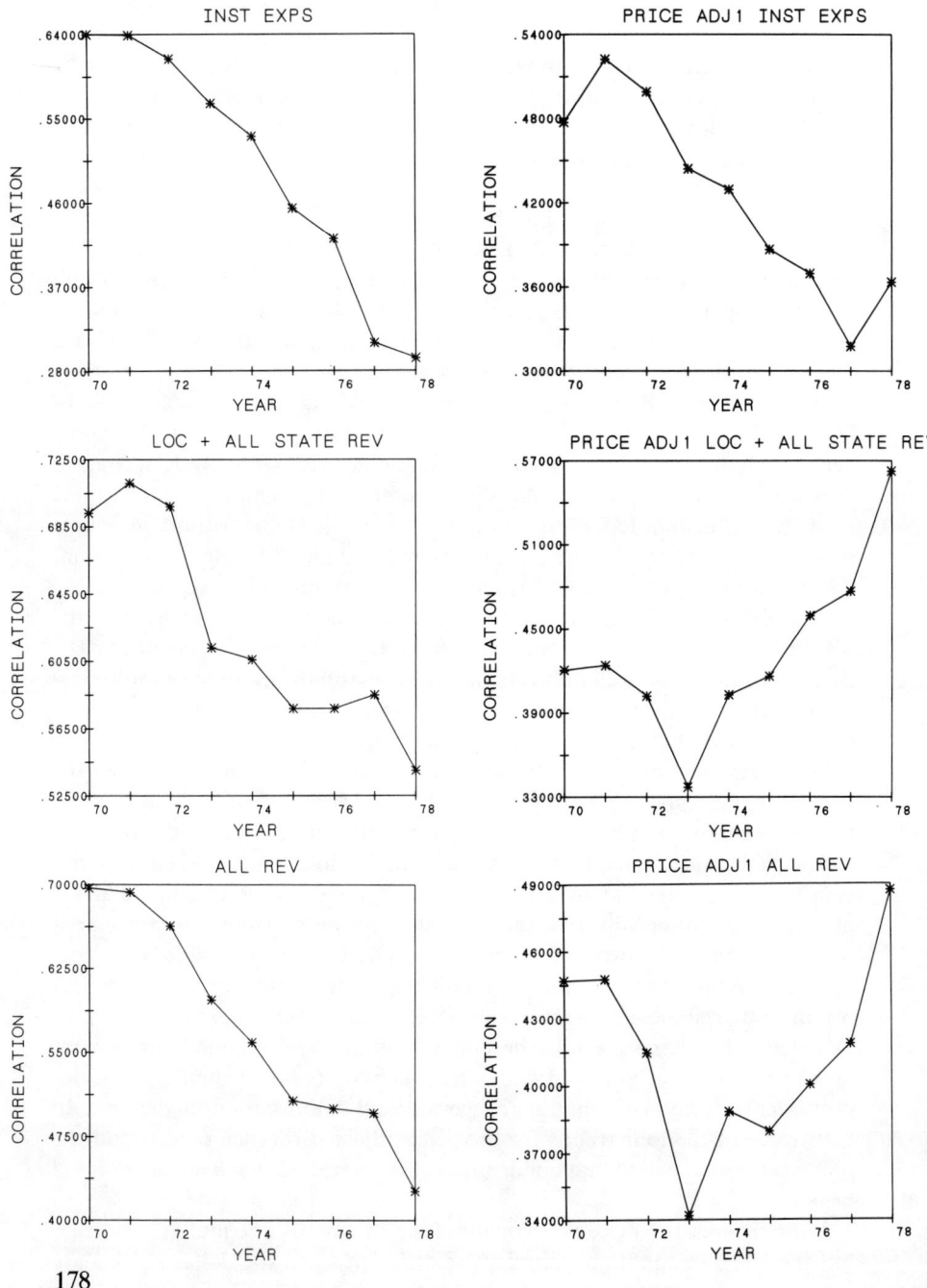

Figure 8.5 Michigan: Comparisons among Input-Based Dollar and Price-Adjusted Dollar Objects Using the Correlation as the Equal-Opportunity Measure with Respect to Wealth

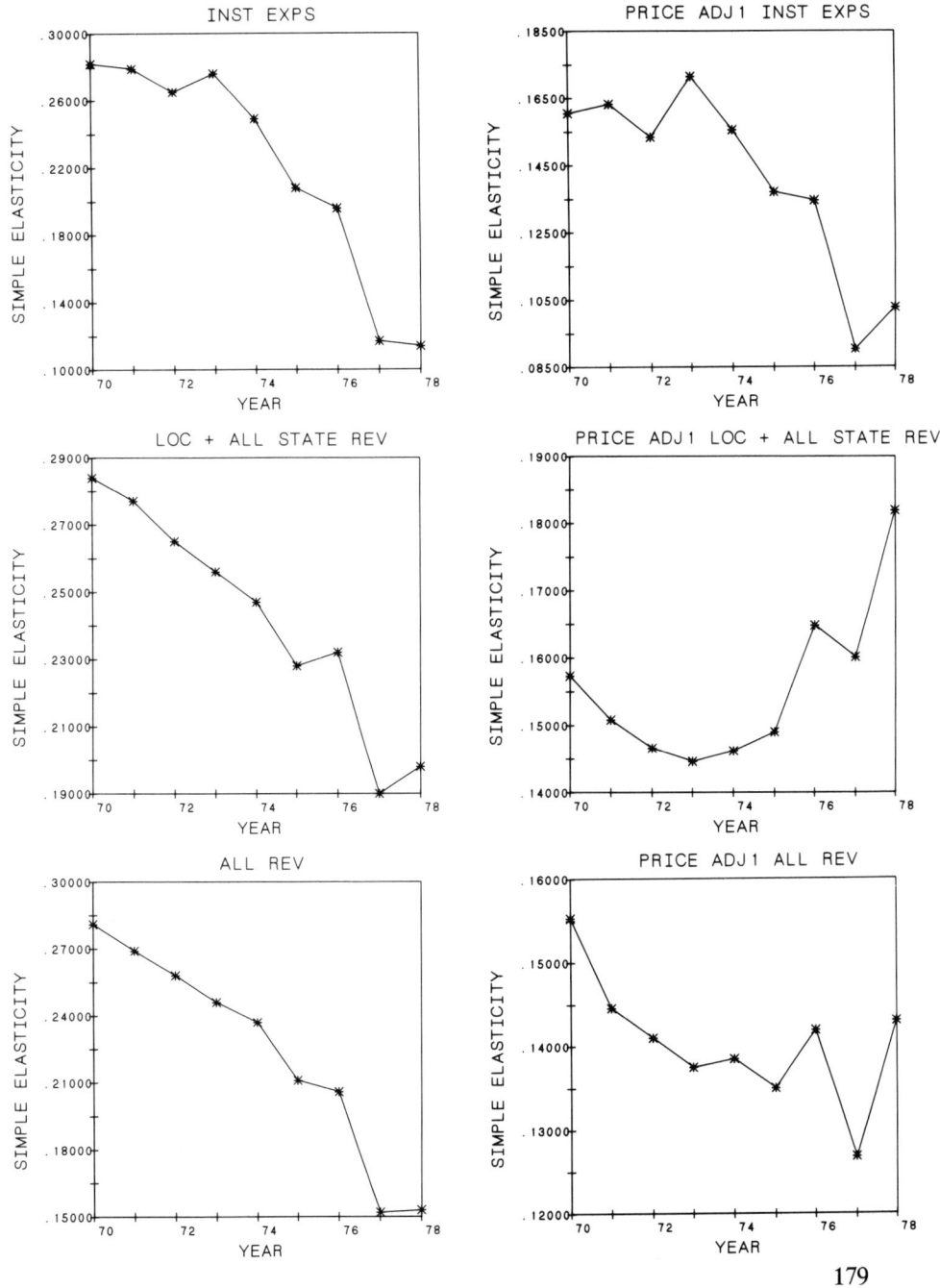

Figure 8.6 Michigan: Comparisons among Input-Based Dollar and Price-Adjusted Dollar Objects Using the Simple Elasticity as the Equal-Opportunity Measure with Respect to Wealth

price adjusted. For a given measure and object, greater equal opportunity usually exists with the price adjustment than with the unadjusted object. When instructional expenditures are the object, equal opportunity is always greater after the price adjustment, except for the last two years with the correlation as the measure. Both adjusted and unadjusted instructional expenditures improve over time, with adjusted instructional expenditures almost always showing greater equal opportunity.

The two revenue objects also show greater equal opportunity after the price-index adjustment. In all cases, the revenue objects show substantially more equal opportunity at the beginning of the period when the revenues are price-adjusted than for unadjusted revenues. And even at the end of the period, despite the fact that the trends in equal opportunity are opposite, the unadjusted revenues still display less equal opportunity than the price-adjusted revenues. Again, the only exception is the last year when the simple correlation is the equal-opportunity measure. Thus, some of the unequal opportunity observed with respect to wealth at the beginning of the study period can be attributed to intrastate price differences.

This comparison of dollar and price-adjusted dollar objects demonstrates the substantial difference that price indexes can make. Dramatic differences in the trends and levels of equal opportunity occur with sufficient frequency to justify the conclusion that price-adjusted dollar objects are not the same as unadjusted dollar objects. Not only are price-adjusted objects preferred conceptually, but their inclusion also affects empirical findings.

Do Trends or Levels Differ for Resource Objects Compared to Dollar and Price-Adjusted Dollar Objects? The third broad category of input-based objects examined in this assessment of equal opportunity with respect to wealth is comprised of direct measures of resources. Although conceptually all resources used as inputs in the education process could be analyzed, only teachers per 1,000 pupils is employed in this chapter as an example. In addition, although data on two measures of teachers per 1,000 pupils for six years are available, the differences between the two measures are very minor, and only the more inclusive measure, all classroom teachers per 1,000 pupils, is presented here. All classroom teachers includes K-12 teachers, special education teachers, and vocational education teachers.

Figure 8.7 shows the trends in equal opportunity with respect to wealth when all classroom teachers per 1,000 pupils is the object, utilizing four equal-opportunity measures. When figure 8.7 is compared with figures 8.5 and 8.6, the differences between the resource object and the dollar and price-adjusted dollar objects are easily seen.

First, in terms of the trend in equal opportunity over time, the pattern of the resource object is neither the generally improving trend displayed by the unadjusted dollar objects and the price-adjusted expenditure object nor the worsening situation depicted by the price-adjusted revenue objects. The resource object shows an improving-worsening-improving pattern that is not

Figure 8.7 Michigan: Equal Opportunity with Respect to Wealth Using All Teachers per 1,000 Pupils as the Object and Four Equal-Opportunity Measures

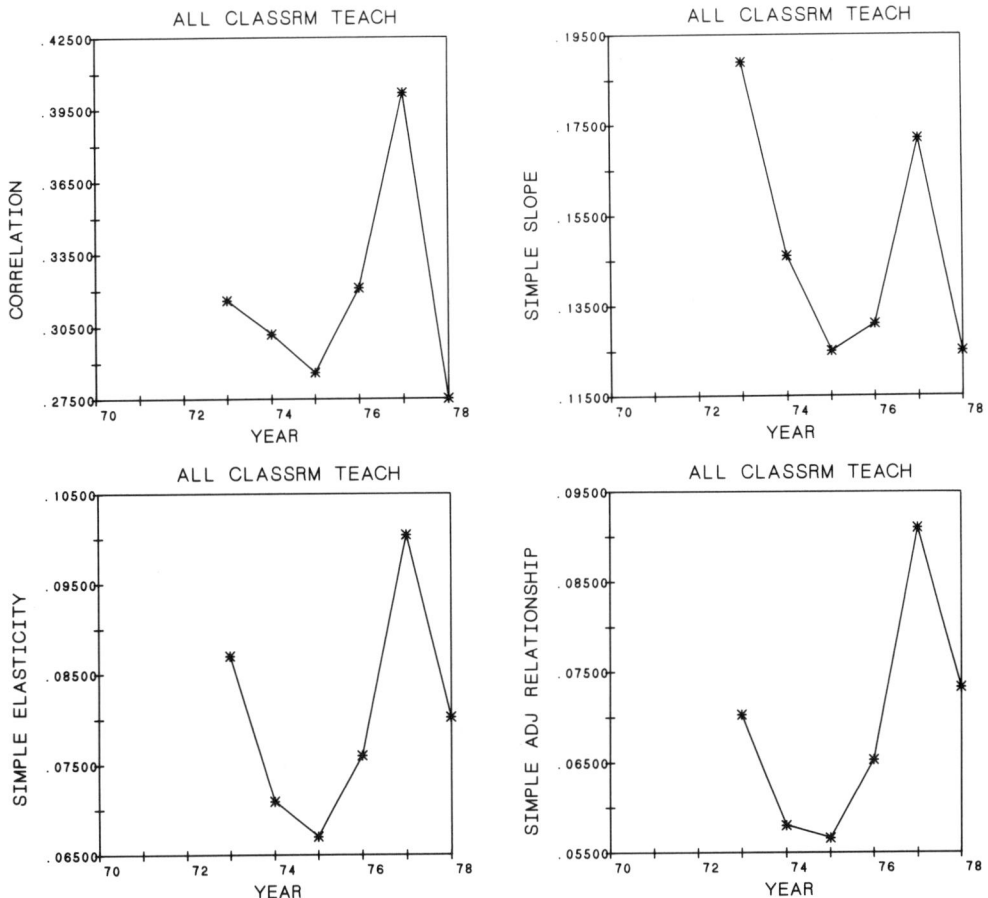

even closely related to any of the previously examined trends in equal opportunity with respect to wealth over the comparable six-year period.

A second dimension for comparisons between resource object and dollar objects is the level of equal opportunity at various points in time. Since the correlation, the simple slope, the simple elasticity, and the simple adjusted relationship measure are insensitive to percentage changes in the dependent variable, the absolute levels of these measures can be compared across objects. A comparison of resource object with dollar and price-adjusted dollar objects shows that, with very few exceptions, equal opportunity with respect to property wealth is greater with the resource object than with either dollar or price-adjusted dollar objects over the entire six years.

Equal Opportunity with Respect to Income

Equal opportunity with respect to property wealth can be viewed as one way to assess the broader concern of equal opportunity with respect to ability to pay. While property wealth is the most common measure of ability to pay in school-finance analyses, this should not be interpreted to mean that it is the only or the "correct" measure of ability to pay. Research in school finance[1] and in public finance[2] has explored the effects of and the rationale for a variety of ability-to-pay concepts, and in many cases the alternatives include a measure of income. Furthermore, seven states now utilize income and property wealth to measure school-district ability to pay in their state aid formulas.[3]

Since income has been recognized as an important ability-to-pay measure, the effects of alternative measures and education objects on equal opportunity with respect to income in Michigan are investigated in this part by answering the four questions posed at the beginning of this chapter. Before beginning the analysis, however, a few comments on the definition of income are in order.

In this analysis, income is measured according to the census definition of money income, because these data are available on a school-district basis for 1969. Money income is less inclusive than personal income, since imputed income such as the rental value of homes and food grown on farms is not included in money income. Also, money income includes social security taxes paid by employees, while personal income does not.

Although income data for 1969 are the most up-to-date on a school district basis, the per-capita-income data used here have been updated using the more recent per-capita-income figures from counties and incorporated places in 1975 and 1977 that are prepared by the U.S. Bureau of the Census for revenue-sharing allocations. Since school districts in Michigan are not coterminous with municipalities, several assumptions and approximations were

---

1. The school-finance literature is most often concerned with the way alternative concepts of wealth affect the distribution fo state aid. See, for example, Allan Odden, *Alternative Measures of School District Wealth* (Denver, Co.: Education Commission of the States, 1976); Robert J. Thornton, "Towards the Development of More Comprehensive Measures of School District Wealth," in Esther O. Tron, ed., *Selected Papers in School Finance, 1981* (Washington, D.C.: Department of Education, National Institute of Education, 1981), pp. 357-444; and Walter W. McMahon, "A Broader Measure of Wealth and Effort for Education Equity and Tax Equity," *Journal of Education Finance* 4, no. 1 (summer 1978): 65-88.

2. The public-finance literature focuses on the rationale for the alternative measures of wealth and the empirical differences among the measures. See, for example, John S. Akin, "Fiscal Capacity and the Estimation Method of the Advisory Commission on Intergovernmental Relations," *National Tax Journal* 26, no. 2 (June 1973): 275-91; Advisory Commission on Intergovernmental Relations, *Measuring the Fiscal "Blood Pressure" of the States—1964-1975* (Washington, D.C.: Advisory Commission on Intergovernmental Relations, 1977); and John S. Akin, "Estimates of State Resource Constraints Derived from a Specific Utility Function: An Alternative Measure of Fiscal Capacity," *National Tax Journal* 32, no. 1 (March 1979): 61-71.

3. See Allan Odden and John Augenblick, *School Finance Reform in the States: 1980* (Denver, Co.: Education Commission of the States, 1980), p. 4.

used to update the 1969 income data.[4] Per capita income in Michigan (pupil weighted) was $3,066 and $5,528 in 1970 and 1978 respectively.

Are There Differences in Trends Due to Alternative Measures? Do the Measures Form Empirical Groupings? Although major differences among the equal-opportunity measures were not found when per-pupil property wealth was the independent variable, we cannot assume that these findings will be replicated with a different independent variable. In this part, the eleven measures of equal opportunity are compared over the nine years in Michigan with per capita income as the independent variable.

The eleven equal-opportunity measures with respect to income for the nine-year study period are graphed in figures 8.8 and 8.9. The correlation and the elasticities are presented in figure 8.8, and the slopes and the adjusted relationship measures are included in figure 8.9. A comparison of these eleven equal-opportunity measures shows that most of the measures are quite similar on most dimensions, but the measures are not perfect matches. The similarity can be seen in the improvement in equal opportunity between 1970 and 1972 and the deterioration in equal opportunity between 1972 and 1975. This consistency across measures does not hold between 1975 and 1978. Most measures show an improvement in equal opportunity from 1975 to 1978. However, the correlation shows an uneven but generally worsening trend between 1975 and 1978, and the simple elasticity and the simple adjusted relationship measure display a relatively level pattern.

Thus, although the differences are not dramatic, the measures and the functional form do matter in some instances. At a general level, the correlation displays a different pattern than the other ten measures. Furthermore, it appears that the functional form of the regression can also affect the trends, judging by the relatively level pattern over the last four years for the simple elasticity and the simple adjusted relationship measure.

These results suggest that differences can appear among the equal-opportunity measures, and a second dependent variable is therefore examined to see if the findings are replicated. Although the graphs are not presented here, similar findings emerge when we examine equal opportunity with respect to

4. The per-capita-income figures were updated differently, depending upon whether the school district is coterminous with an incorporated place in Michigan. For the school districts that are coterminous with incorporated places (most of which are in Wayne County), per-capita-income data from the incorporated place from 1969, 1974, and 1977 were used to calculate average annual growth rates for the 1969 to 1975 period and the 1975 to 1977 period. These annual growth rates were then applied to the per-capita-income figures for each school district. Thus, the average annual growth rate is used to obtain yearly estimates of per capita income in the school districts.

For school districts that are not coterminous with incorporated places, a less precise procedure was employed. Essentially, the average annual growth rates in per capita income were calculated for the counties in Michigan using data from 1969, 1975, and 1977, and these growth rates were applied to each school district in the county. However, in the counties that contain school districts that were covered under the coterminous category, the income and population for the coterminous incorporated places were excluded from the calculation of the county's average annual per-capita-income growth rate.

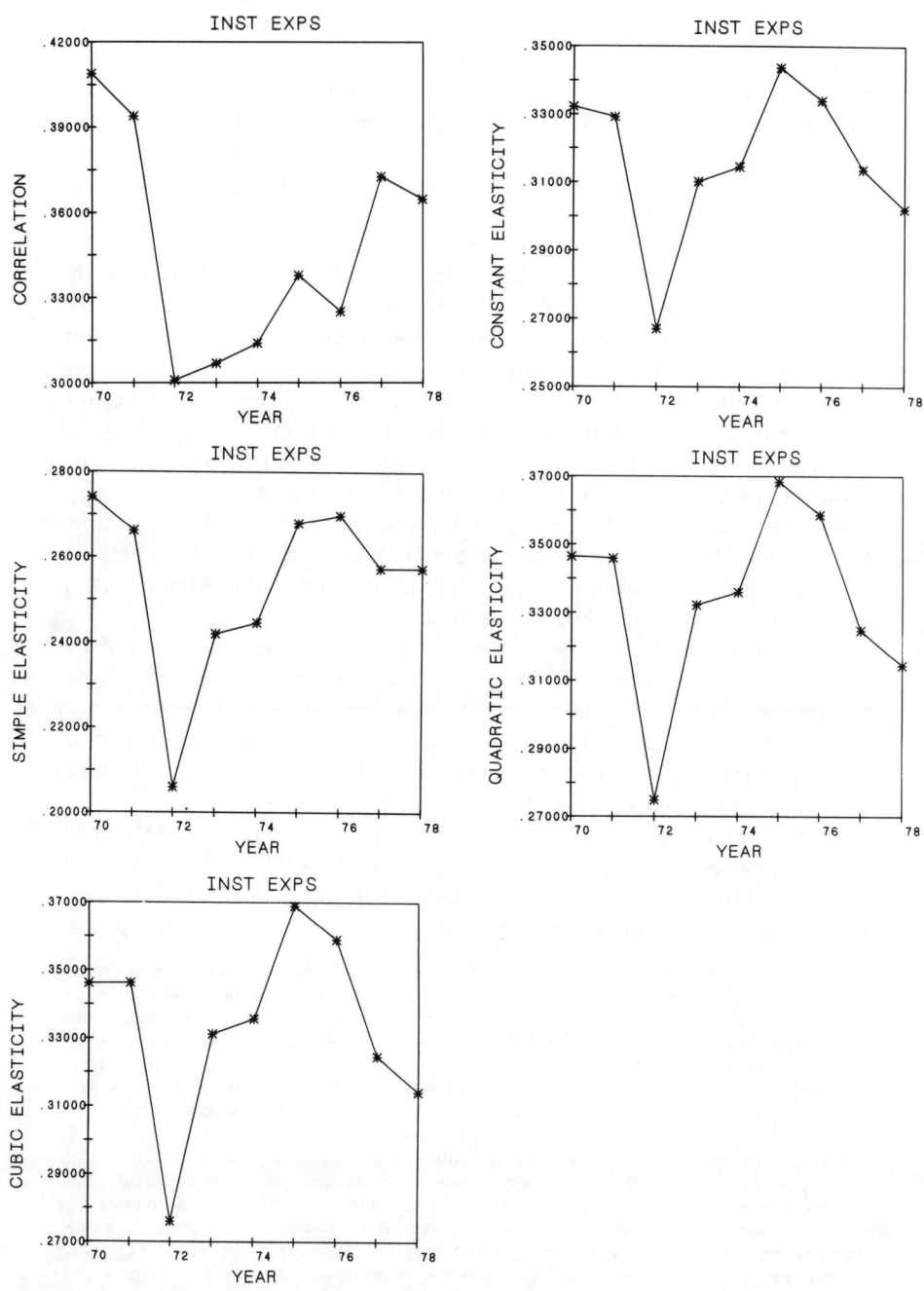

Figure 8.8 Michigan: Equal-Opportunity Measures for Instructional Expenditures with Respect to Income—Correlations and Elasticities

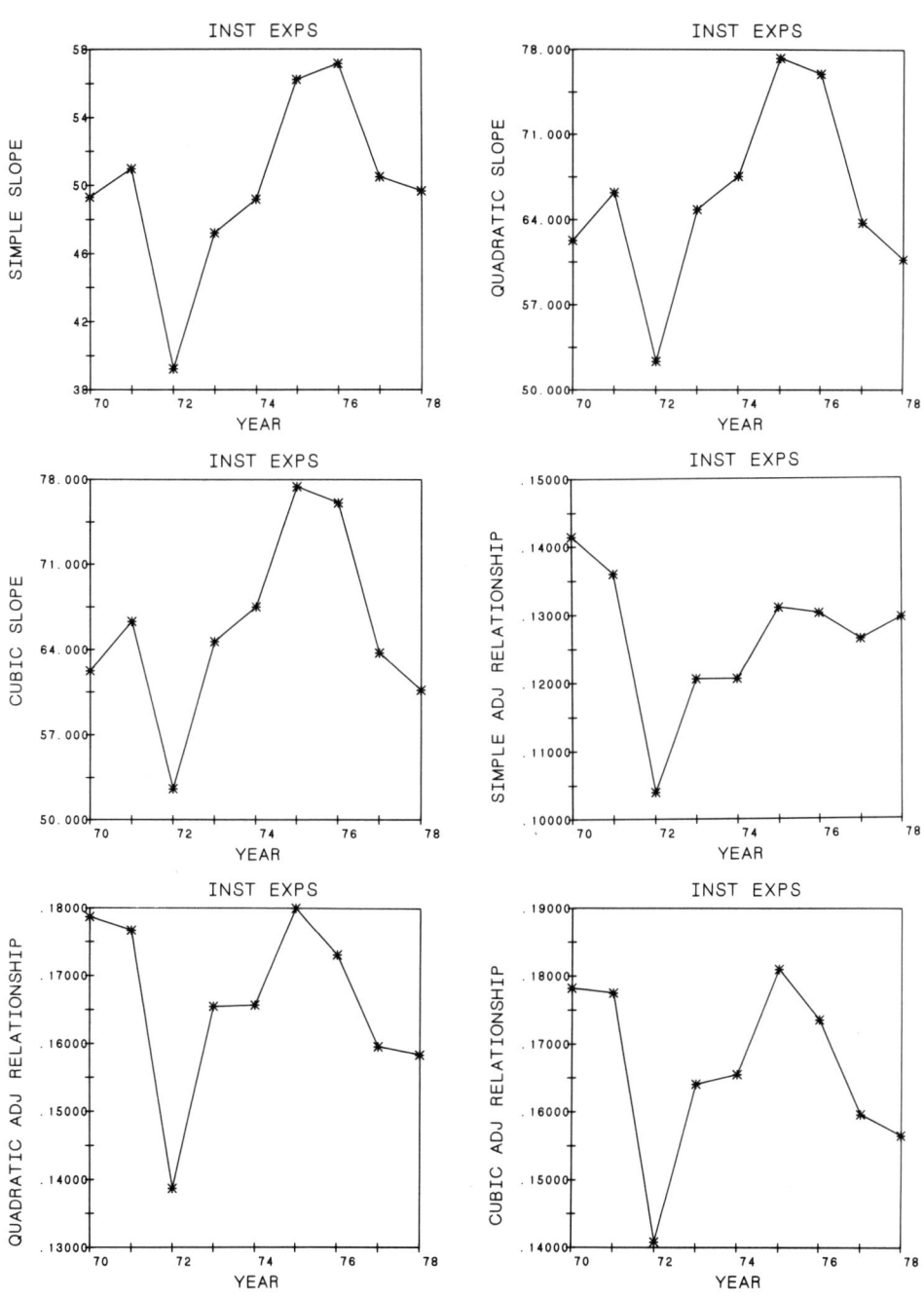

Figure 8.9 Michigan: Equal-Opportunity Measures for Instructional Expenditures with Respect to Income—Slopes and Adjusted Relationship Measures

185

income with local plus total state plus total federal revenues as the dependent variable. For the most part, the elasticities and the adjusted relationship measures are quite similar and are somewhat different from either the correlation or the slopes. Within particular groupings such as the elasticities and the adjusted relationship measures, there are minor variations due to the functional form of the regression.

Using equal opportunity with respect to income as our focus, the answer to the first question is that there are differences among the equal-opportunity measures, but the differences are hardly radical. Further, these modest differences emerge across types of measures as well as across functional form. For both dependent variables, the elasticities and the adjusted relationship measures are fairly similar, and the correlations and, to a lesser degree, the slopes are modestly different compared to the other measures. The differences among measures of equal opportunity in Michigan are slightly greater for income than those that were found when wealth was the independent variable.

Are There Differences Either in the Trends or in the Levels Due to Alternative Input-Based Dollar Objects? The next issue to be considered for equal opportunity with respect to income is whether there are differences among the alternative input-based dollar objects. Four objects are examined: instructional expenditures, local plus state membership revenues, local plus total state revenues, and local plus total state plus total federal revenues. Only two measures are displayed, the simple correlation and the simple elasticity in figures 8.10 and 8.11, respectively. Results for the simple slope and the simple adjusted relationship measure are similar to those for the simple elasticity.

As has been the case in several previous analyses, there are definite similarities in the trends in equal opportunity regardless of the object. Specifically, in almost every case there is an initial period of improvement in equal opportunity, followed, somewhere in the study period, by a period when equal opportunity worsens. Furthermore, relative to the overall variation in equal opportunity over the nine-year period, the levels of equal opportunity in 1970 and 1978 are often similar.

Figure 8.10, which uses the correlation as the measure of equal opportunity, contains little in the way of differences among the objects in the trends in equal opportunity. The trends are not a perfect match, but there is a basic U shape from 1971 to 1977.

There is somewhat less similarity among objects for the simple slope, the simple elasticity, and the simple adjusted relationship measure. In most cases the differences between instructional expenditures and the other three revenue objects are the most obvious for each measure, and this can be seen for the simple elasticity in figure 8.11. These differences appear when the trend in instructional expenditures over the six years from 1973 to 1978 is compared to the trend in the revenue objects over the same period, for all measures except the correlation. Often, equal opportunity worsens and then improves

Figure 8.10 Michigan: Comparisons among Four Input-Based Dollar Objects Using the Correlation as the Equal-Opportunity Measure with Respect to Income

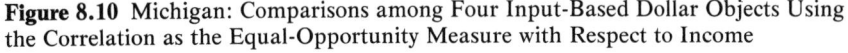

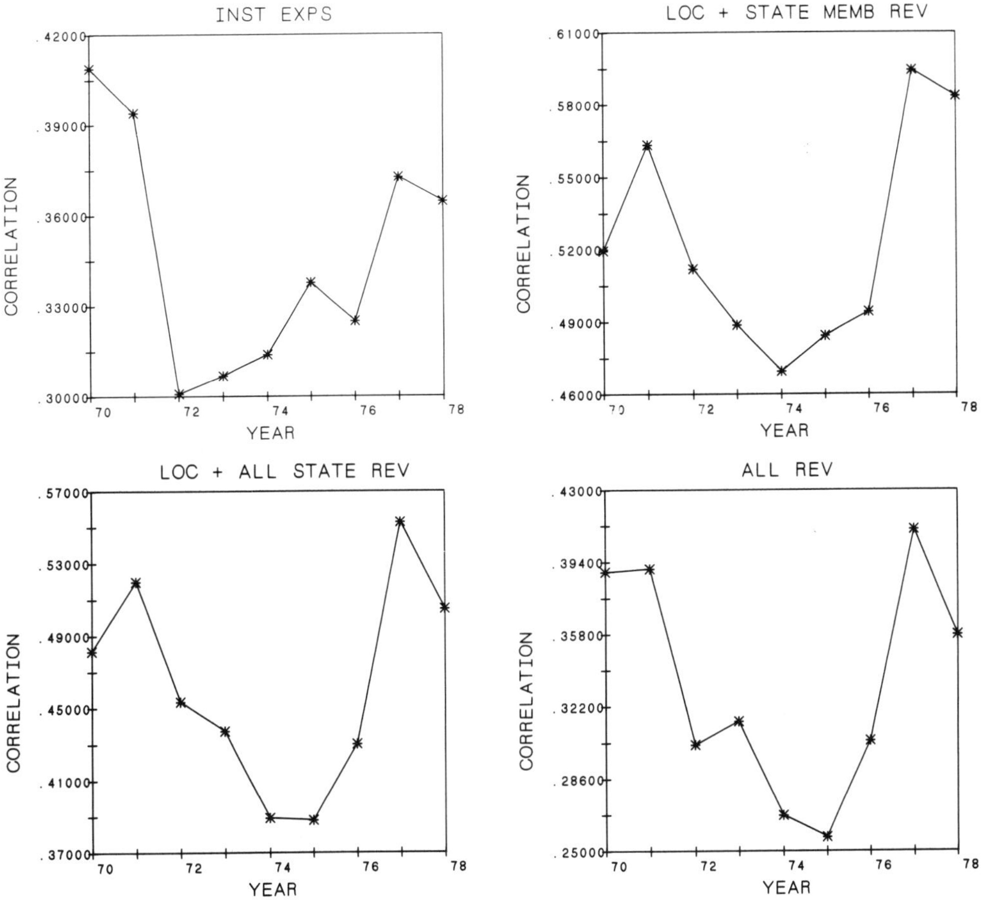

for instructional expenditures over the six-year period, while the revenue objects usually improve between 1973 and 1974, stay relatively constant for a year, and then worsen. The discrepancy between the expenditure and the revenue objects is a replication of the findings from previous examinations of the input-based dollar objects.

The levels of equal opportunity can also be compared across objects, and consistent differences are apparent. In virtually all cases, instructional expenditures and local plus total state plus total federal revenues show greater equal opportunity with respect to income than the remaining two revenue objects, local plus state membership revenues and local plus total state revenues. Federal revenues, when added to state and local revenues, reduce the

Figure 8.11 Michigan: Comparisons among Four Input-Based Dollar Objects Using the Simple Elasticity as the Equal-Opportunity Measure with Respect to Income

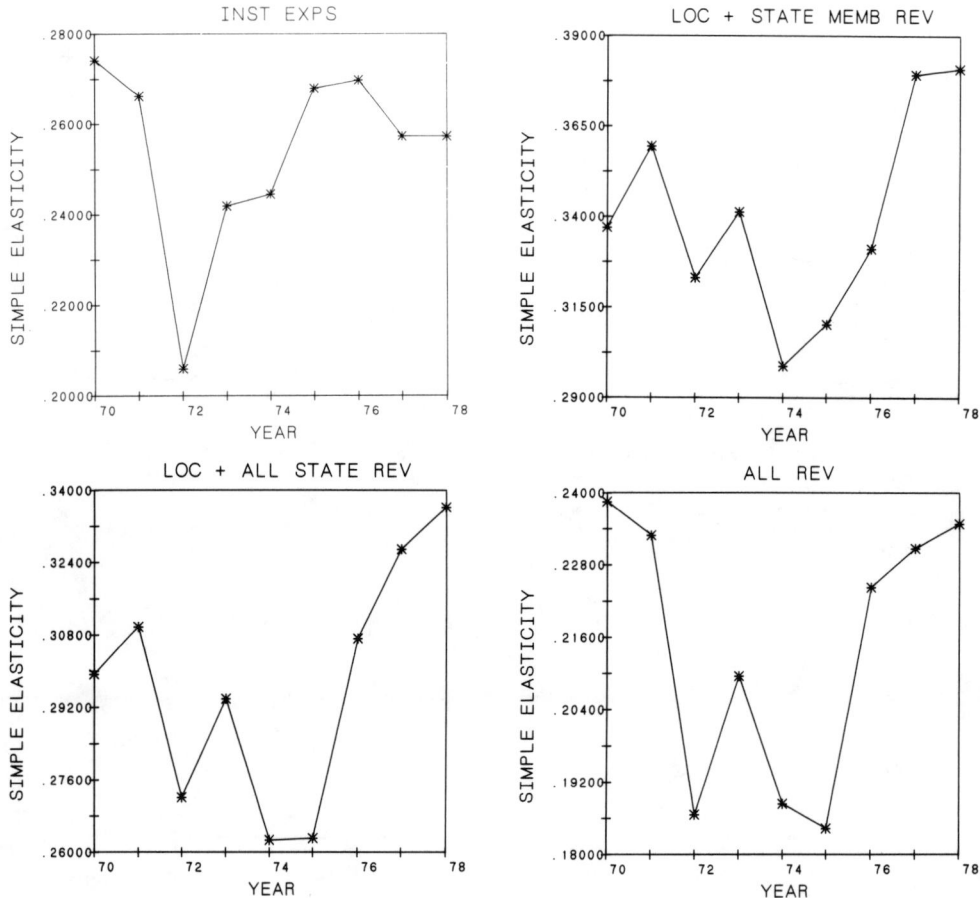

relationship between dollars and income considerably, and this is consistent with the design of several federal programs that are distributed in part in inverse proportion to income. Also, since the level of equal opportunity of instructional expenditures is roughly equal to total revenues, dollars devoted to classroom and nonclassroom activities are probably related in a similar manner to income.

Although the differences are not dramatic, the assessment in this subpart suggests that the selection of an input-based dollar object may affect both trends and levels in equal opportunity with respect to income. At a general level the patterns across objects are similar, but for part of the study period, differences emerged between the expenditure and the revenue objects. Further differences are revealed when the levels of equal opportunity are compared across objects, and these are important not only in the single-state intertemporal analyses but in comparisons across states as well.

How Does the Adjustment of the Input-Based Dollar Objects by Price Indexes Affect the Trends in and Levels of Equal Opportunity? Earlier in this chapter, when dollar objects were adjusted with a price index, both the trends and the levels in equal opportunity with respect to property wealth were substantially altered as a result. In this subpart, dollar and price-adjusted dollar objects are compared in a similar fashion, with the focus on the equity principle of equal opportunity with respect to income rather than property wealth.

The differences between dollars and price-adjusted dollars are examined with one price index (Index 1), three objects (instructional expenditures, local plus total state revenues, and local plus total state plus total federal revenues), and four measures of equal opportunity (correlation, simple slope, simple elasticity, and simple adjusted relationship measure). However, only two measures are displayed in graphs. Figures 8.12 and 8.13 display the trends in equal opportunity with respect to income for three dollar and three price-adjusted dollar objects, with the simple correlation in figure 8.12 and the simple elasticity in figure 8.13.

The adjustment by the price index has very little effect on the trends in equal opportunity over the nine-year period in Michigan. In every case the major features of the pattern are recognizable with and without the price index. There are a few small differences, such as the flattening of the 1975 and 1976 peak for instructional expenditures for all measures except the correlation, but by and large, the price adjustment does not alter the trends in equal opportunity over time.

In contrast, the price index has a consistent effect on the level of equal opportunity over time in Michigan. In every case the price-adjusted object shows substantially more equal opportunity than the unadjusted object, holding the measure constant. In fact, for all objects and measures except the correlation and instructional expenditures, the year during the nine years with the least equal opportunity (the highest point on the graph) with the price-adjusted object is always more equitable than the year during the nine years that shows the most equal opportunity (the lowest point on the graph) with the unadjusted object. While the price index affects the level of equal opportunity, it does not change the relative equity of the three objects. Both with and without the price adjustment, local plus total state plus total federal revenues is the most equitable and local plus total state revenues is the least equitable, with instructional expenditures usually in between.

Thus, the most pronounced effect of price-index adjustments is an alteration in the level of equal opportunity with respect to income. Actually, the improvement in the price-adjusted measures is such that at times, particularly 1975, the two price-adjusted revenue objects are close to zero, signifying an absence of a relationship between the object and income. Despite these

Figure 8.12 Michigan: Comparisons among Input-Based Dollar and Price-Adjusted Dollar Objects Using the Correlation as the Equal-Opportunity Measure with Respect to Income

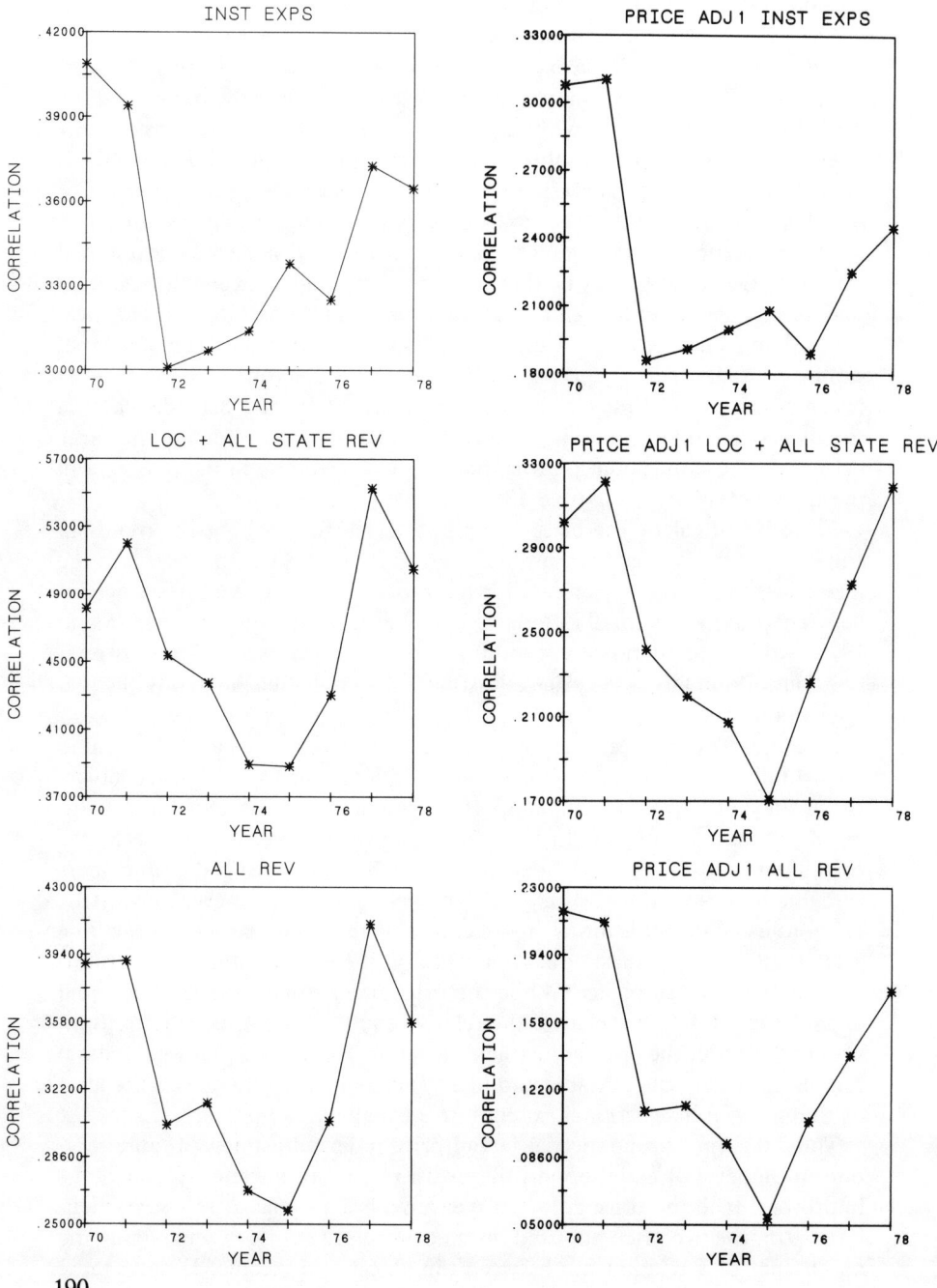

Figure 8.13 Michigan: Comparisons among Input-Based Dollar and Price-Adjusted Dollar Objects Using the Simple Elasticity as the Equal-Opportunity Measure with Respect to Income

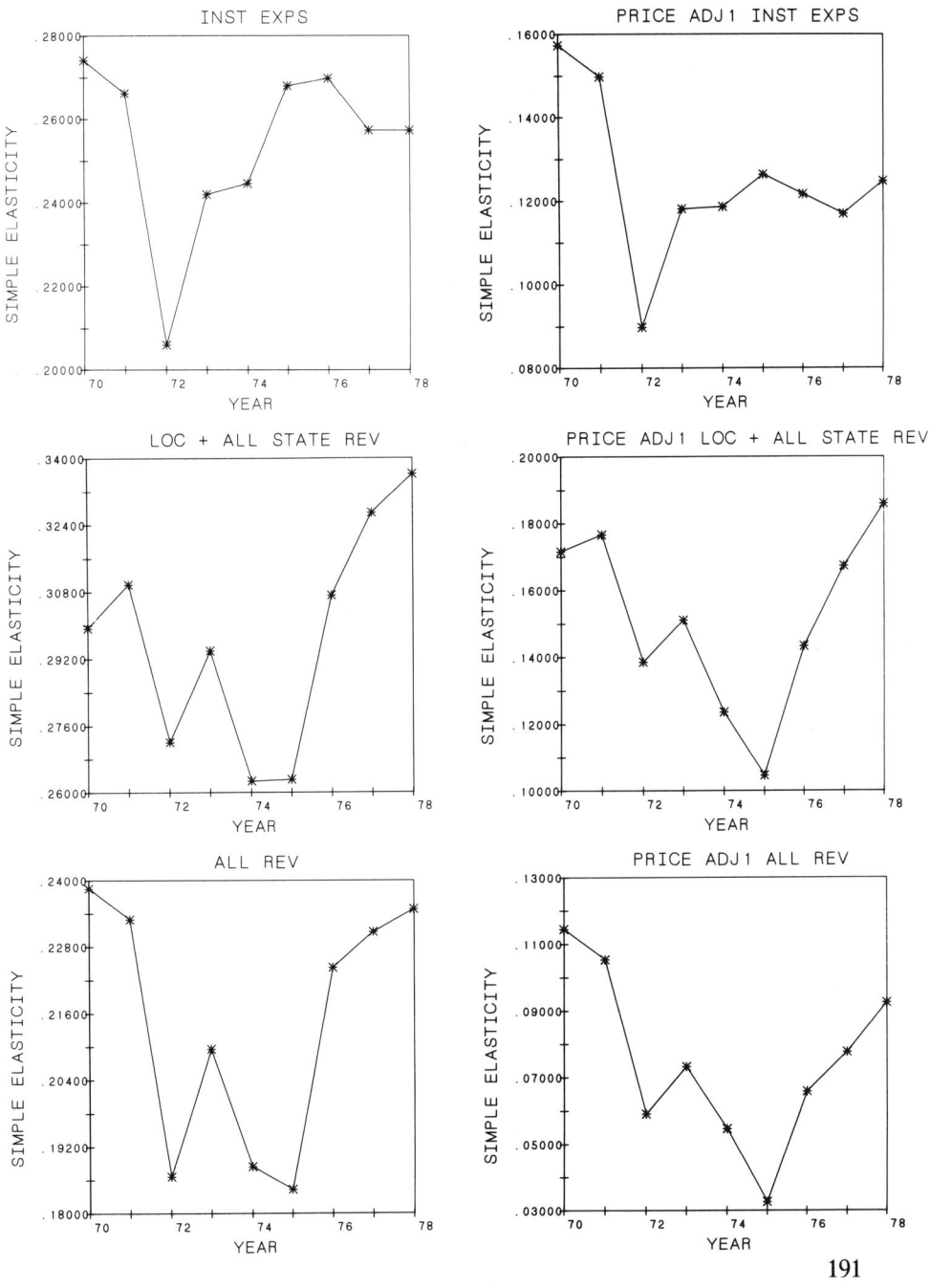

substantial effects on the level of equal opportunity, the price index has a negligible effect on the trend in equal opportunity over the nine-year period.

Do Trend or Levels Differ for Resource Objects Compared to Dollar and Price-Adjusted Dollar Objects? Direct measures of resources represent a group of input-based objects that is conceptually different from either dollars or price-adjusted dollars. In this subpart, the trends in equal opportunity with respect to income are examined using all classroom teachers as the object. Figure 8.14 displays these trends for all classroom teachers with the four measures of equal opportunity that are utilized in the previous two analyses. Data are available for six years, and the trends shown in figure 8.14 can be compared to those shown in figures 8.12 and 8.13 for the dollar and the price-adjusted dollar objects over the same six-year period.

Figure 8.14 Michigan: Equal Opportunity with Respect to Income Using All Teachers per 1,000 Pupils as the Object and Four Equal-Opportunity Measures

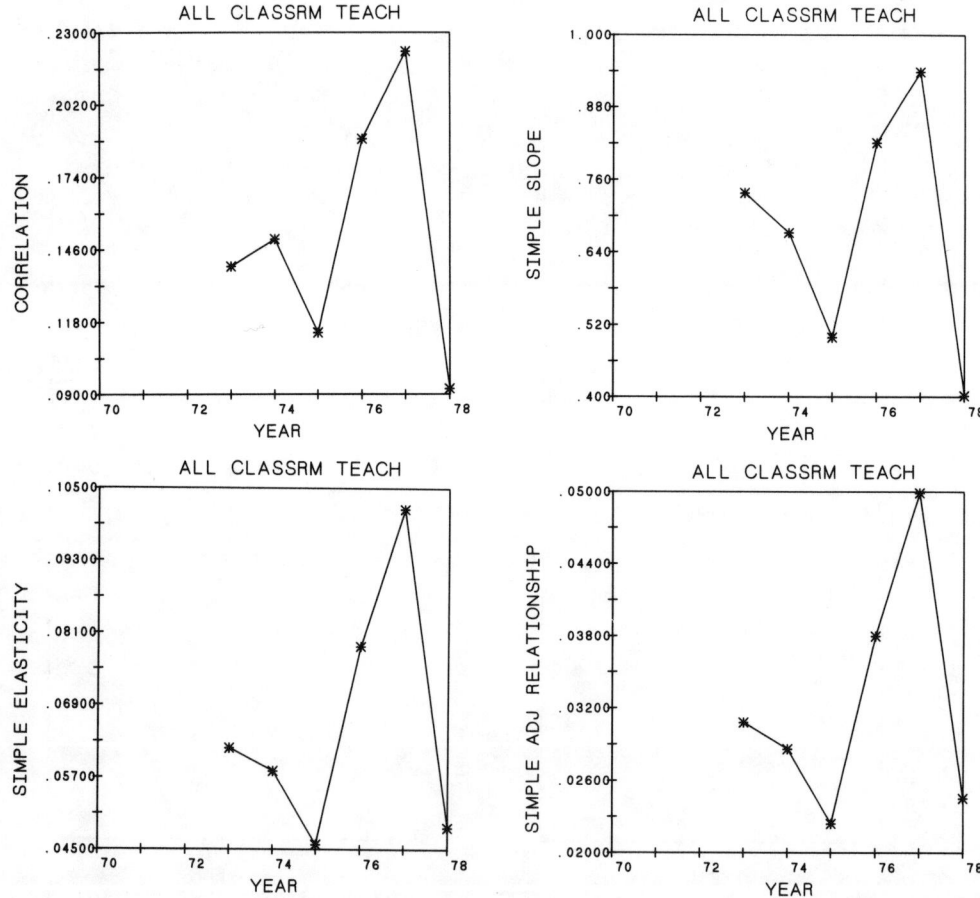

The trends in equal opportunity for all teachers is very different from those in unadjusted and price-adjusted instructional expenditures from 1973 to 1978, when comparable data are available. The expenditure objects show relatively less equal opportunity around 1975, while the teacher object is relatively more equitable in 1975. Also, the instructional expenditure objects do not show the considerable improvement in equal opportunity between 1977 and 1978 that occurs for the teacher object, regardless of the measure. The differences between the trends in the teacher object and the unadjusted and price-adjusted revenue objects are less pronounced. Almost all of these objects show a U- or V-shaped pattern between 1973 and 1977, although there are certain minor discrepancies. The most obvious difference again occurs between 1977 and 1978, where the revenue objects generally show worsening equal opportunity, while the teacher objects display an increase in equal opportunity. Thus, the trends in equal opportunity for the teacher objects more closely resemble those for the revenue objects than those for the expenditure objects, but in all cases there is evidence that resource and dollar objects are not interchangeable.

In previous analyses of horizontal equity and equal opportunity with respect to property wealth in Michigan, the resource objects were more equitable than the price-adjusted or the unadjusted dollar objects. In this case, the differences are not as clear-cut. In fact, the levels of equal opportunity with respect to income for the teacher object are comparable with the levels for price-adjusted local plus total state plus total federal revenues. While the portunity. Thus, the trends in equal opportunity for the teacher objects more closely resemble those for the revenue objects than those for the expenditure objects, but in all cases there is evidence that resource and dollar objects are not interchangeable.

Equal Opportunity with Respect to Region

Michigan, like most large industrial states, is heterogeneous with respect to demographic and economic characteristics across regions. Established regional breakdowns are often used in analyses of, and political decision-making about, school-finance policies. Since a priori there is no reason why one region should receive more education resources than any other, equal opportunity would require no differences across regions. Of course, those who advocate differences have in mind that variables such as price levels or percentages of handicapped pupils will be correlated with the regions. Until such correlations are documented, however, there is no equal-opportunity basis for differences.

In Michigan, the regional breakdowns used in this analysis are (1) the Upper Peninsula (UP); (2) the Detroit metropolitan area, including the school districts in the counties of Wayne, Oakland, and Macomb (Detroit Metro); (3) the middle-city school districts, meaning the medium-sized cities outside the Detroit metropolitan area (Middle Cities)[5]; and (4) all of the rest of the lower-peninsula districts that lie outside the Detroit metropolitan area and the middle cities (Rest of Lower Peninsula).

In this section, we look at differences across these regions based on two alternative dollar-input objects, two price-adjusted dollar objects, and one resource object. Only two dollar objects are used, rather than four, because the results are not significantly different for the omitted two. The following three questions are addressed:

1. Are there differences in regional equal opportunity due to alternative input-based dollar objects: local plus total state revenues versus instructional expenditures, holding the measure constant?

2. How does the adjustment of input-based dollar objects by a price index affect trends in equal opportunity with respect to region?

3. How do the trends in and levels of equal opportunity differ with input-based resource objects compared to input-based objects measured in dollars and price-adjusted dollars?

The methodology used to study regional equal opportunity differs from that used to study property wealth and income equal opportunity. For regions, the mean values of pupil-weighted objects by region are compared, with the expectation that identical mean values will be found if perfect equal opportunity exists. The mean values by region are obtained via multiple regression with dummies, which yields results identical to a one-way analysis of variance. The (pupil-weighted) regression equation is of the form:

$$\$Object = b_0 + b_1 \binom{Regional}{Dummy\ 1} + b_2 \binom{Regional}{Dummy\ 2} + b_3 \binom{Regional}{Dummy\ 3}.$$

Region 4 is left out, and its mean is represented by the constant, b_0. From such a regression, the mean value for each region can be determined as follows:

Mean of region 1 = $b_0 + b_1$
Mean of region 2 = $b_0 + b_2$
Mean of region 3 = $b_0 + b_3$
Mean of region 4 = b_0

Primarily, the results for each object are presented using graphs, although certain results are discussed but not graphed.

Are There Differences in Regional Equal Opportunity Due to Alternative Input-Based Dollar Objects? Figure 8.15 shows the graphs for equal opportunity with respect to region in Michigan for instructional expenditures and local

---

5. The middle-city districts include the following: Ann Arbor, Battle Creek, Bay City, Benton Harbor, Flint, Grand Rapids, Jackson, Kalamazoo, Lansing, Midland, Monroe, Muskegon, Portage, Port Huron, Saginaw, Traverse City, and Pontiac. Pontiac is in the Detroit metropolitan area, but is included here by tradition.

plus total state revenues. The three lines on each graph plot the ratio of the mean value for a region (Detroit metropolitan area, middle cities, or rest of lower peninsula) to the mean value of the Upper Peninsula. A ratio greater than 1.0 indicates a mean value for the region in the numerator that is greater than the mean of the Upper Peninsula. For example, using the graph for instructional expenditures, the value of 1.29 for middle cities/Upper Peninsula in 1970 indicates that mean instructional expenditures in the middle cities were 1.29 times mean instructional expenditures in the Upper Peninsula in that year.

Figure 8.15 indicates that for both objects, the middle cities have the highest and the Detroit metropolitan area has the second highest mean object. For local plus total state revenues, the rest of the lower peninsula is the third highest and the Upper Peninsula is the lowest region. For instructional expenditures, these latter two regions reverse positions. In both cases the Upper Peninsula and lower peninsula regions are very close together, which indicates that the rank ordering of regions remains essentially identical no matter which object is analyzed.

How Does the Adjustment of Input-Based Dollar Objects by a Price Index Affect Trends in Equal Opportunity with Respect to Region? Figure 8.16 displays trends for price-adjusted instructional expenditures and price-adjusted local plus total state revenues respectively, using Index 1. The patterns revealed by price-adjusted instructional expenditures are quite different from the unadjusted ones. Although the middle cities still have the highest average object, the Upper Peninsula now moves into second place. Both the Detroit metropolitan area and the rest of the lower peninsula are below the Upper Peninsula means, and the means for the former two regions are close to one an-

Figure 8.15 Michigan: Ratios of Average Instructional Expenditures per Pupil and Average Local Plus Total State Revenues per Pupil, by Region

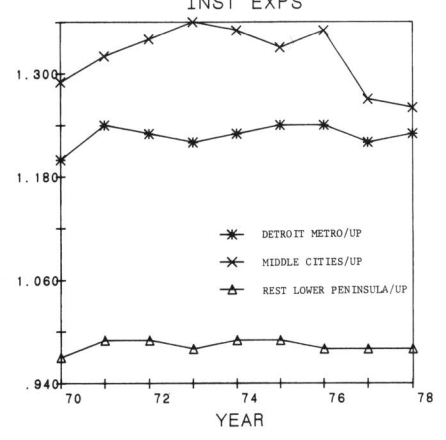
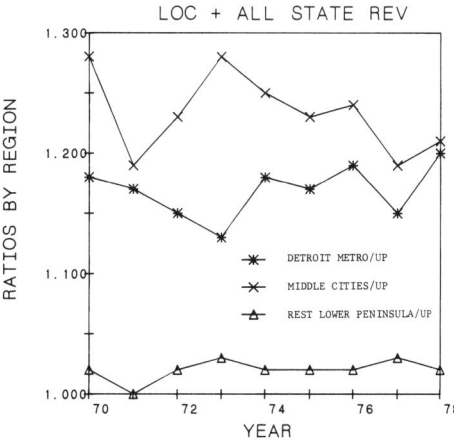

Figure 8.16 Michigan: Ratios of Average Price-Adjusted Instructional Expenditures per Pupil and Average Price-Adjusted Local Plus Total State Revenues per Pupil, by Region

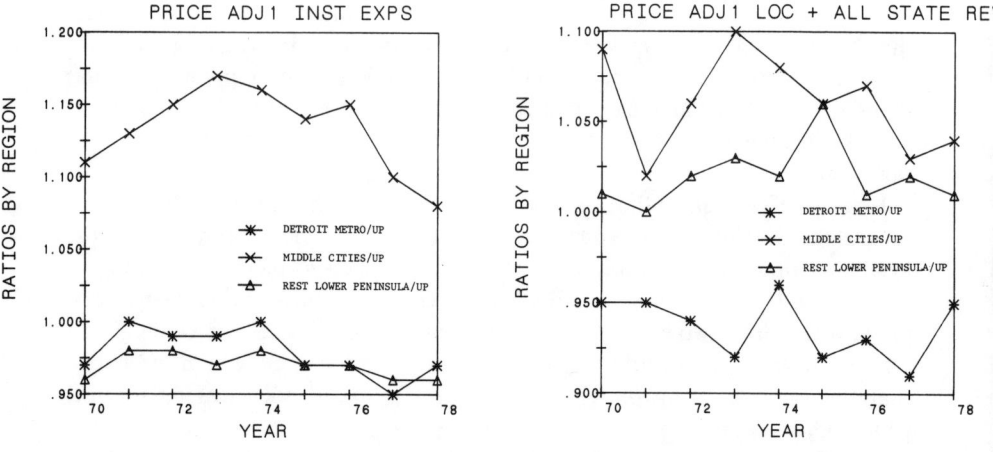

other. In addition, the mean values for all regions are considerably closer together when instructional expenditures are price adjusted, meaning that regional equal opportunity improves when this object is corrected for price differences.

Price-adjusted local plus total state revenues shows yet another pattern, as exhibited in figure 8.16. The middle cities remain in first place, but the rest of the lower peninsula moves into second place, closely followed by the Upper Peninsula region. The Detroit metropolitan area has the lowest average object, with between 93 and 96 percent of the Upper Peninsula mean value. As with instructional expenditures, the price adjustment for local plus total state revenues reduces the disparities in the regional means and thus results in an improvement in equal opportunity. Also similar to instructional expenditures, the price adjustment most changes the relative positions of the Detroit metropolitan area, the Upper Peninsula, and the lower peninsula. While the middle cities mean value is reduced, it still remains highest in all cases.

How Do Trends in Equal Opportunity Differ with Input-Based Resource Objects Compared to Input-Based Objects Measured in Dollars? Figure 8.17 displays the trends in equal opportunity for one resource object—all classroom teachers per 1,000 pupils. For the first time, the middle cities no longer have the highest average value; instead, the Upper Peninsula moves into first place. The middle cities are second, and the Detroit metropolitan area is last. The direction of these changes was anticipated by the price-adjusted patterns displayed in figure 8.16, although for both objects in figure 8.16 the middle cities remained in first place. The last year of the time series shows a noticeable widening of the gap between the Upper Peninsula and the other three regions,

Figure 8.17 Michigan: Ratios of Average All Classroom Teachers per 1,000 Pupils, by Region

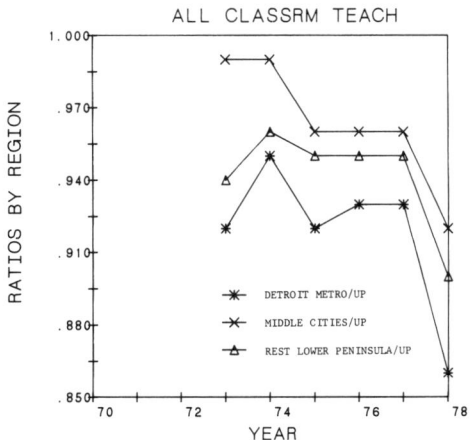

which is largely due to the significant increase in the mean Upper Peninsula value. While little can be made of a one-year movement, such a large change was also evident for all classroom teachers for equal opportunity with respect to property wealth and income.

Equal Opportunity with Respect to Race

For the last thirty years, there has been an explicit awareness that the public education system discriminates against certain racial groups. While discrimination varies by place and may have abated over time, concern over equal opportunity for minority groups is still very much with us. Most of the debate over racial equal opportunity in public education has revolved around questions of segregation, often within districts. Especially over the last decade, however, questions were asked concerning a state's school-finance equity with respect to minority groups.[6] In terms of our equity framework, this issue can be phrased as a question of whether there is a relationship between the education object and a measure of a school district's racial composition.

Using the pupil-weighted district-level approach employed throughout the book, an examination of equal opportunity with respect to race can be carried out analogously to the treatment of equal opportunity with respect to wealth, income, and region. For racial equal opportunity, the independent variable is defined as the percent of a district's enrollment that is comprised of minority

---

6. For examples, see Robert Brischetto and David Vaughan, *Minorities, the Poor, and School Finance Reform: An Impact Study of Six States* (San Antonio, Tex.: Intercultural Development Research Association, 1977), and Stephen J. Carroll, Millicent Cox, and William Lisowski, *The Search for Equity in School Finance: Results from Five States* (Santa Monica, Ca.: Rand, March 1979).

group members. In terms of equity, the absence of a negative relationship between the education object and the percent of the district's enrollment that is comprised of minority group members signifies equal opportunity with respect to race.

The four methodological questions raised at the beginning of this chapter are addressed in this part with "percent minority" as the independent variable. But first, a brief description of the available data on minority enrollment in Michigan is presented. Data on the number of minority pupils in Michigan's school districts were obtained from Michigan's Department of Education. Data were available for only three years: 1972-73, 1976-77, and 1977-78. Since a district's percent of minority enrollment is unlikely to change drastically from year to year, the available data were used to compute equal-opportunity measures for all nine years in the study period in the following manner. First, the percent of enrollment comprised of minority group members was computed for each district for 1973, 1977, and 1978. Second, the percent minority in 1973 was assumed to hold for 1970 through 1974, the percent minority in 1977 was assumed to hold for 1974 through 1977, and the percent minority in 1978 was used for 1978. Minorities include the following: (1) American Indian or Alaskan Native or Native American; (2) Asian or Pacific Islander; (3) Black, not of Latino or Hispanic origin; and (4) Latino or Hispanic.

For the state of Michigan, minority enrollment increased over the study period. Minority enrollment as a percent of total enrollment was 16.0, 18.5, and 19.0 in 1973, 1977, and 1978 respectively. These statewide figures are significantly influenced by the Detroit school district. Detroit's minority enrollment as a percent of the total was 69.1, 81.4, and 84.2 for 1973, 1977, and 1978 respectively. Thus, although about 12 percent of all pupils in the state in 1978 resided in Detroit, 61 percent of the state's minority pupils attended Detroit's schools. The data on minority enrollment cover the same set of over five hundred K-12 districts included in the previous analyses. Data on minority enrollments were not available for eight districts in 1973 and 1977 or for eleven districts in 1978, but these contain less than one half of one percent of all pupils in 1973 and 1977, and less than one percent of all pupils in 1978.

Are There Differences in Trends Due to Alternative Measures? Do the Measures Form Empirical Groupings? As we have already shown in this chapter, there are alternative ways to measure equal opportunity, and in this subpart, the analysis focuses on whether the choice of a measure affects trends in equal opportunity with respect to race. The independent variable in this section is expressed as the percentage of each district's enrollment that is comprised of minority group members, and this variable differs from those previously used in the measurement of equal opportunity. The independent variables used to measure wealth and income were expressed in dollars, and dummy variables were used to represent regions. Since racial composition is expressed as a percentage, the measures of equal opportunity used here are not identical to those analyzed earlier in the chapter.

First, the regression-based measures that were utilized in the assessment of equal opportunity with respect to income and wealth can be used to measure equal opportunity with respect to race. The measures are based on regressions that are estimated with the education object as the dependent variable and the "percent minority" as the independent variable. In this case, since the independent variable is a percentage, only the simple regressions are estimated, and the correlation, the simple slope, the simple elasticity, and the simple adjusted relationship measure are computed from the simple regression.

Second, because the independent variable is a percentage, two relationship measures introduced in chapter 2 under the vertical-equity discussion can be reconsidered as equal-opportunity measures. In chapter 2 a measure called the averaged implicit weight was defined as the ratio of the object for pupils who are in a special group to the object for pupils who are not in the special group. Although the measure was developed with handicapped pupils as the special group, it can be computed in an identical manner with minority enrollment as the group of concern. In this analysis, the ratio of the average value of per-pupil objects for minorities to the average value of per-pupil objects for nonminorities is computed for each year and each object. This measure was called the averaged implicit weight in chapter 2, but is called the minority-nonminority ratio here. If this measure is less than one, it indicates that on the average, minorities statewide are receiving less of the education object than nonminorities, and therefore, according to this measure, equal opportunity for minorities does not exist.

Finally, when a simple regression is estimated with a percent as the dependent variable, an additional measure can be computed. Since the regression line predicts the level of the education object, that line can be used to predict the level of the object both in a district with no minority pupils and in a district with all minority pupils. The ratio of the predicted objects, minority to nonminority, can be used as an equal-opportunity measure that signifies an inequitable situation when the ratio is less than one. Although this measure was called the implicit weight in chapter 2, when used here as an equal-opportunity measure it is called the regression-based minority-nonminority ratio.

We now turn to an examination of the consistency among the following six measures: the correlation, the simple slope, the simple elasticity, the simple adjusted relationship measure, the minority-nonminority ratio, and the regression-based minority-nonminority ratio. The measures can be compared in two ways. First, we focus on the most basic question, Do the measures agree on the direction of the relationship between the object and race? Since all measures except the minority-nonminority ratio are based on the simple regression, the question boils down to whether the regression-based measures differ from the minority-nonminority ratio in terms of the existence of unequal opportunity with respect to race. Second, the trends in the magnitude of the measures can be compared to determine whether they agree on the relative changes in equal opportunity over time.

The answer to the first question, Do all measures agree on the existence of equal opportunity with respect to race? is yes. Regardless of the object, when the correlation, the slope, the elasticity, and the adjusted relationship measure are positive (negative), the minority-nonminority ratio and the regression-based minority-nonminority ratio are greater (less) than one. For example, with instructional expenditures as the object, equal opportunity with respect to race exists in all nine years, but with local plus state membership revenues, equal opportunity only exists in four of the nine years. But regardless, the findings of the existence of equal opportunity with respect to race are not affected by the choice of a measure. Thus, if the only question is whether equal opportunity with respect to race exists, the choice of a measure does not appear to matter for these data in Michigan. Again, when no differences arise, it is difficult to confidently generalize beyond the sample, but in the next chapter, when vertical equity is examined, we will see that this conclusion on the measures is replicated.

The second question is whether the actual trends in equal opportunity depicted by the six measures are consistent with each other. Figure 8.18 shows the trends in equal opportunity for the six measures for instructional expenditures per pupil, and there are some instances of disagreement. In particular, the slope for instructional expenditures differs from the other five measures, and there are a few other minor differences among the measures. Recall that of the six measures displayed, the slope is the only one that changes as a result of inflation in the object, and it is therefore not useful when there is inflation. Although graphs for local plus state membership revenues, local plus total state revenues, and local plus total state plus total federal revenues are not shown, the differences across measures are quite small in these cases. Thus, with the possible exception of the slope, the equal-opportunity measures do not differ appreciably in the way they represent the trends in equal opportunity with respect to race over time. These findings are somewhat at odds with the earlier findings on equal opportunity with respect to property wealth and income, where the correlation often displayed a trend that varied from the other measures. The consistency among the measures in this case must be viewed with caution, since the independent variable, percent minority, did not vary in every year. But for these data the choice of a measure has little or no effect on the findings on equal opportunity with respect to race.

Are There Differences Either in the Trends or in the Levels Due to Alternative Input-Based Dollar Objects? The second methodological question addressed is whether the choice of an input-based dollar object affects conclusions regarding equal opportunity with respect to race. Again, the question is exam-

Figure 8.18 Michigan: Equal-Opportunity Measures for Instructional Expenditures with Respect to Race

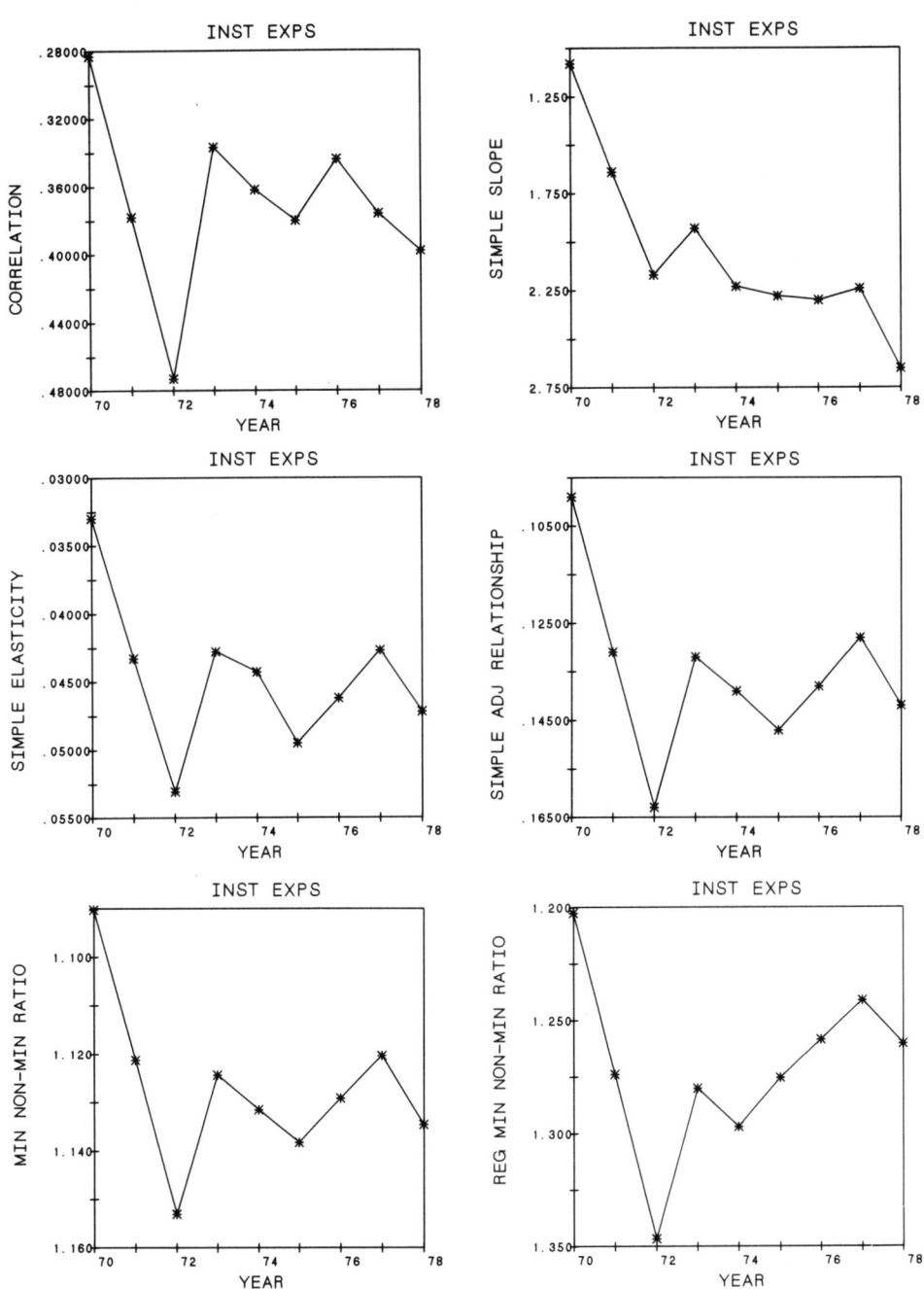

ined in terms of whether equal opportunity with respect to race exists, as well as in terms of the trends in equal opportunity.

Whether equal opportunity with respect to race exists in a given year for a particular object is shown in table 8.1. Recall that since all six measures agree on whether or not equal opportunity is present, there is no need to specify a measure. This table illustrates that the selection of an object does affect the conclusion regarding the presence of equal opportunity. Using instructional expenditures and local plus total state plus total federal revenues (total revenues), every year in Michigan shows a positive relationship between dollars and percent of minority and, therefore, exhibits equal opportunity. For the other two revenue objects, the conclusions differ. Only four of the nine years display equal opportunity with respect to race for local plus state membership revenues, and seven of the nine are equitable for local plus total state revenue.

The way in which equal opportunity varies across objects is consistent with what we know about the distribution of the objects. It is not surprising that when state categoricals and all federal dollars are added to local and state membership revenues, equal opportunity improves in terms of the number of years in which it exists. These funds are distributed on variables such as need and income, which are known to be positively correlated with race. Furthermore, it is reassuring to see that what goes on in the classroom, as measured by instructional expenditures, exhibits equal opportunity. Nevertheless, from a methodological perspective, the results in Michigan strongly suggest that the choice of an input-based dollar object affects conclusions on equal opportunity with respect to race.

Table 8.1. Michigan: Equal Opportunity with Respect to Race for Alternative Input-Based Dollar Objects

	Year								
Object	1970	1971	1972	1973	1974	1975	1976	1977	1978
Instructional expenditures	Yes	Yes	Yes	Yes	Yes	Yes	Yes	Yes	Yes
Local plus state membership revenue	Yes	No	No	No	Yes	Yes	Yes	No	No
Local plus total state revenue	Yes	Yes	Yes	No	Yes	Yes	Yes	No	Yes
Local plus total state plus total federal revenue	Yes	Yes	Yes	Yes	Yes	Yes	Yes	Yes	Yes

Note: Each entry in the table is an answer to the question, "Does equal opportunity with respect to race exist in Michigan?" for a particular object and year.

An entry of Yes (No) indicates that the correlation, the simple slope, the simple elasticity, and the simple adjusted relationship measure are positive (negative) and the minority-nonminority ratio and regression-based minority-nonminority ratio are greater (less) than one.

The trends in the four input-based dollar objects can also be compared to determine if these too are influenced by the choice of an object. The findings in this case are the same regardless of which measures are utilized, so as an example, the trends in equal opportunity with respect to race for four objects using the correlation are displayed in figure 8.19. The most clear-cut differences can be seen between instructional expenditures and the other three revenue objects. Although there are minor differences among the three revenue objects, as a group they depict a different pattern over the nine-year period than that of instructional expenditures.

This assessment of the effects of alternative input-based dollar objects has

Figure 8.19 Michigan: Comparisons among Four Input-Based Dollar Objects Using the Correlation as the Equal-Opportunity Measure with Respect to Race

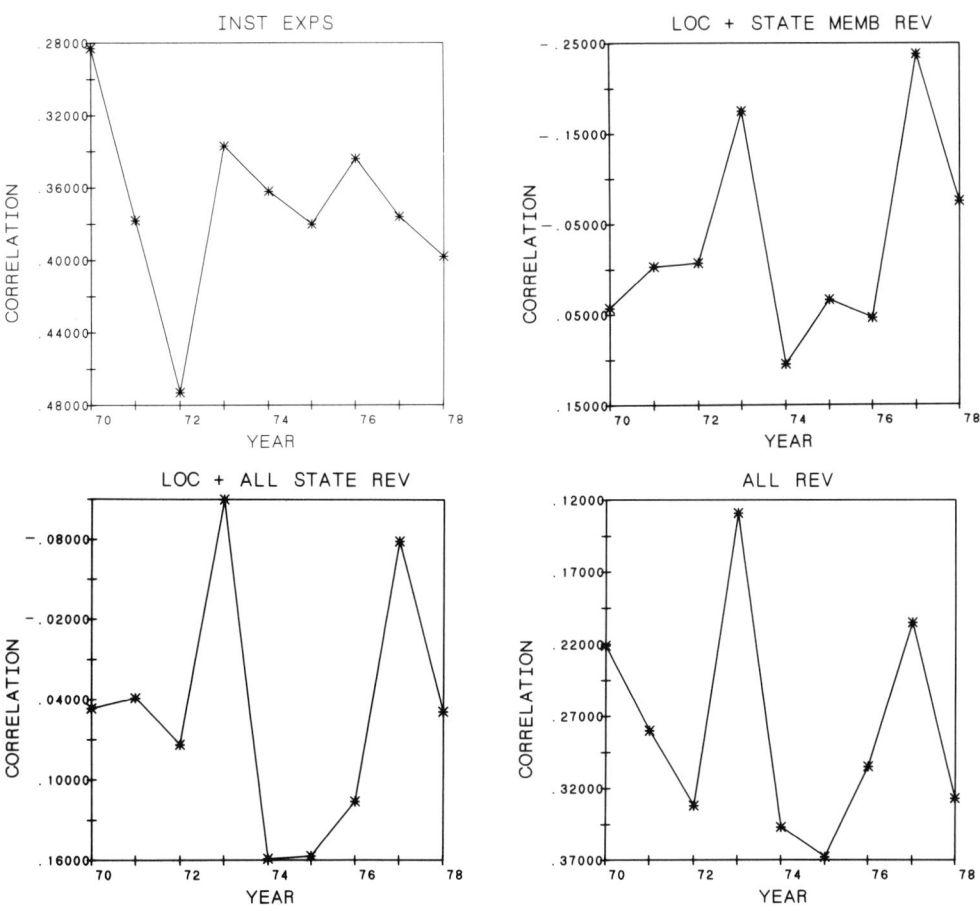

found differences from two perspectives. First, if the question is whether equal opportunity exists, then the choice of an object matters. Second, if trends in the measures over time are compared, different objects yield different trends. Thus, the choice of a dollar object is critical in this assessment of equal opportunity with respect to race in Michigan.

How Does the Adjustment of the Input-Based Dollar Objects by Price Indexes Affect the Trends in and Levels of Equal Opportunity? The question addressed in this subpart is whether the existence of or trends in equal opportunity with respect to race are affected by price adjustments. Are the results different for dollar objects compared to price-adjusted dollar objects?

An examination of the existence of equal opportunity with and without price adjustments is analogous to the question of whether price adjustments affect the level of equal opportunity. In each of the previous parts, price adjustments have had a sizable effect on equal opportunity, and the same findings hold here. Table 8.2 is designed to show the existence of equal opportunity in Michigan during the nine-year study period for three price-adjusted objects. The results are rather uniform, with only one entry (instructional expenditures in 1972) showing the existence of equal opportunity with respect to race for price-adjusted dollar inputs.

These results lead to a substantially different conclusion from the one drawn without price adjustments, which was summarized in table 8.1. Of course these results are based on the relationship between price, dollar objects, and race in Michigan, and they are not guaranteed to occur in other states. In this case, the high price indexes for the Detroit school system undoubtedly played a large role in the results. But from a methodological point of view, these results demonstrate that price indexes have the potential to change the direction of the relationship between education objects and race

Table 8.2. Michigan: Equal Opportunity with Respect to Race for Alternative Price-Adjusted Input-Based Dollar Objects

	Year								
Object	1970	1971	1972	1973	1974	1975	1976	1977	1978
Price-adjusted (Index 1) Instructional expenditures	No	No	Yes	No	No	No	No	No	No
Price-adjusted (Index 1) local plus total state revenue	No	No	No	No	No	No	No	No	No
Price-adjusted (Index 1) local plus total state plus total federal revenue	No	No	No	No	No	No	No	No	No

Note: Each entry in the table is an answer to the question, "Does equal opportunity with respect to race exist in Michigan?" for a particular object and year.

An entry of Yes (No) indicates that the correlation, the simple slope, the simple elasticity, and the simple adjusted relationship measure are positive (negative) and the minority-nonminority and regression-based minority-nonminority ratio are greater (less) than one.

and, therefore, to alter conclusions on the existence of equal opportunity with respect to race.

The question of whether price indexes alter the trends in equal opportunity is also of concern. Figure 8.20 displays three dollar and three price-adjusted dollar objects for the correlation. The trends for this measure are representative of the effects for the other measures as well. In a few cases, most noticeably for instructional expenditures, there are minor changes in the trends in equal opportunity with respect to race resulting from the application of the price index. But for the most part, the price-index adjustments leave the trends unaltered over the nine years, although the effects of the price index on the levels of equal opportunity with respect to race are also evident in the graphs.

For Michigan between 1970 and 1978, price adjustments have a substantial effect on the existence of equal opportunity with respect to race, but do not change the trends over time. This has been a consistent finding for the equal opportunity principle, where the effect on the level is more pronounced than the effect on the trends, although in certain cases (wealth) the effects on the trends have also been substantial.

Do Trends or Levels Differ for Resource Objects Compared to Dollar and Price-Adjusted Dollar Objects? The final question in this part is whether resource objects behave similarly to dollar or price-adjusted dollar objects. Figure 8.21 displays the trends in equal opportunity with respect to race for all teachers per 1,000 pupils using the six measures of equal opportunity. This figure can be used to assess whether equal opportunity exists and to compare the trends with the other objects.

Since the correlation, the simple slope, the simple elasticity, and the simple adjusted relationship measure are always negative, and the minority-nonminority ratio and the regression-based minority-nonminority ratio are always less than one, equal opportunity with respect to race for all teachers did not exist in Michigan during the six years from 1973 to 1978. For this resource-based object, the levels of the measures are comparable to those for the price-adjusted dollar objects. This consistency in the level of equal opportunity between the resource-based object and the price-adjusted dollar objects has been found repeatedly throughout this chapter.

The trends in equal opportunity over the six years where comparable data are available are somewhat different for resources compared to dollar and price-adjusted dollar objects. The first few years in the trends for resources resemble the three revenue objects, while the last few years are similar to some of the instructional-expenditure trends. But no single dollar or price-adjusted dollar parallels the resource trends consistently over the six years. For example, 1978 is the most inequitable year of the six for the resource objects, but this is not true for any of the dollar or price-adjusted dollar objects. Thus, as has been the case before, the trends in equal opportunity with respect to race for the resource objects are unlike those for the other objects.

Figure 8.20 Michigan: Comparisons among Input-Based Dollar and Price-Adjusted Dollar Objects Using the Correlation as the Equal-Opportunity Measure with Respect to Race

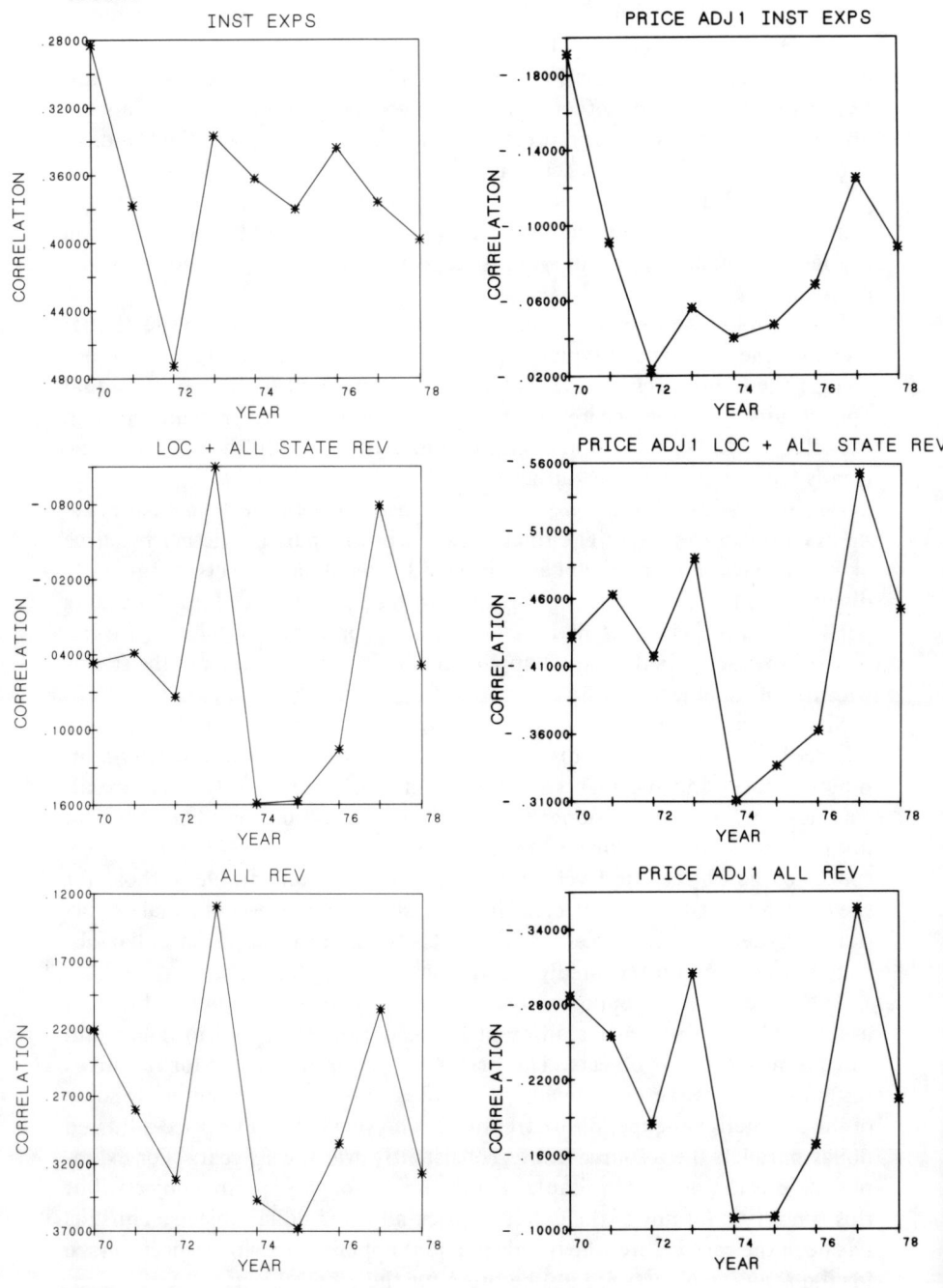

Figure 8.21 Michigan: Equal Opportunity with Respect to Race Using All Teachers per 1,000 Pupils as the Object and Six Equal-Opportunity Measures

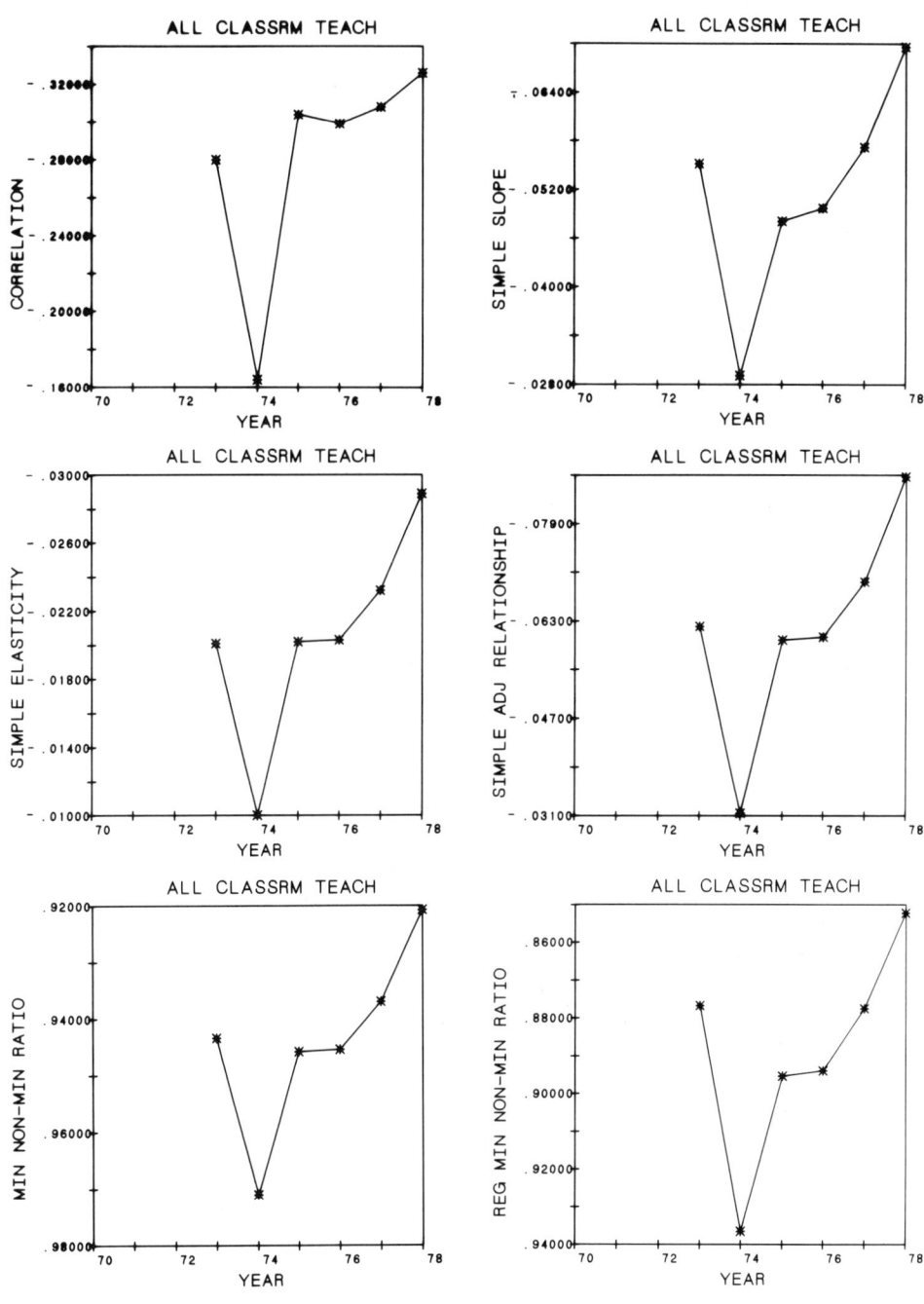

AN ASSESSMENT OF EQUAL OPPORTUNITY IN NEW YORK

In New York, available data permit the assessment of equal opportunity with respect to property wealth, income, and region, but not percent minority. The first three parts of this section are devoted to each of the three available independent variables, in the order just listed. As in chapter 7's analysis of New York's horizontal-equity trends, two objects, current operating expenditures per enrolled pupil (COE) and price-adjusted current operating expenditures per pupil (PRICE ADJ COE), are used throughout the assessment of equal opportunity. The availability of these two objects alone means that only two of the four questions posed for Michigan are relevant for New York. The two relevant questions are:

1. Are there differences in trends in equal opportunity due to alternative measures? Do the measures form empirical groupings that are indentical or similar to the conceptual groupings identified in chapter 2?

2. How does the adjustment of input-based dollar objects by price indexes affect the trends in equal opportunity holding the measure constant? Does the price index alter the trends in equity, the absolute levels of equity, or both?

Both of these questions are answered in each of the three sections that follow.

Equal Opportunity with Respect to Property Wealth

Equalized assessed value of property wealth per pupil in New York was $29,630 in 1965 and $67,167 in 1978. Thus, property values climbed over the time period, although not at a steady rate. Over the entire period they grew by 127 percent, but that growth was considerably slower in the first seven years (27 percent) than in the last seven years (67 percent).

Are There Differences in Trends Due to Alternative Measures? Do the Measures Form Empirical Groupings? In this section, we hold the object constant by focusing on COE in order to observe possible differences in equity trends that could be attributed to equal-opportunity measures. Eleven equal-opportunity measures, calculated on the basis of regression equations, are estimated for each year in the time series, and figures 8.22 and 8.23 display the measures graphically. Figure 8.22 shows the correlation and all four elasticity measures. Figure 8.23 displays the three slopes and the three adjusted relationship measures. In chapter 2, the equal-opportunity measures were conceptually combined into four groupings based on value judgments: correlation, elasticities, slopes, and adjusted relationship measures. Figures 8.22 and 8.23 show that empirically the measures within each group behave similarly. It is also true that the patterns of each group are not distinct. Instead *all* of the measures show nearly the same pattern. Therefore, one could conclude that empirically there is only one group of measures. We would be reluctant

Figure 8.22 New York: Correlation and Constant, Simple, Quadratic, and Cubic Elasticity for Current Operating Expenditures per Pupil with Property Wealth per Pupil

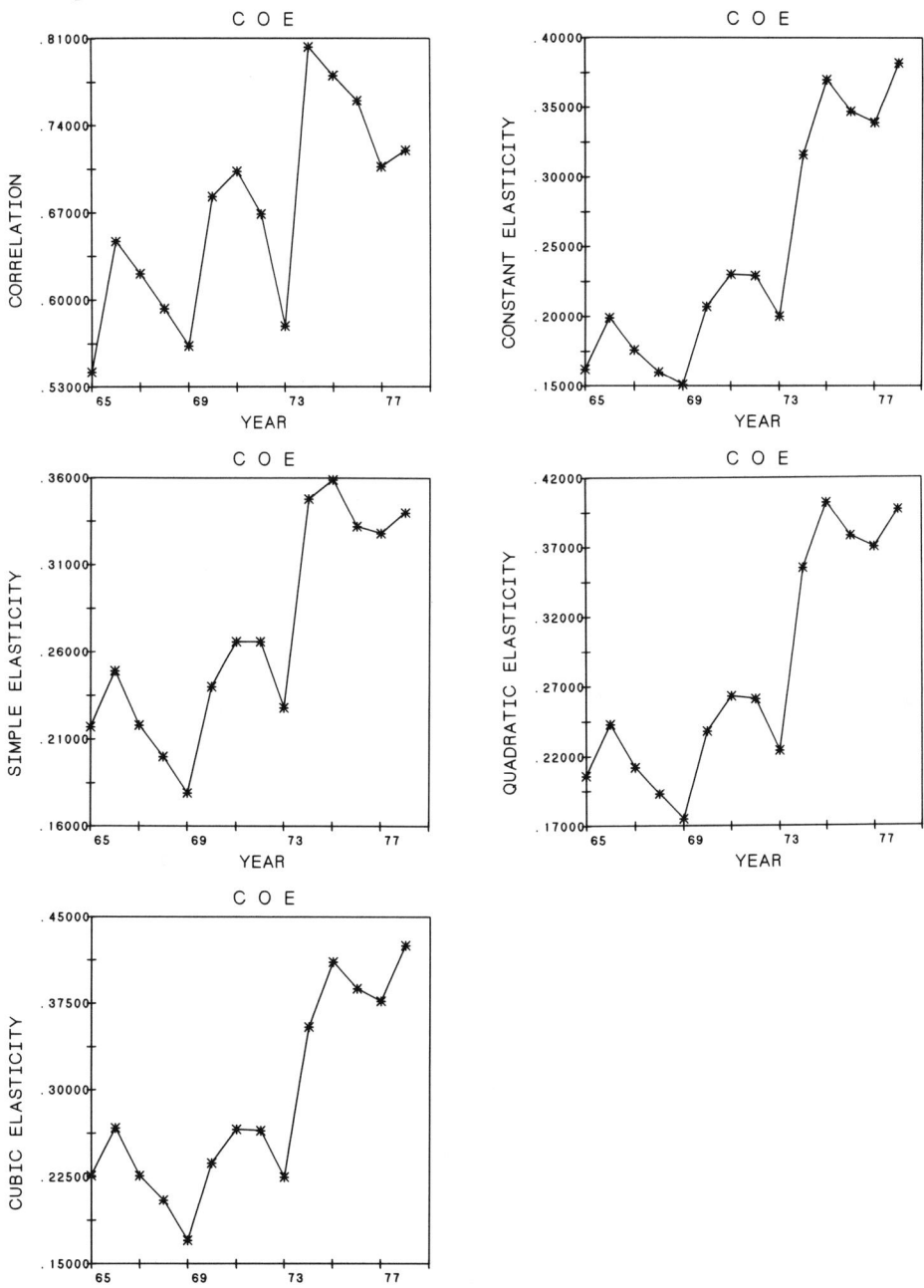

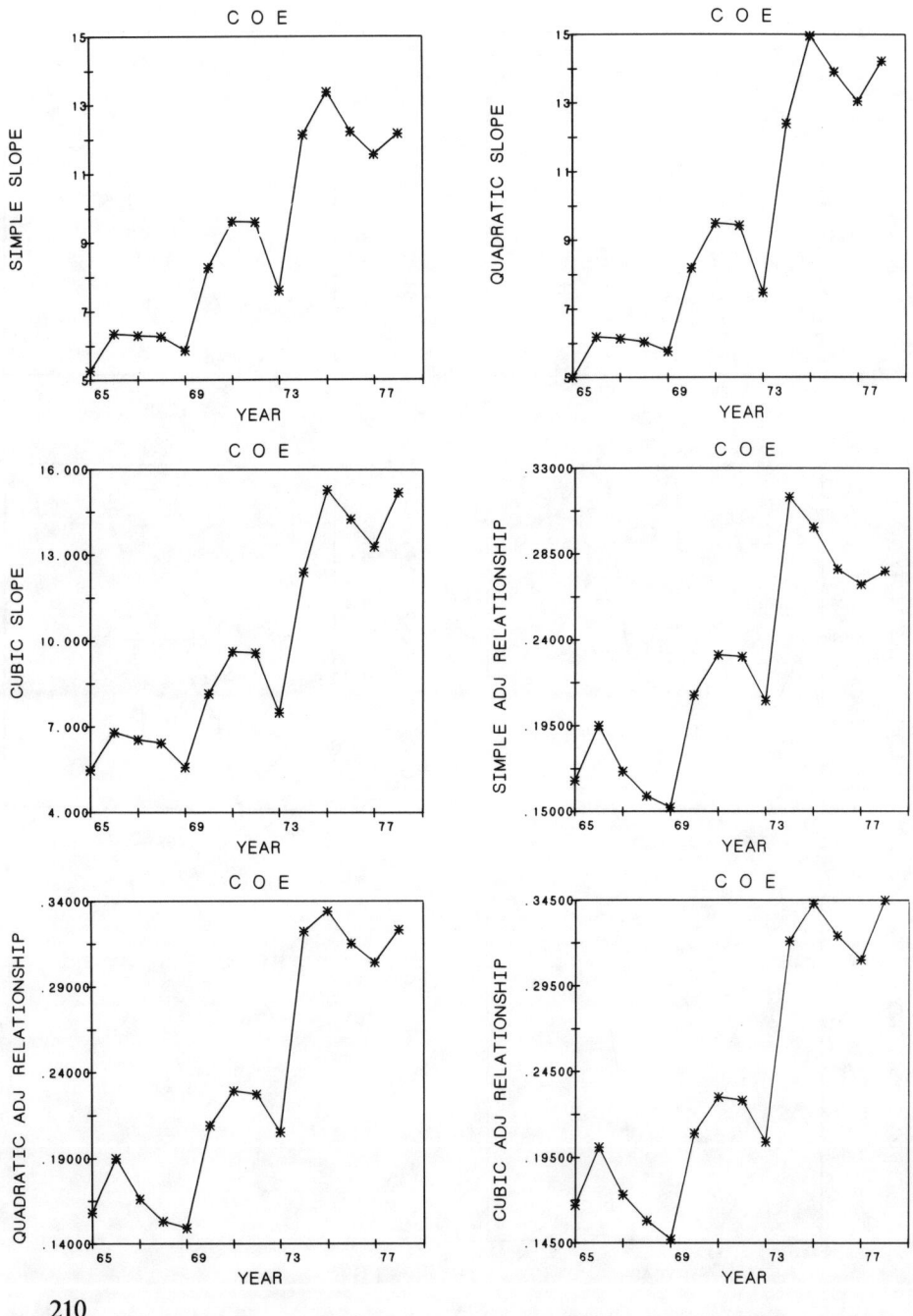

Figure 8.23 New York: Simple, Quadratic, and Cubic Slope and Simple, Quadratic, and Cubic Adjusted Relationship Measure for Current Operating Expenditures with Property Wealth per Pupil

to generalize such a conclusion for other years or other states, because there are circumstances when the differing values would have an impact. For example, if a state changes its assessment or equalization rates substantially in a given year, the measures are likely to diverge in that year. Thus, we prefer to analyze trends in equal opportunity using at least one measure from each group. The four measures presented in all the analyses that follow in this section are: the correlation, the simple slope, the simple elasticity, and the simple adjusted relationship measure.

Figures 8.22 and 8.23 reveal not only similarities in patterns among measures, but also a distinguishable trend over time. Although not monotonic, due to fairly consistently registered improvements in equity in 1969, 1973, and 1977, the overall trend is clearly toward a worsening of equal opportunity from the 1960s to the 1970s. In addition, the trends shown in figures 8.22 and 8.23 are quite similar to those found for horizontal equity in chapter 7.

How Does the Adjustment of the Input-Based Dollar Objects by Price Indexes Affect the Trends in and Levels of Equal Opportunity? Figure 8.24 displays trends in four measures of equal opportunity with respect to wealth when price-adjusted current operating expenditures is the object.[7] As with current operating expenditures, the trends all reveal a worsening of equal opportunity with respect to property wealth between the 1960s and 1970s. The level of equity for all measures is better when current operating expenditures is price-adjusted than for current operating expenditures. This can be seen when the graphs in figures 8.22 and 8.23 are compared with those for comparable objects in figure 8.24. The differences in levels tend to be more pronounced early in the period.

Equal Opportunity with Respect to Income

Property wealth is the most common fiscal-capacity measure used in school-finance studies, largely because it serves as the base for the major part of local school tax revenues. As discussed in the sections on Michigan, property wealth is not conceptually the only, or even necessarily the best, fiscal-capacity indicator. A strong contender is income. In this section, equal opportunity with respect to income is analyzed. Income in New York is imperfectly measured as adjusted gross income from state income taxation returns per return for 1978. The data were obtained from The Education Commission of the States as a by-product of their work as staff to the New York State Special Task Force on Equity and Excellence in Education. Gross income per return has a number of problems that make it a less than ideal measure of income.[8] Its numerator (income) omits several kinds of income,

---

7. Although not shown here, the patterns within and between groups of measures, when all measures are displayed, are the same as those found when current operating expenditures was the object.

8. For an in-depth analysis of the problems and alternatives to gross income per return as an income measure, see E. Kathleen Adams, "Analyses of New York Income Measures," Research Report for the New York State Special Task Force on Equity and Excellence in Education, Education Finance Center, Education Commission of the States, Denver, Col., October 24, 1979.

Figure 8.24 New York: Correlation, Simple Slope, Simple Elasticity, and Simple Adjusted Relationship Measure for Price-Adjusted Current Operating Expenditures with Property Wealth per Pupil

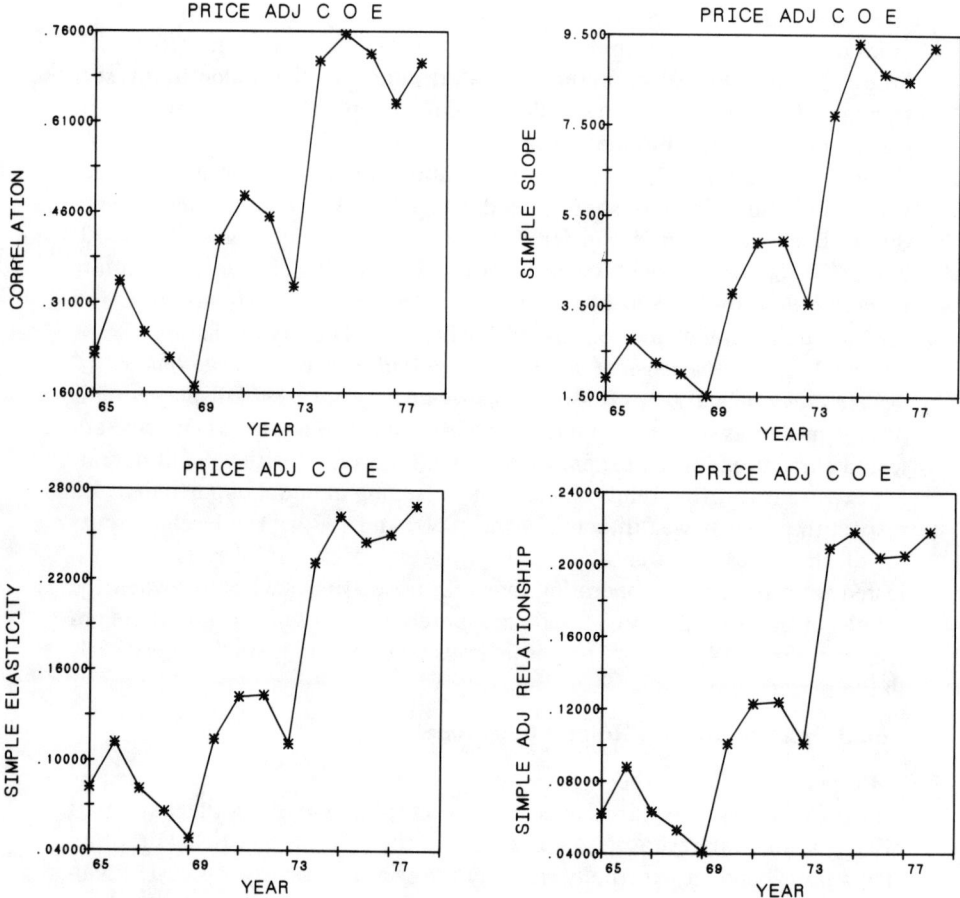

including transfer payments (public assistance, unemployment insurance benefits, social security, veterans benefits), unrealized capital gains, 40 percent of realized gains, and nonmonetary income such as rental value of owner-occupied homes. No available income measure, however, includes all of these sources. The denominator of the income measure (returns) is a proxy for households and is imperfect because some married couples that should be a household file separate returns. In an analysis of alternative income measures in New York, E. Kathleen Adams pointed out that this feature affects low-income households more than high-income ones. This, to some extent, counters the bias toward higher income in the income numbers created because the low-income households file returns less frequently than the high-income households.

While other measures of income are possible—for example, census-money income or personal income, per capita or per pupil—none is overwhelmingly superior on conceptual grounds to gross income per return. In addition, E. Kathleen Adams found that all the available measures of income in New York are highly correlated with one another (.82 or higher).[9] While it would have been preferable to use gross income per return for each year of our time series, 1965 through 1978, this was not possible, because the data by school district first became available in 1978.[10] The (pupil-weighted) statewide mean gross income per return in 1978 was $15,353. The rest of this section is devoted to analysis of the two questions that were previously addressed for property wealth as an independent variable.

Are There Differences in Trends Due to Alternative Measures? Do the Measures Form Empirical Groupings? The income-based equal-opportunity measures are regression based, as were the property wealth-based ones, and since empirically it was found that the functional form of the regression does not affect the measures, only the correlation, the simple slope, the simple elasticity, and the simple adjusted relationship measure are displayed. These four measures are graphed in figure 8.25. As was true when property wealth was the independent variable, the groups of income-based measures that are identified by similar value judgments display similar patterns within their group, i.e., the elasticities, the slopes, and the adjusted relationship measures. Unlike the wealth-based measures, however, there are some easily noticeable differences across groups. The correlation shows more shifts up and down than the other measures, and the slopes show a much smoother upward trend than either the elasticities or the adjusted relationship measures. The latter two groups, on the other hand, are similar in pattern to one another, as they were for the property wealth-based measures. Combining the results for property wealth and income measures, we can conclude that the measures do empirically form groups based on their value judgments.

In addition to the groupings of measures by value judgments, all the graphs in figure 8.25 except the simple correlation show that equal opportunity has worsened from the mid-1960s to the end of the 1970s. The trend is most uniform for the slope measures and less monotonic for the other two groups. The correlation ends the period at a lower level than it began, but there does not appear to be a trend toward either improvement or worsening.

How Does the Adjustment of the Input-Based Dollar Objects by Price Indexes Affect the Trends in and Levels of Equal Opportunity? Figure 8.26 displays four equal-opportunity measures with respect to income when current operating expenditures is price adjusted. For each measure except the correlation, the patterns, and thus the trends, of the measures with current operating expen-

---

9. Ibid., p. 17.
10. The other measures of income are either unavailable on a school-district basis (i.e., personal income) or available for only one year (i.e., census money income for 1969). While it is possible to estimate yearly school-district income in the same way as was done for Michigan, resources to do so for New York were unavailable.

214 THE MEASUREMENT OF EQUITY IN SCHOOL FINANCE

Figure 8.25 New York: Correlation, Simple Slope, Simple Elasticity, and Simple Adjusted Relationship Measure for Current Operating Expenditures per Pupil with Income per Return

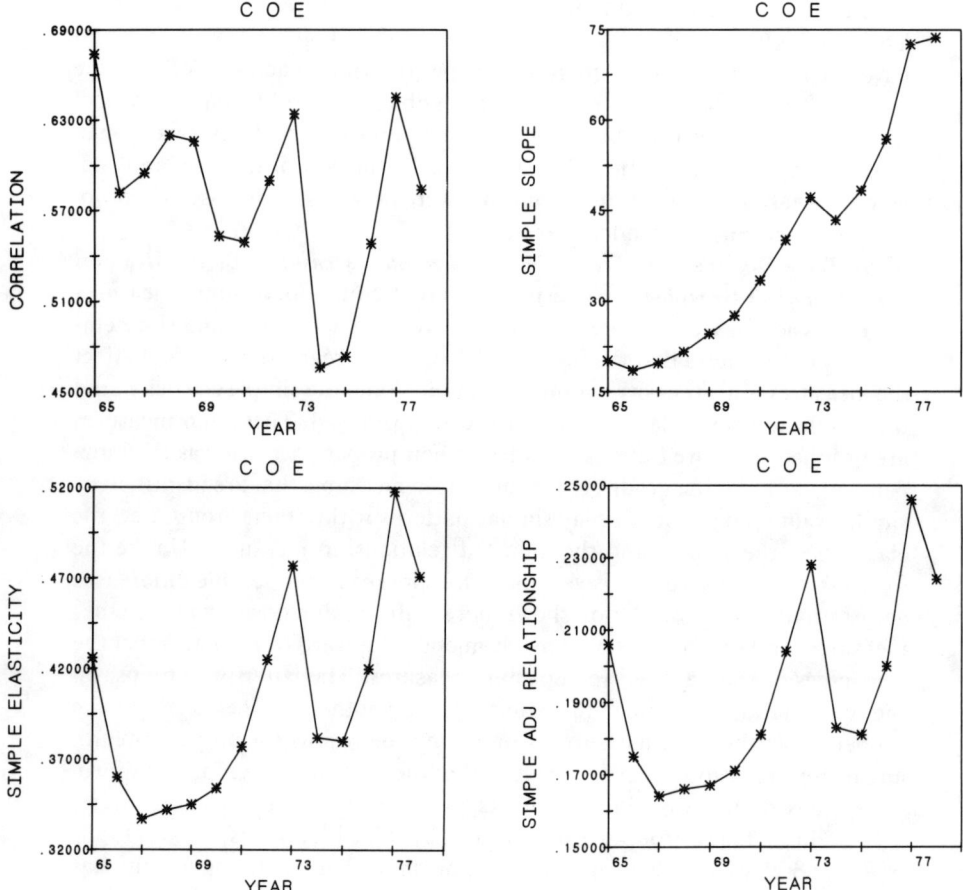

ditures and price-adjusted current operating expenditures as objects are practically identical. The price-adjusted correlation measure exhibits a somewhat smoother pattern in the 1960s than does the unadjusted measure. Again, with the exception of the correlation, the price-adjusted measures are all more equitable in any given year than the unadjusted measures.

Equal Opportunity with Respect to Region

The third independent variable to be analyzed in New York is region. Most states have politically and historically established regional breakdowns that are used by legislatures, executive branches, and interest groups when assess-

Figure 8.26 New York: Correlation, Simple Slope, Simple Elasticity, and Simple Adjusted Relationship Measure for Price-Adjusted Current Operating Expenditures per Pupil with Income per Return

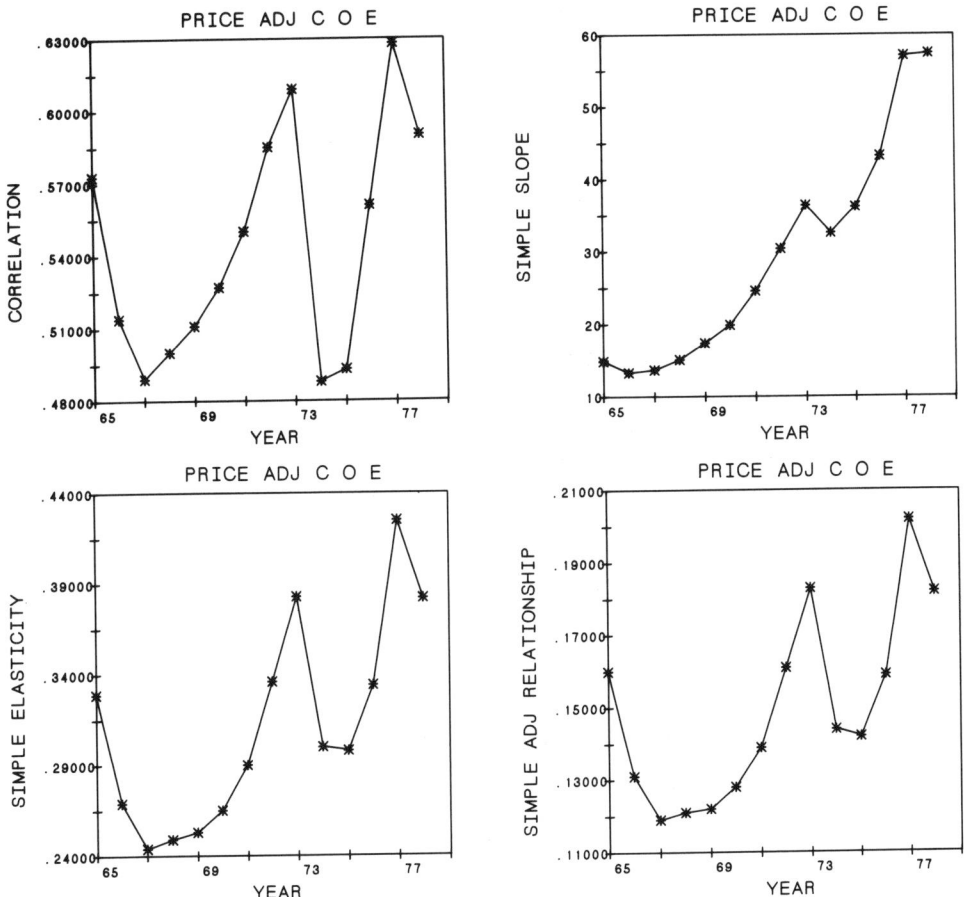

ing the impacts of state programs. In New York, the most common regional division is the downstate-upstate one, meaning the New York City metropolitan area (with its suburbs) versus all other areas in the state. For purposes of this study, two further subdivisions are made. The downstate region is divided into New York City (NYC) and all the school districts in the suburban counties of Nassau, Suffolk, Westchester, and Rockland (downstate suburbs). The upstate region is divided between the school districts of its four major cities of Albany, Rochester, Buffalo, and Syracuse (big four) and all other upstate school districts (upstate nonurban).

Since there is no a priori reason why any one region should obtain more educational resources than the others, perfect equal opportunity would imply no differences in objects between regions. In order to assess how closely the New York school-finance system has approached this goal over time, the average pupil-weighted expenditures per pupil are compared across regions. This is carried out via a regression analysis, with regional dummies, although the same results could have been obtained from a one-way analysis of variance. Two objects, current operating expenditures and price-adjusted current operating expenditures, are used in the regional analyses.

What Are the Trends in Regional Equal Opportunity with Current Operating Expenditures as the Object? The upper part of figure 8.27 graphically displays the trends for regional equal opportunity when current operating expenditures is the object. The downstate suburbs consistently have the highest ratios, and the ratios rise over time, indicating a relatively faster rise in their current operating expenditures compared to the upstate nonurban current operating expenditures. With the exception of the big four in 1965 and 1966 (when their ratio falls below 1.0), the upstate nonurban districts have the lowest regional current operating expenditures throughout the time series. New York City never attains the current operating expenditures of its suburbs and only twice falls below the big four current operating expenditures. New York City shows the most erratic movement of all four regions. This may be because New York City is one district, while the other regions are averages of several or many districts. Nevertheless, only the downstate suburbs contain more pupils than New York City, so that the relative standing of New York City affects significant numbers of pupils. The three trends in ratios are not

Figure 8.27 New York: Current Operating Expenditures per Pupil and Price-Adjusted Current Operating Expenditures per Pupil, by Region (with Upstate Nonurban Region as Denominator)

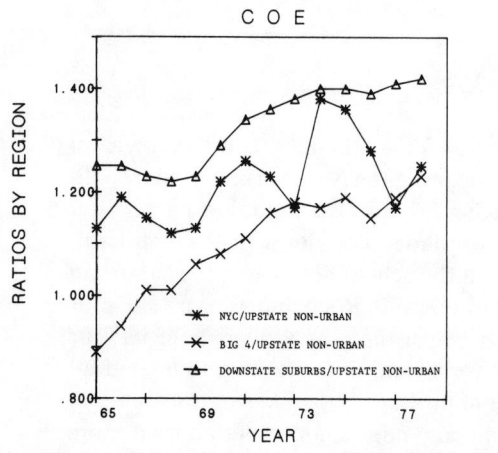
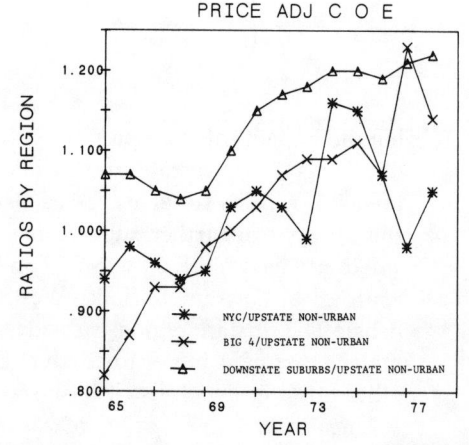

approaching 1.0 over time, and thus perfect equal opportunity across all four regions is not being approached. In addition, both the big four and the downstate suburbs are moving relatively further away from the upstate nonurban region, thus worsening relative equal opportunity for this latter region. Only the downstate suburbs and the big four seem to have made some equalizing progress in the early part of the time series, when their ratios moved closer together.

What Are the Trends in Regional Equal Opportunity With Price-Adjusted Current Operating Expenditures as the Object? The lower part of figure 8.27 displays trends in the New York ratios for price-adjusted current operating expenditures. Some significant changes in the patterns emerge compared to the figures for unadjusted current operating expenditures. Most striking is the change in New York City, which is now below the current operating expenditures level of the upstate nonurban region in seven of the fourteen years, those years being mostly at the beginning of the time series, but with 1977 also being especially low. As might be expected, uncontrollable price levels are relatively high in New York City, and to the extent that price-adjusted current operating expenditures is a good measure of real resources, New York City fares less well with resources than when nominal dollars are the object. The downstate suburbs once again fare better than the other regions, with the exception of 1977, but their advantage is somewhat reduced by the price adjustment, which brings them closer to the other regions than they were with current operating expenditures. Finally the big four upstate cities are no longer the third highest region, but rather move back and forth between second and third place, trading with New York City. Through 1970, the big four exhibit price-adjusted current operating expenditures that are lower than or equivalent to the upstate nonurban region, but thereafter they are above the upstate nonurban group.

In addition to the changes in position of New York City and the big four, the price adjustment for the most part brings the ratios closer to 1.0 and thus improves overall equal opportunity. Nowhere in the equity analyses, thus far, has the price adjustment made such a difference to the conclusions in New York as it does for regions.

OVERALL CHAPTER CONCLUSIONS

The conclusions reported here are organized in a similar way to those in chapter 7. They are based on the in-depth analyses of Michigan and New York combined and are divided into two parts. First are methodological generalizations about the differences in equity trends or levels that result from alternative measures and objects. Second are substantive conclusions about the trends and levels in equal opportunity.

Conclusions on Methodology

Two methodological questions are addressed throughout this chapter. The first asks if the measure of equal opportunity influences results, holding the object constant. The second reverses the ceteris paribus and asks if the object matters, holding the measure constant. Each of these is discussed in turn.

Does the Measure Make a Difference When Assessing Equal Opportunity Trend? The answer here depends on the version of equal opportunity that is studied, or put another way, on the independent variable. In both Michigan and New York, alternative measures yield similar results when property wealth is the independent variable. Since wealth-based equal opportunity is the most commonly studied equal-opportunity principle and since analysts do not always use the same measure, it is encouraging to find that the measure does not influence the results longitudinally, at least in these two states.

When income is the independent variable, both the Michigan and the New York analyses reveal that the measure can influence the results. For both states, it is generally true that the groups based on value judgments show similar results, but that the correlation in particular is often different from the slopes, the elasticities, or the adjusted relationship measures. In Michigan, the functional form within a group sometimes makes a small difference, and in New York both the slopes and the correlations differ from other measures, and from each other.

Race as an independent variable was studied solely in Michigan, and here it was found that the direction of the relationship between race and the object was the same for all measures. The trends were also fairly consistent across measures, with the exception of a slight difference between the slope and all others.

Does the measure make a difference in these two states? Except when property wealth is the independent variable, the answer is yes. But that yes is somewhat qualified, because the differences are not enormous, and within value judgment groups, the measures are, by and large, consistent no matter what the independent variable is.

Does the Object Make A Difference When Assessing Equal Opportunity? The answer to this question is a clear-cut yes. In New York, only two objects were examined, current operating expenditures and price-adjusted current operating expenditures. While the trends in both objects were similar for income and wealth, the level of equity improved with the price adjustment. When regional equal opportunity was assessed, the ranking of regions changed slightly with the price adjustment. In particular, New York City showed a greater variation and was not always ranked second. Regional equal opportunity did improve with the price adjustment, in that the regions were closer together in average values of price-adjusted current operating expenditures.

The Michigan data allowed the examination of a wider variety of objects, and both trends and levels differed depending on the chosen object. For wealth-based equal opportunity, the major differences were between dollar objects, price-adjusted dollar objects, and resources. For any given year, resources generally displayed the most equal opportunity, unadjusted dollars the least, and price-adjusted dollars were in the middle. The trends over the years were most different when price-adjusted revenues were compared to price-adjusted expenditures and to all dollar objects. Price-adjusted revenues displayed a U-shaped pattern, while the other objects showed improvement, albeit inconsistent, over the years.

For income-based equal opportunity, two major differences in conclusions were found when objects were varied. First, there were rather clear-cut differences within the dollar objects, with total revenues and instructional expenditures more equitable than the other two revenue objects. Second, while the price adjustment had little effect on trends, it did consistently improve the level of income-based equal opportunity. In general, equal opportunity with respect to income, while dependent on the object, was less so than wealth-based equal opportunity.

Perhaps more than anywhere else, trends and levels in equal opportunity with respect to race demonstrate that the choice of an object matters. Among the dollar objects alone, some show a lack of equal opportunity for several years while others exhibit equal opportunity for all years. The presence of equal opportunity across all years occurs with the instructional-expenditures and total-revenues objects, both of which include categorical and federal funds. Since categorical and federal revenues are allocated on the basis of variables that one would expect to be highly correlated with race, this result is to be expected. When dollar objects are compared to price-adjusted dollar objects and resources, more-striking differences result. For the latter two objects, equal opportunity with respect to race does not exist. In other words, the direction of the relationship between the object and percent minority is negative throughout the time period, while it is positive in at least some years for all the dollar objects.

Finally, regional equal opportunity in Michigan is significantly influenced by the choice of object. While the dollar objects show Detroit to be ranked second in average value, the other objects show it to be last. In addition, disparities in equal opportunity narrowed somewhat over the time period for all but the dollar objects.

Least for wealth and most for race—but to some extent true for all independent variables—the object does make a difference in levels and trends in equal opportunity in Michigan. Where the data were available, that result was corroborated in New York.

Conclusions on Equal-Opportunity Trends in Each State

Because the trends and levels in equal opportunity depend on the object in both states, we cannot draw any generalizable conclusions. Nevertheless, for each independent variable, it is usually possible to make some limited conclusions.

We begin with Michigan. Based on dollar objects, equal opportunity with respect to property wealth generally improved over the years 1970 to 1978, but this was less true when the price adjustment was made or for resources. For income-based equal opportunity, the most common patterns were U-shaped and W-shaped ones, both of which showed the state ending the period no better than when it began. With race as the independent variable, equal opportunity did not exist for price-adjusted dollars and for resources; when dollars were unadjusted, the results were mixed. Finally, regional equal opportunity showed Detroit to be least equal and the middle cities most favored for all objects except unadjusted dollars. With the latter object, Detroit fared better, although the middle cities remained best off.

In New York, both property wealth- and income-based equal opportunity worsened over the period 1965 to 1978. When current operating expenditures was price-adjusted, the worsening trend still existed, but the level of current operating expenditures was more equitable. Regional equal opportunity neither worsened nor improved in terms of a narrowing of disparities, but New York City's position did vary, especially for price-adjusted current operating expenditures.

9

VERTICAL EQUITY IN MICHIGAN AND NEW YORK

Over the past decade, as the measurement of the horizontal-equity and equal-opportunity principles have become more sophisticated and more frequent, a recurring criticism of school-finance analysts has been their failure to address the vertical-equity principle. As the discussions and illustrations in earlier chapters suggested, vertical equity is the most difficult principle to articulate and measure and is often subject to data limitations. Despite this, the framework and hypothetical examples presented in chapters 2 through 4 provide a means to specify and measure vertical equity, and in this chapter we use available data to assess vertical equity in Michigan and New York.

Vertical equity can be expressed as the unequal treatment of unequals, and its measurement requires the identification of unequals, the specification of the appropriately unequal treatment, and the measurement of vertical equity based on the prior identification and specification. The focus in this chapter is on the measurement question, and the methodological questions used to organize the analyses in chapters 7 and 8 are relied upon here as well. Although entire books could be devoted to the methodology of identifying unequal groups and specifying unequal treatments, within the context of this analysis some issues are addressed in a more limited fashion. In particular, sensitivity analysis is performed to detect how the answers to the basic methodological questions are affected by alternative specifications of unequals and appropriate treatments.

Thus, where data are available, the following five questions are addressed:

1. Are there differences in the trends in vertical equity due to the alternative measures? Do the measures form empirical groupings that are identical or similar to the conceptual groupings identified in chapter 2?

2. Are there differences either in the trends or in the levels of vertical equity due to alternative input-based dollar objects such as local plus total

state revenues versus instructional expenditures, holding the measure constant?

3. How does the adjustment of input-based dollar objects by a price index affect the trends in vertical equity, holding the measure constant? Does the price index alter trends in equity, the absolute levels of equity, or both?

4. How do the trends in and the levels of vertical equity differ with input-based resource objects compared to input-based objects measured in dollars and price-adjusted dollars, holding the measure constant?

5. To what extent is the measurement of vertical equity affected by the alternative specification of the unequal groups and the appropriately unequal treatment?

Although the vertical-equity principle could incorporate a wide range of definitions of unequals, in this analysis the identification of unequals is based on student needs. For both Michigan and New York, student needs are defined in terms of handicapping conditions and learning deficiencies, where the latter are specified in terms of socioeconomic criteria in Michigan and student-achievement criteria in New York. Agreement with our choices of unequals is not a prerequisite to understanding the methodology, although it is necessary if our substantive findings on the two states are to be believed.

Throughout this chapter, the question of how to determine the appropriately unequal treatment of the unequal groups must also be answered. Original research in this area has not been carried out. Instead, we have relied on the work of others who have translated unequal treatments into pupil weights. In general, other research has attempted to answer the difficult question, How much more educational objects should pupils in special groups receive? Usually, this amount is expressed in terms of additional resources (dollars) for pupils with special needs compared to pupils without special needs, and this can be translated to a pupil weight where the resources of the baseline pupil are assigned a weight of 1.0. For Michigan, a state that has not developed pupil weights as part of its school-finance system, the weights are based on research carried out on a national basis as well as in other states. Our review of this literature reveals a fair degree of consistency across a diverse set of studies. In New York, the State Education Department has recently estimated a set of weights for students in special groups based on a statewide average-cost study, and these weights are used in the assessment of vertical equity in New York.

The remainder of this chapter is divided into three sections. The first section examines the five methodological questions for Michigan where data on alternative objects are available. The analysis of New York is more limited and only questions 1, 3, and 5 are addressed in the second section. The third section contains a summary of the methodological findings on the measurement of vertical equity and also includes substantive findings on what has happened to vertical equity in Michigan and New York over the respective study periods.

AN ASSESSMENT OF VERTICAL EQUITY IN MICHIGAN

Vertical equity in Michigan is analyzed in this section by answering the five questions posed at the beginning of the chapter. The first four questions—namely, differences among measures; dollar objects; dollar and price-adjusted dollar objects; and dollar, price-adjusted dollar, and input-based objects—are answered sequentially. The fifth question, the effects of alternative specifications of the unequal groups, is addressed throughout the chapter.

An explanation of this last issue, the way the unequal groups are defined and measured in Michigan, is presented below, before the actual assessment of vertical equity begins. The selection of the unequal groups of pupils is a value judgment that must be made regardless of the way vertical equity is measured. Furthermore, if vertical equity is measured with weighted dispersion measures, as is done in this chapter, the appropriate unequal treatment for the unequal groups must be specified, usually in the form of pupil weightings.

Often, a state's finance plan will include specific pupil categories and associated weightings that can serve as a potential grouping and weighting scheme for the measurement of vertical equity. This is the case in New York, and the analyses in the next section of the chapter utilize groups defined in the formula and weights developed for a task force that evaluated New York's school finances. In Michigan the school-finance formula does not include specific pupil categories, and weights have not been researched; however, district-level pupil data are available for an extensive set of pupil categories. Therefore, in the analysis of vertical equity in Michigan, some reliance is placed on studies from other states, particularly when the pupil weights are specified.

In chapter 2, the various candidates for inclusion as the unequal groups in the vertical-equity principle were discussed. In the empirical assessments of vertical equity in Michigan (as well as in New York), the unequal groups include two of the more commonly agreed-upon categories: pupils with handicapping conditions and pupils with learning disadvantages or deficiencies. In Michigan, data are available on the number of pupils, measured in full-time equivalents (FTE's), in eleven categories of handicapping conditions in each district. These categories and their definitions are listed in table 9.1.

Note that the handicapped categories defined in table 9.1 explicitly exclude pupils whose unsatisfactory performance is based on their social, economic, and cultural background. Yet many peoples' values are consistent with the special treatment of pupils who, because of their background, are learning disadvantaged. Achievement tests are one way to identify a group of pupils who are learning deficient, and this methodology is employed in the analysis

Table 9.1. Definitions of Categories of Handicapping Conditions in Michigan

1. Educable mentally impaired.
    "Educable mentally impaired" means a person identified by an educational planning and placement committee, based upon a comprehensive evaluation by a school psychologist, certified psychologist or certified consulting psychologist, and other pertinent information, as having all the following behavioral characteristics:
    (a) Development at a rate approximately 2 to 3 standard deviations below the mean as determined through intellectual assessment.
    (b) Scores approximately within the lowest 6 percentiles on a standardized test in reading and arithmetic.
    (c) Lack of development primarily in the cognitive domain.
    (d) Unsatisfactory academic performance not found to be based on his social, economic and cultural background.

2. Trainable mentally impaired.
    "Trainable mentally impaired" means a person identified by an educational planning and placement committee, based upon a comprehensive evaluation by a school psychologist, certified psychologist or certified consulting psychologist, and other pertinent information, as having all the following behavioral characteristics:
    (a) Development at rate approximately 3 to $4\frac{1}{2}$ standard deviations below the mean as determined through intellectual assessment.
    (b) Lack of development primarily in the cognitive domain.
    (c) Unsatisfactory school performance not found to be based on his social, economic and cultural background.

3. Severely mentally impaired.
    "Severely mentally impaired" means a person identified by an educational planning and placement committee, based upon a comprehensive evaluation by a school psychologist, certified psychologist or certified consulting psychologist, and other pertinent information, as having all the following behavioral characteristics:
    (a) Development at a rate approximately $4\frac{1}{2}$ or more standard deviations below the mean as determined through intellectual assessment.
    (b) Lack of development primarily in the cognitive domain.

4. Emotionally impaired.
    "Emotionally impaired" means a person identified by an educational planning and placement committee, based upon a comprehensive evaluation by a school psychologist and social worker, a certified psychologist, a certified consulting psychologist, or a certified psychiatrist, and other pertinent information, as having 1 or more of the following behavioral characteristics:
    (a) Disruptive to the learning process of other students or himself in the regular classroom over an extended period of time.
    (b) Extreme withdrawal from social interaction in the school environment over an extended period of time.
    (c) Manifestation of symptoms characterized by diagnostic labels such as psychosis, schizophrenia and autism.
    (d) Disruptive behavior which has resulted in placement in a juvenile detention facility.

5. Learning disabled.
    "Learning disabled" means a person identified by an educational planning and placement committee, based upon a comprehensive evaluation by a school psychologist or certified psychologist or certified consulting psychologist, or an evaluation by a neurologist, or equivalent medical examiner qualified to evaluate neurological dysfunction, and other pertinent information, as having all the following characteristics:
    (a) Disorder in 1 or more of the basic psychological processes involved in understanding or in using spoken or written language, which disorder may manifest itself in imperfect ability to listen, think, speak, read, write, spell or do mathematical calculation.
    (b) Manifestation of symptoms characterized by diagnostic labels such as perceptual handicap, brain injury, minimal brain dysfunction, dyslexia or aphasia.
    (c) Development at less than the expected rate of age group in the cognitive, affective or psychomotor domains.

Table 9.1. Definitions of Categories of Handicapping Conditions in Michigan (*cont.*)

(d) Inability to function in regular education without supportive special education services.

(e) Unsatisfactory performance not found to be based on social, economic or cultural background.

6. Hearing impaired.

    "Hearing impaired" means a person identified by an educational planning and placement committee, based upon an evaluation by an audiologist and otolaryngologist, and other pertinent information, as having a hearing impairment which intereferes with learning.

7. Visually impaired.

    "Visually impaired" means a person identified by an educational planning and placement committee, based upon an evaluation by an ophthalmologist, or equivalent, and other pertinent information as having a visual impairment which interferes with learning and having 1 or more of the following behavioral characteristics:

    (a) A central visual acuity of 20/70 or less, in the better eye after correction;

    (b) A peripheral field of vision restricted to no greater than 20 degrees.

8. Physically and otherwise health impaired.

    "Physically and otherwise health impaired" means a person identified by an educational planning and placement committee, based upon an evaluation by an orthopedic surgeon, internist, neurologist, pediatrician or equivalent, and other pertinent information, as having a physical or other health impairment which interferes with learning or requires physical adaptation in the school environment.

9. Severely multiply impaired.

    "Severely multiply impaired" means a person identified by an educational planning and placement committee, based upon a comprehensive evaluation by a school psychologist, certified psychologist or certified consulting psychologist and an evaluation by a neurologist, orthopedic surgeon, ophthalmologist, or otolaryngologist and an audiologist, and other pertinent information such as previous medical records and any education history, as having all of the following behavior characteristics:

    (a) Severe multiplicity of handicaps in the physical and cognitive domains;

    (b) Inability or expected inability to function within other special education programs which deal with a single handicap.

    (c) Development at less than the expected rate of age group in the cognitive, affective or psychomotor domains.

10. Homebound and hospitalized.

    "Homebound" means a person certified at least annually by a licensed physician as having a severe physical or other health impairment preventing school attendance.

    "Hospitalized" means a person who cannot attend school because of hospitalization for a physical or medical impairment, exclusive of emotional impairment unless as an accompaniment to a physical or medical impairment.

11. Speech and language impaired.

    "Speech and language impaired" means a person certified by a teacher with full approval as a teacher of the speech and language impaired, who has earned a master's degree and has completed at least 5 years of successful teaching of the speech and language impaired, as having 1 or more of the following speech, oral language and verbal communication impairments which interferes with learning or social adjustment:

    (a) Articulation which includes omission, substitutions or distortions of sound.

    (b) Voice with inappropriate voice pitch, rate of speaking, loudness or quality of speech.

    (c) Fluency of speech distinguished by speech interruptions (blocks), repetition of sounds, words, phrases or sentences which interferes with effective communication.

    (d) Inability to comprehend, formulate and use functional language.

Source: State of Michigan, Administrative Code.

of vertical equity in New York. In Michigan, an alternative approach is utilized, based on poverty as a proxy for learning disadvantaged.

More specifically, for the vertical-equity analysis in Michigan, the number of pupils who are *eligible* for Title I allocations are treated as the number of pupils in each district who are learning disadvantaged.[1] Title I eligibles are defined as the sum of the following three groups:

1. The number of children age five to seventeen inclusive from families below the poverty level on the basis of the most satisfactory data available from the Department of Commerce.
2. Two-thirds of the number of children age five to seventeen from families receiving payments under Aid to Families with Dependent Children greater than the current poverty level for a nonfarm family of four.
3. The number of children age five to seventeen—being supported with public funds—who live in foster homes or in institutions for neglected or delinquent children and depend on the local educational agency for educational services.[2]

For certain vertical-equity measures, the weighted dispersion measures— value judgments that go beyond the identification of the unequal groups—are necessary. Since Michigan does not use a weighted-pupil formula and research has not been carried out to determine weights in Michigan, a survey of studies of weighting schemes in other states was undertaken to formulate weights for Michigan.

Probably the best known study of pupil weightings is the analysis carried out by Rossmiller, Hale, and Frohreich for the National Educational Finance Project (the NEFP study).[3] The NEFP study examined "high quality" special education programs in selected districts in Wisconsin, Florida, California, Texas, and New York to determine weights based on the ratio of special education costs to regular education costs.[4] For many categories of handicapped pupils, the NEFP study proposed a range of pupil weightings that were termed "reasonable." Subsequent to the NEFP effort, numerous cost studies have been carried out, using a sample of districts in a particular state, to determine pupil weightings.[5] Although there are variations in the methodolo-

---

1. Title I refers to title I of the Elementary and Secondary Education Act of 1965.
2. National Institute of Education, *Title I Funds Allocation: The Current Formula* (Washington, D.C.: National Institute of Education, HEW, 1977), p. 104.
3. R. A. Rossmiller, J. A. Hale, and L. E. Frohreich, *Educational Programs for Exceptional Children: Resource Configurations and Costs,*, National Educational Finance Project Special Study no. 2 (Madison: The University of Wisconsin, 1970).
4. For a summary of the NEFP study see C. D. Bernstein, W. T. Hartman, M. W. Kirst, and R. S. Marshall, *Financing Educational Services for the Handicapped: An Analysis of Current Research and Practices* (Reston, Va.: Council for Exceptional Children, 1976).
5. For the results of studies of pupil weightings in various states and cities, see J. J. Marinelli, Jr., "Financing the Education of Exceptional Children," in F. J. Weintraub, A. Abeson, J. Ballard, and M. L. LaVor, ed., *Public Policy and the Evaluation of Exceptional Children* (Reston,

gies and results, the findings in these later studies are similar to the NEFP findings in a majority of the cases.

While methodologies based on costs are not the only ways to determine pupil weights, given the reliance on this methodology in the existing studies and the consistency in their results, the specification of the weightings used in the vertical-equity assessment in Michigan is based on this body of research.[6] Regardless of the methodology, the determination of pupil weights requires value judgments, and therefore, sensitivity analysis is employed to capture the effects of alternative weightings. The reader must agree with the selection of weights in order to accept the substantive findings, but the methodological conclusions, particularly those drawn at the end of this chapter based on Michigan and New York, should not be as sensitive as the substantive findings to the actual weights chosen.

Table 9.2 displays the two weighting schemes that are utilized in the analysis of vertical equity in Michigan. The first scheme, scheme 1, treats only the pupils with handicapping conditions as the unequal group. The weightings in scheme 1 vary by handicapping category and correspond to the high end of the reasonable range recommended by the NEFP.[7] We have selected the high end because it is more consistent with the results in other studies[8] and because a higher weighting is more likely to produce methodological distinctions. In the other weighting scheme, scheme 2, both pupils with handicapping conditions and pupils with learning disadvantages are treated as unequal groups. However, in scheme 2, all handicapped and learning disadvantaged pupils are given a weight of two.

In a world of complete data, the number of pupils in the unequal groups would be available in every year of the vertical-equity analysis. For this assessment of vertical equity, however, data on pupils in the unequal groups are only available for the most recent year of our time series, 1977–78. In order to overcome this data limitation, it has been assumed that the *percentage* of pupils in each district who were in each category of handicapped condition and who were eligible for Title I in 1977–78 is constant over the entire nine-

---

Va.: Council for Exceptional Children, 1976) [deals with Indiana, Illinois, Minnesota, Texas]; J. Leppert and D. Routh, *Weighted Pupil Education Finance Systems in Three States: Florida, Utah, and New Mexico* (Washington, D.C.: National Institute of Education, 1980); L. S. Marriner, "The Cost of Educating Handicapped Pupils in New York City," *Journal of Education Finance* 3 (spring 1977): 82–97; and J. R. Stulz, "The Incidence of Educational Needs and the Cost of Meeting These Needs in the United States in 1980," Ed.D. dissertation, University of Florida, Gainesville, 1974.

6. For an assessment of the National Educational Finance Project (NEFP) methodology and suggested alternatives, see Bernstein et al., *Financing Educational Services for the Handicapped*. See also, W. T. Hartman, "Projecting Special Education Costs," Paper 81–88, Stanford University, Institute for Research in Educational Finance and Governance, June 1981.

7. In two categories, hearing impaired and visually impaired, weights were utilized from other studies, since these categories were not included in the NEFP study. Pupils with speech and language impairments are not included in the empirical analyses, due to data problems.

8. See the studies listed in note 5, above.

Table 9.2. Pupil Weights for Vertical-Equity Assessment in Michigan

	Scheme 1	Scheme 2
Handicapping conditions		
1. Educable mentally impaired	1.50	2.00
2. Trainable mentally impaired	2.00	2.00
3. Severely mentally impaired	2.00	2.00
4. Emotionally impaired	2.70	2.00
5. Learning disabled	1.50	2.00
6. Hearing impaired	2.71	2.00
7. Visually impaired	5.01	2.00
8. Physically and otherwise health impaired	3.00	2.00
9. Severely multiply impaired	1.29	2.00
10. Homebound and hospitalized	1.60	2.00
Learning disadvantaged		
1. Title I eligibles		2.00

Note: These weights represent the additional cost of a pupil in each category. Thus, a weight of 2 indicates that pupils in the special group receive three $(1 + 2)/1$ times the weighting of a regular pupil.

year study period. This is clearly an approximation. The percentage of pupils is not constant in each district over the study period due to real changes, and because districts may alter the methodology employed to count these pupils. Because each district's ability to identify pupils with handicapping conditions and learning disadvantages has probably improved over the nine-year period—due to increased sensitivity to these pupils' needs and increased availability of funding for special programs—if only one year of data is available, then the last year of the time series is the most desirable.

For the vertical-equity measures that utilize the percentage of pupils in the special groups, the regression-based relationship measures and the ratio measure, the percentage of pupils in each district in each category in 1977–78 is utilized in the other eight years of the vertical-equity analysis. To calculate the third type of vertical-equity measure, the weighted dispersion measures, the number of weighted pupils in each district in each year must be estimated. To do this, the ratio of weighted to unweighted pupils was calculated for 1977–78 for each district and each weighting scheme. Then the estimated number of weighted pupils in the other years was obtained by multiplying the ratio of weighted to unweighted pupils by the actual number of unweighted pupils in the particular year. This technique is consistent with the assumption that the percentages of pupils in the special groups remain constant in each district over time.

Because of missing data on handicapped pupils, the number of districts analyzed in this chapter is slightly lower than those in chapters 7 and 8. As a result, when weighted and unweighted dispersion measures are compared later in this section for Michigan, the unweighted measures have been recomputed using only the pupils for which handicapped data are available. With scheme 1, 2 percent of the pupils are in the special group, and the figure for scheme 2 is 17 percent. The percentage of pupils who are handicapped is lower than the available estimates of the percentage of handicapped pupils in the state because the data used here are reported in terms of full-time equivalents, not headcounts, and because one category listed in table 9.1, speech and language impaired, has been excluded due to data inaccuracies.[9]

Are There Differences in Trends Due to Alternative Measures? Do the Measures Form Empirical Groupings?

Different vertical-equity measures were introduced conceptually in chapter 2 and were illustrated with simple numerical examples in chapter 4. In this section, the differences among the measures are assessed using data from the nine-year time series in Michigan. Before beginning the analysis, a brief review of the three types of vertical-equity measures is presented.

One type, the weighted dispersion measures, is calculated similarly to the horizontal-equity measures, except that weighted pupils are utilized instead of unweighted pupils. Any measure used as a horizontal-equity measure can be reformulated as a weighted dispersion measure. Recall that the weighted dispersion measure captures all the inequality in the distribution of objects and can be easily utilized to rank several states in terms of their vertical equity or to determine a trend in vertical equity in one state over time. Furthermore, the weighted dispersion measures can be compared with the unweighted dispersion (horizontal-equity) measures to determine whether the weighting procedure reduces or increases the dispersion.

The second and third types of measures are relationship measures, based on either a regression or an averaging technique. Both types of measures determine whether districts with higher percentages of pupils in the special groups have higher per-pupil objects. The regression-based relationship measures and the ratio measures assess the way in which the objects vary with the special groups, but variation unassociated with the special groups is ignored, unlike the weighted dispersion measures that capture all the variation. The regression-based relationship measures and the ratio measures are well suited to determine whether districts that contain a higher percentage of the deserving groups receive higher per pupil objects. Although these measures have the potential to rank states or to assess the trend in one state over time, it was shown in chapter 4 that when used in this way, problems of interpretation may emerge.

The analysis in this section proceeds as follows. First, weighted dispersion measures (excluding Atkinson's index), regression-based relationship measures, and a ratio measure are presented using one object, instructional ex-

---

9. For example, data gathered by the U.S. Office of Special Education indicate that 6.74 percent of the pupils in Michigan in 1980–81 were served by special education programs. See Comptroller General, *Disparities Still Exist in Who Gets Special Education* (Washington, D.C.: General Accounting Office, September 1981).

penditures, and two weighting schemes, scheme 1 and scheme 2. Second, the relationship and the ratio measures are examined to determine whether the deserving groups receive higher per-pupil objects, and third, the weighted and the unweighted dispersion measures are compared to find out how the inclusion of vertical-equity criteria affects the horizontal-equity measures. Fourth, the trends in the weighted dispersion measures and the relationship measures are analyzed, and finally, this section concludes with a summary of the methodological and substantive findings.

Tables 9.3 and 9.4 display vertical-equity measures and pupil and district data for nine years in Michigan, using the weightings and groups in scheme 1 and scheme 2, respectively. Each table lists the number of districts and of weighted pupils, the mean and the median instructional expenditure per weighted pupil, ten weighted dispersion measures, five regression-based relationship measures, and one ratio measure. All ten of the horizontal-equity measures examined in chapter 7 are reformulated as weighted dispersion measures. The five regression-based relationship measures are based on the simple regression. Note that the fifth regression-based relationship measure, the implicit weight, is the ratio of the predicted object in a district comprised of all pupils in the special group to the predicted object in a district with no pupils in the special group where the prediction is based on the simple regression.[10] The only ratio measure, the averaged implicit weight, is the ratio of the average object for pupils in the special group to the average object for the pupils who are not in the special group.[11]

As a group, the relationship measures can be used to assess whether the pupils in the special groups receive higher levels of per-pupil instructional expenditures. The first issue we shall examine is whether there is agreement among the five regression-based relationship measures and the ratio measure. Because the five regression-based relationship measures are all based on the simple regression, agreement occurs by definition. When the simple correlation is positive, the simple slope, the simple elasticity, and the simple adjusted relationship measure will be positive, and the implicit weight will be greater than one. Therefore, the only possible contradiction can occur between the five regression-based relationship measures and the ratio measure.

Tables 9.3 and 9.4 show that for instructional expenditures in Michigan, using either grouping scheme, there is agreement between the regression-based relationship measures and the ratio measure in judging whether the deserving groups receive higher levels of the object. In all nine years with both scheme 1 and scheme 2, the six measures agree that districts with higher percentages of pupils in the special groups receive higher per-pupil instructional expenditures. In this case agreement is demonstrated by the positive sign on

---

10. In chapter 8, the implicit weight was labeled the regression-based minority-nonminority ratio.

11. In chapter 8, the averaged implicit weight was labeled the minority-nonminority ratio.

Table 9.3. Michigan: Vertical-Equity Measures for Instructional Expenditures Using Group and Weighting in Scheme 1

	1970	1971	1972	1973	1974	1975	1976	1977	1978
Number of districts	480	480	484	485	485	485	485	484	481
Total weighted pupils	2,176,797	2,191,885	2,232,767	2,213,438	2,177,619	2,156,997	2,148,600	2,101,341	2,033,838
Mean per-pupil (weighted) instructional expenditures	530	600	635	691	747	839	899	934	1,030
Median per pupil (weighted) instructional expenditures	546	610	636	686	759	834	905	929	1,021
Range	597	640	686	1,204	1,064	1,148	1,139	1,103	1,041
Restricted range	279	283	301	359	386	414	473	457	498
Federal range ratio	0.6990	0.6202	0.6214	0.6888	0.6751	0.6553	0.6957	0.6514	0.6300
Relative mean deviation	0.1245	0.1297	0.1306	0.1333	0.1322	0.1350	0.1343	0.1243	0.1309
McLoone index	0.8514	0.8576	0.8682	0.8741	0.8652	0.8703	0.8603	0.8804	0.8763
Variance	7,311	9,230	10,244	16,300	18,397	23,030	28,138	21,157	28,337
Coefficient of variation	0.1613	0.1600	0.1593	0.1847	0.1792	0.1809	0.1865	0.1558	0.1635
Standard deviation of logarithms	0.1585	0.1586	0.1586	0.1723	0.1689	0.1710	0.1733	0.1545	0.1601
Gini coefficient	0.0879	0.0884	0.0888	0.0962	0.0940	0.0950	0.0962	0.0861	0.0986
Theil's measure	0.0128	0.0126	0.0126	0.0160	0.0152	0.0155	0.0163	0.0120	0.0131
Correlation	0.4420	0.4765	0.5152	0.4664	0.4959	0.4791	0.4977	0.5286	0.5132
Simple slope	33.2496	40.6607	46.9651	52.8821	59.9362	64.2510	73.4711	68.6142	76.8215
Simple elasticity	0.1241	0.1330	0.1438	0.1477	0.1518	0.1466	0.1563	0.1399	0.1417
Simple adjusted relationship measure	0.1514	0.1630	0.1766	0.1825	0.1894	0.1841	0.1979	0.1779	0.1804
Implicit weight	7.8861	8.5172	9.3125	9.6411	9.9911	9.6450	10.3281	9.2305	9.3768
Averaged implicit weight	1.0472	1.0511	1.0554	1.0577	1.0604	1.0591	1.0640	1.0578	1.0587

Table 9.4. Michigan: Vertical-Equity Measures for Instructional Expenditures Using Group and Weighting in Scheme 2

	1970	1971	1972	1973	1974	1975	1976	1977	1978
Number of districts	480	480	484	485	485	485	485	484	481
Total weighted pupils	2,835,610	2,848,370	2,893,811	2,863,870	2,809,931	2,780,370	2,766,426	2,700,377	2,611,260
Mean per-pupil (weighted) instructional expenditures	407	462	490	534	587	651	698	727	802
Median per pupil (weighted) instructional expenditures	398	450	473	524	569	631	674	713	774
Range	488	544	566	771	855	949	1,084	981	1,064
Restricted range	252	288	293	359	365	419	419	420	473
Federal range ratio	0.8248	0.8061	0.7650	0.8884	0.8126	0.8425	0.7847	0.7568	0.7716
Relative mean deviation	0.1767	0.1692	0.1588	0.1810	0.1766	0.1768	0.1797	0.1642	0.1665
McLoone index	0.8440	0.8568	0.8748	0.8363	0.8506	0.8504	0.8507	0.8526	0.8652
Variance	8,109	9,478	9,168	14,814	16,713	20,758	25,290	22,557	28,485
Coefficient of variation	0.2212	0.2107	0.1954	0.2278	0.2204	0.2214	0.2277	0.2067	0.2105
Standard deviation of logarithms	0.2119	0.2008	0.1878	0.2171	0.2111	0.2105	0.2140	0.1991	0.1987
Gini coefficient	0.1218	0.1155	0.1076	0.1255	0.1205	0.1203	0.1223	0.1138	0.1138
Theil's measure	0.0235	0.0213	0.0184	0.0248	0.0233	0.0234	0.0256	0.0206	0.0211
Correlation	0.2442	0.3211	0.4145	0.2718	0.1983	0.3029	0.2849	0.3147	0.3256
Simple slope	1.7866	2.6716	3.6688	3.0014	3.5475	4.0307	4.2238	4.1224	4.9257
Simple elasticity	0.0574	0.0750	0.0963	0.0718	0.0766	0.0782	0.0761	0.0710	0.0766
Simple adjusted relationship measure	0.0837	0.1099	0.1421	0.1064	0.1139	0.1164	0.1133	0.1059	0.1144
Implicit weight	1.3438	1.4630	1.6152	1.4504	1.4888	1.5021	1.4897	1.4578	1.4992
Averaged implicit weight	1.0373	1.0492	1.0641	1.0479	1.0515	1.0526	1.0511	1.0478	1.0517

the correlation, simple slope, simple elasticity, and simple adjusted relationship measure occurring when the implicit weight and averaged implicit weight exceed one. Although the data are not shown here, agreement between the regression-based relationship measures and the ratio measure occurs for both grouping schemes, in all years in Michigan for local and total state revenues, total revenues, and classroom teachers, regardless of the use of a price adjustment for the input-based dollar objects. This should not be interpreted to mean that the particular finding of a positive relationship between instructional expenditures and special groups is replicated for other objects and with price adjustments. As will be shown in subsequent sections, this is not always the case.

The literature review presented in chapter 5 showed clearly that analyses of school-finance equity usually include an assessment of horizontal equity, often captured by unweighted dispersion measures such as the federal range ratio and the coefficient of variation. It was equally clear from the review that vertical equity is rarely measured. At the same time, critics of the existing studies argue that unweighted dispersion measures are difficult to interpret because the assumption that all pupils are equal is not met and that therefore, weighted dispersion measures should be employed. Implicit in many of these arguments is the hypothesis that weighted dispersion measures would show less dispersion (i.e., more equity) than the unweighted measures used to capture horizontal equity.

This hypothesis can be tested using the nine-year data in Michigan. Since data on the pupils in the special groups are missing for several districts, the comparisons of the weighted and the unweighted measures do not utilize the horizontal-equity measures presented in chapter 7. Instead, comparisons are made between the weighted dispersion measures displayed in tables 9.3 and 9.4 and the unweighted dispersion measures calculated for the same data.[12] For scheme 1, which includes only handicapped pupils in the special group, the weighted dispersion measures do uniformly show a lower dispersion than the unweighted measures. However, the reverse is generally true for scheme 2, where Title I eligibles are also included in the special group. Similar findings occur when local plus total state revenues and total revenues are used as the object.

Several conclusions can be drawn from this comparison. First, any weighting scheme, even if it is reasonable, will not always reduce the dispersion in the unweighted measures. Second, the results for instructional expenditures and the two revenue-based objects demonstrate that the variation in the weighting schemes has the potential to alter the conclusions drawn from an aspect of a vertical-equity assessment. Finally, when the initial assessments of the relationship and ratio measures and the weighted dispersion measures are

---

12. In fact, the results would differ only slightly if the unweighted measures from chapter 7 were utilized. The general conclusions would be unaffected.

examined simultaneously, an empirical difference can be added to the conceptual distinctions previously delineated. While the relationship and ratio measures consistently show that groups thought to deserve unequal treatment receive higher levels of instructional expenditures, this is not necessarily consistent with the comparison of the weighted and unweighted dispersion measures. Specifically, with scheme 2, the weighted dispersion measures generally show a greater dispersion than the unweighted measures. This provides empirical verification that the relationship and ratio measures on the one hand and the weighted dispersion measures on the other are examining different aspects of vertical equity. The analyses of the trends in the vertical-equity measures that are presented next will further our knowledge of the differences in these two types of measures.

One advantage of the weighted dispersion measures is their usefulness in charting the trends in vertical equity over time. The trends for six weighted dispersion measures for instructional expenditures per weighted pupil using weighting scheme 1 are displayed in figure 9.1. Since the trends form groups that are similar to those previously articulated for the unweighted dispersion measures shown in chapter 7, all ten measures are not graphed. The range, the restricted range, and the variance form one group of generally increasing measures, as would be expected due to inflation. The coefficient of variation, the Gini coefficient, Theil's measure, and the standard deviation of logarithms form a second well-delineated group. The McLoone index presents a trend that is not similar to any of the other measures, particularly in the first four years of the time series. Finally, the trends in the federal range ratio and the relative mean deviation resemble, but are somewhat different from, the group including the coefficient of variation.

Although the data for calculation of the weighted dispersion measures differs slightly from the data assessed in chapter 7, it turns out that the trends in the unweighted measures calculated on the data used in the weighted measures are nearly identical to the trends in the unweighted measures presented in figures 7.2 and 7.3. A comparison of the trends in the unweighted dispersion measures presented in chapter 7 with the weighted dispersion measures displayed here shows that only the trend in the federal range ratio has been particularly altered by the introduction of the weighting system incorporated in scheme 1. Thus, for one object (instructional expenditures) and one weighting system (scheme 1), the trends in the weighted dispersion measures generally mirror those for the unweighted dispersion measures.

Although conceptual problems arise when the regression-based relationship and ratio measures are used to plot the trend in vertical equity over time, it is still worthwhile to examine the trends in these measures to know how they differ empirically among themselves and from the weighted dispersion measures. Figure 9.2 shows the trends in the five regression-based relationship measures based on the simple regression and the one ratio measure, the averaged implicit weight, for instructional expenditures and the groups in scheme

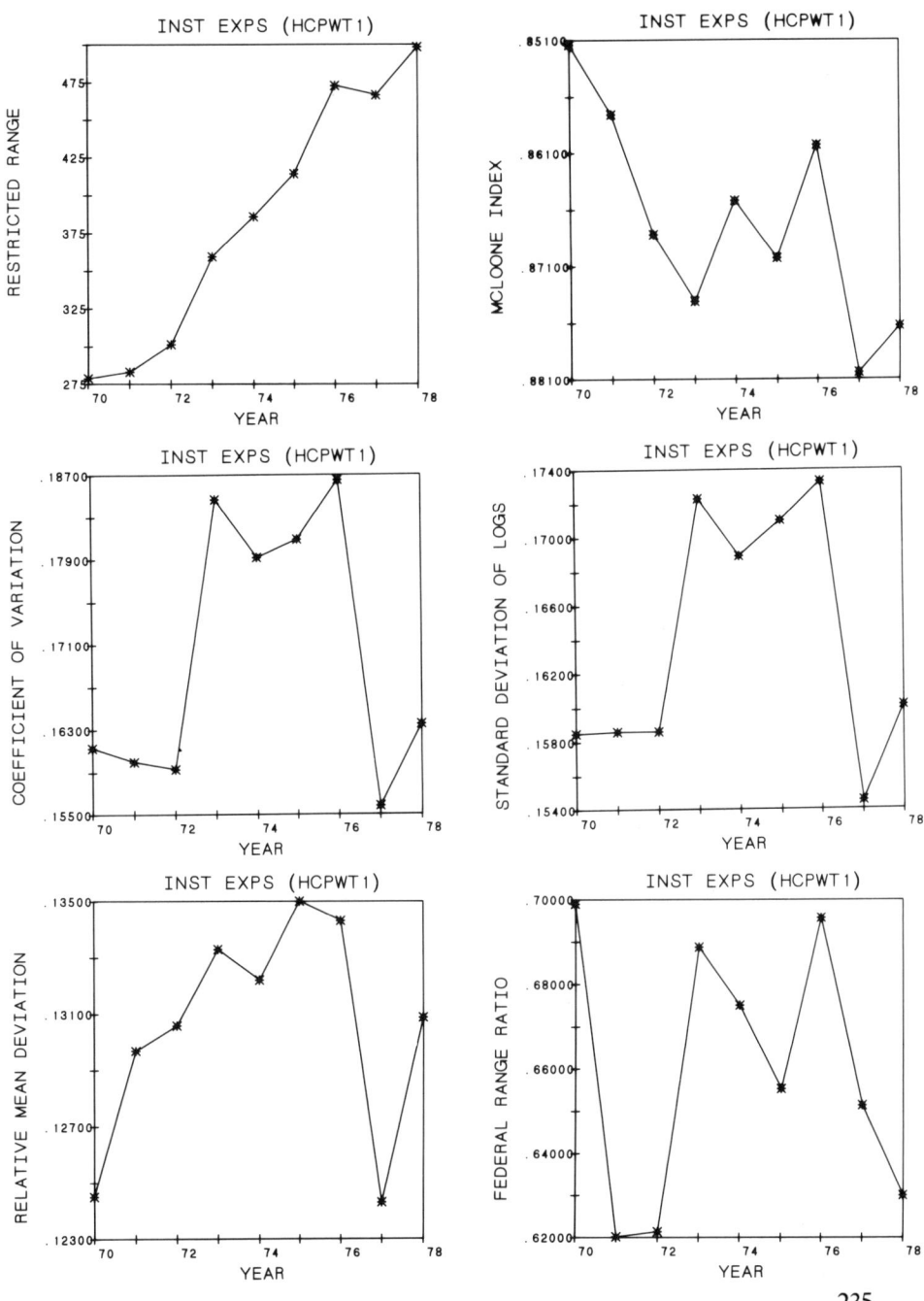

Figure 9.1 Michigan: Restricted Range, McLoone Index, Coefficient of Variation, Standard Deviation of Logarithms, Relative Mean Deviation, and Federal Range Ratio for Instructional Expenditures per Weighted Pupil Using Scheme 1

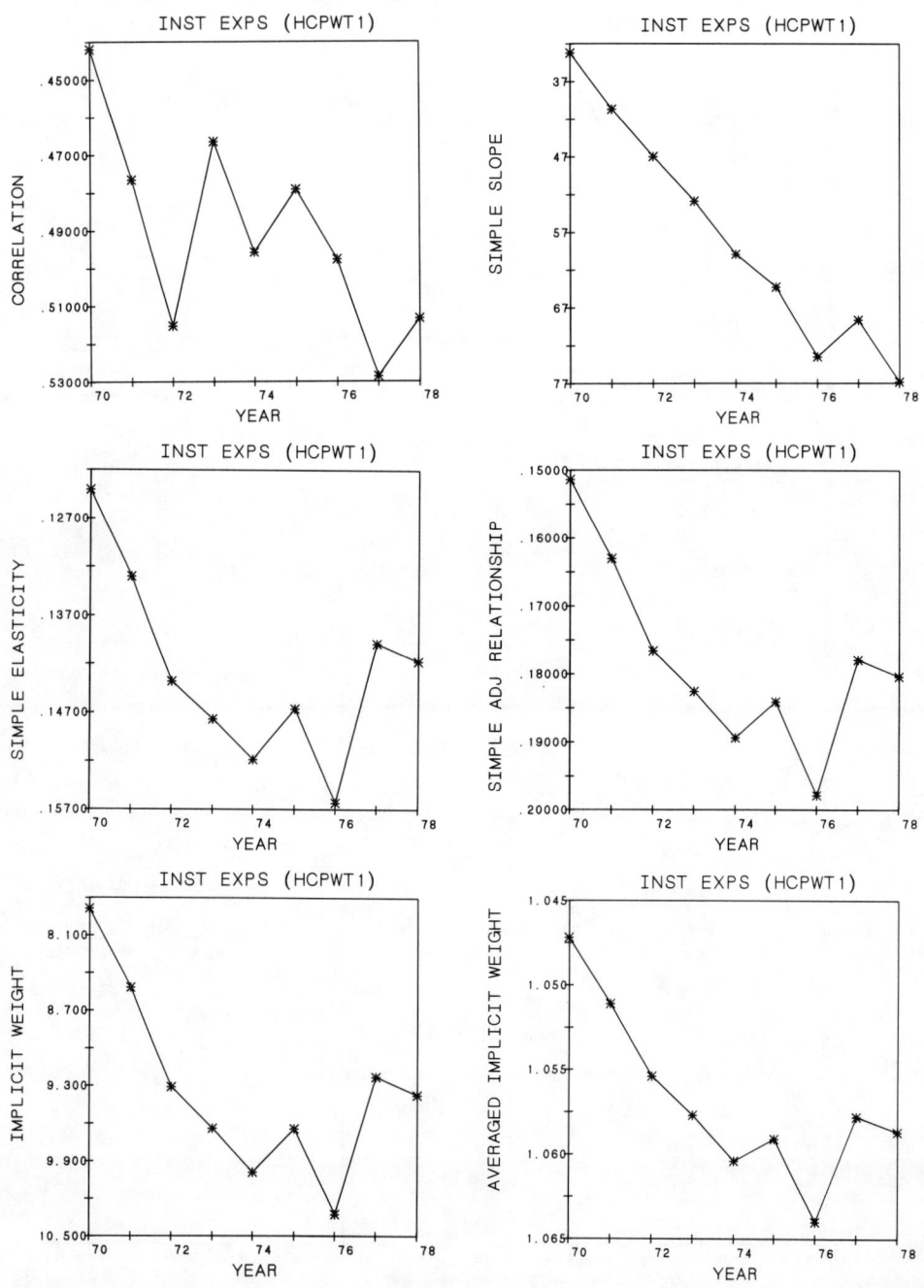

Figure 9.2 Michigan: Correlation, Simple Slope, Simple Elasticity, Simple Adjusted Relationship Measure, Implicit Weight, and Averaged Implicit Weight for Instructional Expenditures per Pupil Using Scheme 1

1. Since higher values for the relationship and ratio measures are indicative of greater equity, at least up to a point, the graphs in figure 9.2 have higher values plotted lower on the graphs. Consistent with all graphs in the book, equity increases as you move down the graphs.

First, the differences in the trends among the six relationship and ratio measures are not pronounced in four of the six cases. The graphs of the simple elasticity, the simple adjusted relationship measure, the implicit weight, and the averaged implicit weight are quite similar. Further, the graph of the simple slope is slightly different at the end of the period, but the correlation shows considerable divergence from the other five measures. All of the measures show a general downward trend over the nine-year period, with the greatest variability in the correlation and the least in the simple slope. Thus, the relationship between the object (instructional expenditures) and the special group (handicapped pupils) became somewhat stronger over the period.

Second, when the trends in the relationship and ratio measures are compared to the trends in the weighted dispersion measures, unmistakable differences are apparent. Only the trend in the McLoone index even moderately resembles those of the relationship and ratio measures. This assessment adds further empirical support to the hypothesis that the weighted dispersion measures assess vertical equity differently then the relationship and ratio measures.

Thus far, the analysis of the trends in the measures has been limited to scheme 1. By examining the trends that result with scheme 2, the question of the replicability of the findings generated for scheme 1 can be addressed. Among the ten weighted dispersion measures, the same general groupings in the trends emerge, and this is also true for the similarity in the trends in the six relationship and ratio measures. When the trends in the measures using scheme 1 are compared to their counterparts using scheme 2, the potential for the weighting scheme to alter the trend in vertical equity is demonstrated. Only in the cases of the restricted range and, to a lesser degree, the coefficient of variation are the trends for the two weighting schemes nearly identical. In other cases, differences caused by the alternative weighting and grouping schemes are revealed. The most noticeable differences occur for the McLoone index, the correlation, and the averaged implicit weight.

The differences in the levels in the vertical-equity measures with scheme 1 and scheme 2 can also be examined using tables 9.3 and 9.4. For many of the weighted dispersion measures, such as the coefficient of variation, the Gini coefficient, and the federal range ratio, vertical equity is greater with scheme 1 than with scheme 2 in every year. This is not true, however, in one year for the McLoone index, and in seven years for the restricted range. With scheme 1, the relationship and ratio measures are consistently larger than the same measures with scheme 2; the only exception is one year for the averaged implicit weight. Thus, the two grouping and weighting schemes alter the trends and yield rather consistent differences in the levels of the vertical-equity measures.

The assessment of alternative measures of vertical equity in this part is based on an analysis of instructional expenditures in Michigan. Alternative objects will be examined in subsequent parts, but the conclusions from this part can be summarized as follows:

1. The five regression-based relationship measures always agree with the ratio measure in judging whether the special groups receive more or less of the object.
2. The weighted dispersion measures do not always show greater equity (lower dispersion) than the unweighted dispersion measures.
3. The differences in the trends among the ten weighted dispersion measures are consistent with those found for the unweighted measures.
4. Trends in the simple slope, the simple elasticity, the simple adjusted relationship measure, the implicit weight, and the averaged implicit weight are quite similar. The trend in the correlation is somewhat different from the other four regression-based relationship measures and the ratio measure.
5. Trends in the relationship and ratio measures are different from the trends in the weighted disparity measures. The differences are considerably more pronounced with scheme 1 than with scheme 2.
6. In several cases the alternative grouping and weighting schemes alter the vertical-equity findings.

Thus, the differences among the alternative vertical-equity measures are well documented. Although the distinctions among the measures are complex, the conceptual difference between the weighted dispersion measures and the relationship and ratio measures is very evident empirically.

Are There Differences Either in the Trends or in the Levels Due to Alternative Input-Based Dollar Objects?

The analysis in this part focuses on the effects of alternative input-based dollar objects on the vertical-equity assessment over the nine-year period in Michigan. The two objects examined, local plus total state revenues and local plus total state plus total federal revenues (hereafter referred to as "total revenues"), are included because both contain resources that are intended for the special groups. In the case of local plus total state revenues, many programs for handicapped and learning disadvantaged children are funded by local and general state revenues. In addition, Michigan has categorical programs for compensatory and special education, and these funds are included in total state revenues. Finally, for total revenues, federal funds are included, and a large share of these funds are accounted for by Title I.

First, we ask whether the relationship and ratio measures show that districts with higher percentages of pupils in the special groups receive greater amounts of the revenue-based objects. With scheme 1 the regression-based relationship measures and the ratio measure indicate that districts with higher percentages of handicapped pupils receive higher levels of local plus total state revenues and total revenues. This replicates the findings for instructional expenditures with scheme 1. These results do not hold for scheme 2 for one of the two objects. When local plus total state revenues is the object in five of the nine years in Michigan, districts with higher percentages of handicapped and Title I eligibles do not receive more local plus total state revenues as determined by the relationship and ratio measures. With scheme 2 and total revenues, however, the original results of the special groups receiving more total revenues are replicated.

The second analytical issue addressed in this part is whether the conclusions on the comparisons between the weighted and the unweighted dispersion measures are affected by the choice of an input-based dollar object. When the results from the analysis of the two revenue objects are compared to the results for instructional expenditures, we find that the objects cause minor variations in the comparisons of the weighted and the unweighted dispersion measures. The differences appear for the federal range ratio and the McLoone index, although no differences are apparent for the coefficient of variation, the Gini coefficient, and Theil's measure. In most cases, the weighted dispersion measures show less dispersion with scheme 1 and more dispersion with scheme 2, but at least the potential for differences among the objects is demonstrated.

Trends in the weighted dispersion measures and the relationship and ratio measures are examined next to see whether the trends are affected by the dollar object. Since the general groupings among the weighted dispersion measures and the relationship and ratio measures documented earlier in the chapter occur for the revenue objects assessed in this part, only selected measures that represent the different groupings are presented at this time. Figures 9.3 and 9.4 display the trends in the vertical-equity measures using scheme 1 for local plus total state revenues and for total revenues respectively.

Comparisons of the trends in the two revenue-based dollar objects—displayed in figures 9.3 and 9.4—with the trends in instructional expenditures shown in figures 9.1 and 9.2 document the ability of alternative objects to affect the trends in vertical-equity measures. The trend in the restricted range does not differ greatly across the three objects. The other five measures presented in figures 9.3 and 9.4 are not similar for all three objects. For example, the trend in instructional expenditures is unlike the trend in the two revenue objects for the coefficient of variation, the correlation, and the averaged implicit weight. In addition, the trends in the federal range ratio and the McLoone index vary across all three objects, although less systematically.

The findings are consistent when scheme 2 is utilized; thus, the graphs of the measures are not presented. Differences of varying magnitude exist in the trends of the revenue and instructional expenditure objects for the federal

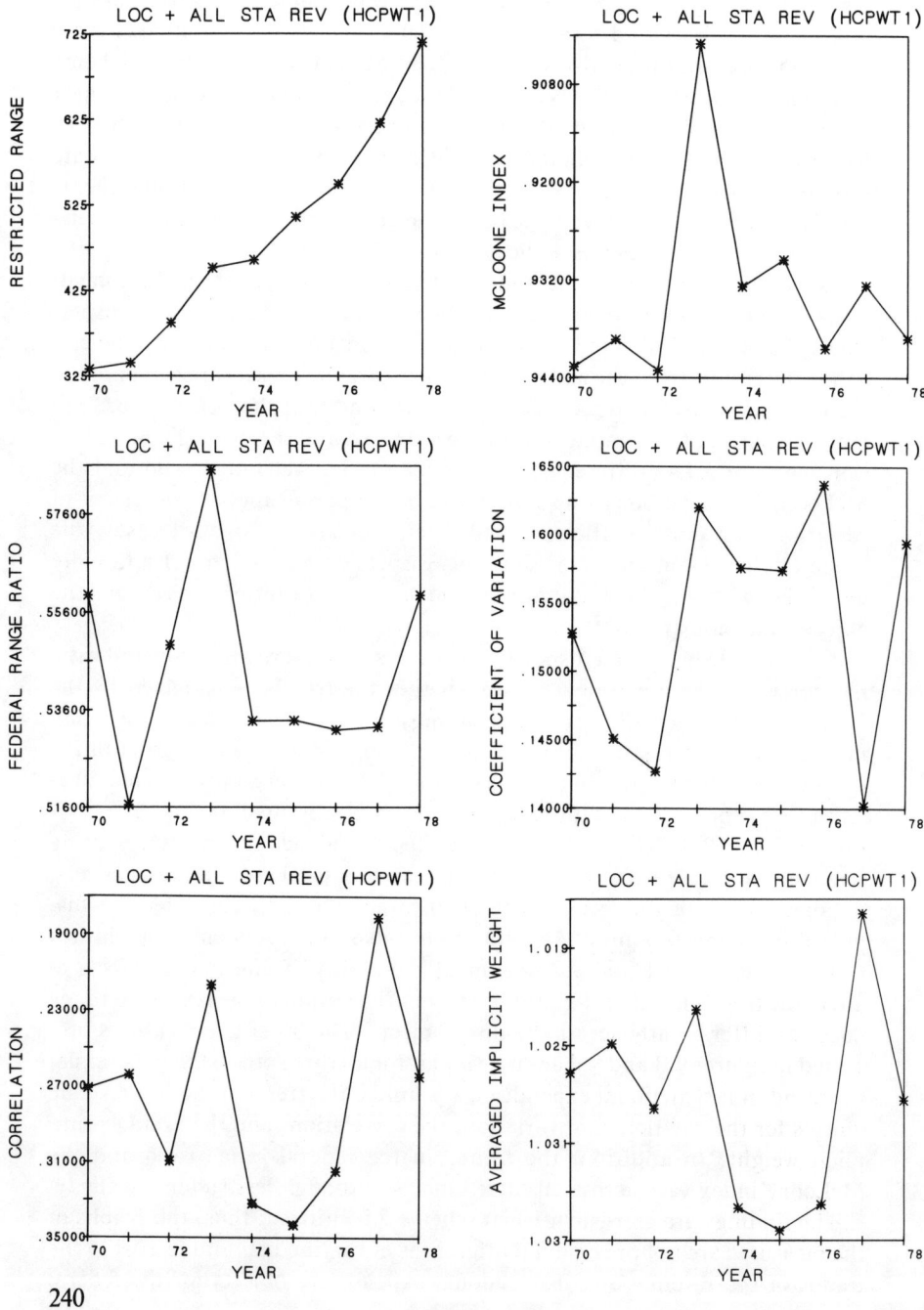

Figure 9.3 Michigan: Vertical-Equity Measures for Local Plus Total State Revenues Using Scheme 1—Restricted Range, McLoone Index, Federal Range Ratio, Coefficient of Variation, Correlation, and Averaged Implicit Weight

Figure 9.4 Michigan: Vertical-Equity Measures for Total Revenues Using Scheme 1—Restricted Range, McLoone Index, Federal Range Ratio, Coefficient of Variation, Correlation, and Averaged Implicit Weight

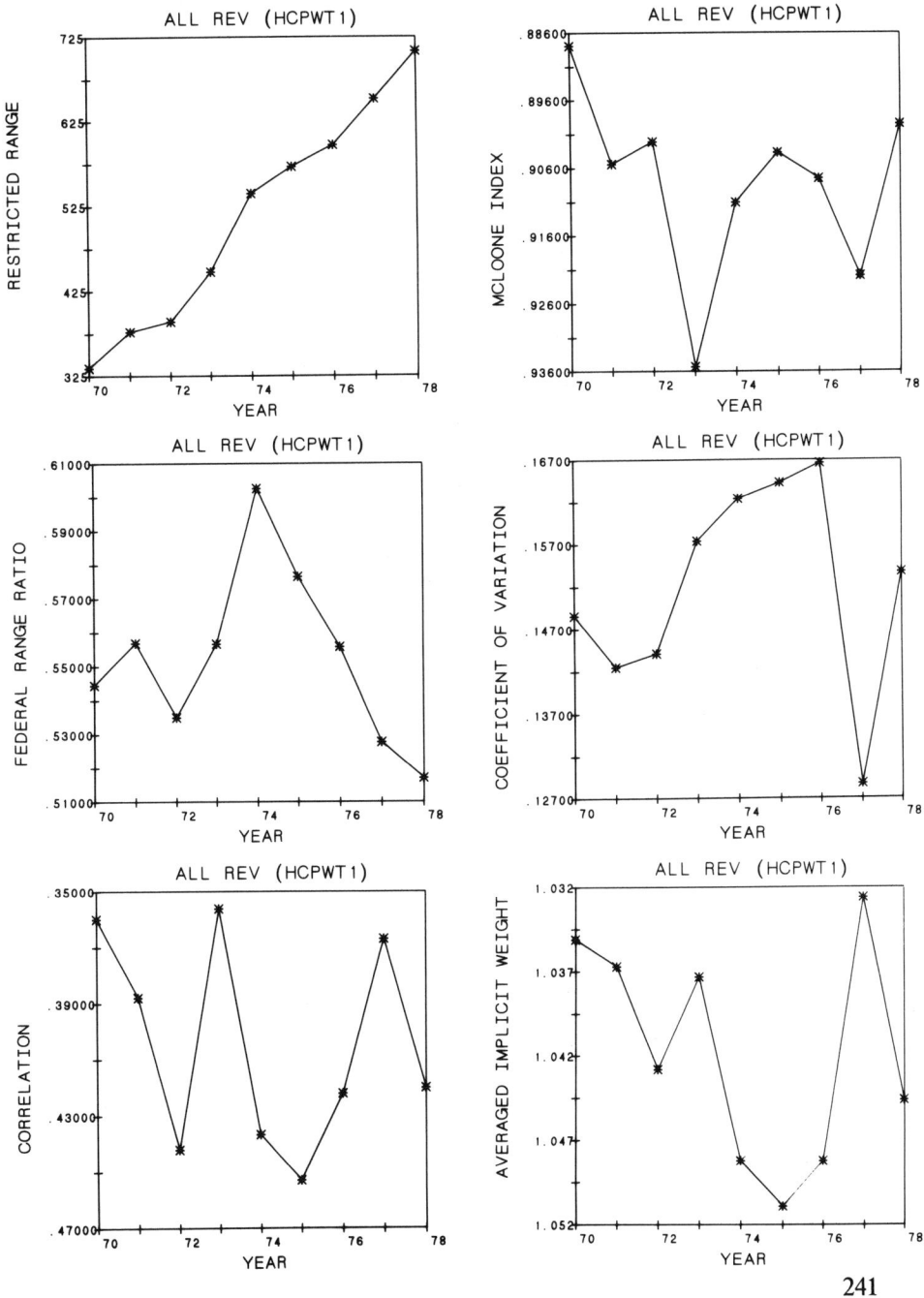

range ratio, the McLoone index, the coefficient of variation, the correlation, and the averaged implicit weight. For both groupings and weighting schemes, therefore, changes in the input-based dollar object often yield different trends in the vertical-equity measures.

In addition to the effect on the trends, the alternative objects alter the levels of vertical equity. Although one object is not consistently more equitable for every measure and every weighting scheme, a few patterns emerge. For example, with scheme 1, the revenue objects are almost always more equitable in a given year than instructional expenditures when the federal range ratio, the McLoone index, and the coefficient of variation are used as the measures. Using scheme 2, local plus total state revenues is usually the least equitable in a given year with the federal range ratio, the McLoone index, and the coefficient of variation. Finally, for both grouping schemes, the addition of federal revenues to local plus total state revenues always increases the relationship between revenues and the percentage of pupils in the special groups in each district.

The analysis of alternative input-based dollar objects with the vertical-equity principle can be summarized by stating that the object matters. The empirical evidence accumulated to this point in the chapter supports the idea that the measure, the grouping and weighting scheme, and the object affect conclusions regarding vertical equity. A summary of the specific findings of this part are as follows:

1. The selection of the object can alter the determination of whether the special groups receive greater amounts of the object. Shifts in the relationship measures occurred in five of the nine years in Michigan using scheme 1 and the two revenue objects.

2. The alternative input-based dollar objects often yield different trends in a given vertical-equity measure, holding the grouping and weighting scheme constant. Differences often arise between the two revenue objects and the expenditure object.

3. Although the differences are not uniform, the alternative input-based dollar objects affect the levels of the vertical-equity measures. One consistent effect is the increase in the relationship measures when federal revenues are added to local plus total state revenues.

4. The conclusions on the vertical-equity measures presented in the previous part are replicated in this part.

5. The grouping and weighting schemes are capable of influencing vertical-equity conclusions. Most of the findings regarding effects on trends and levels documented in the previous part are replicated in this part. An important exception is the finding that the grouping scheme can alter the conclusions from the relationship and ratio measures when judging whether the deserving groups receive more of the object. This occurred for local plus total state revenues in five of the nine years.

How Does the Adjustment of Input-Based Dollar Objects by Price Indexes Affect the Trends in and Levels of Vertical Equity?

In earlier chapters, price indexes have been used to neutralize the effects of intrastate price differences on input-based dollar objects. In this part, the question addressed is whether the utilization of price indexes to adjust dollar inputs alters the conclusions on vertical equity in Michigan. Space constraints forbid an analysis of several objects with different grouping and weighting schemes and the use of alternative price indexes. Instead, one object, instructional expenditures, is analyzed with one price index, Index 1. Although only one object and one price index are utilized in this analysis, the conclusions are not affected by this restriction. Both grouping and weighting schemes, scheme 1 and scheme 2, are employed here.

The issues in this part are examined in a manner similar to the analysis of alternative objects. First, the assessment of the existence of vertical equity with the relationship and ratio measures using the price-adjusted object is presented, followed by a comparison of the weighted dispersion measures with and without the price adjustment. Then the trends in the weighted dispersion measures and the relationship measures with the price-adjusted object are compared to the trends in these measures for the object without the price adjustment.

By examining the relationship and ratio measures and comparing them to the measures for instructional expenditures without the price adjustment, a consistent price-adjustment effect emerges. In every year for all measures and both grouping schemes, the price index lowers the relationship between the object and the special groups for instructional expenditures. This effect of the price index is replicated for local plus total state revenues and total revenues with both scheme 1 and scheme 2. Apparently, unadjusted dollar objects are related to the deserving groups in a more positive way than price-adjusted objects.

The effect of the price index can also be seen in the *direction* of the relationship between instructional expenditures and the special groups. For scheme 1, although the price index lowers the relationships, the special groups still receive higher price-adjusted instructional expenditures. However, this is not the case for scheme 2, since in seven of the nine years the relationship between instructional expenditures and the deserving groups changes from positive to negative when the price index is employed. Again, this latter effect is also present for local plus total state revenues with scheme 1 in six of nine years, for total revenues with scheme 1 in the three years where the unadjusted relationship is positive, and for total revenues with scheme 2 in all nine years. Thus, in terms of the relationship and ratio measures, the price index has a consistent and substantial effect.

The second question addressed in this part is the effect of the price index on the weighted dispersion measures. One way to answer this question is to compare the *weighted* dispersion measures for an object with and without the price adjustment. The results of such a comparison for instructional expenditures show that the price index does affect the weighted dispersion measures, but the effects vary by weighting scheme. With scheme 1, the price-adjusted weighted dispersion measures are uniformly more equitable than the weighted dispersion measures for unadjusted instructional expenditures. The opposite occurs for most of the weighted dispersion measures computed with scheme 2. These findings for instructional expenditures generally hold for local plus total state revenues and total revenues, although for scheme 1, there are often several years in which the weighted dispersion measures for the price-adjusted revenue objects are less equitable than the weighted dispersion measures for the unadjusted revenue objects. In the case of scheme 1, note that the general direction of the effect of the price index is opposite to the effect observed for the relationship and ratio measures, while the direction of the effect of the price index with scheme 2 is similar for the dispersion and relationship measures. In both cases, the effect of the price index on the level of the weighted dispersion measures is evident.

The next question is whether the price index similarly affects vertical-equity trends. Figure 9.5 presents the trends in vertical equity for price-adjusted instructional expenditures with scheme 1. When the trends in Figure 9.5 are examined next to the trends in the comparable measures without the price-adjustment (in figures 9.1 and 9.2), only minor to moderate differences are apparent. In general, each trend is unaffected, although there are a few differences in the case of the McLoone index and the correlation. With scheme 2, the differences in the trends are almost nonexistent and therefore are not presented.

Thus, for instructional expenditures, the trends in the weighted dispersion measures and the relationship and ratio measures are only affected in minor ways by the price adjustment. Furthermore, although the trends in the two revenue objects are not displayed, the conclusions drawn from a comparison of these objects with and without price adjustments are virtually the same.

The accumulated evidence strongly supports the idea that price adjustments affect vertical-equity measurement. The effects are more pronounced in some ways than others, and the specific findings are as follows:

    1. The use of a price adjustment lowers the relationship and ratio measures in every case. Furthermore, in many instances, the districts with greater percentages of the deserving groups receive lower amounts of the price-adjusted object even though the deserving groups receive greater amounts of the unadjusted objects.

    2. The price adjustment affects the levels of the weighted dispersion measures, although the effect varies by weighting scheme and measure. Most of the weighted dispersion measures improve with price adjustments using scheme 1 and worsen with price adjustments using scheme 2.

Figure 9.5 Michigan: Vertical-Equity Measures for Price-Adjusted Instructional Expenditures Using Scheme 1—Restricted Range, McLoone Index, Federal Range Ratio, Coefficient of Variation, Correlation, and Averaged Implicit Weight

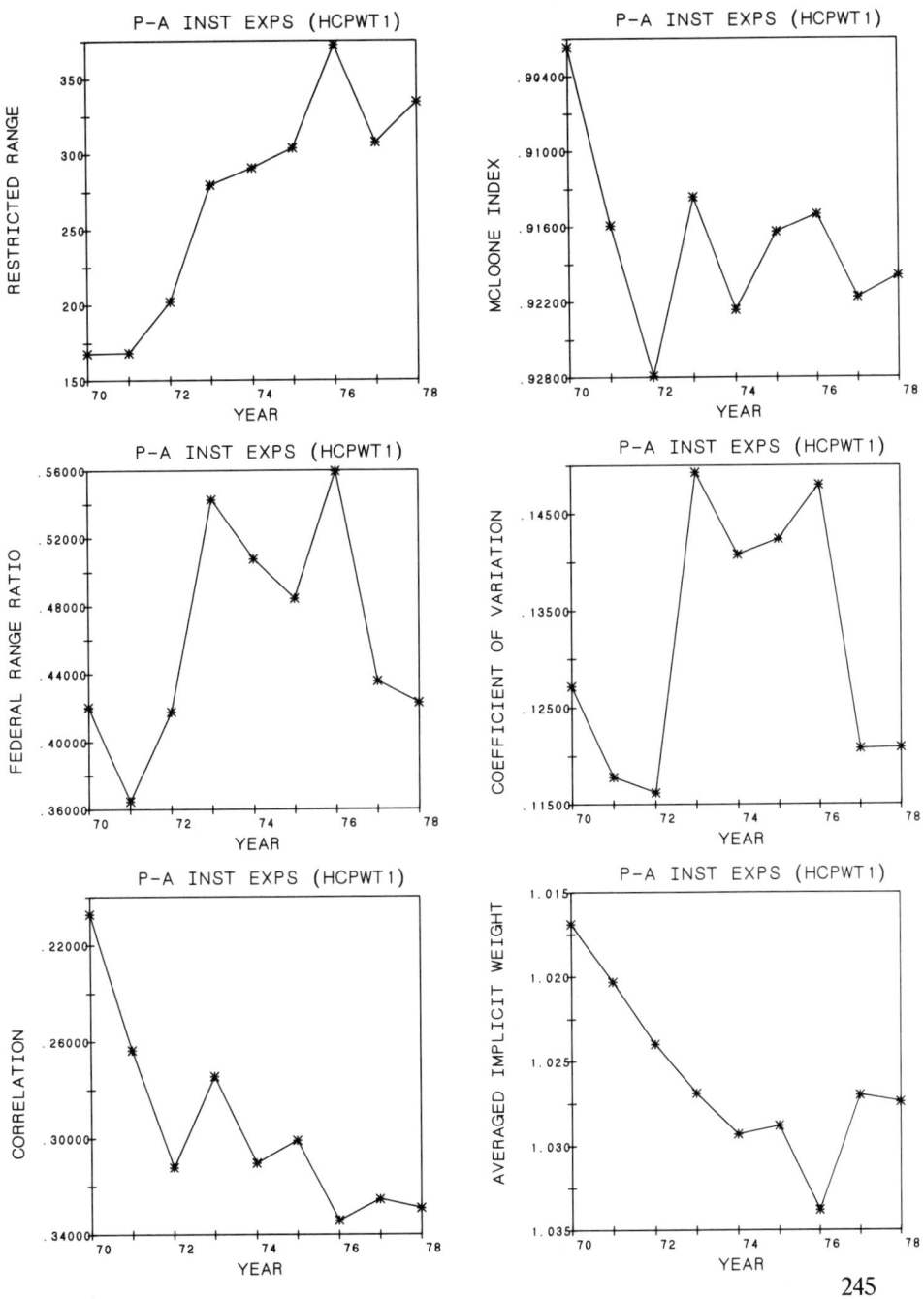

3. Based on the two preceding conclusions, the price adjustments cause most of the vertical-equity measures to improve using scheme 1, but using scheme 2 the price adjustment causes improvement in only the relationship and ratio measures and worsening in the weighted dispersion measures. This highlights the potential differences between the dispersion and relationship measures as well as the possible effects of the grouping and weighting scheme.

4. The price indexes do not have a substantial effect on the trends in the vertical-equity measures. There are a few exceptions, but in general the effects on the trends are small.

5. None of the findings on the behavior of the measures or the effects of the grouping and weighting schemes documented in the earlier parts of this chapter are changed as a result of this analysis.

Do Trends or Levels Differ for Resource Objects Compared to Dollar and Price-Adjusted Dollar Objects?

The final methodological question addressed in this section is whether the substitution of a resource object for dollar and price-adjusted dollar objects affects conclusions on vertical equity. The resource object is all classroom teachers per 1,000 pupils, which includes K–12 teachers, special education teachers, and vocational education teachers. The issues examined with the resource object are the same as those analyzed with the dollar and price-adjusted dollar objects, except that only six years of data rather than nine are available. In this analysis, the resource object, all classroom teachers, is compared to instructional expenditures and price-adjusted instructional expenditures, since the dollars for classroom teachers are always included in, and comprise a major portion of, instructional expenditures.

First, the relationship and ratio measures are examined to determine if the districts with higher percentages of pupils in the special group receive more resources. With scheme 1, the relationship between the resource object and the deserving group is positive in four years and negative in the other two years. This can be compared to the results with instructional expenditures and price-adjusted instructional expenditures, where the relationship is positive in all six years with scheme 1. When scheme 2 is utilized, there is a negative relationship between classroom teachers and the deserving groups in all six years. This occurs for price-adjusted instructional expenditures as well, but the relationship is always positive in the case of unadjusted instructional expenditures with scheme 2.

These findings show that the use of a resource object has the potential to alter the conclusions concerning whether the deserving groups receive greater amounts of the object. Since the price adjustments uniformly reduce the relationship between the unadjusted dollar objects and deserving groups, the reduction of the relationship when the resource object replaces the dollar object can be viewed as a similar effect. In fact, when the grouping scheme and year are held constant, the relationship between instructional expenditures and the deserving group is always greater than the relationship between price-adjusted instructional expenditures and the deserving group, which, in turn, is always greater than the relationship between the resource object and the deserving group.

The effect of the use of a resource object on the weighted dispersion measures is the next issue addressed. When the weighted dispersion measures using all classroom teachers per 1,000 pupils are compared with the weighted dispersion measures with price-adjusted instructional expenditures as the object, vertical equity is generally greater for the resource objects. While the relationship and ratio measures show less vertical equity when resources replace price-adjusted dollars, the results for the weighted dispersion measures generally point in the other direction. The findings do not hold in every year, but for most measures, years, and weighting schemes, the weighted dispersion measures with the resource object are more equitable than the weighted dispersion measures with price-adjusted instructional expenditures as the object. These results provide an additional example of the differences between the weighted dispersion measures and the relationship and ratio measures, in addition to demonstrating the potential differences caused by the resource object.

The trends in the vertical-equity measures may also be altered by the use of a resource object rather than a dollar or a price-adjusted dollar object. Figure 9.6 shows the trends in vertical-equity measures for scheme 1. When these trends are compared to those presented earlier for dollar and price-adjusted dollar objects, virtually no similarities emerge. The trends in all classroom teachers per 1,000 pupils are clearly distinct from the other objects, and this holds for scheme 2 as well. Thus the switch from a dollar or price-adjusted dollar object to a resource object can substantially alter the trends in vertical equity.

This brief analysis of one resource object shows that vertical equity conclusions from a dollar or price-adjusted dollar object may differ from conclusions based on a resource object. More specifically, the conclusions on the resource object are the following:

1. When the relationship and ratio measures are used to determine whether the deserving group receives greater amounts of the object, the results for a resource object differ, at times, from a dollar or price-adjusted dollar object. In Michigan, the relationships between all classroom teachers and the deserving groups using scheme 1 and scheme 2 are uniformly less than the relationships between both instructional expenditures and price-adjusted instructional expenditures and the deserving groups, in comparable years.

2. The levels of the weighted dispersion measures are also different with a resource object compared to a dollar or a price-adjusted dollar object. In most instances the weighted dispersion measures for all classroom

Figure 9.6 Michigan: Vertical-Equity Measures for All Classroom Teachers per 1,000 Pupils Using Scheme 1—Restricted Range, McLoone Index, Federal Range Ratio, Coefficient of Variation, Correlation, and Averaged Implicit Weight

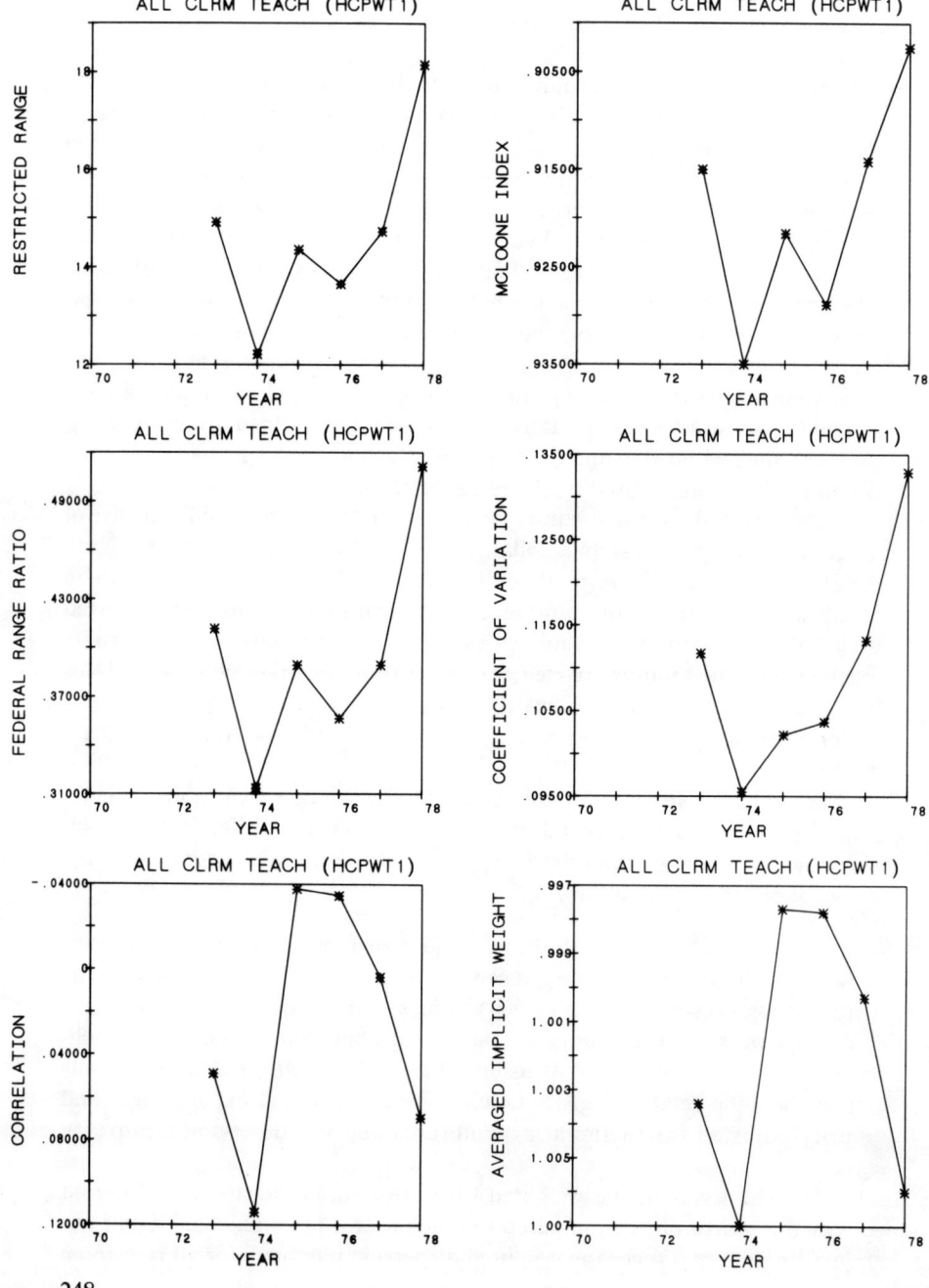

teachers are more equitable than for price-adjusted instructional expenditures.

3. For all classroom teachers per 1,000 pupils, the trends in the weighted dispersion measures and the relationship and ratio measures do not resemble the trends for comparable measures using dollar and price-adjusted dollar objects.

4. None of the methodological findings concerning the measures and the grouping and weighting schemes documented in earlier parts of this section are altered by the analyses of all classroom teachers per 1,000 pupils.

Thus, the analysis in Michigan shows that the measure, object, and grouping and weighting scheme influence the measurement of vertical equity, and we now turn to New York to reanalyze these issues.

AN ASSESSMENT OF VERTICAL EQUITY IN NEW YORK

The examination of vertical equity in New York is limited to three of the five questions posed at the beginning of this chapter, due to data availability. More specifically, questions 1, 3, and 5, the issues of the effects of alternative measures, adjustment by price indexes, and variation in the specification of unequal groups are addressed in this section. The practice that was followed in the previous section of analyzing the effects of alternative unequal groups throughout, rather than separately, is continued in this section.

Before launching into the investigation of vertical equity in New York, it is useful to review the way in which the special groups of pupils are defined and the weights are formulated in New York. As part of the research by New York's Special Task Force on Equity and Excellence in Education, studies were carried out to determine the number of pupils in various groups and the excess costs associated with them. Since this research is extensive and relatively up-to-date, we will rely upon it to assess vertical equity in New York. The reader may agree or disagree with the actual groups and weightings devised by the task force, but this should not affect the validity of the methodological findings of this section.

The task force identified three groups of pupils who should receive unequal treatment and, therefore, could be considered within the vertical-equity principle. In the past, New York has provided state aid for pupils in all three groups. The first group is pupils with handicapping conditions, and these are defined as pupils who are "trainable mentally retarded, educable mentally retarded, visually impaired, physically handicapped, severely speech impaired, or emotionally disturbed, as defined by the Commissioner and who attend district-operated special educational programs that meet the criteria established by the Commissioner."[13] Thus, for purposes of analysis, these are the handicapped pupils who are served by programs in the school districts; pupils served elsewhere, such as in regional facilities, are not included.

The second group of special pupils are those who are disadvantaged educationally. New York State has a category of pupils called "*P*upils with *S*pecial *E*ducation *N*eeds" (PSEN's), and each district's count of PSEN's comprises the second group. PSEN's are defined as the number of pupils in each district that fall below specified competency levels in reading and mathematics as determined by a statewide test. Actually, the number of PSEN's in a district is determined by multiplying the percentage of third and sixth graders who fall below the competency levels by the total number of pupils in the district. Thus, this group is not based on pupils in the special group who are actually served by a program.

The third and final group are pupils who need special treatment because of their limited English-language ability. As defined in New York, these pupils are "from a bilingual background who by reason of limited English proficiency have sufficient difficulty speaking, reading, writing or understanding the English language to deny such individuals the opportunity to learn successfully in classrooms where the language of instruction is English."[14] The count of bilingual pupils used in this research is based on pupils actually in bilingual programs.

One set of vertical-equity measures, the weighted dispersion measures, requires the specification of weights that represent the additional treatment that pupils in the special groups should receive. While for Michigan these weights were derived from many national and state-level studies, the weights in New York are based on the research of the task force, since their estimates are state-specific, aligned with the available data on numbers of pupils in the special groups, and the results of extensive research. In order to analyze the effects of various school-finance schemes, some of which included weighted pupils, the task force carried out research studies to determine the costs of pupils in these three special groups compared to pupils who are not in these groups.[15] In each case the costs for pupils in the special groups were determined by examining samples of actual district-level programs and costs.

In the handicapped-pupil group, weights were estimated for pupils in three subgroups. Handicapped pupils in special classes received an additional

---

13. New York State Education Department, "Providing State Aid for the Education of Children with Handicapping Conditions Based on a Study of Program Costs," a report required by chapter 789 of the Laws of 1978, pt. 2, November 1979, p. 27.

14. James M. Gaughan and Richard J. Glasheen, "Study on Special Pupil Needs, Interim Report" (New York State Special Task Force on Equity and Excellence in Education, November 1979), pp. 1–2, available from New York State Education Department.

15. See the studies cited in the two preceding notes, and for a summary, see memo from Allan Odden to task force dated September 22, 1980, "October 1, 1980, Meeting—*Second Afternoon Topic*; Pupil Needs: Handicapped, PSEN, and Grade Level Differences," available from author at Education Commission of the States, Denver, Colorado.

weight of 2.0 for each full-time equivalent (FTE) pupil, handicapped pupils in resource rooms received an additional weight of 1.0 for each FTE pupil, and speech-impaired pupils received an additional weight of 0.15 for each FTE pupil. For the educationally disadvantaged, each PSEN pupil received an additional weight of 0.35, and each pupil in a bilingual program received an additional weight of 0.40. Note that the handicapped weights are roughly comparable to those used for Michigan. However, since in New York the number of Title I participants and PSEN participants are fairly equal, the weight of 0.35 for the educationally disadvantaged in New York is probably less extreme than the weight of 2.0 for Title I eligibles in Michigan.[16]

Although the pupil counts and cost-based weightings in New York are likely to be quite accurate, one significant data limitation is that pupil counts are only available for one year. Data on the number of handicapped, PSEN, and bilingual pupils are available for the 1979-80 school year. We have assumed that the proportion of pupils in each district in each category that existed in 1979-80 is constant for the entire fourteen-year study period. This is similar to the assumption that was made for Michigan and is justifiable for similar reasons. Because of these data limitations and assumptions, the percent of pupils in the special groups is constant in each district during the fourteen-year period, and the ratio of weighted to unweighted pupils in each district is the same in each year as well. Both are fixed at the 1977-78 levels, which in turn is based on the 1979-80 data.[17]

With the data available in New York, three different specifications of the special pupils deserving of unequal treatment are employed in the assessment of vertical equity. The first specification, called scheme 1, only includes handicapped pupils. In scheme 1 the percent of pupils in the special group is the percent of FTE pupils falling in the three handicapped subgroups: special classes, resource rooms, and speech impaired. When weighted dispersion measures are used with scheme 1, the three handicapped subgroups are weighted 2.0, 1.0, and 0.15, respectively. Using scheme 1, the percent of pupils in the special group (in other words the percent of the pupils who are handicapped) statewide in 1978 equals 5.85. Although this figure is comparable to other data on the percent of pupils in New York in special education programs, it is less than the national estimates of the prevalence of handicapped pupils, regardless of whether or not they are served in special pro-

---

16. See Gaughan and Glasheen, "Study on Special Pupil Needs," table 2, p. 6.

17. Actually the *number* of pupils in the special groups are 1979-80. Since the audited, comparable pupil counts are only available for 1977-78, the special pupil counts for 1979-80 are divided by the regular, total pupil counts for 1977-78 to obtain the percent of special pupils in each category in each district. Similary, the ratio of weighted to unweighted pupils was calculated by combining the special pupil counts from 1979-80 and the count of regular, total pupils in 1977-78. The percent of pupils in the special groups and the ratio of weighted to unweighted pupils was also recalculated using unaudited pupil counts from 1979-80 and the differences, compared to the numbers used in the analyses, were quite small and unlikely to affect the vertical-equity analysis.

grams.[18] Using scheme 1 in 1978, there are 3,439,766 weighted pupils in the state compared to 3,183,607 unweighted pupils.

The second specification, scheme 2, adds the educationally disadvantaged to the special group. Thus, the percent of pupils in a district in the special group is the percent of pupils who are in the three handicapped subgroups plus the percent of PSEN's. In addition to the handicapped weights used in scheme 1, PSEN's receive an additional weight of 0.35. With scheme 2, the percent of pupils in the special group, statewide in 1978, equals 29.81, indicating that 23.96 percent of the pupils are categorized as PSEN's. Again, this is similar to a different estimate (26 percent) reported for 1973.[19] The number of weighted pupils in the state in 1978, using scheme 2, is 3,705,979.

The third and final specification, scheme 3, adds pupils in bilingual programs to handicapped pupils and PSEN's. Thus, the special group according to scheme 3 includes all the pupils identified as handicapped, PSEN, or bilingual. In addition to the handicapped weights and PSEN weight employed in scheme 2, scheme 3 includes a bilingual weight of .40. In 1978 in New York State utilizing scheme 3, the percent of pupils in the special group equals 33.05, and the number of weighted pupils is 3,747,081.

With this description of the special groups and pupil weights behind us, we can now turn our attention to the assessment of vertical equity in New York. The first issue is the effect of alternative measures of vertical equity.

Are There Differences in Trends Due to Alternative Measures? Do the Measures Form Empirical Groupings?

Three general types of vertical-equity measures were assessed in chapter 2, and vertical equity in Michigan was analyzed in the first part of this chapter using all three types of measures. In this part, the three types of vertical-equity measures are compared using data for fourteen years in New York. In addition, the issue of whether alternative definitions and weightings of special groups affect conclusions on vertical equity is addressed and the substantive findings in New York are reported. The three definitions of the groups and weightings described above—scheme 1, scheme 2, and scheme 3—are used throughout this analysis.

The three general types of measures are the weighted dispersion measures, the regression-based relationship measures, and the ratio measures. Recall that the types of measures approach the vertical-equity principle differently,

---

18. In New York in 1972, 6.2 percent of the pupils in public elementary and secondary schools were in special education programs. See William H. Wilken and David O. Porter, *State Aid for Special Education: Who Benefits?* (Washington, D.C. National Institute of Education, December 1977), table 1-6, p. I-52. Wilken and Porter (p. I-14) also report that the Bureau of the Handicapped estimate of the prevalence of handicapped pupils was 10 percent in 1972 and 12 percent in 1977.

19. See Charles D. Bernstein, Michael W. Kirst, William T. Hartman, and Rudolph S. Marshall, *Financing Educational Services for the Handicapped* (Reston, Va.: Council for Exceptional Children, 1976), table 4, p. 33.

since the weighted dispersion measures are capable of assessing the levels and trends in vertical equity, while the relationship and ratio measures are useful in disclosing whether the special groups are receiving more or less of the object.

Table 9.5 displays the basic statistics and vertical-equity measures for scheme 1. The table lists basic statistics including the number of districts and weighted pupils, the mean and median current operating expenditures, ten weighted dispersion measures, five regression-based relationship measures, and one ratio measure. The ten weighted dispersion measures include all of those discussed in chapter 7. The five regression-based relationship measures are those based on the simple regression. The implicit weight is the ratio of the predicted object in a district comprised of all pupils in the special group to the predicted object in a district comprised totally of pupils not in the special group, where the prediction, in this case, is based on the simple regression.[20] The single ratio measure, the averaged implicit weight, is the ratio of the average current operating expenditures for pupils in the special group to average current operating expenditure of the pupils not in the special group.[21]

Since the relationship and ratio measures can determine whether the districts with higher percentages of pupils in the special groups are receiving more current operating expenditures per pupil, agreement among these measures on this dimension can be assessed from table 9.5 for scheme 1. In this case, vertical equity exists when the correlation, the simple slope, the simple elasticity, and the simple adjusted relationship measures are positive and the implicit weight and the averaged implicit weight are greater than one. By definition, all of the regression-based measures will agree, so that the only possible disagreement is between the ratio measure, the averaged implicit weight, and the five regression-based relationship measures. Table 9.5 shows that, for scheme 1, the averaged implicit weight always agrees with the regression-based measures. This holds true in all years for scheme 2 and scheme 3 as well.

The examination of the relationship measures and the ratio measure leads to two additional findings, one substantive and one methodological. If vertical equity is defined to exist when pupils in the special groups receive greater amounts of the object, then New York exhibits vertical equity in all years except 1965 under scheme 1 and in all years except 1965 and 1977 under scheme 2. Although this may be a relatively imprecise assessment of vertical equity, for some people the relationship and ratio measures may accurately capture their preferences for the way in which vertical equity should be measured. On a more methodological note, these observations provide us with the first comparison of the three definitions of the special groups. Judging only from the

---

20. In chapter 8, the implicit weight was labeled the regression-based minority-nonminority ratio.
21. In chapter 8, the averaged implicit weight was labeled the minority-nonminority ratio.

Table 9.5. New York: Vertical-Equity Measures for Current Operating Expenditures Using Group and Weighting in Scheme 1

	1965	1966	1967	1968	1969	1970
Number of consolidated K–12 districts	672	672	673	674	674	674
Total weighted pupils	3,376,188	3,434,280	3,511,349	3,593,603	3,669,303	3,717,112
Mean per-pupil (weighted) Current Operating Expenditures	662	723	824	894	1,012	1,109
Median per-pupil (weighted) Current Operating Expenditures	657	741	826	882	999	1,138
Range	1,042	803	963	1,172	1,320	1,452
Restricted range	341	353	361	374	438	512
Federal range ratio	0.6652	0.6198	0.5377	0.5023	0.5262	0.5709
Relative mean deviation	0.0943	0.0986	0.0840	0.0845	0.0851	0.1017
McLoone index	0.9157	0.8829	0.9150	0.9320	0.9332	0.8782
Variance	10,783	11,498	12,754	14,412	18,520	27,013
Coefficient of variation	0.1569	0.1483	0.1370	0.1344	0.1345	0.1482
Standard deviation of logarithms	0.1458	0.1425	0.1273	0.1230	0.1227	0.1380
Gini coefficient	0.0751	0.0745	0.0672	0.0646	0.0645	0.0743
Theil's measure	0.0116	0.0106	0.0089	0.0084	0.0084	0.0104
Correlation	−0.0494	0.0278	0.0635	0.0734	0.1341	0.1774
Simple slope	−2.1873	1.3219	3.1478	3.8405	8.0656	13.3716
Simple elasticity	−0.0183	0.0101	0.0210	0.0236	0.0437	0.0660
Simple adjusted relationship measure	−0.0151	0.0084	0.0175	0.0196	0.0363	0.0548
Implicit weight	0.7009	1.1702	1.3597	1.4061	1.7689	2.1918
Averaged implicit weight	0.9967	1.0018	1.0038	1.0043	1.0080	1.0121

1971	1972	1973	1974	1975	1976	1977	1978
674	674	675	675	677	678	678	678
3,766,832	3,781,453	3,748,329	3,696,389	3,668,254	3,648,241	3,567,698	3,439,766
1,256	1,339	1,405	1,616	1,807	1,918	1,987	2,222
1,295	1,354	1,371	1,695	1,924	1,977	1,922	2,233
1,740	1,855	2,606	3,196	3,599	3,725	5,322	4,578
635	723	803	913	982	1,055	1,222	1,332
0.6414	0.6930	0.7251	0.7718	0.7308	0.7167	0.7952	0.7968
0.1098	0.1090	0.1164	0.1427	0.1360	0.1185	0.1256	0.1174
0.8661	0.8830	0.9166	0.8196	0.8140	0.8586	0.9178	0.8792
39,114	50,555	63,427	88,612	106,060	112,880	143,585	173,232
0.1575	0.1679	0.1793	0.1842	0.1802	0.1752	0.1907	0.1874
0.1474	0.1537	0.1598	0.1788	0.1743	0.1627	0.1695	0.1717
0.0797	0.0831	0.0857	0.0969	0.0941	0.0876	0.0914	0.0925
0.0117	0.0131	0.0147	0.0164	0.0157	0.0144	0.0166	0.0163
0.1950	0.1853	0.1449	0.2424	0.2526	0.2090	0.1519	0.2162
17.8460	18.9905	16.2403	34.0973	38.9415	32.5942	25.7301	41.2470
0.0776	0.0773	0.0629	0.1144	0.1168	0.0921	0.0701	0.1004
0.0643	0.0640	0.0521	0.0949	0.0966	0.0761	0.0578	0.0828
2.4224	2.4192	2.1394	3.2006	3.2532	2.7286	2.2861	2.9061
1.0142	1.0141	1.0014	1.0209	1.0213	1.0167	1.0127	1.0181

assessment of whether the special groups receive more, the three schemes do not agree perfectly. Contradictory results occur in only two years, however, 1965 and 1977. Thus, the definition of the special group may matter, and other analyses in this part will provide a more complete assessment of the differences among the definitions and weighting of the special groups.

Before turning to the graphs of the measures of vertical equity over time, some knowledge of the weighted dispersion measures can be gained by comparing them to the unweighted dispersion measures. When horizontal equity is measured by dispersion measures, a common criticism is its failure to include any recognition of special needs—in other words, the vertical-equity principle seems to be preferred by some people to the horizontal-equity principle, at least implicitly. This criticism often stems from the belief that the weighted dispersion measures, when used to assess vertical equity, would show greater equity (less dispersion) than the unweighted dispersion measures that were utilized to measure horizontal equity. This belief can be empirically tested for New York.

A comparison of the weighted dispersion measures with the horizontal-equity measures in chapter 7 reveals which of the unweighted or weighted dispersion measures show less dispersion. In New York, the results depend on the grouping and weighting scheme as well as on the measure. For example, with the coefficient of variation, the weighted measures are more equitable than the unweighted measures in twelve of the fourteen years with scheme 1, five of the fourteen years with scheme 2, and ten of the fourteen years with scheme 3. On the other hand, with the McLoone index, the weighted measures are more equitable than the unweighted measures in all years with all three weighting schemes. The fact that the weighted dispersion measures are often, but not always, more equitable than the unweighted dispersion measures illustrates that there are differences among the grouping and weighting schemes and among the dispersion measures as well.

Thus far, the differences among the vertical-equity measures have been examined by comparing the regression-based relationship with the ratio measures, and the unweighted dispersion measures with the weighted dispersion measures. In neither case, however, was the analysis based on the trends in vertical equity, which we turn to now. Since the ten measures form the same groupings we reported previously, figure 9.7 only includes the graphs for six weighted dispersion measures for current operating expenditures per weighted pupil, where scheme 1 is used for the weighting. Although the range and variance are not shown, they form a group with the restricted range. The McLoone index is unlike any of the other nine measures. The coefficient of variation, the Gini coefficient, the standard deviation of logarithms, and Theil's measure form a group, as was the case in chapter 7, and furthermore, the trends in the federal range ratio and the relative mean deviation rather closely conform to this group as well. Therefore, the differences among the

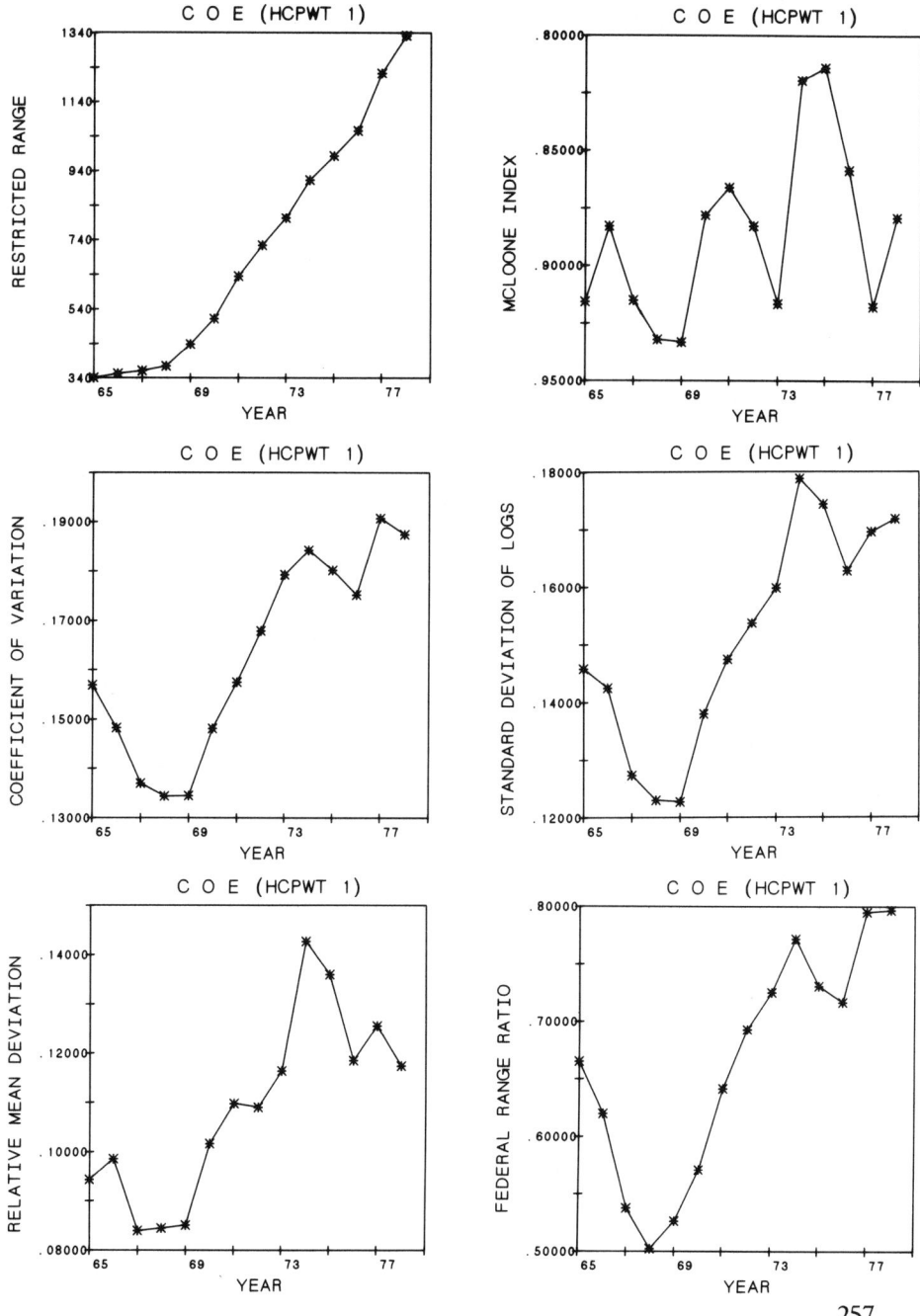

Figure 9.7 New York: Restricted Range, McLoone Index, Coefficient of Variation, Standard Deviation of Logarithms, Relative Mean Deviation, and Federal Range Ratio for Current Operating Expenditures per Weighted Pupil Using Scheme 1

trends in the weighted dispersion measures closely parallel the conclusions drawn for the unweighted dispersion measures.

Throughout this book, the differences between the weighted dispersion measures on the one hand and the regression-based relationship measures and ratio measures on the other have been stressed. The two sets of measures incorporate different approaches to vertical equity, and as a result, they do not interpret vertical equity similarly. The weighted dispersion measures capture the trends and levels in vertical equity and the relationship and ratio measures indicate whether the special group is treated as desired, but because this latter set of measures is a set of continuous numbers, it is useful to know whether the trends in the relationship and ratio measures are consistent with the trends in the weighted dispersion measures. If this were the case, then the relationship and ratio measures would contain the same information as in the weighted dispersion measures. This was not the case in Michigan, and the same question is now raised for New York.

The five regression-based relationship measures based on the simple regression and the one ratio measure, the averaged implicit weight, are graphed for current operating expenditures per pupil in figure 9.8, using the special group inherent in scheme 1, handicapped pupils. As was the convention when these measures were graphed for Michigan, higher values of the measures are assumed to be more equitable, since handicapped pupils should receive more objects. Furthermore, higher values are plotted lower in the graphs, so that greater equity coincides with the bottom of the graph, as is the case throughout the book.

Figure 9.8 can be used to make two points. First, as was the case for Michigan, the trends revealed by these six measures of vertical equity are quite similar. For New York, with scheme 1, each measure shows improvement in vertical equity from 1965 to 1971 and then fluctuations from 1971 to 1978. Also, 1974 and 1975 are the most equitable years for all measures except the slope. Thus, leaving aside the slope because of its sensitivity to inflation, the trends in the five remaining measures are very much alike. Second, the trend traced out by these six measures is not at all similar to the trends in any of the weighted dispersion measures. In fact, on a major dimension the trends are exactly opposite, since many weighted dispersion measures show less equity in the latter part of the fourteen-year period, while the trends in the relationship and ratio measures show the reverse. This second conclusion adds further support to the distinction between the weighted dispersion measures and the relationship and ratio measures. These measures are capturing different things, and for Michigan and New York there is little similarity between them.

This analysis of the trends in the vertical-equity measures has focused on the measures utilizing scheme 1. A complete reanalysis of the measures is not presented for scheme 2 and scheme 3, since the results are identical in terms of the behavior of the measures. However, in order to assess how the trends in

Figure 9.8 New York: Correlation, Simple Slope, Simple Elasticity, Simple Adjusted Relationship Measure, Implicit Weight, and Averaged Implicit Weight for Current Operating Expenditures per Pupil Using Scheme 1

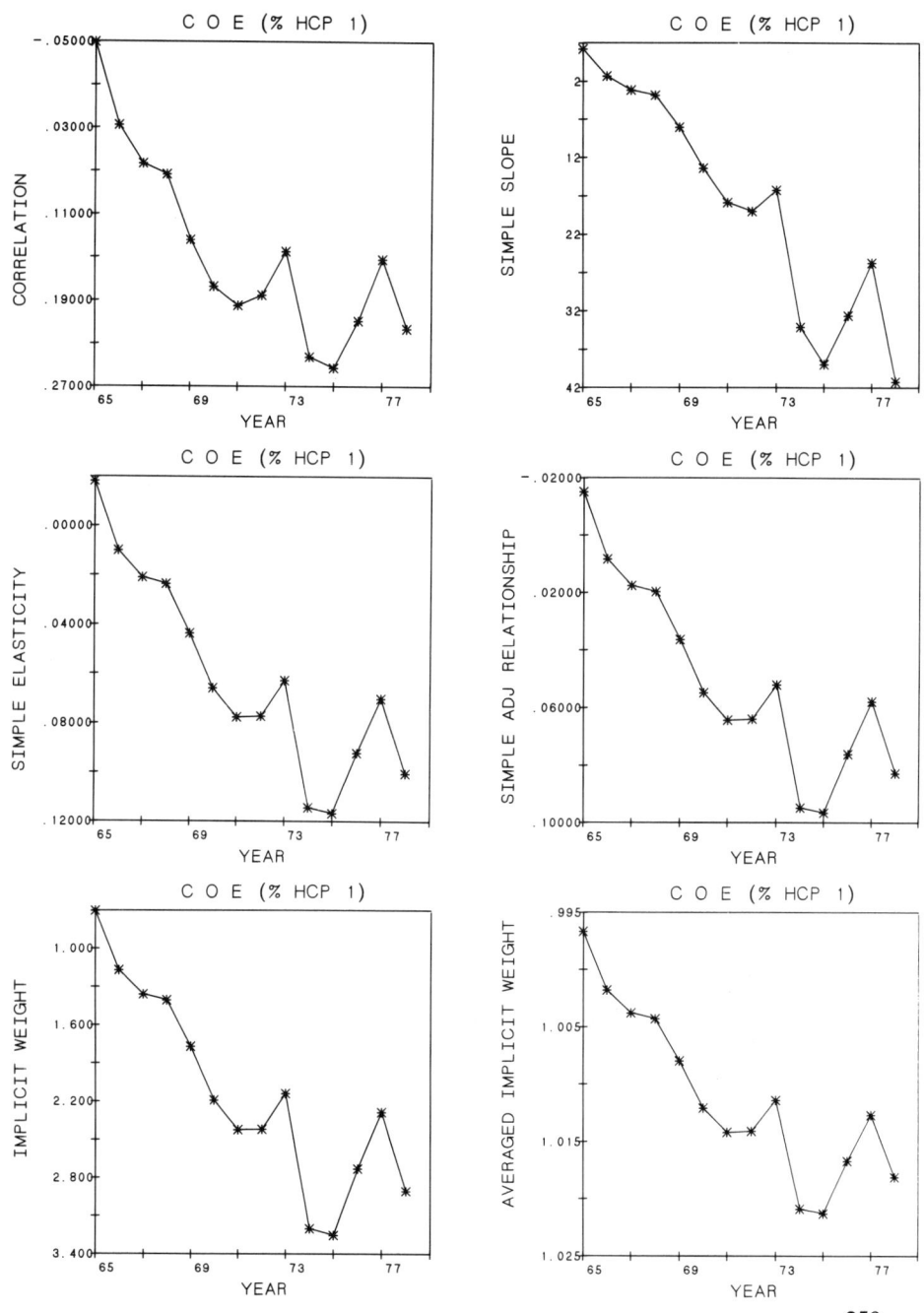

the measures are affected by the grouping and weighting schemes, trends for several of the measures are presented. Figure 9.9 displays the graphs of four weighted dispersion measures (the restricted range, the McLoone index, the federal range ratio, and the coefficient of variation), the correlation, and the averaged implicit weight for scheme 2. The graphs for these measures using scheme 3 are not shown, since the trends are almost identical with those for scheme 2. The weighting schemes have a very minor effect on the trends in the weighted dispersion measures. The small differences among the restricted range, the McLoone index, the federal range ratio, and the coefficient of variation for the two weighting schemes are representative of the other weighted dispersion measures as well. The differences for the correlation and the averaged implicit weight are more pronounced. In particular, the trends in these two measures for scheme 2 (and scheme 3) fluctuate considerably more than the trends for scheme 1, displayed in figure 9.8. Furthermore, the differences hold for the other regression-based relationship measures not shown in figure 9.9.

In addition to the trends, the levels of vertical equity that result from the three schemes can be examined, holding the measure constant. A comparison of the levels of vertical equity across weighting schemes does not yield a consistent pattern. For some measures—the coefficient of variation, for example—vertical equity with scheme 1 is consistently the most equitable, and with scheme 3, the least equitable. For other measures, such as the McLoone index, vertical equity with scheme 3 is the most equitable, and with scheme 1, the least equitable. And finally, in some cases the relative equity changes by scheme, as can be seen from the correlation. Thus, the weighting scheme has some effect on the levels of the measures, but the direction of the effects are not consistent by weighting scheme.

Our analysis of the vertical-equity measures in New York leads to the following six conclusions:

1. The five regression-based relationship measures always agree with the ratio measure on the question of whether the special groups receive more or less of the education object.

2. The weighted dispersion measures do not always show greater equity than the unweighted dispersion measures. Furthermore, there are differences among the dispersion measures when the weighted and unweighted dispersion measures are compared.

3. The trends in the weighted dispersion measures are different and show the same general groupings as in previous analyses.

4. The trends in the five regression-based relationship measures and the ratio measure are quite similar.

5. The trends in the five regression-based relationship measures and the ratio measure are unlike any of the trends in the weighted dispersion measures.

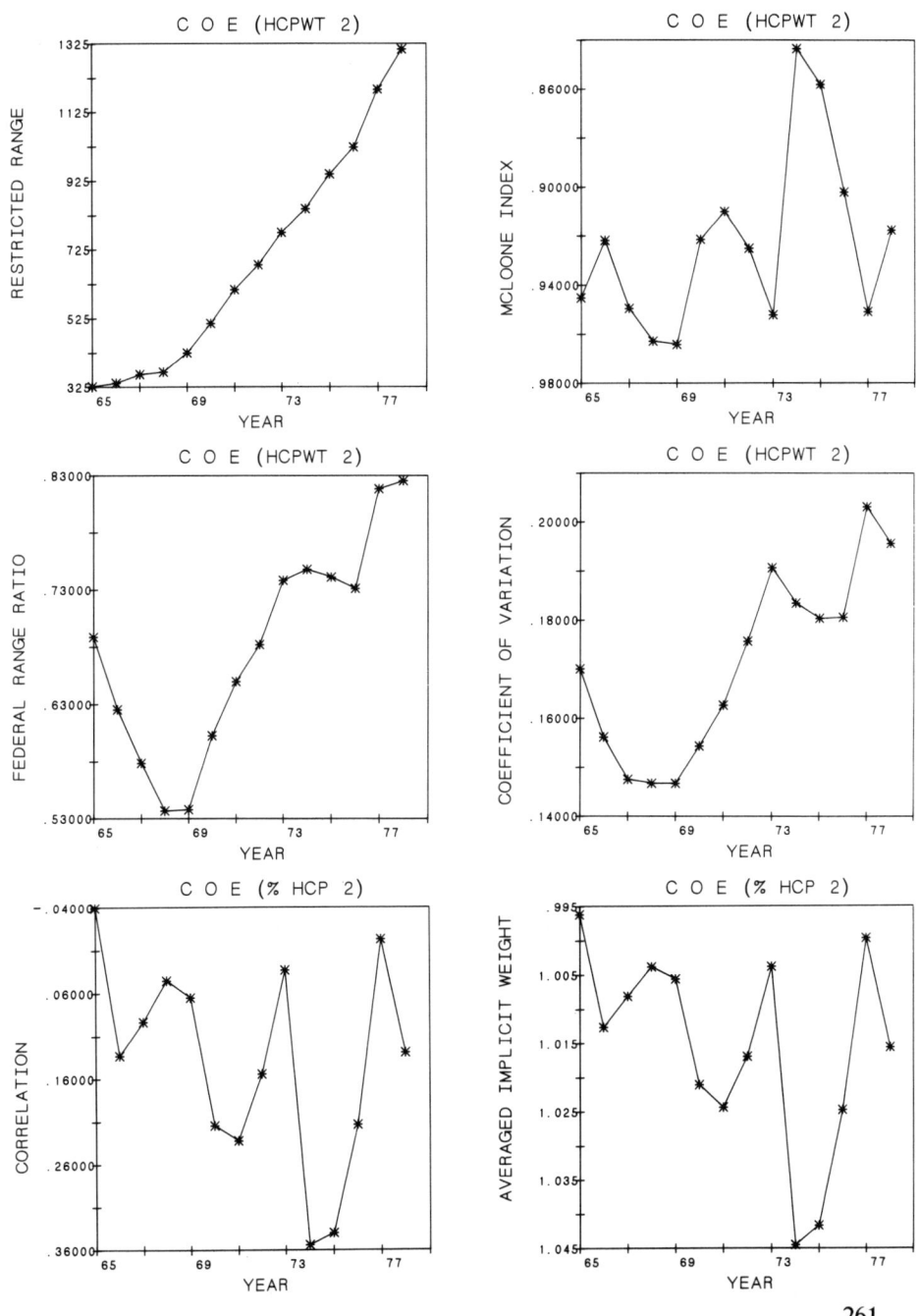

Figure 9.9 New York: Vertical-Equity for Current Operating Expenditures per Pupil Using Scheme 2—Restricted Range, McLoone Index, Federal Range Ratio, Coefficient of Variation, Correlation, and Averaged Implicit Weight

6. The weighting and grouping schemes are capable of affecting the results, but the effects vary according to the question being investigated.

How Does the Adjustment of Input-Based Dollar Objects by Price Indexes Affect the Trends in and Levels of Vertical Equity?

Price adjustments have been used throughout the book to remove intrastate price differences from the education objects, and in this part the influences of the price-index adjustment on the measurement of vertical equity are explored from three perspectives. First, do the price adjustments affect the conclusions on the measures of vertical equity, documented in the preceding part? Second, do the substantive findings on vertical equity in New York differ with and without price adjustments? And third, are the conclusions on the differences among the three grouping and weighting schemes replicated for the price-adjusted objects?

The analyses in this part parallel those in the previous part. The relationship and ratio measures are examined first to see if the price adjustments alter the conclusions on the presence or absence of vertical equity. Next, the weighted dispersion measures with and without the price indexes are compared to see if the price index affects the levels of the weighted dispersion measures. Third, the trends in all the vertical-equity measures with price-adjusted objects are examined and compared to the trends in the measures for objects without price adjustments.

The regression-based relationship and ratio measures are capable of determining whether or not districts with higher proportions of the special groups receive relatively more of the object. With this approach to vertical equity, the relationship and ratio measures showed that vertical equity prevailed in New York in all but one or two years of the study period for current operating expenditures without price adjustments. The situation changes with price adjustments, since the relationship and ratio measures indicate that vertical equity does not prevail in five of the fourteen years, 1965 through 1969, using scheme 1. Furthermore, vertical equity does not prevail in twelve of the fourteen years for price-adjusted current operating expenditures with scheme 2 and scheme 3. In all cases the relationship and ratio measures agree on the conclusions regarding the presence or absence of vertical equity.

A second way to see the effects of the price indexes is to compare the relationship and ratio measures with and without the price index. In New York, for all three weighting schemes, the relationship and ratio measures are always *lower* when the object is price-adjusted. Thus, if higher values of the relationship and ratio measures are thought to be more vertically equitable, then the price-adjusted objects are *less* vertically equitable than the unadjusted objects when vertical equity is measured with the relationship and ratio measures. This replicates the results from Michigan.

Before turning to the weighted dispersion measures, one other point is worth noting. The preceding analysis again demonstrates that the grouping and weighting scheme has the potential to make a difference. Conclusions about whether or not the special groups receive more or less of the objects are reversed in seven years for scheme 2 and scheme 3 compared to scheme 1.

Although the weighted dispersion measures do not assess the presence or absence of vertical equity, their levels can be compared with and without price-adjusted objects to determine how the price index affects these measures in New York. Recall from chapter 7 that when the unweighted dispersion measures were compared with and without the price adjustment in New York, all the measures that are not sensitive to equal percentage increases showed less dispersion with the price index. The findings are not as clear-cut for the weighted dispersion measures, since the price index does not uniformly reduce the dispersion for these measures. While the weighted dispersion measures generally show less dispersion for the price-adjusted, compared to the unadjusted, objects, this holds for all fourteen years only for the federal range ratio and the McLoone index with scheme 1, and for the federal range ratio with scheme 2 and scheme 3. Usually in one or two years with scheme 1, the price-adjusted objects show greater dispersion than the unadjusted objects, and this is the case in four or more years with scheme 2 and scheme 3.

Thus the price adjustment affects the level of the weighted dispersion measures, but does not always lessen the dispersion. However, the dominant effect of less dispersion (greater vertical equity) is opposite the effect observed for the relationship and ratio measures. This analysis also provides additional evidence for the difference in the weighting schemes, especially for scheme 1 in comparison with the other two schemes.

Additional knowledge of the effects of the price index on the measures of vertical equity can be obtained by examining the trends in the vertical-equity measures. Figure 9.10 displays the trends in six weighted dispersion measures for price-adjusted current operating expenditures with scheme 1. Since the trends in the weighted dispersion measures form groups that are similar to those in the previous analyses, all ten dispersion measures are not displayed. The range, restricted range, and variance belong in one group, and the McLoone index is in a group by itself. The Gini coefficient, Theil's measure, the standard deviation of the logarithms, and the coefficient of variation form a third group, and the federal range ratio and the relative mean deviation are related to, but not identical with, this third group.

For all of the measures except the range, the restricted range, and the variance, the price adjustment has an effect on the trends in equity over time. For example, the coefficient of variation, the standard deviation of logarithms, and the relative mean deviation displayed in figure 9.7 without the price adjustment show a period of relative inequity from about 1972 through 1978. When these same measures are plotted with the price adjustment in figure 9.10, the period of inequity from 1972 through 1978 is much less pronounced. A change in the pattern of equity over time is also evident for the McLoone

Figure 9.10 New York: Restricted Range, McLoone Index, Coefficient of Variation, Standard Deviation of Logarithms, Relative Mean Deviation, and Federal Range Ratio for Price-Adjusted Current Operating Expenditures per Weighted Pupil Using Scheme 1

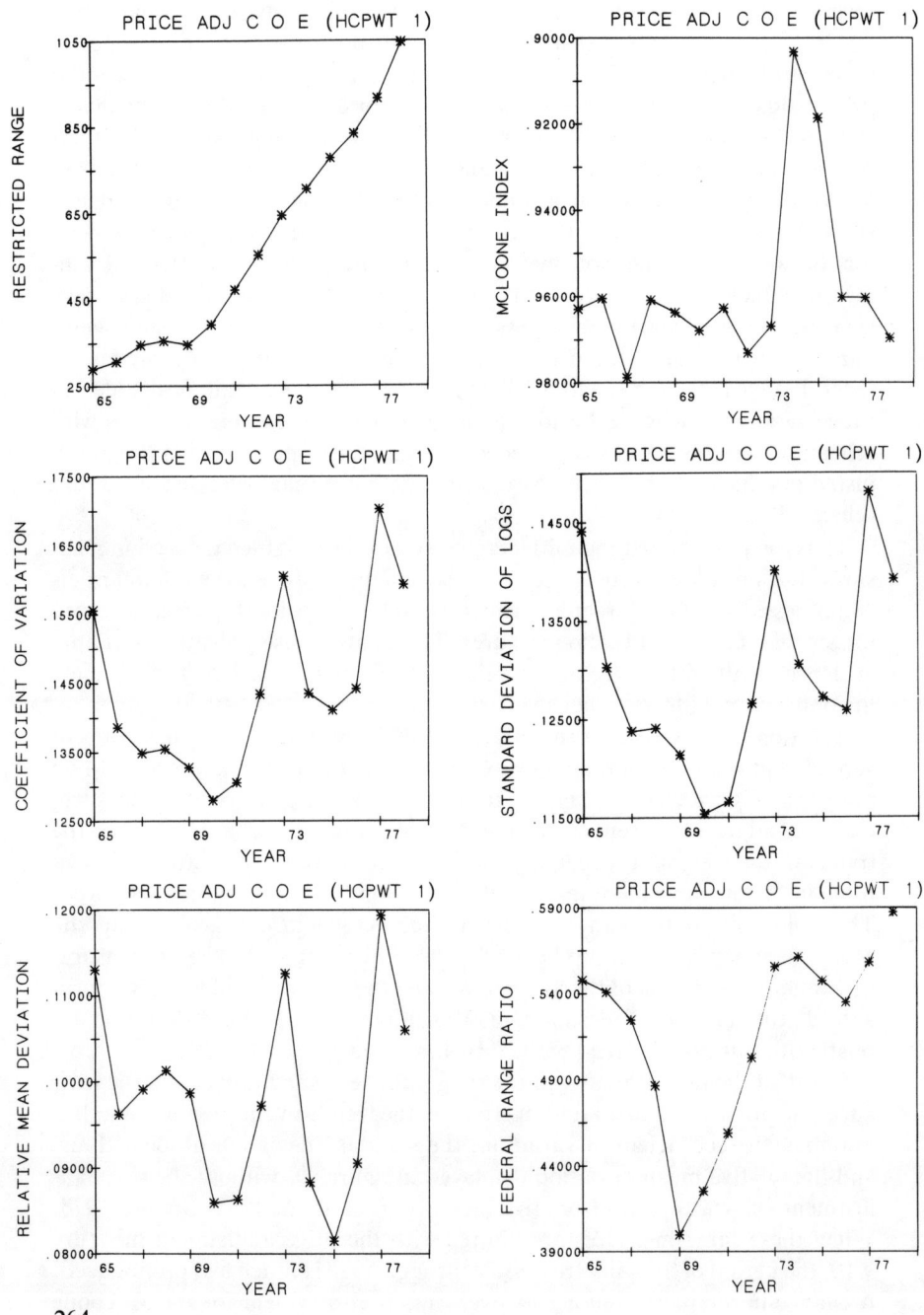

index. Without price adjustments the graph of the McLoone index in figure 9.7 varies over a much wider range than the variation shown in figure 9.10 for all years with price adjustments except 1974 and 1975. These comparisons, therefore, document the potential for the price adjustment to alter the trends in the weighted dispersion measures.

The final set of trends for price-adjusted objects, with scheme 1, are those formed by the regression-based relationship and ratio measures, and these are graphed in figure 9.11. With some minor exceptions in the slope, the similarity of the trends among these measures prevails. Furthermore, as opposed to the noticeable effects of the price index on the trends in the weighted disparity measures, the price index does not affect the trends in the relationship and ratio measures. This can be seen quite clearly by comparing the trends in figure 9.8 with those in figure 9.11. Despite the dramatic change (documented earlier) in the levels of the relationship and ratio measures caused by the price-index adjustment, the trends are unaffected by the price index.

All of the conclusions reached for the trends in vertical-equity measures with price-adjusted objects were formulated utilizing grouping and weighting scheme 1, but they also hold for scheme 2 and scheme 3. It is unnecessary to present the graphs of all the vertical-equity measures using scheme 2 and scheme 3; only selected measures with scheme 2 are presented to illustrate the potential differences among the grouping and weighting schemes. Four vertical-equity measures are graphed in figure 9.12 for scheme 2. Comparisons of these trends with those presented for scheme 1 show that the effects of the alternative weighting schemes vary from moderate to none at all.

On the one hand, the most noticeable effect of the weighting and grouping scheme is evident in the trend in the relationship and ratio measures (shown by the correlation) and the McLoone index for price-adjusted current operating expenditures. For example, the trend in the correlation with scheme 2 shown in figure 9.12 varies substantially more from year to year than the trend in the correlation with scheme 1, displayed in figure 9.11. Also, the McLoone index with scheme 1 graphed in figure 9.10 varies over a rather narrow range for most years compared with the McLoone index with scheme 2, presented in figure 9.12. On the other hand, almost no differences across weighting schemes occur for the coefficient of variation, shown in figures 9.10 and 9.12. Finally, there are minor differences across the weighting schemes for the federal range ratio, as shown in figures 9.10 and 9.12.

This brief assessment has demonstrated that the weighting schemes have the potential to influence the trends in the relationship and ratio measures and in some of the weighted dispersion measures. Furthermore, the most consistent differences have, again, occurred between scheme 1 and the other two weighting schemes.

The conclusions on the analysis with price-adjusted objects can be divided into three groups: conclusions on the effect of the price-index adjustment, conclusions on the vertical-equity measures themselves, and conclusions on

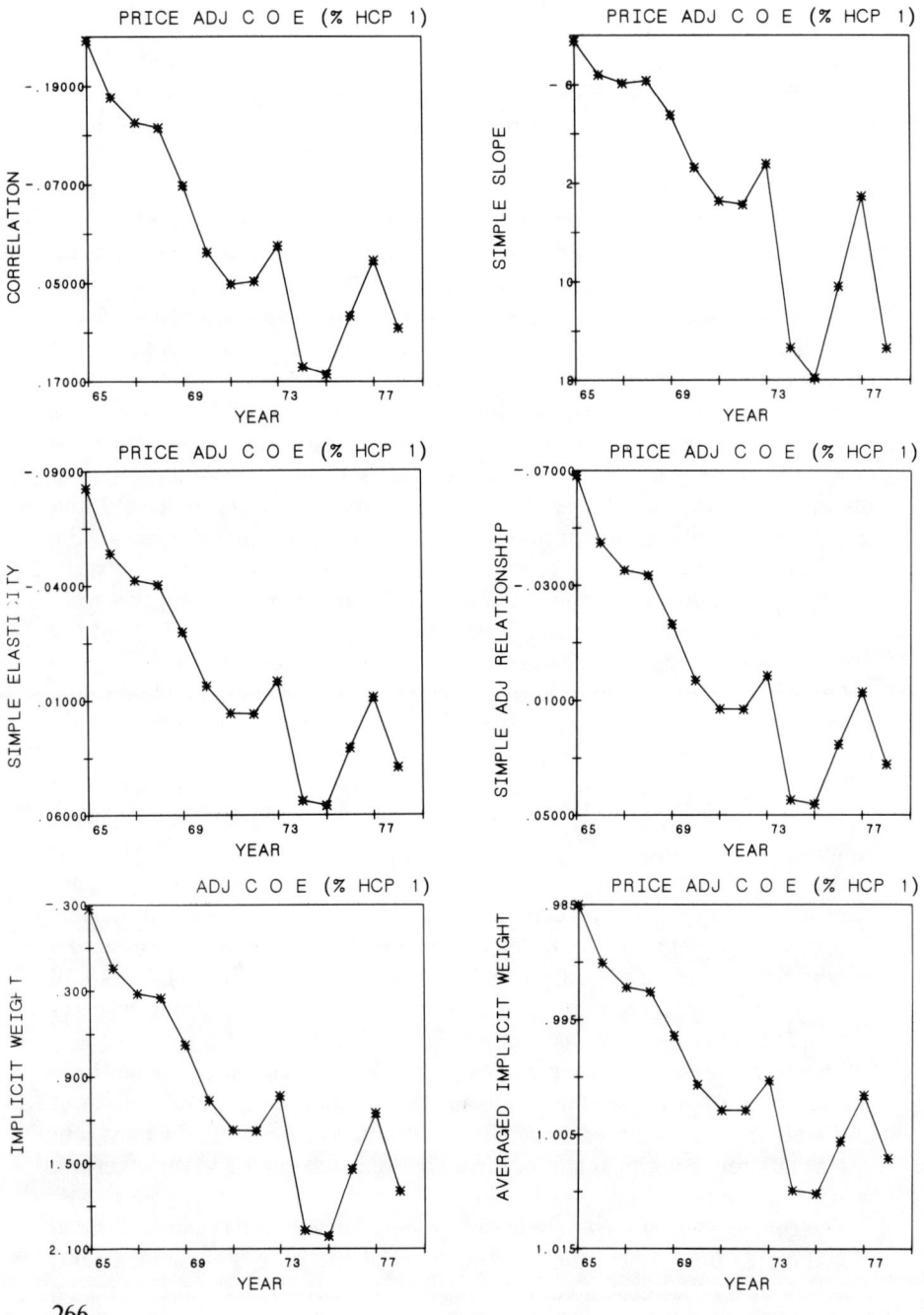

Figure 9.11 New York: Correlation, Simple Slope, Simple Elasticity, Simple Adjusted Relationship Measure, Implicit Weight, and Averaged Implicit Weight for Price-Adjusted Current Operating Expenditures per Pupil Using Scheme 1

Figure 9.12 New York: Vertical-Equity Measures for Price-Adjusted Current Operating Expenditures per Pupil Using Scheme 2—Coefficient of Variation, Federal Range Ratio, McLoone Index, and Correlation

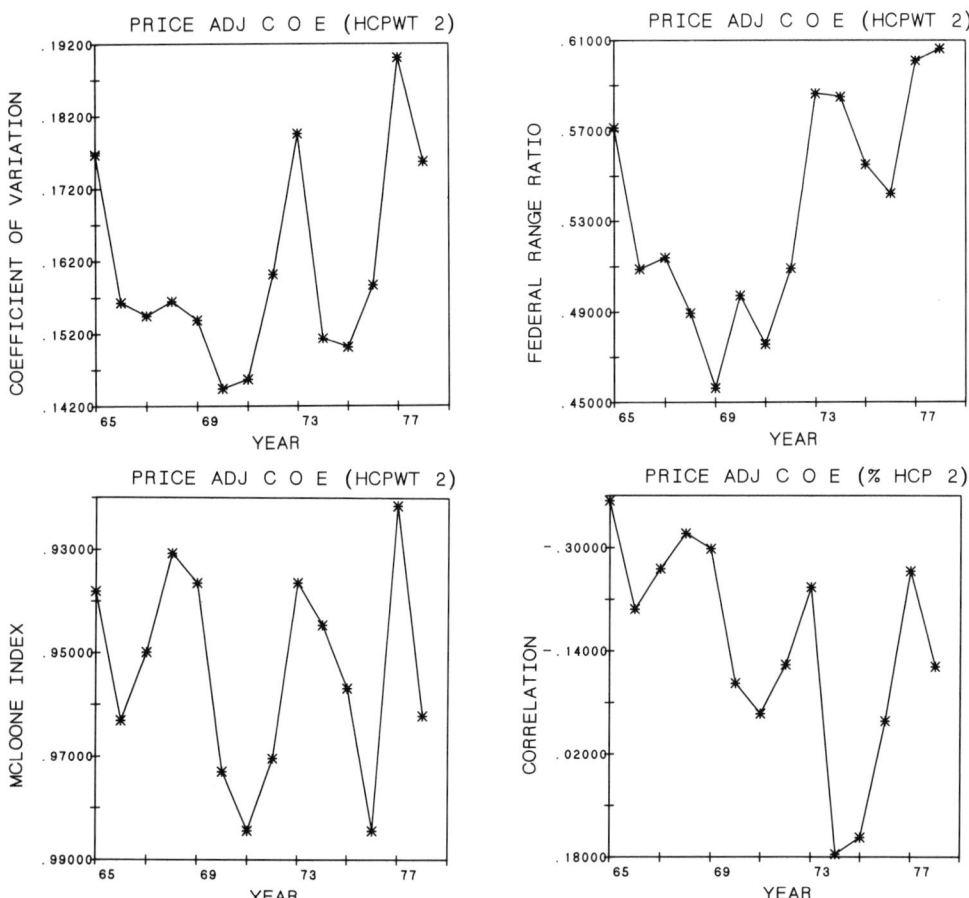

the differences across weighting schemes. In essence, the price index has an effect in several ways, and the conclusions on the measures and weighting scheme reached in the last part are replicated here. More specifically, the following conclusions can be drawn:

1. Price-index adjustments influence the findings on the existence of vertical equity as measured by the relationship and ratio measures. For some grouping schemes (2 and 3), the unadjusted objects show the prevalence of vertical equity in almost all of the fourteen years, but the price-adjusted objects show the opposite. In all cases the relationship and ratio measures with the price-adjusted object are lower than the same measures with the unadjusted object for every year in the study.

2. Price-index adjustments alter the levels of the weighted dispersion measures. In most cases the dispersion is lower with the price-index adjustment, but this is not a uniform effect, particularly for the early part of the study period.

3. The direction of the effects of the price-index adjustments on the relationship and ratio measures are, therefore, opposite the direction of the effects on the weighted dispersion measures. The price-index adjustments move the relationship and ratio measures in a less equitable direction, and the weighted dispersion measures in a more equitable direction.

4. The price index affects the trends in some of the weighted dispersion measures, but none of the trends in the relationship and ratio measures. For some of the weighted dispersion measures, the inequitable trend in evidence for the unadjusted objects is moderated by the price-index adjustment.

5. The major methodological conclusions reached in the previous part are replicated in this analysis with price-adjusted objects.

6. Some differences occur across the grouping and weighting schemes, and the differences show that scheme 2 and scheme 3 are quite similar, but are different from scheme 1 in certain analyses. The most noticeable variation across schemes is when the relationship and ratio measures are used to assess the presence or absence of vertical equity. Differences also surfaced in the trends in some of the weighted dispersion measures (the McLoone index, for example) and in the trends in the relationship measures.

OVERALL CHAPTER CONCLUSIONS

Here we summarize the methodological and substantive conclusions for both Michigan and New York, emphasizing the similarities and differences in the two states. For both states, everything matters methodologically—the measure, the price index, the grouping and weighting scheme, and, for Michigan, the objects. Levels as well as trends in vertical equity are influenced by choices of these variables. For both states, there are differences between the weighted dispersion measures and the relationship and ratio measures. While the relationship and ratio measures often show that vertical equity exists, the weighted dispersion measures are at times more inequitable than the unweighted ones. Within groups, the weighted dispersion measures tend to form the same four or five groupings as the unweighted ones do, and the relationship measures likewise behave similarly to relationship measures in previous chapters.

In Michigan, where there are a variety of objects available for study, the difference in object affects whether there is more or less equity, the trends, and the levels in equity. In both chapters 7 and 8, similar results were found for horizontal equity and equal opportunity.

The use of a price index influences conclusions in both states. The price-adjusted relationship and ratio measures generally show less equity than the unadjusted ones in both Michigan and New York. In New York, the price-adjusted weighted dispersion measures usually exhibit more vertical equity than the unadjusted ones, but in Michigan the direction of the influence is not consistent and depends on the weighting scheme. In Michigan, the price adjustment does not generally affect trends in vertical equity, but in New York trends are affected.

The weighting and grouping schemes affect levels and trends in vertical equity in both states. This is particularly true when the handicapped scheme alone is compared to schemes that include one or more of the following: learning disadvantaged or Title I, bilingual.

Finally, the substantive results on trends in equity depend, in both states, on the methodological choices one makes. In Michigan, many times the group of measures that includes the coefficient of variation exhibits two tendencies. First, the measures often begin and end the period at the same level, and second, there is generally a span of relative inequity during the nine-year period, although not necessarily during the same years for each object. For a wide number of measures in New York, the 1970s show less vertical equity than the late 1960s. This trend is moderated somewhat by the price adjustment.

10

SUMMARY AND CONCLUSIONS

Throughout the Twentieth century, the criterion of fairness has been continually applied to the American system of education. In a society where a dominant belief is that a child's future chances in life should not be unduly constrained by his parent's wealth and influence, the equitable provision of education is a necessity. The importance of education and equity is captured by Judge Fuchsburg of the State of New York Court of Appeals:

> In any meaningful order of priorities, it is in the impact education makes on the minds, characters and capabilities of our young citizens that we must find the answer to many seemingly insoluble societal problems. In the long run, nothing may be more important—and therefore more fundamental—to the future of our country. Can it be gainsaid that, without education there is no exit from the ghetto, no solution to unemployment, no cutting down on crime, no dissipation of intergroup tension, no mastery of the age of the computer? Horace Mann put it pragmatically that education is not only "the greatest equalizer of men," but, by alleviating poverty and its societal costs, more than pays for itself.[1]

The specific words of the judge embody America's hopes for the educational system. Meanwhile, the involvement of the judicial system itself has encouraged our society to move toward its goal of equity in education. The Supreme Court in its 1954 decision in *Brown v. Board of Education* signaled

---

1. From Judge Fuchsburg's dissenting opinion in *Levittown v. Nyquist*, June 23, 1982 (Board of Education, Levittown, etc. v. Nyquist, Ct. App., 453 N.Y.S. 2d 643 in West Publishing Co., *New York Supplement*, 2d ser. vol. 453 N.Y.S. 2d (St. Paul, Minn.: West Publishing Co., 1983) p. 455). The majority decision of the Court of Appeals overturned the two lower court rulings of unconstitutionality of New York State's school-finance system. However, in the majority opinion that decided that New York's system is constitutional, Chief Justice Jones did not dispute that "education is of primary rank in our hierarchy of societal values"; in fact, Jones went on to state, "all recognize and support the principle that it is." See majority opinion of the State of New York Court of Appeals in *Levittown v. Nyquist*, June 23, 1982, p. 21, note 9. The majority, while recognizing the inequities in the state's system of school finance, decided it was up to the legislature, and not the judicial branch, to find a remedy.

SUMMARY AND CONCLUSIONS   271

to the nation that inequality along racial lines was unacceptable. Judicial interest in educational equity continues to be high. Beginning in the 1970s many state courts evaluated the equity of state school-financing systems; some such systems were declared to be unconstitutional. Even in states whose systems were found to be constitutional or where no legal challenge was brought, the anticipation of judicial actions served to foster equity goals in school finance.

The special role of equity in school finance and the intervention by the courts are reflected in current public-policy analysis and research. Equity is continuously assessed in many states, particularly when the state's policymakers contemplate changes in the state's school-financing system. For example, during the last decade, over half of the fifty states have "reformed" their state finance systems by changing the way in which state aid is distributed. Equity goals usually comprise a significant component of the rationale for these changes. Furthermore, despite the political and fiscal climate of the 1980s, a number of individual states are continuing the quest for more equitable school-financing systems.

The federal government has also begun to examine equity in school finance, in part to determine the effectiveness of its programs. While less than 10 percent of all revenues for public primary and secondary education are provided by the federal government, federal aid has frequently evolved from specific equity concerns. Federal aid programs for educationally disadvantaged, handicapped, and bilingual students are designed to eliminate or reduce inequities that develop from a purely state and local financing system.

Equity in education is not affected solely by policies especially designed to distribute state or federal aid. Tax policies also have a direct or an indirect impact on school-finance equity. The imposition of tax and expenditure limits such as California's Proposition 13 and Massachusetts's Proposition 2½ have profound effects on equity in education. Moreover, demographic trends such as declining birth rates and relative rises in the size of the elderly population indirectly affect equity in education through enrollment changes in the case of the former and through preferences for spending on education in the case of the latter.

Thus, for a multiplicity of reasons, equity in school finance changes continuously and is constantly being assessed. Despite the abundance of equity studies, they often employ methodologies that are inadequate, resulting in misleading findings. The objective of this book was to improve the measurement of equity in school finance by analyzing the complex issues involved in assessing equity and by presenting and comparing alternative methodologies. This was accomplished through theoretical development, a literature review, hypothetical illustrations, and comprehensive empirical studies.

In the first five sections of this chapter, we present the principle findings of our research. Equity in school finance involves value-laden choices. The four-dimensional framework used to organize and assess alternative concepts of equity, including their associated value judgments, is presented in the first section. The second section describes our findings on the alternative measures of equity, while the third section summarizes our study of the effects of variation in what is distributed by the education system. The equity framework includes three broad equity principles, and our conclusions on these are the subject of the fourth section. In order to compare alternative measurement techniques, we have conducted an evaluation of school-finance equity in the states of Michigan and New York over nine and fourteen years, respectively; the methodological findings contained in the second, third, and fourth sections are based on this research. In the fifth section we shift gears from a methodological perspective to present the major substantive conclusions on school-finance equity in Michigan and New York. That is, how has equity changed, over time, in the two states? In the sixth and final section of the chapter, we identify future issues for research in educational equity.

A FRAMEWORK FOR ASSESSING EQUITY IN SCHOOL FINANCE

Equity concerns emanate from many sources, but all have one thing in common. All incorporate specific values, either implicitly or explicitly, where values are preferences for what should be and for what should not be. In many cases equity analyses are unnecessarily confusing, in part because the values embedded in the assessment are hidden or suppressed. To clarify and improve equity analyses, we have developed a four-dimensional framework in which each dimension helps bring certain kinds of value judgments to the forefront.

The four-dimensional framework enables the analyst to sort out the critical components of any approach to equity measurement and to confront the value judgments that must be made when equity is assessed. This framework is a critical part of our findings and analysis, and we therefore summarize it here.

The first dimension of the framework is the group that comprises the target of equity concerns. When making a determination of equity or fairness, the analysis may differ, theoretically and empirically, depending upon the answer to the question, "Equity for whom?" In school finance, both children and taxpayers are plausible answers to this question. Children are often selected because they are the recipients of the benefits of education, and taxpayers are logical targets since, when viewed as members of households, they simultaneously pay the costs of education through taxes and receive the benefits of that education for their children.

The choice between children and taxpayers as the target for a school-finance equity analysis is made on the basis of values. Furthermore, the selection of either children or taxpayers as the target group divides the framework into two parts. Since the empirical analyses presented in the book focus exclusively on children's equity, the conclusions presented below, as well as this discussion of the framework, are limited to equity for children.[2]

The second dimension of the framework is the issue of what should be equitably distributed. Another way of viewing this dimension is as the answer to the question, "Equity of what?" In order to refer to this dimension generally, without specifying a particular answer to that question, we have chosen to use the term, *object*. The choice of an object (or objects) for a children's equity assessment must be made on the basis of values. For example, should school-finance equity be analyzed in terms of inputs to the education system, because inputs are the objects most directly distributed by the public policy process? Or should equity be judged by focusing on the outputs of the education system, since knowledge and skills are what we hope children acquire through schooling? Or should equity be analyzed according to the activities that take place inside schools, such as types of classes or programs, or access to specific experiences such as art, computers, and automobile-repair shops?

Even within broad categories such as inputs or outputs, there are further choices that must be made, and these too are based on values. One object within the input category is the dollars that are available to purchase the inputs to the education process. An alternative is to utilize the inputs themselves, such as teachers or textbooks, but here the technical problem of how to combine these diverse units must be overcome. Finally, since the dollars available to each school district in a state do not purchase the same quantity of inputs, due to price variations across the state, price-adjusted dollars should be used as the object in equity assessments. In sum, by including the object as the second dimension of the framework, we are emphasizing the point that alternative value choices are involved.

The principles used to assess whether the objects are distributed fairly or equitably among the group—in our case, children—comprise the third dimension of the equity framework. For children's equity in school finance we have identified three principles, each of which incorporates different values. First, horizontal equity asks whether equally situated pupils are treated equally. This principle is concerned with the equality or disparities in objects for children who are judged to be deserving of equal treatment. We demonstrated in our literature review that of three principles, horizontal equity is the most frequently utilized in equity assessments. By enumerating two additional principles, however, we stress the important point that equity is more than just equality. Equality is only appropriate when comparing children judged to be deserving of equal treatment.

The second principle is based on the idea that certain of the ways in which children differ should *not* lead to systematic differences in the distribution of the object among children. In school finance, concern is often expressed that

---

2. A more complete description of the framework, including the part focusing on taxpayers' equity, is presented in chapter 2.

children in school districts with high levels of property wealth (equalized assessed value per pupil) receive more objects (usually dollars) than children in low-property-wealth districts. Expressed in this way, the second principle assesses whether there is a systematic relationship between the objects and a second variable, in this case property wealth. Equity, according to this principle, exists when there is *no* relationship between the object and the variable of concern.

In order to identify this principle, we use the term *equal opportunity*. But since the equal-opportunity principle involves not only the object but also a second variable, the principle is often stated as equal opportunity with respect to X, where X in the above example is property wealth. Clearly the decision to use this principle is a value judgment, but the specification of the variables of concern is a value judgment as well.

The third and final children's equity principle, vertical equity, is defined as the unequal treatment of children who are unequally situated. If, for example, a handicapped or a gifted child is judged to be deserving of greater amounts of the object, vertical equity would be the appropriate principle to assess such a concern. Thus, in order for a situation to be vertically equitable, *inequality* in the objects across children may have to prevail. The expression of the vertical-equity principle usually requires decisions on which children are deserving of unequal treatment and the nature of the unequal treatment that is desirable.

The fourth dimension of the framework consists of the measures used to assess equity for a particular principle. For each principle, alternative measures are available, and the choice of a measure is also based on value judgments. For example, horizontal equity is assessed by alternative dispersion measures, where the measures incorporate value judgments that lead to ways to differentiate among the measures. The same is true for the various relationship measures based on regression techniques used to assess equal opportunity and for the modified dispersion and relationship measures capable of analyzing vertical equity.

Thus, the measurement of equity can be viewed along four dimensions, where choices within each dimension rely heavily on values. When the issue of values is ignored, equity analyses become overly complicated and confused. The framework is designed to make the selection of values an explicit action. In the next three sections, we examine the differences that result from choices within specific dimensions.

DIFFERENCES AMONG MEASURES IN SCHOOL-FINANCE-EQUITY ANALYSES

We have studied two broad categories of measures of school-finance equity. Dispersion measures are used to assess horizontal equity and vertical equity, while relationship measures, based on regression techniques, are employed to analyze equal opportunity and vertical equity. In this section the differences among the various measures are assessed by examining whether trends in equity in one state, over time, or in levels in equity at one point in time are affected by alternative measures.[3] The time series analyses of Michigan and New York presented in the preceding three chapters form the basis for our conclusions that the choice of a measure has a substantial effect on equity findings. In both states, data gathered at the district level are utilized, which is the prevailing practice in school-finance-equity research, and we comment further on this practice in the final section of this chapter.

Every measure of school-finance equity has certain theoretical properties that could lead to different conclusions when alternative measures are used to assess the amount of change in school-finance equity over time, or even the direction of the change, when applied in actual cases. For example, certain dispersion measures, such as the McLoone index, the standard deviation of logarithms, and Atkinson's index with high values of E, weight the lower end of the distribution more than the higher end. Other dispersion measures, including the coefficient of variation and the Gini coefficient, do not weight either the low or the high ends of the distribution more heavily. This theoretical difference—whether or not the measure weights the low end of the distribution more—may or may not lead to different conclusions about trends in equity in a state over time. Thus, it is only by comparing the different measures in practice that we can tell whether the choice of a measure affects conclusions about the movement of equity in a particular case over a specified time period. Our analysis shows that the choice of a measure of school-finance equity makes a substantial difference, and we consider first the dispersion measures, then the relationship measures.

Differences among Alternative Dispersion Measures

Alternative dispersion measures incorporate different theoretical properties that can be viewed as value judgments. In our assessment of the dispersion measures, we found first that certain measures could be grouped together from a theoretical perspective. Second, when we examined the measures in the empirical assessment of equity over time, we found that they could be grouped by the way in which they captured the trends in equity. Our research shows that the theoretical and empirical groupings for the dispersion measures are similar, but not identical.

Table 10.1 shows the theoretical and empirical groupings of the dispersion measures. The first theoretical grouping includes the measures that are sensitive to equal percentage increases. These measures will show changes simply as a result of uniform inflation, and thus analysts need to take special care to use other measures insensitive to inflation when assessing trends in equity over time if there are price increases. All the measures that include all of the

---

3. In the next section, a similar approach is utilized to compare alternative objects.

Table 10.1. Theoretical and Empirical Groupings of Alternative Dispersion Measures

Theoretical Groupings	Empirical Groupings
1. Range, restricted range, and variance	1. Range, restricted range, and variance
2. Coefficient of variation, Gini coefficient, Theil's measure, Atkinson's index with low values of E, and relative mean deviation	2. Coefficient of variation, Gini coefficient, Theil's measure, Atkinson's index with low values of E, relative mean deviation, and standard deviation of logarithms
3. Standard deviation of logarithms, McLoone index, and Atkinson's index with high values of E	3. McLoone index
4. Federal range ratio	4. Atkinson's index with high values of E
	5. Federal range ratio

pupils, that are sensitive to mean-preserving transfers, and that are insensitive to equal percentage increases are in the second theoretical grouping. The measures that weight observations at the low end of the distribution more heavily are included in the third theoretical grouping, and the federal range ratio comprises the fourth theoretical grouping by itself.

The difference between the theoretical and the empirical groupings is that the third theoretical grouping does not hold up empirically. Instead, empirical analyses show that the standard deviation of logarithms is similar to the group that includes the coefficient of variation, and that the McLoone index and Atkinson's index (with high values of E) are different from each other and from all other groups as well. This is an important finding, because all these measures conceptually give more weight to pupils at the low end of the distribution. Thus, if one thinks that an equitable school-finance system must be especially responsive to the pupils who receive the least, then the measures that weight the bottom of the distribution will be attractive. But having decided on this value, it will not be possible to choose indiscriminately among the three measures that theoretically emphasize the bottom. However, the other dispersion measures do group as the value judgments inherent in them would predict.

The three measures in the third theoretical grouping, which weight the bottom of the distribution, behave differently from one another. While the standard deviation of logarithms mathematically weights low values relatively more than high values, the extra weights are not great enough to change the equity trends from those evident for the second theoretical grouping, containing the coefficient of variation. For example, trends in horizontal equity in Michigan with instructional expenditures as the object show that the standard deviation of the logarithms behaves similarly to the coefficient of variation, the Gini coefficient, and Theil's measure. Not all objects and principles show in such a clear-cut way the similarity in trends, but most are reasonably represented by this example.

The McLoone index and Atkinson's index with high values of E, again using Michigan's instructional expenditures as the object, document that trends depicted by these two measures are quite dissimilar from one another as well as from the standard deviation of logarithms. The McLoone index almost always behaves uniquely. This measure compares the aggregate of the object received by pupils below the median to the aggregate they would receive if they were all at the median level. Occasionally in our empirical analyses (chapters 7 through 9), the McLoone index has approached perfect equity (as for New York's horizontal equity using price-adjusted current operating expenditures as the object—figure 7.15), and often it has shown erratic swings up and down (for example, New York's vertical equity with current operating expenditures as the object—figure 9.7). Both of these phenomena may result from a few very large school districts moving closer or farther from the median. No other measures exhibit these characteristics.

Atkinson's index can be made to depict very different trends in equity as one of its parameters (E) is set at different values. In fact, were this measure more widely used or more intuitively understandable, it would be a good candidate for a single set of measures, with varying E's. Because most readers of school-finance-equity analyses are more familiar with measures such as the federal range ratio or the coefficient of variation, however, we do not recommend this approach at this time, although continued experimentation appears warranted.

Differences among Alternative Relationship Measures

The second category of measures employed in school-finance-equity analyses is relationship measures. These measures are used in conjunction with both equal opportunity and vertical equity and they are all based on regression analyses of a dependent and independent variable. We examined relationship measures theoretically and empirically; groupings that result are displayed in table 10.2.

Again, the theoretical and empirical groupings are similar but not identical. First, empirically the elasticities and the adjusted relationship measures (theoretical groupings 3 and 4) are not usually differentiated. Second, empirically, the slopes are sometimes differentiated from the other groups and

Table 10.2. Theoretical and Empirical Groupings of Alternative Relationship Measures

Theoretical Groupings	Empirical Groupings
1. Correlation	1. Correlation
2. The slopes	2. The slopes
3. The elasticities	3. The elasticities and adjusted relationship measures
4. The adjusted relationship measures	

sometimes not. To be safe, evaluators should keep the slope groupings separate until evidence from their own analyses warrant a combination with theoretical groupings 3 and 4. Also, because slopes will show changes due to inflation, analysts need to use other measures when assessing equity over times of inflationary changes. Finally, empirically the correlation often shows quite a different trend from the other groupings.

Empirically, the relationship measures are not as differentiated among themselves as their theoretical groupings would predict. The only measure that consistently shows trends different from the other measures is the correlation. The correlation also differs most in terms of inherent value judgments. For example, it alone among relationship measures does not change when either equal-percentage or constant-amount additions are made to the object every pupil receives. Since the correlation is one of the most commonly used relationship measures in school-finance-equity studies, its uniqueness is important to acknowledge.

DIFFERENCES AMONG OBJECTS IN SCHOOL-FINANCE-EQUITY ANALYSES

Three categories of input-based objects have been examined in earlier chapters. The most commonly measured input-based object is simply the dollars used to purchase inputs for the education process. Some objects in the dollar category capture the "revenues" raised to purchase inputs, while others are based on the "expenditures" for the inputs themselves. Two problems with dollar objects are that a dollar does not always purchase the same quantity and quality of inputs at different locations in a particular state or in different years. The second category of input-based objects, price-adjusted dollars, uses econometrically derived price indexes to adjust dollars for intrastate price differences. Finally, the third category of input-based objects, which corrects for the problem of unequal purchasing power of dollars over space and time, is the resources that actually comprise the inputs. In our research, the most important resource used in the education process, teachers, serves as the example of a resource object.

Thus, the question we examine is whether the choice of one or more objects influences findings on school-finance equity. Due to the improvements offered by price-adjusted dollars as compared to dollars and the technical difficulties of adding together resources of different types, the comparison between dollars and price-adjusted dollars is particularly important. When there are price differences across locations in a state, then dollars are not comparable across districts because a dollar does not purchase equal inputs. For this reason, price-adjusted dollars are conceptually preferable to unadjusted dollars. As we indicated in chapter 5, however, unadjusted dollars, rather than price-adjusted dollars, are currently used in virtually every study of equity in school finance. Since techniques to estimate price adjustments are now available, it is important to know whether a conceptually preferred object alters the results of the less preferred, but more frequently used, object. If there are no empirical differences, the superiority of price-adjusted dollars is not as crucial. If there are empirical differences, it is important for evaluations of school-finance equity to use the price-adjusted object. We begin by summarizing the major findings for the three categories of input-based objects and then turn our attention to the differences within specific categories, particularly dollars.

Differences among Categories: Dollars, Price-Adjusted Dollars, and Resources

A major finding of our research is that conclusions from school-finance-equity analyses *are* profoundly influenced by the category of object employed. Dollars, price-adjusted dollars, and resources are not interchangeable. The differences among the three categories are evident in the levels and trends in horizontal equity, equal opportunity, and vertical equity in Michigan and New York. Because levels and trends differ, it is important for analysts to use price-adjusted dollars or resources in their assessments. The results that follow show the instances when the preferred objects of price-adjusted dollars and resources differ from dollars.

The *levels of horizontal equity* vary across the three categories of objects in Michigan and the two categories available for New York. In both Michigan and New York, price-adjusted dollars are generally more horizontally equitable than the conceptually inferior unadjusted dollars. Furthermore, the resource objects in Michigan are also more horizontally equitable than the dollar objects. A comparison of the levels of the price-adjusted dollar and resource objects shows that neither is consistently the most equitable. Put another way, in several instances both of these objects alternate as the most horizontally equitable at different points during the six years when resource data are available.

The *trends in horizontal equity* are only occasionally affected by the price adjustment. On the other hand, trends in horizontal equity measured by resource objects are consistently unlike the trends in horizontal equity of dollars or price-adjusted dollars.

Equal opportunity is assessed with respect to wealth, income, region, and race, and in all four cases the choice of a category of object affects conclusions on *levels of equal opportunity*. In both Michigan and New York, price-adjusted dollar objects almost always improve the level of equal opportunity with respect to wealth and income in comparison with unadjusted dollar objects. For resource objects (again, only in Michigan) the levels of equal opportunity with respect to wealth are improved in comparison with either dollars or price-adjusted dollars, while for equal opportunity with respect to income, levels are improved for resources and price-adjusted dollars in comparison with dollars.

The change to price-adjusted dollars or resources from unadjusted dollars also affects the findings on equal opportunity with respect to region. In both Michigan and New York, the inequality of opportunity with respect to regions is reduced substantially when dollars are price-adjusted. This reduction in inequality of opportunity with respect to region also occurs in Michigan when resources replace dollars as the object.

Finally, the category of object influences conclusions regarding the levels of equal opportunity with respect to race in Michigan. In every instance, the replacement of dollars by price-adjusted dollars or resources lowers the relationship between the object and the percent minority, although not by equivalent amounts in every year. The use of price-adjusted dollars or resources often changes the relationship from positive to negative and thus shows a worsening of equal opportunity with respect to race.

Although there are exceptions, *trends in equal opportunity* with respect to wealth, income, and race are generally similar for dollars and price-adjusted dollars despite the differences in levels. Almost without exception, the trends in equal opportunity with resources as the object are different from the trends for the other two categories.

The general findings for the effects of the categories of objects observed for horizontal equity and equal opportunity hold for vertical equity as well. The effect of the object on the *levels of vertical equity* can be seen most clearly when the relationship measures are used to determine if the districts with needier pupils receive greater amounts of the object. The relationship between district needs and objects is always lower for price-adjusted dollars and resources than it is for dollar objects.

Finally, price-adjusted dollars and dollars have very similar, but not identical, *trends in vertical equity*. Only in the case of resources do the differences in trends appear in a systematic way.

The divergence in trends between the resource and price-adjusted dollar objects reinforces the point that the use of actual inputs is not the same as removing intrastate price differences with price indexes. Future research will be needed to determine what part of the difference is due to the methodology used to compute the price index and what part to the fact that only one input, teachers, is being utilized as the resource object. Perhaps with improved price indexes and more complete resource measures the differences in the trends will be reduced.

These results show clearly that price adjustments influence empirical analyses. For horizontal equity, for equal opportunity with respect to four different independent variables, and for vertical equity, price-adjusted dollars differ from unadjusted dollars in the levels of equity. Furthermore, the direction of the change varies from improvement to worsening. Thus, since empirical differences are documented, the conceptual arguments that favor price-adjusted dollars over dollars cannot be ignored. Instead, school-finance-equity analyses should at the very least use price-adjusted dollars along with dollars. If only one object is used, price-adjusted dollars is preferable.

Differences within Categories: Dollars, Price-Adjusted Dollars, and Resources

Because the differences between the two price indexes and between the two teacher definitions used in our data analyses are relatively small, price-adjusted dollars and resources show only minor intragroup variations. The analysis of the effects of alternative dollar objects in Michigan is considerably more complete, and some substantial intragroup differences result. Since school-finance-equity studies typically utilize different dollar objects, it is important to know whether the choice of this kind of object affects the findings of an equity analysis.

In general, the most significant differences in trends and levels of equity over time using dollars result when a choice is made between expenditures and revenues. Using one of many possible examples, we can examine equal opportunity with respect to wealth in Michigan. While all dollar objects show fairly consistent improvement over the nine-year period, the three expenditure objects generally show greater improvement than the three revenue objects. Although the level of equal opportunity with respect to wealth is similar across all objects in 1970, by 1978 the expenditure objects evidence more equal opportunity with respect to wealth than the revenue objects due to the differences in trends.

Frequently differences in equity trends and levels also result when alternative definitions of revenues are selected. An example that is relevant to policymakers is the differences that occur in vertical equity when federal revenues are added to local and state dollars. The addition of federal revenues always increases the relationship between dollars and needs, thereby showing an improvement in vertical equity. This is a hoped-for result, since federal revenues are generally targeted toward children identified in our analyses as having greater needs. From our analyses of alternative dollar objects in Michigan, examples of which are given above, the fact that the dollar objects are not interchangeable is demonstrated. Assessments of equity not only depend on whether a dollar, price-adjusted dollar, or resource object is employed, but within the dollar category, the choice of a dollar object can lead to different conclusions.

FINDINGS ON THE THREE PRINCIPLES OF EQUITY IN SCHOOL FINANCE

The three school-finance-equity principles are based on different underlying values. Horizontal equity focuses on equality, equal opportunity concentrates on the relationship with other variables, and vertical equity assesses whether unequals are treated as appropriately unequal. Given the very different meanings attached to the three principles, it is not surprising that conclusions about school-finance equity can differ depending upon which principle is used in the analysis. Evidence of these differences was presented for both Michigan and New York. Instead of stressing these empirical findings in this concluding chapter, we highlight the conceptual development of the vertical-equity and equal-opportunity principles that is contained throughout the book.

Our literature review in Chapter 5 turned up no fifty-state studies, one multistate study, and only a handful of single-state studies that assessed vertical equity. Yet many researchers as well as users of school-finance-equity analyses consider vertical equity a legitimate and important goal. Furthermore, given the overall societal concern for groups such as the handicapped, federal intervention on their behalf in the education system, and the expanding role being played by the courts, there is a good chance that vertical equity will become a more important concern for the future. Observers of school-finance-equity assessment probably characterize the absence of vertical-equity measurement as the most serious flaw in the literature.

To meet this perceived need, we have systematically developed alternative measures of vertical equity by using relationship and dispersion measures. Vertical equity is the most complex of the principles to measure, and each of these two categories of measures assesses the principle somewhat differently. Both the relationship and the dispersion measures require that the special group deserving of special treatment be identified and quantified. The relationship measures then assess whether districts that include higher percentages of the special groups receive greater or lesser amounts of the object. If the special group is handicapped pupils, then vertical equity would require a positive relationship between the object and the percentage of pupils in the special group.

When measuring vertical equity with dispersion measures, more than the identification and quantification of the special group is required. In addition, the appropriately unequal treatment that the special group should receive must be determined, so that members of the special group can be weighted more (or less) heavily compared to pupils not in the special group. Continuing the example of handicapped pupils, a decision may be made (e.g., by studying the learning process) that handicapped pupils should receive twice the level of objects received by pupils who are not handicapped. This would lead to a weighting of two to one for handicapped to nonhandicapped pupils. With the added specification of the pupil weights, the dispersion measures used to assess horizontal equity can be converted to weighted dispersion measures to analyze vertical equity.

The theoretical underpinnings of the two types of vertical-equity measures are shown to be empirically important when vertical equity is analyzed in Michigan and New York. The trends and levels of vertical equity measured by the relationship measures differ repeatedly from those measured by the weighted dispersion measures. Furthermore, the finding that the identification of the special groups and the determination of the appropriate weights also influence conclusions on vertical equity increases the complexity of measurement. Despite the inherent complexity, the methodology developed here should be useful for future school-finance studies because it fills such an obvious gap. School-finance-equity studies should include vertical-equity assessments in the future.

Heretofore, the most common relationship analyzed in equal opportunity has been that between dollars per pupil and property wealth per pupil. In this study we have expanded this concept to include relationships between a variety of objects and other independent variables such as income, region, and race. Income is often cited as superior to wealth as an ability-to-pay measure, and our analyses show that the two can result in different trends and levels of equity. Regional differences are important politically, especially in large geographically diverse states such as Michigan, New York, Pennsylvania, Illinois, and California, and we present a way to proceed with such analyses that is easily comprehended and executed. Race is an example of a characteristic (much like sex and age) that for both historical and legal reasons has been the subject of much equal-opportunity concern both in school finance and in other public-policy areas as well. Our analyses show what can be said using race alone as an independent variable, and we also point out some pitfalls of such analyses.

FINDINGS ON EQUITY TRENDS AND LEVELS OVER TIME IN MICHIGAN AND NEW YORK

The status of equity in New York and Michigan is somewhat difficult to summarize, since our methodological assessment demonstrated that choices concerning the principle, object, and measure affect conclusions on equity trends and levels. Some of the choices can be omitted a priori, either because the measures are inappropriate to use over time in the presence of substantial inflation (viz range, restricted range, and variance) or because the object is conceptually inferior (viz dollars). Many other choices, however, are value judgments. Where necessary because of differences in conclusions, we present results only for certain objects and measures but even with these limited choices, conclusions sometimes vary. After presenting the choices and our findings for each principle in each state, we summarize the most robust results for each state. Only results for the children's group are reported, since no empirical analyses of taxpayers' equity were carried out. Furthermore, when choices are necessary among objects, we generally report on price-adjusted dollars. The bases for this selection are that the use of a price adjustment is conceptually superior to unadjusted dollars, and that since most analyses omit this adjustment, our findings may be of particular interest. When choices among dispersion measures are necessary, we report results for the coefficient of variation because it embodies a set of value judgments that, once made explicit, are likely to appeal to a substantial group of readers and because the empirical performance of several of the other dispersion measures is similar to the coefficient of variation. In addition, we report the results for the McLoone index because there appears to be heightened interest on the part of policymakers and researchers for pupils in the bottom part of the distribution, and this measure weights pupils at the bottom end more heavily. We summarize conclusions for all three principles, but for vertical equity we use only weighted dispersion measures and not relationship measures, because the former are more easily interpreted and understood.

Michigan

Horizontal Equity. Data for Michigan were collected for the years 1970 through 1978. When using dispersion measures such as the coefficient of variation and the McLoone index that are insensitive to equal percentage increases and do not change simply as a result of inflation, the levels of horizontal equity for the price-adjusted objects are often similar in 1970 and 1978. Occasionally, the McLoone index shows a moderate improvement from 1970 to 1978. Furthermore, for both measures it is common for horizontal equity to worsen and then improve during the nine-year period, although the precise trends for the coefficient of variation do not always parallel those for the McLoone index. The focus of the McLoone index on the lower half of the distribution compared to the coefficient of variation's inclusion of the entire distribution probably accounts for the discrepancies in the trends.

Note that the trends in horizontal equity reported above do not hold for the range, the restricted range, and the variance, the three measures that are sensitive to equal percentage increases. Since inflation has been considerable over the nine-year study period, the worsening trends over the period depicted by the range, the restricted range, and the variance capture the inflation more than any real change in equity.

Equal Opportunity. Taking equal opportunity with respect to wealth (equalized assessed property value per pupil), the most salient finding is that in all nine years, for every measure and object, educational objects are positively related to wealth. That is, pupils who attend schools with higher per-pupil wealth are more likely to receive greater amounts of the object.

Findings concerning the trends in equal opportunity with respect to wealth in Michigan are not as unambiguous as those for levels. For price-adjusted objects, the trend over time depends on the definition of dollars that is used. For about half of the definitions, the trend over the nine-year period is substantial improvement in equal opportunity with respect to wealth, while for the other half there is no improvement, or a worsening.

A positive relationship between the object and income (per capita) also exists in Michigan in every year using all objects and measures, indicating that equal opportunity with respect to income does not occur in Michigan.

When price-adjusted dollars are the object, the trends in equal opportunity with respect to income are generally **U**- or **W**- shaped over the nine-year period. That is, the trends begin and end at roughly the same level, but there is usually a period of less unequal opportunity during the middle years.

Equal opportunity with respect to regions in Michigan is assessed by comparing objects in the Detroit metropolitan area, the Upper Peninsula, middle city school districts in the lower peninsula, and the remainder of the lower peninsula (excluding the Detroit SMSA and middle cities). With price-adjusted dollar objects, the differences between mean levels of objects across regions are sometimes as great as 20 percent. The middle cities fare the best, and Detroit is often the region with the lowest level of price-adjusted objects.

Finally, in almost every year for all price-adjusted dollar and resource objects, equal opportunity with respect to race in Michigan does not prevail. For price-adjusted dollars, equal opportunity with respect to race usually ends the nine-year period at a level similar to where it began, and there are often several ups and downs during the period.

Vertical Equity. In Michigan, vertical equity, the unequal treatment of unequals, is analyzed using two different definitions of the "unequal" groups. One unequal group is comprised solely of handicapped pupils, while the second consists of handicapped pupils and learning disadvantaged (Title I-eligible) pupils. Conclusions on vertical equity in Michigan often hinge on which definition is used.

Vertical equity can be assessed with weighted dispersion measures if pupils in the unequal groups are weighted prior to calculating the dispersion measures. Weighted dispersion measures are often expected to be more equal than unweighted ones, since the former compensate for certain "planned" inequalities. In Michigan, when weighted dispersion measures are compared to unweighted dispersion measures, the weighted measures are generally more equal than the unweighted measures when handicapped pupils are in the unequal group, and usually less equal than the unweighted measures when handicapped and learning disadvantaged pupils are in the unequal group. Thus, weighting dispersion measures to capture vertical equity does not automatically reduce the dispersion. In Michigan, at least, it depends on the particular definition of the unequal group.

Conclusions on the trends in vertical equity depend upon which of the weighted dispersion measures is used to capture the trends. Like the unweighted dispersion measures used to assess horizontal equity, the trends in the weighted dispersion measures for the price-adjusted objects show that vertical equity often ends the period at a similar level to where it began, eight years earlier. Over the period, however, the trends in vertical equity depicted by the coefficient of variation are somewhat different than those for the McLoone index, again reflecting the different value judgments incorporated in the two measures. The trends in the weighted dispersion measures for the resource objects are different than those for the price-adjusted objects.

New York

Horizontal Equity. The use of a particular horizontal-equity measure affects conclusions on the trends in horizontal equity over the fourteen years studied, 1965 through 1978. For the group of measures including the coefficient of variation, price-adjusted dollars indicate that horizontal equity in New York improved from 1965 to 1968 or 1969, then worsened for five years, and finally was fairly level or improved somewhat from 1974 to 1978. As a result, these trends indicate that horizontal equity during the mid to late 1970s was worse than during the latter part of the 1960s. These findings are not replicated for the McLoone index. The trends in the McLoone index for price-adjusted current operating expenditures indicate that the 1970s are not uniformly less horizontally equitable than the 1960s. In fact, using the McLoone index as the measure, horizontal equity in 1977 is roughly equal to horizontal equity in 1965.

Equal Opportunity. For equal opportunity with respect to wealth in New York, one conclusion is unaffected by the measure. In all fourteen years, there is a positive relationship between both objects and per-pupil equalized property wealth. Thus, equal opportunity with respect to wealth is absent in New York over the fourteen-year period.

Overall, the trends in equal opportunity with respect to wealth show a general worsening over the period, and again the latest part of the period, 1974 to 1978, displays the highest level of unequal opportunity with respect to wealth.

In New York, equal opportunity with respect to income (income per return) does not exist for price-adjusted expenditures in any of the fourteen years studied. That is, there is always a positive relationship between the object and income.

The trends in equal opportunity with respect to income for price-adjusted current operating expenditures depend somewhat on which measure of equal opportunity is employed. For all measures except the correlation, equal opportunity with respect to income is generally worse at the end of the period (1976 through 1978) than in 1967 through 1969. Except for the correlation, the overall trend in equal opportunity with respect to income from 1967 to 1978 is generally worsening, although there are certain years during which improvements are registered. When the correlation is utilized to assess equal opportunity with respect to income for price-adjusted dollars in New York, the worsening trend is somewhat modified.

Equal opportunity with respect to region, the final equal-opportunity principle examined in New York, compares mean levels of the objects in four regions: New York City, downstate suburbs (Nassau, Rockland, Suffolk, and Westchester counties), four upstate cities (Albany, Buffalo, Rochester, and Syracuse), and the upstate, nonurban areas (remainder of the state). When price-adjusted current operating expenditures are assessed across regions in New York, the maximum differences are in the 20 to 30 percent range. The downstate suburbs receive the highest levels of the object; at one time during the fourteen-year period, however, each of the other regions is the region with the lowest levels of the object. New York City is the region with the lowest level of price-adjusted dollars during the last two years of the time series, 1977 and 1978.

Vertical Equity. In the analysis of vertical equity in New York, three definitions of the unequal group are utilized. The first group contains handicapped pupils, the second includes handicapped and educationally disadvantaged pupils, and the third is comprised of handicapped, educationally disadvantaged, and bilingual pupils. When vertical equity in New York is assessed using the weighted dispersion measures rather than the unweighted dispersion measures, the dispersion is reduced more often than it is increased. But the number of years in which the reduction occurs varies by dispersion measure. Thus, measuring vertical equity by weighting the horizontal-equity measures does not unambiguously reduce the dispersion.

Trends in vertical equity in New York, assessed using the weighted dispersion measures, depend upon the particular dispersion measure and the object. With a price-adjusted object and the coefficient of variation as the weighted dispersion measure, vertical equity improves from 1965 to 1969, worsens substantially from 1969 to 1974 or 1975, and stays relatively constant from 1975 until 1978. The mid to late 1970s are less vertically equitable than the late 1960s with this weighted dispersion measure. When the McLoone index is used to assess vertical equity in New York with price-adjusted dollars, no longer are the 1970s clearly less equitable than the 1960s. Furthermore, although the precise trends are not identical, the finding that the 1970s are as equitable as the 1960s holds for another measure that emphasizes the lower end of the distribution, Atkinson's index with high values of E.

Finally, in both Michigan and New York, certain findings reappear frequently. With the caveat that any one person's values may not necessarily lead to the modal conclusions, we present our interpretation of the most recurrent findings. In Michigan, equity often begins and ends the nine-year period at similar levels. A few notable exceptions are evident, such as equal opportunity with respect to wealth, but the most prevalent result is the similarity of levels in 1970 and 1978. The trends between 1970 and 1978, however, are not uniform. By contrast, equity in New York has worsened according to a variety of objects, principles, and measures. Most, but not all, analyses show that the mid to late 1970s are less equitable than the late 1960s.

FUTURE RESEARCH ON EQUITY RELATED TO THE FOUR-DIMENSIONAL FRAMEWORK

There are a number of equity issues where both the appropriate concepts and the data are sufficiently developed to permit relatively straightforward analyses using the four-dimensional framework. By contrast, some policy areas exist where considerable creativity and effort would be required before an assessment of equity could be performed.

Among the issues in which concepts and data are available is the evaluation of the school-finance formula that a state uses to fund local school districts. Each state has in place a finance system for its elementary and secondary schools, and in almost all instances the system involves transfers of funds from the state treasury to local school districts. From time to time, perhaps at the instigation of a new governor or a court case or a citizen pressure group, proposals to change the way the funds are allocated to school districts are advanced. Because one of the primary goals of school-finance systems is equity, the effects of new proposals on equity are always of prime importance. The framework developed in this book is ideal for such political assessments because it allows the explicit choice of alternative values.

A second area with concepts and data already available is the constitutionality of school-finance systems, which have been tried in over half the state courts in the last decade. In the future, some of these cases are likely to return to court for compliance hearings, as happened in California's *Serrano* case in early 1983. If the original ruling in a case involves a finding of violations in equity, then compliance hearings will naturally need to reassess the system with respect to the definition of equity that was violated. This reassessment can be facilitated if the four-dimensional framework is utilized. Since parts of the framework were used to organize testimony in the 1983 *Serrano* compliance case, we illustrate other potential future court cases with examples from this case. The 1974 *Serrano* ruling specified a standard of equity and gave the state six years to reach this standard. In 1983, the plaintiffs returned to court, claiming that the standard had not been met.

The alternative measures of equity and their values were part of the evidence in the 1983 *Serrano* case. The findings in the previous Serrano case involved a statement that "wealth-related disparities in expenditures per pupil among school districts apart from categorical aid, special-needs programs that do not reduce to insignificant differences, which means amounts considerably less than $100 per pupil,"[4] are objectionable. The compliance hearings included evidence on the values implied in utilizing a range number of $100 rather than one of the other disparity measures in this book. In particular, some of the controversy in the compliance hearings was over the value judgment implied in the range, since it is sensitive to equal percentage

---

4. *Serrano v. Priest*, Superior Court of the County of Los Angeles, no. 983, at 54 (August 30, 1974).

changes in dollars received by each child. Because there had been considerable inflation since the original $100 standard was set, one side in the case argued that at a minimum the sensitivity to inflation (an equal percentage increase) should be eliminated via an inflation adjustment. In addition, the judge admitted to testimony a comparison of the values implied in each of the other disparity measures described in this book and in the range. Foremost among the differences between the range measure used in the original judgment and the other disparity measures is the range's sensitivity to inflation. This suggests that an alternative disparity measure would be more appropriate than the range. While every court case is different, various parts of the framework are likely to prove useful in similar cases.

Finally, there are a number of policy issues not directly related to school finance where concepts and data now exist, so that equity assessments using the framework developed here could proceed. For example, the past five years has witnessed several tax- and expenditure-limitation laws. The two most renowned are California's Proposition 13 and Massachusetts' Proposition 2½. In these situations, the framework could help assess equity impacts. A variety of groups, in addition to children, would be of interest (e.g., taxpayers, age groups, income classes). All three equity principles could be applied, all of the objects discussed with respect to school finance in Michigan and New York would be relevant, and all of the measures could be used. In addition, other principles, objects, and measures directly related to taxpayers, and described in chapter 2, would be germane to the equity effects of tax and expenditures limitations. The framework allows a researcher to make a very quick outline of paths to follow in setting up an evaluation. Experience using the framework in contexts other than school finance will result in generalizations similar to those reported in this book about differences and similarities in objects and measures.

There are numerous school-finance issues where concepts and/or data are not now readily available. For these issues it is valuable to consider the costs of developing what is needed versus the benefits of the information on equity that would result. While the analyses described below would be of interest to a variety of groups, we do not advocate their immediate pursuance without some careful thinking about their benefit-cost ratios.

The next revolution in analyses of school-finance systems is likely to involve the collection of data disaggregated to the school, classroom, and individual pupil level. Every researcher craves such data, and in a few instances they have been collected.[5] With such data, school-finance-equity studies could make two important advances. First, the traditional objects (preferably price-

---

5. See, for example, Charles S. Benson, Elliot A. Medrich, and Stuart Buckley, "A New View of School Efficiency: Household Time Contributions to School Achievement," in James E. Guthrie, ed., *School Finance Policies and Practices—The 1980's: A Decade of Conflict* (Cambridge, Mass.: Ballinger, 1980), and Michael Rutter et al., *Fifteen Thousand Hours: Secondary Schools and Their Effects on Children* (Cambridge, Mass.: Harvard University Press, 1979).

adjusted) could be traced to individual pupils, so that instead of assigning pupils the average number of their districts, specific numbers by pupil (classroom or school) would be available. This advance would be particularly important if within-district variation in objects is large relative to between-district variation, a fact that has been suspected by many but rarely shown.

Second, and more important, objects other than dollars and resources could meaningfully be used in an analysis if individual pupils were studied. For example, the intellectual, social, and creative levels and changes of children could be evaluated and their distributions assessed. The idea that equity requires at least minimum fulfillment of individual children's unique capacities is a recurrent theme in the theoretical literature on equity concepts. While individual data are necessary in order to measure this idea, they are not sufficient. In addition, further work on how to conceptualize and measure varieties of children's achievements is required before individual data could be put to their most powerful use. Again, studies where such efforts are made are beginning to appear, but they are far from common due both to their costs and to the inherent conceptual challenges of defining and measuring less objective characteristics, such as learning or creativity.

The discussion in this chapter has shown how—given data that can be collected with reasonable costs and are normally used in studies each year—the analyses of school-finance equity can be considerably advanced beyond the current state of the art. The four-dimensional framework, including the principles of vertical equity and equal opportunity, the use of price-adjusted dollars and the comparison of numerous statistical measures, serves to underscore the wide variety of value choices that must be made in every step of an equity analysis. The use of this evaluative methodology will make school-finance-equity analyses more meaningful to the diverse audiences interested in their outcomes. Furthermore, the methodology also points the way to future advances in data and concepts, while providing a framework in which the advances can be incorporated for public-policy-equity assessments.

We believe that if other analysts of school-finance systems emphasize value choices by utilizing our framework, conclusions on equity will be on firmer ground. But it is also important to us that our approach be useful to policymakers. Unless policymakers choose to make their values explicit, they will not understand why equity studies so often "make no sense" to them. Although making values explicit is politically risky, it may be more risky to hide values behind so-called objective studies of equity. Value judgments cannot be avoided by policymakers, and social science research that highlights the specific influence of values may help in understanding this. At a minimum, poor choices such as the range, the absence of adjustments for price differences, and the failure to measure vertical equity should be avoided.

INDEX

Achievement score measures, 9, 11, 12
Adjusted relationship measure, 72
   Adams, E. K., 212, 213
   computation of, 74-76
   in conceptual and empirical groupings, 277-78
   differentiated from correlation and elasticity, 80-81
   for equal opportunity, 28, 31-32
      in Michigan, 171-80, 199-207
      in New York, 208-11
   value judgments in, 32-35
   for vertical equity, 38-39
      in Michigan, 236-38
      in New York, 254-55, 266
Advisory Commission on Intergovernmental Relations, 182
Age, and vertical equity, 14
Aid to Families with Dependent Children, 226
Akin, J. S., 182
Assessment ratio, 79
Atkinson, A., 13, 21
Atkinson's index
   in conceptual and empirical groupings, 138, 139, 141, 276, 277
   in equity studies, 107
   for horizontal equity, 9, 19, 20-22, 130, 132, 165-66
      in Michigan, 138-41
      in New York, 158-63
   value judgments in, 23-26, 138
Augenblick, J., 182

Behavioral output measures, 9, 11-12
Benson, C. S., 289
Berne, R., 23, 125
Bernstein, C. D., 226, 227, 252
Bilingual pupils, 250, 251, 252
Birth rate, 271
Brischetto, R., 197
Brown v. *Board of Education*, 270-71
Buckley, S., 289

California
   in NEFP study, 226
   Proposition 13 in, 271, 289
   and state court rulings, 3, 288-89
Carroll, S. J., 197
Chambers, J. G., 126
Children, identification of differences among, 13-16
Children's equity, 8-40
   literature review of, 97-116
   measures of, 17-40, 105-6
   principles of, 12-17, 102-4
   in school finance studies, 98-106, 272-73
Choice, and vertical equity, 16
Class size, 119-20
Coefficient of variation, 64
   and alternative objects, 61-62, 142-57, 239-42
   calculation of, 84, 85
   in conceptual and empirical groupings, 133-38, 276, 277
   in equity studies, 105-8

291

Coefficient of variation (*continued*)
  for horizontal equity, 9, 19, 20
    in Michigan, 130, 131, 134-38, 142-57
    in New York, 158-61, 163-66
  and unit of analysis, 56-59
  value judgments in, 23-25, 69-70, 71
  for vertical equity
    in Michigan, 234-42, 245, 248
    in New York, 254-55, 257, 260-63, 265, 267
College preparatory education, 14, 16
Colorado, 3
Compliance, 288
Comptroller General, 229
Correlation measure, 72
  computation of, 73-75
  in conceptual and empirical groupings, 277-78
  differentiated from other measures, 77-82
  for equal opportunity, 27-31, 171-80, 199-211
    with respect to race, 199-207
    with respect to wealth, 171-77, 208-11
  in equity studies, 105-8
  value judgments in, 32-35, 278
  for vertical equity
    in Michigan, 236-42, 244, 245, 248
    in New York, 254-55, 259, 260-62, 265, 266, 267
Cost adjustments, 101
Costs, and vertical equity, 14, 15
Current operating expenditures
  and equal opportunity, 208-11
  and horizontal equity, 143-47, 158-61, 163-64
  in Michigan, 130, 131, 143-47
  in New York, 127-28, 158-61, 163-64
  and vertical equity, 254-55

Data availability, and vertical equity, 35-36
Deciles, 50
Demographic trends, 271
Dispersion measures, 83-94
  calculation of, 83-86
  conceptual and empirical groupings of, 229-38, 252-62, 275-77
  differences among, 274-77
  differentiated from other measures, 258
  weighted, 36-37, 39-40
    operationalization of, 94
    value judgments in, 226
    and vertical equity, 228-49, 250-68
  weighted vs. unweighted, 83-86, 233-34, 256

Dispersion statistics, 13, 18-19
District size, 14, 15
District, as unit of analysis, 19, 109, 126
  vs. pupil as unit of analysis, 51-59
Dollar objects. *See also* Input-based dollar objects
  and children's equity, 9-11
  in equity studies, 278-81
  and horizontal equity, 141-59, 163-64, 166-67
  measurement of, 59-62
  in Michigan data base, 118, 120-23
  in New York data base, 118-19, 127-28
  and vertical equity, 262-68

Economic tax incidence, 41
Economies of scale, 14, 15
Education benefits, 102
Educational quality, 10-12, 119
Education Commission of the States, 118, 126, 127
Education production function, 119
Elasticity, 72
  computation of, 74
  in conceptual and empirical groupings, 277-78
  differentiated from other measures, 74, 77-82
  for equal opportunity, 28-31, 171-80, 208-11
  in equity studies, 105-8
  value judgments in, 32-35
  for vertical equity, 38-39
    in Michigan, 236-38
    in New York, 254-55, 259, 266
Elderly, 271
Elementary and Secondary Education Act, 119, 122
Empirical groupings
  of Atkinson's index, 138, 139, 141
  and conceptual groupings, 133-38, 275-78
  of equal opportunity measures, 171, 183-86, 198-200, 208-11, 213
  of horizontal equity measures, 133-38, 158
  of vertical equity measures, 229-38, 252-62
Equal opportunity
  and alternative objects, 279
  and children's equity, 9, 17
  in Michigan, 169-207, 217-20, 284-85
    with respect to income, 182-193
    with respect to property wealth, 170-81
    with respect to race, 193-207
    with respect to region, 193-97

in New York, 169-70, 208-20, 286-87
  with respect to income, 211-14
  with respect to property wealth, 208-11
  with respect to region, 214-17
Equal opportunity measures, 26-35
  differences among, 71, 77-82
  empirical groupings of, 171, 183-86, 198-200, 208-11, 213
  in equity studies, 102-8, 273-74
  and hypothetical illustrations, 71-82
  in Michigan, 171-80
  in New York, 208-11
  value judgments in, 26, 31, 32-35
Equal-yield-for-equal-effort principle, 42, 104-5, 107
Equity. *See also* Children's equity; Equal opportunity; Horizontal equity; School-finance equity; Taxpayers' equity; Vertical equity
  and fiscal restraint, 1-6
  future research on, 288-90
  time series trends in, 129-32
Equity-measurement methodology, 44-62, 63-96
Equity measures, conceptual and empirical groupings of, 133-38, 275-78
Ethnicity, 14
Expenditures
  and children's equity, 10
  in equity studies, 99-102, 281
  in Michigan, 120-22, 125-26
    Atkinson's index for, 138-41
    equal opportunity measures for, 174-80
    horizontal equity measures for, 133-38, 141-54
    vertical equity for, 229-38
  in New York, 127-28

Federal funding, 2, 3, 271
Federal range ratio, 64, 66
  in conceptual and empirical groupings, 133-38, 276, 277
  for horizontal equity, 9, 19, 20
    in Michigan, 134-38, 142-54
    in New York, 158-66
  value judgments in, 23-26, 69-71
  for vertical equity
    in Michigan, 234-42, 245, 248
    in New York, 254-57, 260-65, 267
Federal revenues
  and horizontal equity, 143-47
  in Michigan, 121, 122-23, 143-47, 238-46
  and vertical equity, 238-46, 281
Fifty-state studies, 110-11

Financial Data for School Districts, 127, 128
Fiscal capacity, 14, 15, 108-9
Fiscal neutrality, 17, 42
Fiscal restraint, 1-6
Florida, 226
Frohreich, L. E., 226
Fuchsburg, Judge, 270

Gaughan, J. M., 250, 251
Gini coefficient, 64, 66-68
  computation of, 67
  in conceptual and empirical groupings, 133-38, 276
  in equity studies, 105-8
  for horizontal equity, 9, 19-21
    in Michigan, 134-38
    in New York, 158-61, 163-66
  value judgments in, 23-25, 69-71
  for vertical equity
    in Michigan, 234-38
    in New York, 254-55, 256, 263-65
Glasheen, R. J., 250, 251
Glass, G. V., 119
Goodness-of-fit measure, 78
Grade level, 14
Graduation measure, 12
Grubb, W. N., 10

Hale, J. A., 226
Handicapping, specification of, 222-29, 237, 249-52
  and horizontal equity, 148-54
  and vertical equity, 14, 256, 263
Hartman, W. T., 226, 227, 252
Horizontal equity
  and alternative objects, 141-47, 279, 280-81
  and Atkinson's index, 138-41
  for children, 9, 13
  in equity studies, 102-8, 273, 274
  and hypothetical illustrations, 45
  for instructional expenditures, 133-38
  in Michigan, 129-57, 165-68, 284
  in New York, 157-64, 286
  and price index, 147-54, 163-64
  for taxpayers, 41-42
  trends in, 167-68
  and unit of analysis, 55-56
  and weighting procedure, 86
Horizontal equity measures, 18-26
  empirical groupings of, 158
  in equity studies, 105-8
  and hypothetical illustrations, 64-71

294　INDEX

Horizontal equity measures (*continued*)
　and inflation, 69
　and value judgments, 22-25, 68-71
Hyman, J., 10
Hypothetical illustration, 44-96
　advantages of, 45-46, 94-96
　assumptions incorporated in, 46-47
　of equity principles, 63-96
　　equal opportunity, 71-82
　　horizontal equity, 64-71
　　vertical equity, 82-94
　in equity studies, 106, 107
　and price index, 123-24
　structure and use of, 46-71
　of units of analysis and objects, 51-63

Impact aid, 122
Implicit weight measure, 86-87, 89, 91-94
　definition of, 253
　and vertical equity, 38, 39
　　in Michigan, 234-42, 245, 248
　　in New York, 253-55, 258, 259, 260-62
Income
　compared to wealth, 283
　definition of, 182
　and dispersion statistics, 13
　equal opportunity with respect to, 182-93, 211-14
　in equity studies, 103-4, 108-9
　and vertical equity, 14, 15
Inequality-in-tax-rates, 104-5, 108
Index 1 and 2, 124, 125. *See also* Price index
Inflation
　and dispersion measure groupings, 275
　and horizontal equity measures, 24-25, 69, 138
　and range, 142, 147, 165
　and *Serrano* v. *Priest*, 288-89
　and slope, 79
Input-based dollar objects
　and equal opportunity trends, 171-207
　　with respect to income, 186-93
　　with respect to race, 198-207
　　with respect to region, 194-97
　　with respect to wealth, 171-81
　in equity studies, 278-81
　and horizontal equity trends, 163-64
　and vertical equity trends
　　in Michigan, 238-49
　　in New York, 163-64, 262-68
Input objects
　and children's equity, 9-11, 98-101
　and horizontal equity measures, 141-47

　measurement of, 59-62
　in Michigan data base, 118-19
　in New York data base, 119
Instructional expenditures, 120, 121
　and Atkinson's index, 138-41
　and equal opportunity, 171-80
　and handicapping, 237
　and horizontal equity, 133-38, 143-57
　and vertical equity, 230-38, 243-49

Jones, Chief Justice, 270
Judicial system, and equity, 270-71

Kirst, M. W., 226, 252

Learning disabilities, 14, 223-29
Legal tax incidence, 41
Leppert, J., 227
Levittown v. *Nyquist*, 270
Litigation, 11, 117
Local funding, 3
Local revenues, 121-23
　and horizontal equity, 143-54
　and vertical equity, 238-46
Long, D., 4

McLoone index, 64, 66
　in conceptual and empirical groupings, 133-38, 276, 277
　in equity studies, 106, 107
　and horizontal equity, 9, 19, 20
　　in Michigan, 134-38, 142-57
　　in New York, 158-61, 163-66
　value judgments in, 23-25, 69, 70, 71
　and vertical equity
　　in Michigan, 234-42, 244, 245, 248
　　in New York, 254-57, 260-65, 267
McMahon, W. J., 182
Magnitude-of-the-relationship measures, 77, 78
Marinelli, J. J., Jr., 226
Mariner, L. S., 227
Marshall, R. S., 226, 252
Massachusetts, 271, 289
Mean, 48-49
　and alternative objects, 61-62
　in equity studies, 105-8
　and unit of analysis, 52-54
Median, 49
　and alternative objects, 61-62
　in equity studies, 105-8

and unit of analysis, 54
Medrich, E. A., 289
Methodologies
  literature review of, 97-116
  in single-, multi-, and fifty-state studies, 110-11
Michigan
  and Atkinson's index, 138-41
  equal opportunity in, 169-207, 217-20, 284-85
  horizontal equity in, 117, 129-57, 168, 284
  vertical equity in, 221-49, 268-69, 285-86
  weighting scheme in, 227-29
Michigan Department of Education, 120
Michigan variables, 118-27
  dollar measures, 118, 120-23
  physical resources, 118, 119-20
  price index, 123-27
Milliken, Governor, 117
Minority-nonminority ratio, 199-207
Mosteller, F., 12
Moynihan, D., 12
Multistate studies, 110-11
Municipal overburden, 15

National Center for Education Statistics, 1
National Education Finance Project (NEFP), 226-27
National Institute of Education, 226
New York
  equal opportunity in, 169-70, 208-20, 286-87
  handicapping in, 223, 226, 249-52
  horizontal equity in, 157-64, 167-68, 286
  in NEFP study, 226
  reasons for choice of, 117-18
  vertical equity in, 221-23, 249-69, 287
New York Special Task Force in Equity and Excellence in Education, 126, 211, 249
New York State Department of Audit and Control, 127, 128
New York State Education Department, 222, 250
New York variables
  dollar measures, 118-19, 127-28
  price index, 118-19

Objects. *See also* Dollar objects; Resource objects
  alternative, 59-62
  in equity studies, 98-102, 273, 278-81
Odden, A., 117, 182, 250
Outcomes, 9, 12, 118

Outputs, 9, 11-12, 118

Phelps, J., 117
Physical resource objects, 9, 11. *See also* Resource objects
Porter, D. O., 252
Poverty level, 226
Preschool preparation, 14
Price index, 10-11, 60
  controllable and uncontrollable variables in, 124-25
  and equal opportunity, 177-80, 211
  in equity studies, 278-81
  and horizontal equity, 167, 147-57, 163-64
  hypothetical illustrations of, 123-27
  measurement of, 60, 61-62
  in Michigan, 123-26
  in New York, 118-19, 126-27
  and vertical equity, 243-46, 262-68
Program differentials, 14, 16
Property-tax limits, 3
Property wealth
  definition of, 171
  and equal opportunity, 26, 29-31, 170-81, 208-11
  in equity studies, 103-4, 108-9
  and value judgments, 32-35
  and vertical equity, 15
Proposition 13, 271, 289
Proposition 2½, 271, 289
Public policy, and equity studies, 271
Pupils with Special Education Needs (PSEN's), 250, 251, 252
Pupil unit of analysis, 18, 51-59, 109
  and horizontal equity, 19, 20, 55-59
  and mean, 52-54
  and median, 54
  and quintiles, 54-55
Pupil weighting, 222-29, 250-52

Quality, educational, 10-12, 119
Quintiles, 50
  and horizontal equity measures, 70-71
  and pupil vs. district unit of analysis, 54-55
  and relationship measures, 76-77

Race
  and equal opportunity, 193-207
  and vertical equity, 14
Range, 64, 65
  conceptual and empirical groupings of, 133-38, 276

Range (*continued*)
  in equity studies, 105-8
  and horizontal equity, 9, 19, 20
    in Michigan, 133-38
    in New York, 158-61, 163-66
  and inflation, 68-69, 138, 142, 147, 165
  in *Serrano* v. *Priest*, 289
  value judgments in, 23-25, 68-69, 70, 71
  and vertical equity
    in Michigan, 234-38
    in New York, 254-55, 256, 263-65
Ratio measure, 92-94
  empirical groupings of, 229-38, 252-62
  and vertical equity, 39-40, 229-38, 252-62
    in Michigan, 228, 238-49
    in New York, 252-68
Region, equal opportunity with respect to, 193-97, 214-17
Regression-based relationship measures
  empirical groupings of, 229-38, 252-62
  and equal opportunity, 26-32
  value judgments in, 32-35
  and vertical equity, 37-40, 86-94, 229-38, 252-62
    in Michigan, 228, 238-49
    in New York, 252-68
Relationship measures
  computation of, 73-77
  differences among, 71, 77-82, 274-75, 277-78
  empirical groupings of, 229-38, 252-62
  and equal opportunity, 26-32
  operationalization of, 94
  value judgments in, 32-35, 77-82
  and vertical equity, 37-39, 86-94, 158-61, 163-66, 229-49, 252-62
Relative mean deviation, 9, 19, 20
  and horizontal equity, 133-38
  value judgments in, 23-25
  and vertical equity, 234-38, 254-57
Resource objects, 9, 11. *See also* Teacher-pupil ratio
  and equal opportunity, 180-81, 192-93, 205-7
  in equity studies, 278-81
  and horizontal equity, 154-57
  measurement of, 60, 61
  in Michigan data base, 118, 119-20
  and vertical equity, 246-49
Restricted range, 64, 65
  conceptual and empirical groupings of, 133-38, 276

  in equity studies, 105-8
  and horizontal equity, 9, 19, 20
  and inflation, 68-69, 138
    in Michigan, 134-38, 148-49
    in New York, 158-61, 163-66
  value judgments in, 23-25, 68-71
  and vertical equity
    in Michigan, 234-42, 245, 248
    in New York, 254-57, 260-65
Revenue disparity measures, 20
Revenues
  and children's equity, 10
  empirical groupings of, 137
  and equal opportunity, 174-77
  in equity studies, 100-102, 281
  and horizontal equity, 137, 141-54
  in Michigan data base, 121, 122-23, 125-26
  and vertical equity, 238-46
Rossmiller, R. A., 226
Routh, D., 227
Rutter, M., 289

School district characteristics, 14, 15
School-finance equity
  framework for assessment of, 7-43, 272-74
  future research on, 288-90
  literature review of, 97-116
School-finance-equity studies
  bibliography of, 112-16
  differences among measures in, 274-78
  equity measures in, 105-8
  equity principles in, 102-5
  fiscal capacity measures in, 108-9
  frequency of children's equity objects in, 98-101
  methodologies in, 110-11
  units of analysis in, 109
School-finance formulas, 288
School-finance systems, 288
Sen, A., 13
Sensitivity analysis, 86, 227
Serrano v. *Priest*, 288
Sex, and vertical equity, 14
Single-state studies, 110-11
Slope, 72
  computation of, 74
  in conceptual and empirical groupings, 277-78
  differences with other measures, 77-80, 82
  and equal opportunity, 28-31, 171-80, 199-211
  in equity studies, 106

and inflation, 79
  value judgments in, 32-35
  and vertical equity, 38-39, 236-38, 254-55, 258, 265, 266
Smith, M. L., 119
Social-welfare function, 21-22
Standard deviation, 106, 107
Standard deviation of logarithms
  conceptual and empirical groupings of, 133-38, 276, 277
  in equity studies, 106
  and horizontal equity, 9, 19, 20, 134-38, 158-61, 163-66
  value judgments in, 23-25
  and vertical equity, 234-38, 254-55, 257, 263
State courts, 3-4
State funding, 1, 2, 3, 288
State revenues, 121-23, 143-54, 238-46
Stiefel, L., 23, 125
Stulz, J. R., 227
Supply schedule, 123-24

Tax-burden equity principle, 41-42
Tax burdens, 40-41, 102
Tax incidence, 41
Taxpayers' equity, 40-42, 97-116, 272-73
Tax policy, 271, 289
Tax rates, 101-2
Teacher-pupil ratio, 119-20, 154-57, 166-67. *See also* Resource objects
Technology, 14, 15
Texas, 226
Theil, H., 21
Theil's measure
  conceptual and empirical groupings of, 133-38, 276
  in equity studies, 106, 107
  and horizontal equity, 9, 19, 20, 21
    in Michigan, 134-38
    in New York, 158-61, 163-66
  value judgments in, 23-25
  and vertical equity, 234-38, 254-56, 263
Thornton, R. J., 182
Title I, 119, 122, 226
Transportation expenditures, 122
Tron, E. O., 182

Unequal groups. *See* Handicapping, specification of
Unit of analysis, 51-59, 109

Urban districts, 15
U.S. Bureau of the Census, 182
U.S. Department of Commerce, 226
U.S. Office of Special Education, 229
U.S. Supreme Court, 270

Value judgments
  and correlation, 278
  in dispersion measures, 275-77
  in equal opportunity measures, 26, 31-35
  in equity studies, 272-74
  in horizontal equity measures, 22-25, 68-71
  and input concerns, 9
  need for explicit, 290
  in specification of unequals, 223, 226, 227
  and taxpayers' equity, 41, 42
  in vertical equity measures, 13-16, 36, 37
Variance
  conceptual and empirical groupings of, 133-38, 276
  and horizontal equity, 9, 19, 20
    in Michigan, 134-38
    in New York, 158-61, 163-66
  and inflation, 138
  value judgments in, 23-25
  and vertical equity, 234-38, 254-56, 263-65
Vaughn, D., 197
Vertical equity, 2, 3
  and alternative measures, 82-94, 229-38, 252-62, 280
  for children, 9, 13
  empirical groupings of, 229-38, 252-62
  in equity studies, 102-8, 274
  and hypothetical illustrations, 82-94
  measures of, 35-40
  in Michigan, 221-49, 268-69, 285-86
  in New York, 221-23, 249-69, 287
  operationalization of, 94
  specification of unequals with, 222-29
  studies of, 282-83
  for taxpayers, 42
  and value judgments, 36, 37
Vocational education, 14, 16

Wealth measures, 3, 170-71, 283. *See also* Property wealth
Weighted dispersion measures, 36-37, 39-40
Weighting schemes, 86, 233-34, 265, 268
Wendling, W., 126
Wilken, W., 252
Wisconsin, 226

Robert Berne is an associate professor of public administration and Leanna Stiefel an associate professor of economics at New York University's Graduate School of Public Administration.

THE JOHNS HOPKINS UNIVERSITY PRESS

The Measurement of Equity in School Finance

This book was composed in Times Roman text and Helvetica display type by Action Comp Company, Inc., from a design by Cynthia W. Hotvedt. It was printed on 60-lb. Lakewood text and bound in Holliston Roxite A by Bookcrafters, Inc.